ISLAMIC LAW OF CONTRACT: APPLICATIONS IN ISLAMIC FINANCE

Dr. Muhammad Tahir Mansoori

PRESS

IPS Press is the publishing arm of Institute of Policy Studies, Islamabad – an independent think tank dedicated to promoting policy-oriented research. Pakistan Affairs, International Relations and Faith and Society are some of the major study areas at IPS.

Islamic Law of Contract: Applications in Islamic Finance

IPS Press
Institute of Policy Studies
Nasr Chambers, 1, MPCHS Commercial Centre, E-11/3,
Islamabad, Pakistan
Tel: +92 51 8438391-3 Fax: +92 51 8438390
Email: publications@ips.net.pk URL: www.ips.org.pk

ISBN: 978-969-448-788-5

Title Designing: Asif Taimuri
Layout Formatting: Abid Hussain

Printed in Pakistan by
Premier Printers, Rawalpindi

Dedication

Dedicated with gratitude and affection to my late father Qazi Muhammad Sarwar. May Allah shower His blessings on his soul.

Table of Contents

Foreword.. xvii

Preface xxi

Part-I

General Theory of Contract

Chapter 1: General Principles of Contracts in the Qur'ān and the *Sunnah* 3

1. Free Mutual Consent 4
2. Prohibition of *Gharar* 5
3. Prohibition of *Ribā* 6
4. Prohibition of *Qimār* (Gambling) and *Maysir* (Games of Chance) 8
5. Prohibition of *Khilābah* and *Ghishsh* (Fraud and Deception) 9
6. Prohibition of Two Mutually Inconsistent Contracts or Contingent Contracts 11
7. Conformity of Contract with the *Maqāsid al- Sharī'ah* (Objectives of the *Sharī'ah*) 12
8. Principle of Liability for Loss and Entitlement to Profit 14
9. Permissibility as a General Rule 15

Conclusion 17

Chapter 2: Meaning of *'Aqd* (Contract) and Other Similar Terms **19**
Meaning of the Terms: *Mithāq*, *'Ahd* and *'Aqd* 19
Definition of *'Aqd* 21
Preferred definition 24
Analysis of the Definition 24
Conclusion 25
Chapter 3: Elements of Contract: Form *(Ṣīghah)* **27**
Form of Contract 28
Meaning of *Ījāb* and *Qabūl* 28
Different Kinds of Form *(Ṣīghah)* 28
Condition Necessary for *Ṣīghah* (Form) 31
Lapse of Offer in Modern Law 34
Causes of Cancellation of Offer *(Ījāb)* 35
Conclusion 36
Chapter 4: Elements of the Contract: Subject-Matter **39**
Condition Relating to Subject-Matter 39
Conclusion 51
Chapter 5: Contractual Capacity of Contracting Parties **53**
Capacity for Execution or *Ahliyyah al-Adā* 53
The Condition of *Ahliyyah-al-adā* 54
Complete and Deficient Capacities of Execution 54
Complete Capacity 56
Circumstances Affecting the Legal Capacity of a Person ... 56
Conclusion 63

Chapter 6: Delegated Authority **65**

1. Contract of Agency *(Wakālah)*....................................... 65

Conditions of Agency... 66

Subject-Matter of an Agency.. 68

Termination of Agency 71

2. Guardianship *(wilāyah)* 78

Conclusion... 82

Chapter 7: *Ṣaḥīḥ*, *Fāsid* and *Bāṭil* Contracts 85

Valid or *Ṣaḥīḥ* Contract.. 86

Kinds of Valid Contract... 87

The *Lāzim* (Binding) and *Jā'iz* (Non-binding) Contract.... 91

Fāsid (Irregular contract).. 92

Causes of Irregularity in *Fāsid* Contracts........................... 92

Difference Between Valid and Irregular Contracts 98

Forms of Irregular Contract 99

The *Bāṭil* Contract.. 100

Causes of Invalidity 101

Conclusion.. 105

Chapter 8: Extrinsic Causes of Invalidity *Gharar* (Uncertainty) **107**

Definitions of *Gharar* 107

Effect of *Gharar* on Contracts 115

Insurance: A Modern Contract of *Gharar* 116

Types of Insurance.. 117

Types of *Gharar* in Insurance 119

View Point of Proponents of Insurance regarding *Gharar* 120

Conclusion 122

Chapter 9: Extrinsic Causes of Invalidity 125

Literal Meaning of *Ribā* 125

Technical Meaning of *Ribā* 125

Other Meanings and Definitions of *Ribā* 127

Ribā in the Qur'ān 128

Forms of *Ribā* al-Qur'ān, i.e. *Ribā al-Jahiliyyah* 131

Ribā in Sunnah 132

Kinds of *Ribā* 134

Ribā al-Faḍl, *Ṣarf* and *Qard* (Loan) 140

Other Forms of *Ribā* 146

Indexation of Loans and *Ribā* 150

Arguments of Proponents 152

Arguments of the Opponents of Indexation 153

The Element of *Ribā al-Faḍl* 155

Conclusion 157

Chapter 10: Defect of Consent and its Effect on Contract 159

I. Mistake *(Khaṭā')* 159

II. Fraud *(Tadlīs, Taghrīr, Khilābah)* 162

Traditional Forms of Fraud in Islamic Juristic Literature 163

Coercion *(Ikrāh)* 167

Conditions of Effective Coercion 168

Kinds of Coercion 168

Effects 169

Conclusion 170

Chapter 11: Extrinsic Conditions and their Effect on the Contract 171

Viewpoint of Ẓāhirī Jurists 172

Ḥanbalī viewpoint 172

Viewpoint of Ḥanafī, Shāfi'ī and Mālikī Jurists 174

Conclusion 177

Chapter 12: Islamic Law of Options *(Khayārāt)* 179

Kinds of Options 179

Conclusion 191

Chapter 13: Classification of Contracts 193

A. Classification According to Function of Contract 193

B. Classification of Contracts with Regard to Time of Completion 198

Conclusion 202

Part-II

Specific Contracts

Chapter 14: Contract of Sale 207

Definition of *Māl* (Subject-matter) 207

Classification of *Māl* 208

Conditions for Validity of Sale 210

Expressly Prohibited Sale Contracts of Islamic law 212

Kinds of Sale Transactions 217
I. *Muqāyaḍah* 217
II. *Bay' Muṭlaq* 218
III. *Ṣarf* 218
Definition of Money 220
IV. *Salam* Contract 223
Difference Between *Salam* Sale and Ordinary Sale 224
The Conditions of a Valid *Salam* 225
Modern Applications of the *Salam* Contract 229
V. *Istisnā'* 231
Difference Between *Istisnā'* and Other Allied Contracts . 232
Modern Applications of *Istiṣnā'* 235
VI. *Murābaḥah* 236
Conditions of *Murābaḥah* 239
Modern Applications of *Murābaḥah* 241
Conclusion 243
Chapter 15: Contract of *Ijārah* (Leasing) 245
Definition 245
Features of *Ijārah* 246
Legitimacy of *Ijārah* 247
Kinds of *Ijārah* 248
Modern Applications of *Ijārah* 254
Ijārah in Islamic Banks 255
Conclusion 257

Chapter 16: Contract of *Mushārakah* (Partnership) **259**

Definition 259

Definition of Partnership in Law 260

Concept of Company in Modern Law 262

Legitimacy of *Sharikah* 264

Kinds of *Sharikah* 265

Kinds of *Sharikat al-'aqd* 267

Sharikat al-amwāl (Investment partnership) 269

Kinds of *Sharikat al-Amwāl* 273

'Inān sharikat al-amwāl 273

Mufāwaḍhah sharikat al-amwāl 280

Sharikat al-a`māl: Work partnership 281

Definition 281

'Inān work partnership 282

Mufāwaḍah work partnership 284

Sharikat al-wujūh (Credit partnership) 286

Modern Forms of Partnership 289

Diminishing Partnership in Islamic Banks 291

Conclusion 293

Chapter 17: Contract of *Muḍārabah* **295**

Various Definitions of *Muḍārabah* 295

Legitimacy of *Muḍārabah* 297

Elements of *Muḍarabah* 299

Conditions of *Muḍārabah* 300

Types of *Muḍārabah* 304

Dissolution of *muḍarabah* 307
Conclusion 309
Chapter 18: Contract of *Kafālah (Suretyship or Guarantee)* .. 311
Definition 311
Elements of *Kafālah* 311
Legitimacy of *Kafālah* 311
Kinds of Suretyship 312
Contract of Guarantee in English Law 314
Rules of *Kafālah* 314
Contract of Guarantee in Islamic Banks 322
Conclusion 324
Chapter 19: Contract of *Ḥawālah (Assignment of Debt)* 327
Validity of *Ḥawālah* 328
Effects of *Ḥawālah* 330
Kinds of *Ḥawālah* 331
Comparison between *Ḥawālah* and Negotiable Instruments 335
Modern Forms of *Ḥawālah* 340
Conclusion 340
Chapter 20: Contract of *Rahn* (Pledge/Mortgage) 343
Definition 343
Legal Status of the Pledged/Mortgaged Property 344
Benefiting from Pledged/Mortgaged Property 349
Rahn in Pakistani Law 353
Rahn in Islamic Banks 354

Conclusion.. 356

Part-III

Issues in Islamic Finance

Chapter 21: Concept of *Ḥiyal* and its Applications in Modern Islamic Finance 359

Treatment of *Ḥiyal* in Islamic Law Schools 362

Use of *ḥiyal* in Islamic Banks 370

Unlawful *ḥiyal* in Islamic Finance.................................. 370

Ḥiyal as *Makhārij* in Islamic Finance 389

Conclusion.. 391

Chapter 22: Investment in Equities: *Sharī'ah* Appraisal of Screening Norms.. 393

Introduction... 393

1. Screening Norms for *Sharī'ah* Compliance 395
2. Viewpoint of Opponents 396
3. Viewpoint of Proponents....................................... 399
4. Rules for Investment in Mixed Business.................. 399
5. Arguments of the Proponents of Mixed Activity..... 403
6. Screens for Acceptable Financial Ratios.................. 404
7. Analysis of Screens... 409

Conclusion.. 411

Chapter 23: Islamic Microfinance: Fundamental Concepts and Principles... 415

Introduction... 415

Concept of Islamic Microfinance 415
Fundamental Beliefs and Values 416
Islamic Social Values in Islamic Microfinance 420
General Principles of Islamic Microfinance 423
Modes of Islamic Microfinance 427
Conclusion 430

Chapter-24: Promise and Bilateral Promise in Islamic Finance 433

Viewpoint of Classical Jurists 433
Viewpoint of Modern Muslim Scholars 435
Promise in Banking Transactions 437
Promise in Currency Exchanges 438
Conclusion 443

Chapter 25: *Takāful*: Concept and Application 445

Different Models of Takāful 447
Takāful Practice in Islamic Financial Markets 450
Working of the *takāful* business 452
General *Takāful* Business 456
Conclusion 459

Chapter 26: Concept of *Maqāṣid al- Sharīʿah* Applications in Islamic Finance 461

Concept of *Maqāṣid* 461
Definition of *Maqāṣid* 462
Analysis of Definitions 462
Sharīʿah Evidence of *Maqāṣid* 464

Textual Evidence for *Maqāṣid* 465
Classification of *Maqāṣid / Maṣālih* in Order of Priority . 468
Revival of the Theory of *Maqāṣid* 473
Applications in Islamic Finance 475
Ideal *Maqāṣid* in Islamic Finance 476
Conclusion 493

Foreword

Sharī'ah is a code of life for human beings. It is a body of beliefs, moral values, legal system, commands and prohibitions ordained by Allah Almighty for mankind for its well-being, success and salvation in this world and the world hereafter. Although, it is commonly perceived as 'Islamic law' or 'Islamic legal system', it is a much broader concept in its scope and application. *Sharī'ah* embraces in its ambit a variety of fields and areas which are not generally held to be in the domain of law. *Sharī'ah* implies that a Muslim is duty-bound to obey the commands of Allah, even if these commands are not enforced through any legal system and state machinery. He is under religious obligation to observe the *Ḥalāl* (permissible) and *Harām* (forbidden) of *Sharī'ah* even if he resides outside Muslim territory.

Islamic commercial law is an important branch of *Sharī'ah* that regulates economic activity of Muslim individuals and society. It provides guidance on means and modes of acquiring property, augmentation of wealth in *ḥalāl* manner, and its disposition. Islam lays great emphasis on lawful earning and prohibits all illegal sources such as theft, usurpation, embezzlement, *riba*, gambling, fraudulent market practices and other unlawful means. Unfortunately, in contemporary Muslim societies enough importance is not given to business transactions (*muamlat*) and emphasis is merely laid on acts of worship (*'Ibādāt*). The fact is that *mu'āmlāt* i.e. civil dealings and business transactions are as important in *Sharī'ah* as *'ibādāt*. The implication of this requirement is that every Muslim should be conversant with Islamic teachings concerning his everyday economic activities and commercial transactions.

The Constitution of Pakistan also lays obligation in this regard. It stresses on the state to provide opportunity to the people to fashion their individual and collective lives in accordance with the precepts and ideals of Islam. Thus, the state is duty bound to implement economic system of Islam, and to mold existing commercial laws according to the principles of *Sharī'ah* as enshrined in the *Qur'ān* and *Sunnah* and interpreted by the Muslim jurists. The Supreme Court of Pakistan in its historic judgement on *riba* in 1999, has declared all forms of interest in the country unIslamic, and has held numerous commercial laws contrary to *Sharī'ah*. The need of producing literature on Islamic commercial and financial law, in the contemporary context increases manifold when seen in this background.

The present work by Dr. Mohammed Tahir Mansoori is a valuable attempt to understand and introduce Islamic law on business contracts and commercial and financial transactions in present day context. The book is divided into three parts. Part I provides discussion on the general principles of business and commercial contracts derived from the *Quran and Sunnah* and interpreted by the leading Muslim jurists. Part II deals with specific contracts and their modern applications. The focus of the author in this part is on the applications of *Sharī'ah* contracts in the sphere of Islamic banking and finance. Part III of the book is devoted to the study of some selected issues of current Islamic finance. *Sharī'ah* issues in the modern Islamic banking practices have been especially discussed in this chapter. The author argues that the focus of modern Islamic finance is more on contract mechanics than the spirit and substance of Islamic law. The *maqasid al-Sharī'ah* have not been given due consideration in the current scheme of Islamic finance. In his analysis, the Islamic finance should be value oriented, based on higher purposes of *Sharī'ah*, and ethical values of Islam.

Although the book has been written primarily to serve as text book for the students of law, economics, finance and business management programs, it is equally useful for the researchers in the field of Islamic commercial law as well as practitioners in the field of Islamic finance.

Dr. Mansoori, is himself an Islamic scholar and a banking practitioner. He is serving as *Sharī'ah* Advisor to a leading bank in Pakistan. With background in *Sharī'ah* studies and by virtue of his practical involvement in Islamic banking, he has developed deep understanding of Fiqh issues relevant to Islamic banking and finance. The Institute of Policy Studies is honored to publish a thoroughly revised and updated version of his book "Islamic Law of Contracts and Business Transactions" which was first published in the initial years of 2000s. We hope this will benefit all those who are interested and involved in the fields of Islamic commercial law, Islamic banking, takaful, Islamic capital market and other areas of Islamic finance as well as those who wish to observe *Sharī'ah* teachings while doing business and commercial activities.

Khalid Rahman
Executive President
Institute of Policy Studies

Preface

The injunctions of the *Sharī'ah* are based upon the interest of man both here and in the hereafter. The aim of the *Sharī'ah* is to preserve religion, life, intellect, progeny and property. These are the five basic interests of man. They are also known as the *maqsid al- Sharī'ah* (objectives of the *Sharī'ah*).

Preservation of property being one of the fundamental interests of man and a basic objective of the *Sharī'ah* occupies a vital and significant place in Islamic legal philosophy. Islam regards the property of a person as sacred and inviolable as his life and honour. The Qur'ān forbids the unlawful devouring of property by a believer. This includes prohibition against theft, usurption, embezzlement, bribery and all other unlawful and impermissible means of acquiring wealth. The Qur'ān also prohibits usurious transactions, which bring undue and unjustified enrichment to one party at the cost of the other party. Contracts involving *gharar* and *aleatory* transactions have also been strictly prohibited in the Qur'ān and the traditions of the Holy Prophet (s.a.w.s.). Aleatory or *gharar* transactions comprise those transactions where both parties and either of the parties to the contract becomes a victim of excessive ignorance with regard to the existence, acquisition, genus, quality, and other necessary attributes of the subject matter. Such ignorance and uncertainty may lead to dispute and litigation among the parties. It also includes uncertainty and lack of knowledge about the material terms of the contract. It is, thus, the requirement of a valid transaction that the- object of the obligation be specifically determined to avoid exorbitant *gharar*.

The Holy Prophet (s.a.w.s) also forbade certain market practices such as withholding of food items in times of scarcity, collusion to bid up prices, purchase from the farmers at lower prices keeping them ignorant about market prices, sale of something, which one does not possess, and the sale of foodstuff before taking it into possession.

Thus, the Qur'ān and the *Sunnah* embody some very basic and important rules with regard to transactions. The purpose of all such injunctions is to preserve property and the material wealth of the people.

It is worth mentioning here that the Qur'ān and the *Sunnah* have not laid down a detailed law of contracts and transactions. They have only provided brand guidelines for economic and commercial activity. It is the *fuqahā'*, who after taking guidance from the principles provided by the Qur'ān and the *Sunnah* developed a comprehensive system of contracts and transactions. They classified contracts into different categories with regard to their objects and principal features and assigned them different nomenclatures. They discussed the elements and conditions of contracts together with the other necessary characteristics and attributes. They exercised *ijtihād* in the sphere of transactions and framed new rules according to the need of the time.

Modern jurists like Dr. 'Abd al-Razzāq al-Sanhūrī, Muṣṭafā Aḥmad al-Zarqā, Shaykh Abū Zahrah, 'Abd al-Salām Madkūr, Dr. 'Abd al-Karīm Zaydān. Dr. Yūsuf Mūsā and many other scholars furthered the process of *ijtihād* in the sphere of business law depending on the principles of public good, custom, original law of permissibility, the redress of harm, and the removal of hardship. They have made valuable contributions to the law of contracts and transactions. The various *fiqh* academies and *Sharī'ah* councils of the Islamic world today are also engaged in further developing and enriching Islamic law. The Muslim ummah, through this collective and institutionalized intellectual effort, has succeeded in finding solutions to a large number of legal problems. It was able through this collective *ijtihād* to develop a viable system of banking and insurance free from elements of *ribā*, hazard and speculation.

It is worth mentioning that present day legal problems are so complex and diverse that their solutions may not always be found in the doctrines of classical schools. Cognizant of this fact, the modern *fiqh* councils and institutions explore solutions to the problems through collective and consultative *ijtihād*.

Accounting and Auditing Organization for Islamic Financial Institutions (AAOIFI) in the last two decades has played significant role in the enrichment of Islamic business and commercial law. AAOIFI has issued over 58 *Sharī'ah* Standards that cover broad spectrum of old and modern issues of *fiqh al-Mu'āmlāt*. I have largely benefited from *Sharī'ah* Standards of AAOIFI in this book.

The present book has been written primarily to serve as text book for the programs for LL.B. *Sharī'ah*, MS Islamic Commercial law, BS Islamic banking & Finance, BBA Management sciences at International Islamic University and Islamic banking programs of other universities. This may, however, be beneficial for the Islamic bankers, Islamic finance practitioners and researchers in the field of Islamic economics, banking and finance.

The book is divided into three parts: The first part deals with the general theory of contracts in Islam where the topics such as general principles of contracts, elements of a contract, delegated authority, classification of contracts into valid voidable and void contracts, *gharar*, *ribā*, extrinsic conditions, defect of consent and the classification of contracts with regard to their subject matter have been discussed. The second part deals with specific contracts such as contracts of sale, leasing, partnership, *muḍārabah*, suretyship, assignment of debt and mortgage. While dealing with these contracts both theory and practice have been discussed. For example, under *murābaḥah* contracts not only the conditions of *murābaḥah* in *fiqh* have been identified, but their applications to banking have also been discussed.

The third part deals with some selected issues of current Islamic finance. In this part the issues such as use of *ḥiyal* (stratagems) in Islamic finance, concept of Islamic micro finance and its models, concept and application of *takāful*, doctrine of *maqāṣid al- Sharī'ah* with reference to modern Islamic finance, issues in screening norm of shares and similar other issues have been discussed. Thus, in this part, the new emerging contested issue of Islamic finance has been discussed. The book is an attempt to introduce *fiqh al mu'āmlāt* as a commercial and business law of 21st century that has the potential to meet the needs of modern commercial activities. This modern Islamic commercial law is not based on the doctrines of a particular legal school; it rather, relies on all schools of Islamic law. *Sharī'ah* verdicts (*fatwā*) issued by the prominent *Fiqh* Councils and academies, have been given prime consideration in the formulation of any opinion on certain issue of Islamic law in the book. This book is an updated version of my early book published in 2003. In this book, I have revised many ideas in an attempt to rectify the shortcomings. Third part has been added to the book which provides a through description and evaluation of current Islamic finance.

In the end, I would like to acknowledge my debt of gratitude to my teacher, late Dr. Mehmood Ahmed Ghazi who encouraged me in 2003 to write a textbook on *Fiqh al Mu'āmlāt* based on the classical and modern juristic literature. He was a source of inspiration and encouragement for me. He was indeed a precious asset for Muslim world. May Allah shower His blessings on his soul. I am also thankful to brother Khalid Rehman, Director General, Institute of Policy Studies for the publication of this book from the platform of Institute of Policy Studies. May Allah reward him for this favour.

Dr. Muhammad Tahir Mansoori

Part I

General Theory of Contract

Chapter 1

General Principles of Contracts in the Qur'ān and the *Sunnah*

The methodology of the *Sharī'ah* in dealing with *'ibādāt* (devotional acts) and *mu'āmalāt*, i.e., (transactions) is somewhat different in character. A thorough study of the Qur'ān and the *Sunnah* on this subject reveals that *'ibadāt* have been dealt with in detail, while *mu'āmalāt* have been discussed in general terms. The wisdom appears to be that *'ibādāt* are held to be universal truths that are unaffected by time and space. They are not subject to modification or change by means of *ijtihād* or otherwise. As these fixed commandments were necessary so they have been provided for. The *mu'āmalāt* are matters pertaining to individuals interacting amongst themselves. The variety of this interaction is neither foreseeable nor it can be complied under a regime of fixed rules. They are also changeable in different epochs of time within various geographical entities.

Imam ibn Taymiyyah explaining the difference between *'ibadāt* and *mu'āmalāt* writes:

The acts and deeds of individuals are of two types: *'ibādāt* (devotional acts) whereby their religiousness is improved and adapt (transactions) with the needs in their worldly matters. An inductive survey of sources of the *Sharī'ah* establishes that devotional acts are sanctioned by express injunctions of the *Sharī'ah*. Thus, what is not commanded cannot be made obligatory. As for transactions, the principle governing them would be permissibility and absence of prohibition. So, nothing can be prohibited unless it is proscribed by Allah and His Messenger (s.a.w.s.).[1]

In view of this, the *Sharī'ah* has laid down rules in connection with *mu'āmalāt* in general terms so that different people at different places and in different times may seek guidance. By giving a general framework, the Lawgiver conceded the right to Muslim jurists to frame specific rules for *mu'āmalāt*, which may be deemed necessary under prevailing circumstances. This methodology envisaged by the *Sharī'ah* provides people a reasonable degree of liberty in their dealings with each other and entering into contracts and transactions.

Keeping such treatment of the *mu'āmalāt* in Islamic law under consideration the broad principles can be elaborated as follows.

1. Free Mutual Consent

Free mutual consent of the contracting parties is a prerequisite for the validity of a contract. This is the cause that brings into being the obligations arising from a contract. The consent that is required for the formation of valid contract is a free consent. A consent that is obtained through coercion, fraud, misrepresentation or some other illegal means renders a contract invalid in the *Sharī'ah*. Similarly, a contract made in a state of intoxication or by way of jest or through mistake is also invalid in Islamic Law. This is because the elements of free consent and the intention of the parties to enter into a contract and accept consequential obligations is missing in such cases.

The principle of free mutual consent has been emphasized in a number of verses of the Qur'ān and *ahādith* of the Holy Prophet (s.a.w.s.). A number of verses and traditions can be cited in support.

[1] Ibn Taymiyyah, *al-Fatāwā al-Kubrā*, Beirut: Dār al-Kutub

يَا أَيُّهَا الَّذِينَ آمَنُواْ لاَ تَأْكُلُواْ أَمْوَالَكُمْ بَيْنَكُمْ بِالْبَاطِلِ إِلاَّ أَن تَكُونَ تِجَارَةً عَن تَرَاضٍ مِّنكُمْ

> O you who believe, devour not your property among yourselves by unlawful means except that it be trading by your mutual consent.[2]

The Holy Prophet (s.a.w.s) said: "The contract of sale is valid only by mutual consent".[3] In another *ḥadīth* the Holy Prophet (s.a.w.s) said: "My people are forgiven for that which they have done through mistake, forgetfulness and under coercion".[4]

The principle of free consent requires that the consenting parties have certain and definite knowledge of the subject matter of the contract and the rights and obligations arising from it.

2. Prohibition of *Gharar*

Prohibition of *gharar* is another principle that governs all contracts and transactions. The Arabic word *gharar* conveys the meanings of indeterminacy, speculation, hazard and risk. As a technical term it is applied to uncertainty about the ultimate outcome of a contract, which may lead to dispute and litigation.

A contract is presumed to suffer from *gharar* if it is about:

(a) an occurrence about which the parties are unaware whether such an event will take place or not;

(b) a thing that is not within the knowledge of the parties.

(c) a thing about which it is not known whether it exists or not;

---

[2] Qur'ān 4:29

[3] Muḥammad ibn Yazīd ibn Mājah, *Sunan,* Istanbul: Dār al-Da'wah, 1952 *ḥadīth* no. 2245.

[4] Nūr al-Dīn 'Alī Haythamī, *Majma' al-zawā'id,* Beirut: Dār al-Kitāb al-'Arabī, 1982, vol. 6, p. 250.

(d) a thing whose acquisition is in doubt; and

(e) a thing whose quantum is unknown.

Examples of transactions based on *gharar* are: sale of fish in water, birds in the air, a fetus in the womb, and fruits of trees at the beginning of season when their quality cannot be established.

Prohibition of *gharar* has occurred in a large number of *ahādith* such as:

(a) Abū Hurairah (r.a.t.a.) narrated that the Holy Prophet (s.a.w.s.) forbade sale by pebbles and the *gharar* sale i.e. indeterminate and speculative transactions.[5]

(b) It is narrated by Anas ibn Malik that God's Messenger forbade the sale of fruits till they were ripe.

c) Allah's Messenger further said: "If Allah spoiled the fruits what right would one party have to take the money of his brother"?[6]

(d) 'Alı reported that the Messenger of Allah forbade forced purchases from a needy person and *gharar* purchase and the purchase of fruit before it reached maturity.[7]

3. Prohibition of *Ribā*

Another principle that governs transactions is that of prohibition of *ribā*. *Ribā* is defined as "an increase that has no

---

[5] Muslim ibn al-ḥajjāj Muslim, *Ṣaḥīḥ,* Beirut: Dār Iḥyā al-Turāth al-Islamī, Kitāb al-Tijārāt, no. 1513, vol. 3, p. 454.

[6] Ibid, *Kitāb al-Buyū'*, no. 1554, vol. 3, p. 1190

[7] Sulayman ibn al-Ash'ath al-Sijistanī Abū Dawūd, *Sunan,* Cairo: Iḥyā al-Sunnah al-Nabawiyyah, 1975, no. 3382, vol. 3, p.676.

corresponding consideration in an exchange of property for property".[8]

A contemporary scholar, Nabil Ṣālih has defined it as "an unlawful gain derived from the quantitative inequality of the counter-value in any transaction purporting to affect the exchange of two or more species which belong to the same genus and are governed by the same efficient cause".[9]

The prohibition of *ribā* appears in a large number of texts of the Qur'ān and the *Sunnah*.

Says the Qur'ān:

وَأَحَلَّ اللّهُ الْبَيْعَ وَحَرَّمَ الرِّبَا

"And Allah has permitted sale and prohibited usury".[10]

يَا أَيُّهَا الَّذِينَ آمَنُواْ اتَّقُواْ اللّهَ وَذَرُواْ مَا بَقِيَ مِنَ الرِّبَا إِن كُنتُم مُّؤْمِنِينَ {278/2} فَإِن لَّمْ تَفْعَلُواْ فَأْذَنُواْ بِحَرْبٍ مِّنَ اللّهِ وَإِن تُبْتُمْ فَلَكُمْ رُؤُوسُ أَمْوَالِكُمْ لاَ تَظْلِمُونَ وَلاَ تُظْلَمُونَ وَرَسُولِهِ {279}

O you who believe: Fear God and give up what remains of your demand for usury if you are indeed believers. If you do it not, take notice of war from God and His Apostle, but if you turn back you shall have your capital sums. Deal not unjustly and you shall not be dealt with unjustly.[11]

---

[8] Muhammad ibn Maḥmūd Bābartī, *al-'Inayah 'ala al-Hidāyah*, Cairo: Muṣṭafā al-Babī al-ḥalabī, 1970, vol.7, p.3.

[9] Nabil Ṣalih, *Unlawful Gain And Legitimate Profit in Islamic Law*, London: Kluwer law International, 1992, p.16.

[10] Qur'ān, 2:275

[11] Qur'ān, 2:278

The Holy Prophet (s.a.w.s.) cursed one who charges *ribā*, gives it, records it, and witnesses it. He said, "They are all equal in their sin".[12]

4. Prohibition of *Qimār* (Gambling) and *Maysir* (Games of Chance)

Qimār includes every form of gain or money the acquisition of which depends purely on luck and chance. As opposed to others equally eligible, one may acquire income as a result of lottery or lucky draws. It also includes any receipt of money, benefit or usufruct that is at the cost of the other party or parties having equal entitlement to that money or benefit.[13]

Maysir literally means getting something too easily or getting a profit without working for it. The form most familiar to the Arabs was gambling by casting lots by means of arrows on the principle of lottery. The arrows were marked and served the same purpose as a modern lottery ticket. An item e.g. the carcass of a slaughtered animal was divided into unequal parts. The marked arrows were then drawn from a bag. Those who drew blank arrows got nothing while other arrows indicated prizes big or small. Whether one got a big share or a small share or nothing, depended on pure luck. Dicing and wagering are rightly held to be within the definition of gambling and *Maysir.*[14] The Qur'ān has explicitly prohibited this practice. It says:

يَا أَيُّهَا الَّذِينَ آمَنُواْ إِنَّمَا الْخَمْرُ وَالْمَيْسِرُ وَالأَنصَابُ وَالأَزْلاَمُ رِجْسٌ مِّنْ عَمَلِ
الشَّيْطَانِ فَاجْتَنِبُوهُ لَعَلَّكُمْ تُفْلِحُونَ

---

[12] Muslim, *Ṣaḥīḥ, Kitāb al-Musaqāt,* no. 1598, vol. 3, p.1219.

[13] Mahmood Aḥmad Ghazi, *Murābaḥah Financing an appraisal,* Paper presented in the Conference on Islamic Corporate Finance: *Sharī'ah* based Solutions, Nov. 21-22, 1998 at Karachi.

[14] 'Abdullah Yūsuf 'Ali, The Holy Qur'ān: Translation and Commentary, al-Rajihi Company, Saudi Arabia: 1983, p.111.

> O you who believe: Intoxication and gambling, dedication of stones, and divination by arrows are an abomination of satan's handiwork. Eschew such abomination, that you may prosper.[15]

5. Prohibition of *Khilābah* and *Ghishsh* (Fraud and Deception)

The Qur'ān and the *Sunnah* disapprove of fraud, cheating and deception in whatever form they might be. The words *khilābah*, *ghishsh* and *taṭfif* have been used in the Qur'ān and the *Sunnah* to convey the meanings of fraud and cheating. Fraud refers to maneuver practiced by one of the parties to induce a person to a contract without which he would have not entered it. It also refers to concealing the defects of and adulteration in merchandise.

Fraud and cheating have been strongly condemned in the Qur'ān and the *Sunnah*. Fraud includes a number of practices such as giving short measure and short weight *(taṭfīf)*, false bidding to raise price of an item *(najash)*, leaving an animal unmilked for a long time to give false impression to buyer about its milk yield *(taṣriyah)*, the practice of meeting villagers at the outskirts of the town in order to purchase their merchandise before they reach the market place *(talaqqī al-rukbān)*, false swearing and hiding defects in sale.

Some texts of the Qur'ān and the *Sunnah* dealing with the topic are as follows:

وَيْلٌ لِّلْمُطَفِّفِينَ {1} الَّذِينَ إِذَا اكْتَالُواْ عَلَى النَّاسِ يَسْتَوْفُونَ {2} وَإِذَا كَالُوهُمْ أَو وَّزَنُوهُمْ يُخْسِرُونَ {3} أَلَا يَظُنُّ أُولَئِكَ أَنَّهُم مَّبْعُوثُونَ {4} لِيَوْمٍ عَظِيمٍ{5}

[15] Qur'ān, 5:90.

> Woe to those that deal in fraud, those who, when they have to receive by measure, exact full measure, but when they have to give by measure or weight to men, give less than due. Do they not think that they will be called to account on a Mighty day.[16]

The Prophet (s.a.w.s) is reported to have said: "If both the parties spoke the truth and described defects of the goods, then they would be blessed in their transactions, and if they told lies and hid something, then the blessing of their transaction would be lost.[17]

> The Holy Prophet (s.a.w.s) also said: "False swearing (by the seller) is beneficial to the trade, i.e. it may persuade the buyer to purchase the goods, but in that way he will be deprived of God's blessing to the earnings."[18]

> It is reported that a person came to Holy Prophet (s.a.w.s.) who was always defrauded in buying. The Holy Prophet (s.a.w.s.) instructed him to say at the time of buying: "There should not be any attempt to deceive, and I have the right to cancel it within three days."[19]

> "The truthful merchant will be on the day of resurrection together with the Prophets, the faithful ones, the martyrs and the pious people".[20]

> The Holy Prophet (s.a.w.s.) once happened to pass by a heap of grain in a market place and on examination

---

[16] Qur'ān, 83:1-6

[17] Muhammad ibn Isma'il Bukhari, *Ṣaḥīḥ*, Beirut: Dar al-Kitab al-'Arabi, 1323 A.H., no. 2079, p.410.

[18] Ibid., no. 2087, p. 412.

[19] Ibn Mājah, *Sunan*, no. 2205, vol. 2, p.743.

[20] Ibid., no. 2139, vol. 2, p.724.

found that the grain beneath the surface was wet while that on surface was dry. He chided the seller for resorting to such deceptive tactics and said: "he who deceives is not one of us".[21]

6. Prohibition of Two Mutually Inconsistent Contracts or Contingent Contracts

This is another principle that relates to transactions. Two mutually inconsistent contracts have been prohibited by the Holy Prophet (s.a.w.s.) in a number of *aḥādith.*

It is narrated by Abu Hurayrah (may Allah be pleased with him) that the Holy Prophet (s.a.w.s.) prohibited from two sales in one sale *(bay'atān fi bay').*[22] The prohibition of bay'tān fī bay' has been interpreted by the *Sharī'ah* scholars in different ways. Some of the modern interpretations are as follows:

A. Inconsistent Combination

- To combine two such transactions which produce mutually inconsistent effects, and lead to *gharar* or *ribā.*
- Example: A sells a house for 10 lac rupees to B on the condition that C sells his house to A. Here second contract has no relevance to the first transaction. Besides, it is a contingent contract because completion of first contract depends upon completion of second contract.
- A sells a house to B on the condition that C lends some amount to A. Here lending from C to A has no relevance to the sale between A and B.

[21] Muslim, *Ṣaḥīḥ*, Ḥadīth no. 102, vol. 1, p.99.

[22] Abu Dāwūd, *Sunan*, Ḥadīth no. 3540, vol. 3, p.769.

B. Combination of Sale and Loan

- To combine lending and selling in such a way that only one party benefits from the transaction.
- Example: A, lends to B Rs. 10 lac on the condition that B sells him a piece of land worth 12 lac rupees for Rs. 10 lac.

  Here A, has got benefit of cheap price because of lending to the needy borrower. This benefit in purchase is *ribā*.

C. Combination Leading to *Ribā*

- *Buy-back Agreement*: This sale is sale intended to obtain usurious loan.
- A buys sugar worth one lac rupees on credit of one year from B, and then sells it immediately to B, for Rs. 80,000 on cash. Here A, has in fact obtained loan of Rs. 80,000 with interest of Rs. 20,000.

7. Conformity of Contract with the *Maqāsid al- Sharīʿah* (Objectives of the *Sharīʿah*)

The aim of the *Sharīʿah* in regard to man is fivefold i.e. to preserve his religion, life, progeny, intellect and material wealth. All the injunctions of the *Sharīʿah* are directed towards the realization of five objectives known as the *maqāsid al- sharīʿah*. These are:

1. Preservation of *Din* (Religion)
2. Preservation of *Nafs* (Life)
3. Preservation of *Nasl* (Progeny)
4. Preservation of *ʿAql* (Intellect)

5. Preservation of *Māl* (Property)

Any transaction or contract that offends or jeopardizes any of these objectives is invalid in the *Sharī'ah*. It is pertinent to note here that the *maqāṣid al- sharī'ah* are alternately referred to as *ḥuqūq Allah* (rights of God) in Islamic Law. The right of God in *Sharī'ah* refers to everything that involves the benefit of the community at large. Taftazani defines *ḥuqūq Allah* in the following words: "By rights of God is meant that which comprehends a public benefit, not peculiar to any individual. It is referred to God because of the greatness of its significance and generality of benefit."[23] Thus, *ḥuqūq Allah* in this sense corresponds with public rights, or public policy in the modern law. The objectives of *Sharī'ah* have been emphasized in a large number of texts of the Qur'ān and the *Sunnah*. The following verses on this topic can be cited.

مِنْ أَجْلِ ذَلِكَ كَتَبْنَا عَلَى بَنِي إِسْرَائِيلَ أَنَّهُ مَن قَتَلَ نَفْسًا بِغَيْرِ نَفْسٍ أَوْ فَسَادٍ فِي الأَرْضِ فَكَأَنَّمَا قَتَلَ النَّاسَ جَمِيعًا وَمَنْ أَحْيَاهَا فَكَأَنَّمَا أَحْيَا النَّاسَ جَمِيعًا

On that account, we ordained for the children of Israel that if any one slew a person, unless it be for murder or for spreading mischief in the land, it would be as if he slew the whole people, and if anyone saved a life, it would be as he saved the life of whole people.[24]

وَلَكُمْ فِي الْقِصَاصِ حَيَاةٌ يَاْ أُولِيْ الأَلْبَابِ لَعَلَّكُمْ تَتَّقُونَ

In the law of equality, there is saving of life to you, o men of understanding.[25]

يَا أَيُّهَا الَّذِينَ آمَنُواْ لاَ تَأْكُلُواْ أَمْوَالَكُمْ بَيْنَكُمْ بِالْبَاطِلِ

---

[23] Mas'ūd ibn 'Umar Taftāzanī, *al-Talwīḥ,* Cairo: Maktabah Muḥammad 'Alī Ṣabīḥ, 1957, vol.2, p.151.

[24] Qur'ān, 5:32.

[25] Qur'ān, 2:179.

> O you who believe, devour not your property among yourselves in vanities.[26]

In a *ḥadīth* the Holy Prophet (s.a.w.s.) said: "Allah has made the life, and property and honour of each one of you unto the other sacred and inviolable like this day of this month in this territory."[27]

The requirement of the conformity of contract with the objectives of the *Sharī'ah* is similar to the requirement of modern law that an agreement should not be against public policy.

8. Principle of Liability for Loss and Entitlement to Profit

Another principle that governs contracts and commercial transactions is the principle of liability for loss and entitlement to profit. This principle has been enunciated in the following texts. The Holy Prophet (s.a.w.s.) said:

1. "*Usufruct* devolves with liability"[28]

2. "A loan with a sale is not permitted, nor two conditions in a sale nor a profit of a thing allowed which is not in one's liability, nor the sale of what you do not have in your possession.[29]

This principle provides that a person is entitled to profit only when he bears the risk of loss. The principle operates in a number of contracts such as contract of sale, hire or partnership. A businessman is entitled to profits and gain in his business

---

[26] Qur'ān, 4:29.

[27] Bukhārī, *Ṣaḥīḥ,* Ḥadīth no. 7447, p.1562, no. 7447, p.1562.

[28] Abū Dawūd, *Sunan,* no. 3508, vol. 3, p.777.

[29] Abū 'Abd al-Raḥmān ibn Shu'ayb Nasā'ī, *Sunan,* Istanbul: Dār al-Da'wah, Kitāb al-Tijārah, Ḥadīth no. 4625, 4644, vol. 7, p.33.

because he is ready to bear loss. Similarly, the landlord of a house is entitled to rent of his house in the hiring contract because he subjects himself to the risk of its destruction and damages to it. This risk makes him the rightful owner of its rent.

All profit that has accrued to the partners in a partnership contract is also attributable to this principle of liability. On the other hand, any excess over and above the principal sum paid to the creditor by the debtor is prohibited because the creditor does not bear any risk with regard to the amount lent.

9. Permissibility as a General Rule

In the field of transactions and contracts everything that is not prohibited is permissible. This rule has been emphasized in a number of verses of the Qur'ān. Some of which are as follows:

وَسَخَّرَ لَكُم مَّا فِي السَّمَاوَاتِ وَمَا فِي الْأَرْضِ جَمِيعًا مِّنْهُ

> And God has made of service unto you whatever is in the heavens and what so ever is in the earth; it is all from him".[30]

قُل لاَّ أَجِدُ فِي مَا أُوْحِيَ إِلَيَّ مُحَرَّمًا عَلَى طَاعِمٍ يَطْعَمُهُ إِلاَّ أَن يَكُونَ مَيْتَةً أَوْ دَمًا مَّسْفُوحًا أَوْ لَحْمَ خِنزِيرٍ فَإِنَّهُ رِجْسٌ أَوْ فِسْقًا أُهِلَّ لِغَيْرِ اللهِ بِهِ فَمَنِ اضْطُرَّ غَيْرَ بَاغٍ وَلاَ عَادٍ فَإِنَّ رَبَّكَ غَفُورٌ رَّحِيمٌ

> Say: I find not in that which is revealed unto me prohibited to an eater that he eats thereof, except it be carrion, or abomination which was immolated to the name of other than God. But who is compelled (thereto) neither craving nor exceeding the limit, Lo, your Lord is forgiving, merciful.[31]

---

[30] Qur'ān, 45:13.

[31] Qur'ān 6:145.

قُلْ مَنْ حَرَّمَ زِينَةَ اللهِ الَّتِي أَخْرَجَ لِعِبَادِهِ وَالْطَّيِّبَاتِ مِنَ الرِّزْقِ

> Say (O Muhammad): Who has forbidden the adornment of God, which he has brought forth for His bondsmen, and the good things of His providing.[32]

The principle of permissibility referred to above establishes the fact that all agreements and conditions contained in them are permissible as long as they do not contradict any explicit text of the Qur'ān and the *Sunnah.* This broad principle gives ample scope to different communities to frame laws for them in order to meet new and changed situations.

"He has explained to you that which is forbidden"[33]

The *aḥādīth* of the Holy Prophet (s.a.w.s.) also highlight permissibility as a general rule to be adhered to in the sphere of *mu'āmalāt.* The Holy Prophet (s.a.w.s.) says: "Muslims have to abide by their conditions except those that make the unlawful lawful or the lawful unlawful."[34] This *ḥadīth* points to the fact that every agreement is basically lawful so long as it does not oppose any explicit text of the Qur'ān and the *Sunnah.*

The Quranic commandment of the fulfillment of contractual obligations contained in the first verse of *Sūrah al-Mā'idah*[35] also provides that subject to any prohibition and limitation set down in the Qur'ān and the *Sunnah* all contracts are to be fulfilled. Ibn Taymiyyah writes. "If proper fulfillment of obligations and the respect for covenants are prescribed by the Lawgiver, it follows that the general rule is that contracts are valid. It would have been meaningless to give effect to contracts and recognize

---

[32] Qur'ān 7:32.

[33] Qur'ān, 6:119.

[34] Haythamī, *Majma' al-Zawā'id,* vol. 4, p.205.

[35] O believers: fulfill your contracts. Qur'ān 5:1.

the legality of their objective, unless these conditions were themselves valid".[36]

Conclusion

The Qur'ān and the *Sunnah* have dealt with *'ibādāt* (devotional acts and the matters of ritual obedience) in detail and *mu'āmalāt* (civil transactions) in general terms.

Some important principles governing commercial contracts and transactions are as under:

(a) The contract should be by free mutual consent.

(b) It should be devoid of *gharar* (uncertainty, indeterminacy)

(c) it should be free from *ribā*

(d) It should not contain an attribute of *qimār* (gambling) and *maysir* (games of chance)

(e) It should be free from *ghishsh*, and *khilābah* (fraud and cheating)

(f) Two mutually inconsistent contracts are not permissible.

(g) a contract should not be contrary to objectives of the *sharī'ah*.

(h) Entitlement to profit depends upon liability for risk.

(i) What is not explicitly prohibited is permissible. All the agreements are permissible unless they contradict any text of the Qur'ān or the *Sunnah*, or oppose the objectives of the *sharī'ah*.

---

[36] Ibn Taymiyyah, *Fatāwā*, vol.3, p.387.

Chapter 2

Meaning of *'Aqd* (Contract) and Other Similar Terms

Meaning of the Terms: *Mithāq*, *'Ahd* and *'Aqd*

Three Arabic terms used to designate contract and convey the sense of undertaking and obligation are *mithāq*, *'ahd* and *'aqd*

Mithāq

Mīthāq is a contract that signifies earnestness and firm determination on the part of parties to fulfill the contractual obligation. In other words, *mithāq* is a contract considered to be sacred by the contracting parties and has more sanctity than the ordinary contracts. The examples of *mithāq* include; the very first covenant between man and God at the outset of creation, treaties by the Muslims with other nations, and the contract of marriage. The word *mithāq* has been used in the Qur'ān in a number of verses.

الَّذِينَ يُوفُونَ بِعَهْدِ اللهِ وَلاَ يِنقُضُونَ الْمِيثَاقَ

> These who are true to their bond with God and who never break their covenant.[1]

وَإِنِ اسْتَنصَرُوكُمْ فِي الدِّينِ فَعَلَيْكُمُ النَّصْرُ إِلاَّ عَلَى قَوْمٍ بَيْنَكُمْ وَبَيْنَهُم مِّيثَاقٌ
وَاللهُ بِمَا تَعْمَلُونَ بَصِيرٌ

> But if they seek your aid in religion, it is your duty to help them except against the people with whom you have a treaty of mutual alliance.[2]

---

[1] Qur'ān, 13:20
[2] Qur'ān, 8:72

إِلاَّ الَّذِينَ يَصِلُونَ إِلَىَ قَوْمٍ بَيْنَكُمْ وَبَيْنَهُم مِّيثَاقٌ

> Except those who join a group with whom you have a treaty.[3]

وَكَيْفَ تَأْخُذُونَهُ وَقَدْ أَفْضَى بَعْضُكُمْ إِلَى بَعْضٍ وَأَخَذْنَ مِنكُم مِّيثَاقًا غَلِيظًا

> For how can you take it back (dower), when you have lain with each other, and entered a firm contract?[4]

The commentators of the Qur'ān hold that the word *mithāq* in this last verse refers to the contract of marriage. Thus marriage is a sacred contract enjoying the sanctity of religion.

'Ahd

'Ahd means a unilateral promise or undertaking although it also includes a bilateral obligation. The Qur'ān has used this word in both senses. Some verses in which the word has occurred are given below:

وَأَوْفُواْ بِالْعَهْدِ إِنَّ الْعَهْدَ كَانَ مَسْؤُولاً

> And fulfill every engagement, for every engagement will be enquired into (on the day of reckoning).[5]

وَأَوْفُواْ بِعَهْدِي أُوفِ بِعَهْدِكُمْ

> And fulfill your covenant with me as I fulfill my covenant with you.[6]

وَالْمُوفُونَ بِعَهْدِهِمْ إِذَا عَاهَدُواْ

> But righteous are those who fulfil the contracts, which they have made.[7]

---

[3] Qur'ān, 4:90
[4] Qur'ān, 4:21
[5] Qur'ān, 17:34
[6] Qur'ān, 2:40
[7] Qur'ān, 2:177

'Aqd

'Aqd is synonymous with the word "contract" found in modern law. It is of common occurrence in Islamic legal literature. It implies obligation arising out of a mutual agreement.

The literal meaning of the word *'aqd* is "to join" and "to tie". The term *'aqd* has an underlying idea of conjunction as it joins the intentions and declarations of two parties. The Qur'ān has used the word in this sense in different places.

وَلاَ تَعْزِمُواْ عُقْدَةَ النِّكَاحِ حَتَّىَ يَبْلُغَ الْكِتَابُ أَجَلَهُ

> And resolve not on the marriage tie until the prescribed period *('Iddat)* reaches its end.[8]

لاَ يُؤَاخِذُكُمُ اللّهُ بِاللَّغْوِ فِي أَيْمَانِكُمْ وَلَكِن يُؤَاخِذُكُم بِمَا عَقَّدتُّمُ الأَيْمَانَ

> Allah will not call you to account for what is void in your oaths, but will call you to account for the oath, which you take in earnest.[9]

يَا أَيُّهَا الَّذِينَ آمَنُواْ أَوْفُواْ بِالْعُقُودِ

> O you who believe! Fulfil your contracts.[10]

Definition of *'Aqd*

In Islamic legal literature *'aqd* is used in two senses i.e. general and specific.

In the general sense, *'aqd* is applied to every act which is undertaken in earnestness and with firm determination regardless of whether it emerges from a unilateral intention *(irādah munfaridah)* such as *waqf*, remission of debts, divorce, undertaking an oath, or it results from mutual agreement, such

---

[8] Qur'ān, 2:235
[9] Qur'ān, 5:88
[10] Qur'ān, 5:1

as sale, hire, agency and mortgage,[11] *'aqd* in this sense is applied to an obligation irrespective of the fact that the source of this obligation is a unilateral declaration or agreement of two declarations.

In the specific sense it has been defined in different ways. However, the common feature of all definitions is that it is a combination of an offer and acceptance which gives rise to certain legal consequences.

It is pertinent to note that modern Muslim scholars are inclined to apply *'aqd* only to bilateral contracts as it is the case in Western laws. Rayner attributes this inclination to an increasing tendency towards uniformity with the West in the field of obligations. In the view of this author, it is an evidence of the fact that Muslim scholars are clearly moving away from the wider Islamic interpretation of the term towards the more precise definitions employed in western systems.[12]

Now we take up some important definitions of *'aqd* in the modern sense of bilateral obligations.

a) ***Murshid al-Ḥayrān:*** "Conjunction of an offer emanating from one of the two contracting parties with the acceptance of the other in a manner that it affects the subject-matter of the contract".[13]

b) ***Majallat al-Ahkām al-'Adliyyah:*** "It is where the two parties undertake obligations in respect of any matter. It is affected

[11] See Wahbah al-Zuhayli, *al-Fiqh al-Islami wa adillahtuhu*, Damascus: Dar al-Fikr, 1984, vol. 4, p.80.

[12] Rayner, *The Theory of contracts in Islamic Law*, London, Graham and Trotman. 1991, p. 80.

[13] Qudrī Pashā, *Murshid al-Ḥayrān*, Cairo: 1933, art. 186, p. 27.

by the combination of an offer *(ijāb)* and acceptance *(qabūl)*".[14]

In'iqād (making of *'aqd)* has been defined in Section 104 of the *majallah.* It reads: "*In'iqād* is to connect an offer with acceptance in a legal manner from which flow legal consequences with respect to subject matter".[15] It seems that the term *'aqd* as used in the *majallah* is equivalent to the term "agreement" in the contract Act of 1872. Law considers a simple agreement contract only when it is enforceable. *In'iqād,* on the other hand, signifies that the contract has actually taken place. Thus the difference between *'aqd* and *in'iqād* is that the latter expresses the additional condition of being legal, i.e., enforceable by law.

c) ***Al-'Ināyāh:*** "Legal relationship created by the conjunction of two declarations, from which flow legal consequences with regard to the subject matter".[16]

d) ***Shaykh Abū Zahrah:*** "*'Aqd* is a conjunction between two declarations or that which substitutes them" (i.e., conduct creating a legal effect".

e) ***'Abd al-Razzāq al-Sanhuri:*** "Contract is concurrence of two wills to create an obligation or to shift it or to relinquish it."

Sale and hire contracts are examples of contract meant for creating an obligation. The contract of *ḥawālah,* i.e., assignment of debt serves as a means of shifting liability from a principal debtor to a third party, which assumes the role of new debtor.

---

[14] Commission of Ottoman Jurists (1867-77) *Majallht al-Aḥkām al-'Adliyyah,* Istanbul, 19305A.H., Art. 153.

[15] Ibid., art. 154

[16] Babarti, *'Inayah 'ala Fath al-Qadir,* vol. 5, p. 47.

Preferred definition

Contemporary Muslim scholars prefer the definition of *al-'Ināyah* referred to above, because it is much more comprehensive, and covers all the ingredients of contract: (1) agreement based on offer and acceptance, (2) contracting parties; (3) completion of offer and acceptance in a legal manner; and (4) subject matter.

Analysis of the Definition

The definition offered by the author of *al-'Ināyah* can be broken into the following ingredients:

- Existence of two parties: The definition implies that there must be two parties to the contract. Thus a contract cannot be concluded through a unilateral declaration although such declaration may have legal effects. An example of a unilateral declaration is divorce, which issues forth from the husband only but has legal consequences. An endowment *(waqf)* also comes into being through a unilateral declaration. Thus, though a unilateral declaration may have legal consequences in many cases, it cannot be called a contract *('aqd)* on the basis of this definition.

- Issuance of outward act depicting internal willingness. There must issue forth from the contracting parties that which makes manifest the intention or willingness of parties to enter into a contract. Such willingness may be communicated by way of speech, an action or any other indication. What issues forth first from either of the parties is termed the offer *(ijāb)* while that which follows is termed the acceptance *(qabūl)*. The offer and acceptance are declaration of the internal willingness of the parties.

- There must be a legal *(shar'ī)* union between two declarations. The offer and acceptance must agree with each other in the manner prescribed by the *Sharī'ah*. This agreement or conformity or union cannot take place unless certain conditions are fulfilled, like the issuance of *ijāb* and *qabūl* in the *majlis,* the conformity of the offer to the acceptance, the existence of the offer till the acceptance linked with it.

- The appearance of the effects of the conjunction of the offer and acceptance in the subject matter. The contract when formed produces legal effects in the subject matter. Thus the legal status or position of the subject matter either stands modified or shifts from one state to another. In the contract of sale, for example, the ownership of the goods stands transferred from the seller to the buyer, while in a mortgage the possession of the property passes from one party to another.

Conclusion

The preceding discussion may be summarized as follows:

- Three Arabic terms *mithāq, 'ahd"* and *'aqd* are used to convey the sense of undertaking and obligation.

- *Mithāq* is a contract that signifies earnestness and firm determination on the part of parties to fulfil a contractual obligation. *Mithāq* has been used in Qur'ān in the sense of covenant, treaty of mutual alliance with non-believers and for marriage contract.

- *'Ahd* conveys the sense of unilateral promise or undertaking.

- *'Aqd* implies obligation arising out of mutual agreement. *'Aqd* is defined as legal relationship created by the conjunction of two declarations, from which flow legal consequences with regard to the subject-matter.

Chapter 3

Elements of Contract: Form *(Ṣīghah)*

The majority of the Muslim Jurists hold that the essential elements of a contract are three: the form i.e. offer and acceptance *(ṣīghah)*; the contracting parties (*'āqidān)*; and the subject matter (*ma'qūd 'alayh)*. Ḥanafī jurists hold that there is only one element of a contract; namely, the *ṣīghah* (form). This, however, implies the existence of other elements. From the practical point of view, there is not much difference between the opinion of the Ḥanafīs and that of the majority. It is pertinent to note that some modern Muslim jurists have dealt with the object of contract or the motivating cause of contract as an independent element of contract. They did not consider it a part of the subject matter. As such the elements of a contract are four instead of three.[1]

Sanhūrī,, an eminent contemporary Muslim jurist, has cited seven component elements in a contract: They are (1) the concurrence of offer and acceptance; (2) the unity of the *majlis* of contract; (3) plurality of contracting parties; (4) reason (*'aql*), or the power of distinction (*tamyīz*) of the contracting parties; (5) That the subject *(maḥall)* is susceptible to delivery; (6) the object *(maḥall)* defined; and (7) the beneficial nature of the object that it is permitted for trading.[2] We have however, followed the scheme of the earlier jurists.

---

[1] See Zuhaylī, *al-Fiqh al-Islamī wa Adillahtuhū*, vol. 4, p. 94.

[2] Sanhūrī, *Maṣādir al-haq* , *vol.* 4, pp. 134-135.

Form of Contract

Form is the instrument or the means by which a contract is made. It consists of *ījāb* (offer) and *qabūl* (acceptance).

Meaning of *Ījāb* and *Qabūl*

In the Majallah, *ījāb* has been defined as "a declaration that is made first with a view to creating an obligation, while the subsequent declaration is termed *qabūl*.[3]

In Islamic Law, *ījāb* signifies the willingness of a party to do something positive. Islamic Law is silent on whether the willingness of a party to abstain from a thing also constitutes *ījāb* or not. The Council of Islamic Ideology in Pakistan is of the view that only the commission of an act forms *ījāb*. Abstinence from an act cannot be regarded as *ījāb*.[4] The Federal Shariat Court, on the other hand, has held a different viewpoint. It is of the opinion that a contract may be to do anything or to abstain from doing it.[5] This meaning of *ījāb* conforms to the meaning of *ījāb* in the Contract Act of 1972. The Contract Act defines it in the following words: "When one person signifies to another his willingness to do or to abstain from doing anything, with a view to obtaining the assent of that other person to such an act or abstinence, he is said to make a proposal."[6]

Different Kinds of Form *(Ṣīghah)*

In Islamic Law offer and acceptance can be conveyed in a number of ways namely:

---

[3] *Majallah,* Art. 101.

[4] Council of Islamic Ideology, *14th report on Contract Act 1872, 1984.*

[5] Federal Shariat Court, *Suo moto examination of laws in the contract* Act. 1986, p.5.

[6] Mullah, D.F., *The Contract Act,* 1872, Lahore: Mansoor Book House, 1987, Section 2.

a) By Words: There is no dispute amongst the jurists as regards the conclusion of contracts through words. The reason for this is that words are considered to be the basis of all kinds of expression and other things can only take their place in cases of necessity.

A basic rule in Islamic Law, however, is that the basis to be considered in contract is the meaning and not words and forms.[7] It is for this reason that the jurists have not fixed particular words for the formation of particular contracts. Whatever conveys the meaning with clarity is considered sufficient for the formation of the contract. It is all the same whether the words are explicit or implicit. However, the Shāfi'īs and Ḥanbalīs exempt certain contracts from the above mentioned rule. Thus, the words used for the contract of marriage are *nikāh* or *ziwāj* rather than gifting or ownership. Thus if a woman were to say. "I gift myself to you" or "I make you my owner" then the contract of marriage will not be deemed to have been concluded according to these schools.[8] From another viewpoint such postulation creates a difficulty for those witnessing such contracts. The Ḥanafīs and Mālkīs do not recognise the above exceptions.[9]

Tense: In order to avoid any degree of uncertainty, Islamic Law requires that the words must convey the past tense. Thus, if A says to B: "I have sold this house to you for Rs. 100,000 and B replies I have accepted", a contract is said to have taken place. A contract concluded in the future tense is invalid. A contract made through the present tense can be concluded if it is

---

[7] 'Abd al-Karīm Zaydān, *al-Madkhal li Dirāsāt al-Sharī'ah al-Islāmiyyah*, Bughdād: Maktaba al-Quds, 1982, p.92.

[8] Shirbīnī *Mughnī al-Muhtāj*,Cairo: Sharikah wa Maṭba'ah Muṣṭafā al-Bābī al-halabī, 1933, vol.3, p.532.

[9] Ibn al-Humām, *Fatḥ al Qadīr*, Cairo: Muṣṭafā al-Bābī al-ḥalabī, 1387/1968, vol. 5 p.76.

accompanied by some other evidence (circumstantial) showing that the intention is to conclude the contract presently and not in the future.

b) Writing: The majority of jurists (except the Ḥanbalīs) are of the view that contracts can be concluded through writing, irrespective of whether the parties are present in one *majlis,* i.e., contracting session or one of them is missing. It is customary in event of absence of one party that an offer may take the form of a letter.

Some of the Shāfi'ī jurists have opposed this opinion maintaining that the one who is capable of contracting through spoken words must not resort to writing. According to these jurists, contract in writing is allowed only when the person is unable to speak.

c) Gesture or indication: The Ḥanafīs and Shāfi'īs are of the opinion that forming contracts through gestures or indications is not allowed for one who can speak or write, because spoken words and writing serve a more powerful form of expression of willingness than gesturing. The Mālikī jurists, however, permit such contracts as the rule according to them is that, whatever conveys the willingness of the parties is sufficient, irrespective of whether words are used or not.

d) Conduct: This is termed as *mu'āṭāh* in Islamic Law. For example, A says to B: "I sell you this book for Rs.10 B places Rs.10 on the counter and picks up the book. The majority of jurists allow this form of concluding a contract, but with the following conditions:

i- Conduct must be from both sides: Delivery of counter values must be from both sides. Like a buyer asks the seller the price of an item and the seller mentions a price. The buyer then hands over the money and the seller delivers the item to him.

ii- There must be an intention: Conduct should be based on consent of the parties to the extent that no presumptive evidence that exists negates the existence of consent.

iii- That the item must be of small value: The Muslim jurists are of the view that in order to form a contract through conduct it is necessary that the subject matter of the contract must be of a small value like bread meat etc. and not expensive, like house, land, gold or silver. However, Mālikī jurists allow even in expensive items. The above conditions depend mostly on customs prevailing in the area.[10] The Shāfi'ī jurists do not allow the formation of contracts through conduct.[11]

Condition Necessary for *Ṣīghah* (Form)

As stated earlier, the *sīghah* (form) comprises an offer *(ījāb)* from one party and an acceptance (*qabūl*) from the other. Muslim jurists, however, have laid down certain conditions for offer and acceptance without the fulfilment of which the contract cannot be concluded. These conditions are:

(a) conformity of the offer and acceptance on the same subject matter; and

(b) issuance of the offer and acceptance in the same session (*majlis*).

(1) Conformity of the offer and acceptance on the same subject matter: It is necessary that the acceptance must conform to the offer in all its details irrespective of whether such conformity is express or implied.

(2) Issuance of the offer and acceptance in the same session of contract: According to the jurists when an offer is made, it must

[10] Ibn Qudāmah, *al-Sharḥ al-Kabīr*, Beiut: Dār al-Fikr,1405/1985, vol.3 p.3.

[11] Shirbīnī, *Mughnī al-Muḥtāj*, vol.2, p.3.

be accepted in the same meeting. However, the promisee is allowed to think over the offer for some time. The basis of this viewpoint is a precept of the Holy Prophet (s.a.w.s.). "The contracting parties have the right of option until they separate."[12]

Opinion is divided among scholars in regard to the interpretation of the phrase "until they separate". According to Imām Abū Ḥanīfah it is the separation from a particular topic and not from the place of session. This means that if the parties complete the offer and acceptance and then start discussion on some other topic, the contract is not liable to be cancelled at option. Ḥaḍrat 'Umar said: "Sale is either a concluded deal or deal subject to option". Imām Shāfi'ī and Imām Aḥmad, on the other hand, hold that separation should be bodily separation from the place of negotiation.

However, both these group are unanimous on the point that a contract must be completed by offer and acceptance in the same meeting unless one party reserves for itself the right to think over to ratify or to revoke the contract later.

Commenting on the condition of unity of contract session the Federal Shariat Court has observed the following:

> A narrow interpretation of *majlis* would mean that the offer of the promisor should be accepted without any delay and without giving the promisee any opportunity to think or consult someone in order to make up his mind. This may be practicable in small transactions but will fail in bigger transactions, which may require considerable inquiry. Thus, if an offer is made for sale of a factory, it will require inquiry into the title, power to sell, value of machinery, value of building, its liabilities, if any, profitability etc. If the

---

[12] Bukhārī, *sahīh, Kitāb al-Buyū'*, no.2112, p.417.

> *majlis* is interpreted to mean single session, no one will consider purchasing a property.[13]

The Court further noted:

> The language of the above-mentioned tradition demonstrates that it was only meant to denote the law of revocation, thus if two parties agree to enter into a contract in one meeting, each of them shall have a right to retract from it till they separate. This appears to be the object. Its other object is that the offer must be taken seriously. To some modern scholars the word "meeting" is only a legal fiction in that whatever time is taken by the promisee to communicate his acceptance may be called the continuance of the same meeting.[14]

Does this *ḥadīth* pose a practical problem for entering into bigger transactions as the Federal Shariat Court has observed? The answer is 'No'. The reason is that even if the contracting parties conclude the transaction in one session and observe the requirement of *majlis*, they still have the right to think over the transaction and revoke it within a specified time. This right is known in Islamic Law as "option of stipulation" (*Khiyār al-sharṭ).* The option of stipulation is the power by virtue of which one of the two contracting parties can give his final assent to the contract within a specified time. Islamic Law recognizes this right for the contracting parties. As such, if a purchaser, while giving his consent to the offer, retains the right to accept or reject it within three days, the contract will not be binding on him during that period. This means that Islamic law provides a

---

[13] *Fedral Shariat Court of Pakistan, Suo-Moto examination of Laws in the Contract Act*, 1986, p.8.

[14] Ibid.

mechanism to overcome the problem caused by the restriction of unity of session.

It is pertinent to point out here that the requirement of unity of session does not apply to contract of agency, making bequest and appointment of an executor (*'Īṣā*) for the property of minor.

Lapse of Offer in Modern Law

The Contract Act of Pakistan does not fix any time or place during which or when the offer remains effective for the promisee to accord his acceptance. Section 5 and 6 deal with the question of revocation of offer. Section 5 provides that the revocation of proposal can be made before communication of the acceptance to the proposer by the promisee. Similarly, the acceptance can be revoked before its communication. Section 6 deals with the modes of revocation. Thus revocation can be affected:

(1) through communication of a notice of revocation;

(2) by lapse of time prescribed for acceptance in the proposal for acceptance;

(3) by lapse of reasonable time;

(4) by failure of the acceptor to fulfil a condition precedent to acceptance; and

(5) by death or insanity of the proposer, when the fact of his death comes to the knowledge of the acceptor before his acceptance.[15]

This method can be followed by Islamic Law also since it facilitates the contract. Moreover, it is in the interest of the public. It goes without saying that realisation of the public interest is an objective of the *Sharī'ah*. Such methods may also

---

[15] See *Contract Act, 1872,* Section 5,6.

be justified under the rule: "Hardship causes giving of facility"[16] and the rule: "What is not prohibited is permitted".[17]

Causes of Cancellation of Offer *(Ījāb)*

There are five causes due to which an offer ceases to exist. These are:

1. **Withdrawal of offer by the maker:** The majority of Muslim jurists are of the opinion that an offer can be withdrawn at any time before its acceptance by the other party. The Hanafīs call this the "option of withdrawal". It is permissible to them, as the rights of the other party have not been linked with the subject matter as yet. The Mālikīs on the other hand do not give the maker of an offer the right of withdrawal. If the other party accepts the offer after the withdrawal but within the same session, the contract becomes binding.

2. **Death of a party or loss of its capacity:** The death of either party before acceptance causes the offer to lapse. Similarly, if there occurs a loss of capacity or the party becomes insolvent, the offer ceases to exist. The 'Ibāḍiyyah, a sect of the Khawārij, however, hold that the offer once issued does not cease to exist due to death or loss of capacity but can be accepted by the other party to complete the contract. They also maintain that an acceptance can be made by survivors of a party to whom the offer was made. In other words, rights can be inherited.

3. **Refusal of the offer:** The offer can be rejected by words or conduct.

---

[16] Mohammad sidqī al-Būrnū, *al-wajīz fi- īḍāh Qawā'id al-Fiqh al-Kulliyyah*, Beriut: Mu'ssasah al-Risālah, 1st edition 1404/1983, p.129.
[17] Ibid, p.109.

4. **Termination of the majlis:** The offer will be deemed cancelled by the termination of *majlis* before acceptance from the other party.

5. **Destruction of the subject matter:** The destruction of the subject matter wholly or in part leads to the lapse of the offer. Thus the existence of the subject matter is a condition for the existence of an offer.[18]

Conclusion

The above discussion leads to the following conclusions:

- A Contract has three elements: form (offer and acceptance), the contracting parties and subject matter.
- *'Ījāb* (offer) in juristic literature signifies the willingness of a party to do something positive. The literature is silent on whether abstinence of a party from doing something also forms *ījāb* or not. In our view *ījāb* in the sense of abstinence is also acceptable in the *Sharī'ah* on the basis of the rule of permissibility discussed in the first chapter of this book, which provides that everything is permissible unless explicitly prohibited.
- Offer and acceptance can be conveyed by spoken words, in writing or through indication and conduct.
- It is a requirement of Islamic Law that acceptance should conform to offer in all its details and that the offer should be accepted in the same meeting.
- The requirement of unity of session has been interpreted in different ways. To the modern jurists, whatever time is taken

[18] Ḥassān, Ḥussain Ḥāmid, *al-Madkhal li Dirāsah al-Fiqh al-Islāmī*, pp.252-254.

by the promisee to communicate his acceptance may be called continuance of the same meeting.

- Option of stipulation (*Khiyār al-Sharṭ*) is a mechanism provided by Islamic Law to overcome the problem caused by the restriction of unity of session. This option or right makes a contract non-binding for the party, which has reserved that right within a specified period.

Chapter 4

Elements of the Contract: Subject-Matter

The second essential element of a contract is its subject matter, which includes a number of things; namely, commodity, performance, consideration and object of the contract. The term "subject-matter" is applied to all of these things. Islamic Law does not hold consideration as an independent element of contract. The reason is that the contractual obligation of one party according to Islamic Law is consideration for the contractual obligation of another party. In a contract of sale, the commodity is the consideration for the purchaser and the price is the consideration for the seller. The object of the contract is also covered under subject matter.

Condition Relating to Subject-Matter

Islamic law has laid down the following conditions for the subject matter.

1. Legality of subject-matter

The commodity, service or performance must not include things prohibited by the *Sharīʿah* like wine, pork, intoxicants, and prostitution. It is forbidden for a Muslim to acquire or transfer through contract anything that the *Sharīʿah* has declared *ḥarām*. Since adultery, obscenity and immorality are prohibited by the *Sharīʿah,* any contract or transaction that entails these evils or promotes them in any way is also forbidden. From this it is established that the subject matter of a contract must be such in which transactions are legally permissible. The list of things prohibited by the *Sharīʿah* has been affirmed in the Qur'ān and the Sunnah. This includes wine, flesh of swine, blood or animals, which have died naturally or have not been slaughtered according to Islamic teachings. Contracts involving such things are not permissible, especially when the contracting parties are Muslims. Muslim jurists are divided on the sale of milk of a woman and the hair of human beings. Some jurists allow it because according to them, milk and hair are pure and beneficial. Other jurists disallow this sale on the basis that these are a part of man. Musical instruments are also included in the things proscribed by Islamic Law, provided the contracting parties are Muslims.[1] Contracts for wine, swine and musical instruments are, however, allowed for non-Muslim citizens of an Islamic state. Sale of human blood today for the purpose of transfusion and donation and the sale of human eyes can be covered by the principle of necessity.

Articles of public property also constitute forbidden commodities in private transactions. Thus, a mosque cannot constitute the subject matter of a contract of sale, because its use cannot be passed on to an individual.[2]

The legality of subject matter further requires that the commodity should be owned by someone. Thus, public property is excluded and cannot be the subject matter of a contract. The same applies to other things, which are yet to be owned like fish in the sea etc. As regards public property, however, the state is nowadays considered similar to a person capable of owning property.

Legality of subject matter also requires that there should be no encumbrance or right attached to it. An example in this regard is sale of mortgaged property to which the rights of the creditor/mortgagee are linked.

---

[1] Kāsānī, *Badā'i' al-Sanā'i'*, vol. 5, p.144.

[2] Abū Zahrah, *al-Milkiyyah wa Nazriyyat al-'Aqd*, p.255.

2. Existence of subject-matter

The subject matter should either be in actual existence at the time of contract or it should be capable of being acquired and delivered to a prospective buyer in the future. Transactions, which involve an element of uncertainty and risk with regard to the existence and acquisition of the subject matter, are forbidden in Islamic Law. Examples of such transactions are as follows:

(a) fruits on tree at the beginning of the season when their quality is yet to be established;

(b) sale of fish still in water;

(c) milk in the udders of an animal;

(d) sale of standing crops (which are not free from getting spoiled); and

(e) foetus yet in the mother's womb.

Commenting on the practice of selling fruit trees before they begin to blossom, Anwar Iqbal Qureshi writes:

> It is unfortunately a custom with us that fruit trees are sold before they begin to have blossoms upon them. This is known as spring sale. This spring sale, for instance, of mangoes is affected before trees begin to have blossoms. The natural consequence of this is a definite loss to one of the parties in the transaction. What happens usually in such transactions is that people make a general estimate of the produce in fruits. But no one can be aware of the unknown in which case this amounts to a form of gambling.[3]

[3] Anwar Iqbal Qureshi, *Islam and Theory of Interest*, Lahore; Sh. Muhammad Ashraf publishers, 1991, p.90.

As regards non-existent object, Muslim jurists, in general, hold the view that their sale is invalid. They base this opinion on the following tradition of the Holy Prophet (s.a.w.s): 'Sell not what you do not have'.[4] The only exception to this rule is *salam* sale where the purchaser pays price in advance while delivery of the subject matter is postponed to a specified future date. They restrict *salam* to those commodities, which can be determined in terms of quality and quantity. This means that future goods are not saleable in ordinary sale.

Wahbah Zuhāylī explains the viewpoint of the *fuqahā'* on this issue in the following words:

> The object of contract must be present during the contracting session. Contracting over a non-existent object is invalid, like selling crop before it is visible, on the assumption that the crop might not appear. Equally prohibited are cases involving what is known as "the fear of non-existence (*khaṭar al-'adam*) like the assumption that a foetus might not survive upon birth...This requirement is mandatory in the Ḥanafī and *Shāfi'ī* schools, regardless of whether the transaction involves commutative (*mu'āwaḍāt*) or gratuitous (*tabarru'āt*) contracts.[5] Any transaction involving *ma'dūm* is void whether the case is sale (*bay'*), gift (*hibah*) or pledge (*rahn*). This view is based on a tradition of the Prophet (s.a.w.s.) wherein he is reported to have prohibited the sale of the foetus of an animal (*bay' ḥabl al-ḥablah*)[6] as well as the sale of an

[4] Abū Dāwūd, *Sunan*, no.3503.

[5] Kāsānī, *Badā'i' al-ṣanā'i'*, vol. 5, p.187, Shiribīnī, *Mughnī al-Muḥtāj*, vol. 2, p.20.

[6] Shawkānī, *Nayl al-Awṭār*, Lahore; Anṣār al-Sunnah al-Muhammadiyyah, n.d. vol. 5, p.156.

> embryo (*al-maḍāmīn*)[7] and sperm (*al-malāqīḥ*).[8] He is also reported to have prohibited people from dealing in transactions where the seller did not possess the object. This is because object was treated as *ma'dūm* during the contract. They have established an exception to this general rule, i.e., the prohibition of *bay'al-ma'dūm* in cases pertaining to sale by advance (*salam*), contract of manufacturing (*istiṣnā'*). These transactions are approved, despite the absence of the object of contract, by way of *istiḥsān* (juristic preference) in order to cater for the needs of mankind".[9]

Ibn al-Qayyim, an eminent Ḥanbalī Jurist, has differed with the majority opinion. He is of the view that non-existence of an object does not constitute a reason for prohibition. He tries to denounce the confusion between uncertainty and non-existence. He says:

> "There is nothing in the Qur'ān nor in the *Sunnah* that asserts the view that contracting over a *ma'dūm* (non-existing object) is disallowed. What is available in the *Sunnah* regarding transactions involving existent commodities is contained in the *ḥadīth*: "do not sell what is not with you (i.e. not in your possession)". The *ḥadīth* indicates that the *'illah* (legal effective cause) here is not *'adam* or non-existence but *gharar* (uncertainty). The uncertainty is due to the inability to deliver the subject matter of the contract, for instance a runaway camel (*al-ba'īr al-shārid*). Whenever the *'illah* is removed the *ḥukm* too stands removed, for are you not aware that the Lawgiver has

---

7 Haythamī, *Majma' al-Zawā'id*, vol.4, p.104.

8 Ibid, vol.4, p.104.

9 Zuḥaylī, *al-Fiqh al-Islāmī wa Adillahtuhū*, vol.4, pp.173-174.

> permitted *'ijārah* and *al-musāqāh* because of the absence of uncertainty? The Lawgiver, instead, disallowed the sale of a runaway camel because of the element of *gharar* inherent in it even though it is in existence. Similarly, the Lawgiver has disapproved the hire of a camel in cases where the owner of the camel cannot deliver the animal for use. Above all, this principle applies to all forms of commutative contract in contrast with *al-waṣiyyah* (bequests). *Al-waṣiyyah* is a pure gratuitous contract to which *gharar* does not apply. Thus a contract concerning a will created over an absent subject-matter is a valid contract.[10]

As regards the *ḥadīth*: "Sell not what is not with you", other jurists have advanced three different interpretations, which are as follows:

1. "Sell not what is not with you" means not to sell what you do not own at the time of sale. Many prominent *'ulamā'* of the various schools have recorded the view that the seller must own the object of sale when he sells it, failing which the sale will not be concluded, even if the seller acquires ownership afterwards. The only exception to note in this context is the forward sale of *'salam'* where ownership is not a pre-requisite.

2. The jurists and *'ulamā* of *ḥadīth* have generally held the view that the *hadīth* under discussion applies only to the sale of specified objects but not to fungible goods as these can easily be substituted and replaced. It is thus stated that prohibition in question is confined to the sale of objects in *rem (buyū' al-a'yān)* and does not apply to sale of goods by description. Hence when *Salam* is concluded over fungible

---

[10] Ibn al-Qayyim, *I' lām al-Muwaqqi'īn* Cairo: Maktabah al-Kulliyyah al-Azhariyyah, 1968, vol. 1, p.358.

goods that are commonly found in the locality, it is valid even if the seller does not own the object at the time of contract. Imām Shāfi'ī has also held that one may sell what is not with him provided that it is not a specified object, for delivery of a specified object cannot be guaranteed if the seller does not own it.

3. The third position some 'ulamā have taken on the interpretation of this *ḥadīth* is that sale of 'what is not with you' means sale of what is not present and the seller is unable to deliver. This is the view of Ibn Taymiyyah and the Mālikī jurist al-Bājī.[11] They contend that the emphasis in the *hadīth* is on the seller's inability to deliver, which entails risk-taking and uncertainty. If the *hadīth* were to be taken on its face value, it would proscribe *Salam* and a variety of other sales, but this is obviously not intended. It is quite possible that the seller owns the object and yet is unable to deliver it or that he possesses the object but does not own it, in either case he would fall within the purview of this *ḥadīth*. The emphasis in the *ḥadīth* is, therefore, not on ownership, nor on possession, rather it is on the seller's effective control and ability to deliver. Thus the effective cause (*'illah*) of the prohibition is *gharar* on account of inability to deliver.[12]

Among modern writers, Yūsuf Mūsā, 'Alī 'Ābd Al-Qādir and Yūsuf Al-Qaraḍāwī have drawn attention to the fact that the market place of Madīnah during the Prophet's (s.a.w.s.) time was so small that it did not offer assurance of regular supplies at

---

[11] Abū al-Walīd Muḥammad ibn Aḥmed, Ibn Rushd, *al-Muqaddimāt*, Cairo: Maṭba'ah al-Sa'ādah, 1325/1907, vol.2, p.221; Ibn Taymiyyah, *al-Qiyās fī al-Shar' al-Islāmī* Cairo: Maktabah al-Salafiyyah, 1328AH. pp. 26-27.

[12] Zainuddin Zafar, *"Bay' al-Ma'dūm: An analysis*, paper presented in International Islamic Capital Market Conference Malaysia 1997.

any given time. The *hadīth*, therefore, prohibited sale of objects that were not available at the time of sale. This is perhaps, what is indicated, in the *hadīth* in which Ḥakīm b. Ḥizām said that people would come to him asking to sell them what he did not have. In contrast, the modern markets are regular and extensive which means that the seller can find goods at almost any time and make delivery as may be required. We also note that the contract normally operates on a deferred basis that gives the seller a fair amount of time to buy what is required in order to make delivery, if necessary, within the contract period. When we compare the Madinah market at the time of the Prophet (s.a.w.s) with a modern market, we are faced with a different reality. Given the means and facilities that are available today, the fear of failure to find the goods and make delivery, which was the basic rationale behind the original prohibition, no longer exists.[13]

3. Certainty of delivery

The ability or capacity to deliver the subject-matter of the contract at the time of conclusion of a contract is an essential condition to make a valid contract. If such a capacity is lacking, the contract is void and this position is not altered by the fact that the seller was able to deliver the goods after the time of contract. This condition is applicable to contracts of sale as well as mortgages and pledges. The condition is dictated by the nature of the contract and the purpose, which such contract is supposed to serve. Thus, in a contract of sale the purpose is that the buyer should be able to exercise the authority and benefits of an owner. If such a capacity is lacking the purpose fails. The Muslim Jurists, therefore, prohibit the sale of a stray animal, whose whereabouts are not known, or fish in the sea or birds in the air.[14]

---

[13] Ibid.

[14] Kāsānī, *Badā'i' al-Sanā'i'* vol. 5, p.147.

4. Precise determination of subject matter

The general principle in Islamic Law is that the subject matter must be precisely determined as regards its essence, quantity and value. Similarly, if the subject matter is an obligation or performance, it must be precisely determined at the time of the contract otherwise the contract will be invalid. Indetermination in a contract belongs to variety of things i.e. genus, specie, quality, price, and value. An example of indetermination with regard to genus is where a seller was to say: "I am selling you an ewe from this flock or a dress from this bundle". Such sale is irregular (*fāsid*) because the particular ewe or dress has not been indicated.[15] Similarly, if price of an item is not fixed or its fixation is left to the arbitration of a third party, this too is indetermination. This indetermination renders a contract *fāsid.* The subject matter is ascertained by the acquisition of such knowledge that does away with all uncertainty and vagueness likely to lead to dispute among contracting parties.

There are two ways, in the opinion of the Jurists, to determine subject matter.[16]

First Method: Examination

The subject matter becomes known and specified when the parties to a contract see and examine it at the time of contract. If the subject- matter is present at the session (*majlis*) of a contract, then the majority holds its examination to be necessary. Failure of the parties to examine the subject-matter while it is present invalidates the contract.

---

[15] See Siddīq al-Darīr, *al-Gharar fī al-'Uqūd*, Islamic Development Bank, Jeddah, p.20.

[16] Ḥassān, *al-Madkhal*, p.311.

Second Method: Sale by description

The second method of sale acknowledged by the Jurists is sale by description. Such description must be detailed enough to do away with any vagueness and uncertainty. If the goods or property to be sold are already known, like a house or horse of a seller who has only one house or horse, a description highlighting its specification or characteristics would be deemed to be sufficient. But if the sale is of fungible (*mithlī*) goods then genus, kind and quantity must be described. This method is applicable where the goods are not present in the *majlis* of the contract. The majority of the jurists allow it. The *Shāfi'īs*, however, do not allow it and stipulate actual examination at the time of the contract as a necessary condition. Examination is the sole medium through which sale is possible according to these jurists.[17]

Some jurists allow a sale even if the goods have not been examined or described. This is achieved by granting to the buyer the option of sight or examination after the contract. In this case the buyer can reject the goods on examination. This option can also be exercised when the goods have been sold by description only. Some of the jurists give an absolute right to reject the goods on sight even if they conform to the description.[18] Others restrict such right to a case where the goods do not conform to the given description.[19]

We can conclude from the above that the majority of the jurists allow sale by description and it is only the *Shāfi'īs* who insist on examination and sight at the time of the contract. The jurists distinguish between fungible goods and non-fungible goods.

---

[17] Shīrāzī, *al-Muhadhdhab*, vol. 1, p.263.

[18] kāsānī, *Badā'i' al-sanā'i'* vol. 5, p.292.

[19] Dasūqī, *Ḥāshiyah al-Dasūqi* vol.3, pp.23-24, Shīrāzī, *al-Muhadhdhab* vol.1, p.264.

5. Legality of object and underlying cause

The validity of contract requires that the object and the underlying cause must be legal. Thus a contract made for the use of a property in commission of an offence, when the parties know this fact, is unlawful. Similarly, selling a weapon to a person who will kill an innocent man with it is illegal if the seller has knowledge of this fact. It means that the intended objectives of the contract should not oppose the will and intention of the Lawgiver.

Modern law also lays emphasis on this point. Thus, all contracts which promote immorality, or are against public policy, or harmful to a person or property of a third party, or which are forbidden by law are deemed void and of no legal effect. It is for this reason that courts do not countenance a claim to enforce a promise to pay for any criminal act.[20] Under Kuwaiti law, this concept is contained in Article 167 that governs *maḥall* (subject-matter). It reads: "The motivating purpose must be legal".[21]

The Egyptian Civil Law provides that if there is no cause of obligation, or if a cause is contrary to the general system or morals the contract will be invalid. Thus, the sale of weapons whose import is prohibited is invalid on account of the illegality of the cause and knowledge of the seller regarding this prohibition. Likewise, a contract of loan intended for getting money for gambling is invalid, when the moneylender knows about this intention. The sale or leasing of a house is also invalid if the purchaser or lessee intends to turn it into a brothel when the seller or lessor knows of this intention".[22]

---

[20] *Business Law*, London: Cavendish publishing ltd. p.73.

[21] *Kuwaiti Civil Code, 1980,* section 167.

[22] See ʻAbd al-Razzāq Sanhūrī, *Maṣādir al-Haq,* Cairo: Dar al-Marifah, 1968, vol.4, p.30.

In declaring a contract invalid on account of illegality of cause, Islamic law stipulates that both the contracting parties must have knowledge of such illegality. Thus, ignorance of such a fact on the part of either of the contracting parties would not render the contract invalid. This is to ensure the security and stability of contracts.

Muslim jurists have decided on the above basis that the sale of grapes to a person, who will extract wine from them, is invalid, because the intention and motivating cause is unlawful. Likewise, a contract of marriage to facilitate re-marriage between divorced couple is invalid, because such a contract does not intend to bear the consequences of marriage. At the same time intention in such a contract disagrees with the intended objectives of the Lawgiver. On the same grounds, a contract to sell something on credit say, for Rs. 100/- and buy it back for say, Rs. 80/- with immediate payment, is held to be invalid, because the purpose of the parties is to conclude a usurious transaction which is prohibited in the *Sharīʿah*. The mere form of the sale does not exclude it from purview of usurious loan contracts.

In this regard the eminent jurists, Imām Ibn al-Qayyim write:

> The proofs and rules of the *Sharīʿah* indicate that intentions are taken into account in contract, that affect their validity and invalidity, and lawfulness and unlawfulness of a contract, but more seriously that it affects the action which is not a contract with respect to making it lawful and unlawful. The same item becomes lawful sometimes and unlawful at other times depending on variation of intention and intended objectives.[23]

[23] Ibn al-Qayyim, *I'lām al-Muwaqqi'īn*, vol.3, p.96.

Conclusion

- The subject- matter, i.e., commodity or performance or service should be lawful.
- The object of contract should be either in actual existence at the time of contract or it should be capable of being delivered in future.
- Contracting over a non-existent object is disallowed only when there is grave uncertainty regarding its acquisition and delivery to the buyer.
- The object of contract should be deliverable.
- The subject-matter should be precisely determined at the time of contract.
- The subject-matter can be determined either by the examination or by the description.
- The validity of contract requires that its motivating cause should also be according to requirements of the *Sharī'ah.*

Chapter 5

Contractual Capacity of Contracting Parties

A basic requirement for conclusion of a valid contract is the necessity that the contracting parties should be qualified to enter a contract. Thus, such parties are required to possess legal capacity *(ahliyyah)* for this purpose. The capacity which is required for concluding a contract is termed in Islamic Law as capacity for execution or *ahliyyay al-adā*.

Capacity for Execution or *Ahliyyat al-Adā*

The capacity for execution is defined as the "capacity of a human being for the issuance of words and performance of deeds to which the lawgiver has assigned certain legal effects."[1] On the basis of this definition the capacity for execution is considered by the jurists to be of three kinds.

i) Capacity for the *Khiṭāb Jinā'ī*: This is the capacity for the issuance of words and the performance of deeds the legal effects of which are worldly punishments. In other words, whosoever possesses such a capacity can acquire through his words and deeds a liability for punishment. This is termed as the capacity for punishment or the capacity for the *khiṭ āb jinā'ī*.

ii) Capacity for the *Khiṭāb of 'Ibādāt*: It is the capacity for the issuance of words and performance of deeds, the legal effects of which are produced in the shape of reward or *thawāb* in Hereafter and as well as the fulfillment of one's obligation in the

---

[1] Ḥassān, *al-Madkhal*, p.320.

present world. This is termed as the capacity for *'Ibādāt* or the capacity for the *khiṭāb* of *'ibādāt.*

iii) Capacity for the *Khiṭāb of Mu'āmlāt*: This is the capacity for issuance of words and performance of deeds the legal effects of which are exercise of rights and fulfillment of obligations for contracts and other transactions. It may be called the capacity for transactions or the capacity for the *khiṭāb* of *mu'amalāt.*[2]

The Condition of *Ahliyyah-al-adā*

The requirement for *ahliyyah al-adā`* is reason and discretion. The method to check whether a person possesses faculties of reasons and discretion the lawgiver has associated such powers with puberty. This is the view of the majority.

The Ḥanafīs on the other hand acknowledge a deficient capacity of execution for purposes of some transactions for a person who has attained some degree of discretion though his mental faculty is not fully developed. Thus, a minor who possesses discretion can be assigned such a capacity. Here, again there is no certain way of determining that the minor has attained this capacity. The Ḥanafī jurists, however, fix the age of seven years for the assignment of such a capacity. Anyone over seven who has not attained puberty may be assigned such a capacity. A deficient capacity is also assigned by the Ḥanafīs to one who has attained puberty but his mental faculty is not fully developed mentally, like the *ma'tūh* (lunatic).

Complete and Deficient Capacities of Execution

The capacity of execution is then divisible into two kinds:

[2] Ibid, p.328.

Deficient capacity is assigned to a non-pubert who possesses some discretion and to the *ma'tūh (*lunatic*)* who has attained puberty yet lacks complete mental development.

A person who possesses a deficient capacity is not subject to the *khiṭ āb jinā'ī*. Thus he cannot be held criminally liable. The reason for this is that the *khiṭ āb jinā'ī* is applicable only to that person who can understand the *khiṭ āb* fully.

As regard *'ibādāt* the *fuqahā'* are unanimous that the communication of Lawgiver addressed to the minor is by way of recommendation and that there is reward (*thawāb)* for the performance of the *'ibādāt* by such person. We are now concerned with the capacity of such persons for the purpose of transactions. The Ḥanafīs divide transactions into three kinds:

a) Purely beneficial transactions: These are like the acceptance of a gift or of *sadaqah* and are allowed to a non-pubert who can discriminate and has been permitted to do so by his guardian.

b) Purely harmful transactions: The granting of divorce, manumission, *sadaqah, qarḍ, hibah, waqf* and *wasiyyah* are not to be entered into by the *sabī mumayyaz* (minor possessed with discretion).

c) Transactions equally likely to result in profit or in loss: These are the sale, hire, and partnership. They are considered as valid if permission of the guardian is granted. Thus, a deficient capacity for execution is granted by the Ḥanafīs to the *sabī mumayyaz.* Other jurists refuse to acknowledge any kind of capacity for the *sabī mumayyaz*. The *Khiṭ āb* according to them is not directed towards the non-pubert at all; hence it makes no difference whether the transactions are beneficial or harmful[3].

[3] Aḥmad Ibrāhīm Bik, *al-ltazāmāt fī al-Shar' al-Islāmī*, Cairo: Dār al al-Anṣār, *1944*, pp.120-121.

Complete Capacity

Complete capacity is established for a human being when he attains full mental development and acquires the ability to discriminate. Thus, the requirement of this capacity is reason (*'aql*) and discretion (*rushd).* Such a stage has been associated with an external standard by the Lawgiver. This standard is puberty. The sign of puberty is ejaculation in a male, and menstruation in a female. In the absence of these signs puberty is presumed to have occurred by the age of 15 in both male and female according to the majority of the jurists and at 18 years for a male and 17 years for a female according to Imam Abū Ḥanīfah.

Attaining puberty in itself alone is not sufficient evidence that a person has acquired complete capacity for execution. In addition to puberty, the possession of *rushd* or maturity of action is also deemed necessary.

Circumstances Affecting the Legal Capacity of a Person

There are certain factors, which impair legal capacity of a person and prevent him from concluding contracts and making dispositions in his property. These are as follows:

1 ***Junūn* (Insanity):** "*Junūn* is the mental derangement which, except in rare cases, prevents a person from and dispositions utterances". It is divided into two kinds:

(i) *Aṣlī* (regular) when a person attains puberty during his lunacy.

(ii) *Ṭārī'* (casual): which appears after a person has attained puberty and developed sanity together with mature understanding.[4]

[4] Zaydān, *al-Madkhal*, p.317.

Insanity eliminates the legal capacity of an individual because its basis is intelligence and discrimination, and Insane is destitute of that. As regards legal effects of the utterances and dispositions of Insane, he is like a minor without discretion *(ṣabī ghayr mumayyaz)*, which do not produce any effect. Islamic Law puts an insane person under a guardian who looks after his affairs.

2. *'Atah* (lunacy or partial insanity): *Ma'tūh* is partial or temporary insane person who sometimes acts like a sane person and some other times like an insane person.

" '*Atah* is defined as 'the mental derangement of a person who is confused in his speech and who speaks sometimes like sensible person and sometimes like lunatics".[5]

Ma'tūh is treated like a minor possessed with discretion (*sabī mumayyaz*). Thus, he is not allowed to enter contracts, which are disadvantageous for him. However, he is allowed to conclude beneficial transaction. As regards transactions that may equally result in benefit and loss, his transactions will be considered valid subject to verification by his guardian.

3. Forgetfulness: Forgetfulness is defined as: "A circumstance that befalls a man without his volition causing loss of remembrance of something.[6]

The majority of jurists are of the opinion that a contract concluded through mistake or forgetfulness is not a contract at all. They rely for this on the words of the Holy Prophet (s.a.w.s) contained in a Hadīth in which he said: "My Ummah is forgiven

---

[5] 'Ubaid Allah ibn Mas'ūd, Sadr al-Sharī'ah, *al-Tawḍīh,* al-Maktabah al-Khayriyyah,1322 H., vol. 2, p.168.

[6] Ḥassān, *al-ḥukm al-Shar'ī 'īnda al-Uṣūliyyīn*, Dār al-Nahḍah al-'Arabiyyah, 1972, p.186.

for that which they have done through mistake or forgetfulness or under coercion".[7]

The Ḥanafīs oppose the majority and declare that statements made by mistake or forgetfulness are valid for the formation of contracts. They maintain that the door will otherwise swing open for setting up false defenses and the security of transactions demands that this should not be allowed.

4. *Safah* (Prodigality and weakness of intellect): *Safah* has been defined as follows:

(i) "*Safah* is that weakness of intellect which urges a person to act with respect to his property contrary to the dictates of reason."[8]

(ii) "*Safah* is the disposition of wealth contrary to the dictates of the intellect and the *Sharī'ah* by spending it without righteous purpose".[9] *Safah* is opposite of the word *rushd* which signifies handling of financial matters in accordance with the dictates of reason. Thus, *rashīd* is a person who can identify avenues of profit as well as loss and act accordingly to preserve his wealth. This is majority viewpoint. The Shāfi'ī Jurists, on the other hand, maintain that *rushd* is maturity of actions not only with regard to financial matters but also in matter of *dīn*. Thus, a person who attains puberty and handles his business sensibly but he doesn't abide by the rules and prohibitions of Lawgiver, is not *rashīd* in the opinion of Imām Shāfi'ī. An eminent Shāfi'ī jurist Imām Nawawī declares *rushd* to be present in a person in the following circumstances:

---

[7] Haythamī, *Majma' al-Zawā'id,* vol. 6, p.250.

[8] Amīr Bādshāh, *Taysīr al-Taḥrir,* Cairo:Muṣtafā al-Bābī al-Ḥalabī, 1351AH, vol.2, p.300.

[9] Ḥassān, *al-ḥukm al-Shar'ī 'īnda al-Uṣūliyyīn,* p.210.

(i) when he is able to perform his religious duties properly;

(ii) when he behaves reasonably in his personal affairs;

(iii) when he abstains from every thing that brings him reproach; and

(iv) when he is not a spendthrift, i.e., he does not waste his wealth by allowing himself to be deceived in commercial transactions by obvious fraud.[10]

A person is considered eligible to take charge of his wealth if he is both *bāligh* and *rashīd*. This is the general view. However, Imām Abū Ḥanīfah maintains that a person who attains the age of 25 years, must be given his property irrespective of the fact that he attained *rushd* or not. He also maintains that if property is given to one who attains majority and *rushd* and subsequently loses his *rushd* while yet under 25, will not be subjected to interdiction (*ḥajr*).[11] Kuwaiti Civil Code provides that transactions of the *safīh* will, after determination of the judgement be treated in the same way as that of a minor without discernment. Any transaction arising from him before he is proclaimed *safīh* is neither *bāṭil* nor voidable except where the contract has been concluded in collusion with anticipation of the restriction, that is fraudulently and with knowledge of the impending lack of capacity.[12] The *safīh* may validly make *waqf* or bequest dispositions if the court authorizes him to do so.[13]

The court has the power to give absolute or limited authorization to a *safīh* to handle his affairs whether wholly or

---

[10] Nawawī ,Muhiyyuddīn Abū Zakariyyah, Minhāj al-Ṭālibīn, translated into English by: E.C. Howard, London:1977, p.167.

[11] 'Abd al-Sattār al-Jibālī, *Ahkām 'Aqd al-Bāy'*. Cairo: Jami'ah al-Azhar, 1993, p.49

[12] *Kuwaiti Civil Code,* Art, 101 (1)

[13] Ibid, 102.

in part. In special cases it may require the *safīh* to give account of his affairs.[14] The court may also restrain or withdraw his authorization if it sees just grounds for doing so.[15]

A *safīh* who has been given permission to administer personal affairs, also has capacity to enter into transactions out of the bounds of that permission set by the court especially for him.[16]

Procedure for exercise of interdiction

The opinion of Ḥanafī jurists is divided on the issue as to whether the interdiction should be by orders of court or the existence of (*safah*) itself.

Imām Muhammad holds that a *safīh* should be prevented from disposing his property by the mere existence of *safah* without necessitating the order of the court. Therefore, the existence of stupidity in a person presupposes interdiction and its non-existence requires its removal.

According to Abū Yūsuf interdiction will be imposed and lifted by the order of the court. The result of this disagreement becomes manifest in the dispositions of a *safīh* prior to placing him under interdiction. These dispositions are valid and enforced according to Imām Muhammad. According to Abū Yūsuf they remain suspended until the decision of the court.

The Iraqi Civil Code favours the opinion of Imām Abū Yūsuf, hence, when a *safīh is* placed under interdiction by the court, he becomes like a minor possessed with discretion. Iraqi Law allows him to make bequest to the extent of one-third of his property.

---

[14] Ibid., 103 (1).
[15] Ibid., 103 (2).
[16] Ibid., 64.

5. Intoxication: Intoxication is a condition, which overtakes a man on account of taking an intoxicant, and along with it his intelligence remains suspended, being neither lost nor diminished.[17]

The drunken person is one who is in a state of intoxication due to the consumption of liquor and does not know what he is saying. The Majority is of the opinion that a contract is established by the statement of a drunken person and gives rise to all kinds of rights and obligations of the contract. They argue (i) that he became intoxicated out of his own choice, (ii) that he knew that drinking was prohibited and a crime should not absolve a person of the duties acquired by him.

The Ḥanbalī jurists are of the opinion that the statement of an intoxicated person is not to be taken into account at all as he does not intend what he is saying. He is just like an insane person or one under duress. Some other jurists try to distinguish between intoxication caused by illegal means and that caused by lawful means. Intoxication is caused by lawful means in the following cases:

(i) when a person drinks intoxicating liquor without knowing that it is forbidden liquor;

(ii) when he is forced to do so under duress;

(iii) when he is about to die of thirst and no other drink is available; and

(iv) when intoxicant is caused by drugs taken medicinally.

Those who prefer the stand of the Ḥanablīs give the following arguments:

[17] Ḥassān, *al-Ḥukm al-Shar'ī*, p.204.

i) The intoxicated person doesn't intend what he says and thus takes the *ḥukm* of one who is insane.

ii) It is not necessary that the intoxicated person is making a bad bargain and in fact he may suffer if the contract is declared invalid.

6. *Taflīs* (Bankruptcy): A person is considered bankrupt when his debts exceed his assets, and court on the demand of his creditors passes a prohibitory order restraining all alienation by him, and directs the sale of his property for the benefit of his creditors. The purpose of this *al-ḥajr* (interdiction), i.e., to restrict *al-muflis* (bankrupt) in the right of disposal of his property, is to safeguard and protect the right of creditors and to prevent him from carrying out transactions detrimental to his creditors. The precedent for such regulation was set by the Prophet (s.a.w.s). It is narrated that Mu'ādh ibn Jabal was a generous man and always gave his possessions away. He was always in debt. His debts were more than his property. So, he came to the Prophet (s.a.w.s) and requested him to ask his creditors to withdraw their claims on the debts. They, however, refused. The Prophet (s.a.w.s), later, sold all Mu'ādh's property to pay the debts, to the extent that he had nothing left.

7. Coercion: Coercion is to compel a person without having such a right, to do a thing without his consent or through fear. It is also defined as an action directed against a person, who suppresses his true consent. The contracts and dispositions made under coercion are not valid according to the majority of Muslim jurist. Ḥanfīs, however, maintain the contract of the person coerced is valid but is suspended, on the extinction of coercion. The *mukrah* (coerced person) has right to ratify it or revoke it. They also hold that the contracts of marriage, divorce, manumission are valid even with coercion.

Conclusion

The above discussion leads to the following conclusions:

1. Legal capacity refers to capacity of human being for the issuance of words and deeds to which the law-giver has assigned certain legal effects.
2. Legal capacity is assigned in Islamic law to a person who attains puberty with sanity.
3. The Hanafi law acknowledges a deficient legal capacity for the purpose of some transactions for a person who has attained some degree of discretion though he has not attained puberty.
4. Certain circumstances effect legal capacity of a person. These circumstances include: Insanity, weakness of intellect, lunacy, intoxication, interdiction by the court, and coercion.

Chapter 6

Delegated Authority

A person sometimes makes transactions on behalf of other people. In such a case, he is required to have, besides legal capacity, proper authority to make a transaction. He derives authority either from the person on whose behalf he enters into a contract or from the Lawgiver. The authority in the former case is called agency while in the latter case it is termed as guardianship.

The nature and scope of both the authorities, i.e., agency and guardianship will be discussed in this chapter.

1. Contract of Agency *(Wakālah)*

Wakālah is to substitute an agent for the principal to perform on behalf of that principal an act, which admits of representation. It creates a fiduciary relationship that exists between two persons, one of whom expressly or impliedly consents that another should act on his behalf. The one on whose behalf the act is done is called the principal *(aṣīl)* and the one who is to act is called agent *(wakīl)*.[1]

A number of legal texts provide justification for the contract of agency. Some of them are produced below:

[1] Zaydān, *al-Madkhal li Dirāsāt al- Sharī'ah al-Islāmiyyah*, p.338; Muḥammad Muṣṭafā, Shalabī, *al-Madkhal li Dirāsat al-Fiqh al-Islāmī*, Beriut: Dār al-Jami' at, *1985*, p.339.

1. Ḥaḍrat 'Alī (r.a.t.a) narrates that once the Holy Prophet (s.a.w.s) ordered him to distribute the saddles and skins of animals he had slaughtered. [2]

2. 'Uqbah ibn 'Āmir narrates that the Prophet (s.a.w.s.) gave him some sheep to distribute among his companions and a male kid was left after distribution. He informed Holy Prophet (s.a.w.s) about it, and he said "Sacrifice it on my behalf".[3]

3. 'Urwah al-Bariqī (r.a.t.a.) narrated that the Holy Prophet (s.a.w.s.) gave him a *dīnār* to buy a sheep for him. He bought two sheep by it and sold one of them for one *dīnār* on the way. He said: When I brought a *dīnār* and a sheep to the Holy Prophet (s.a.w.s.), he said to me, "May Allah bless the bargain of your right hand".[4]

These traditions prove that a person can delegate his business to an agent to perform it on his behalf. Ḥaḍrat 'Alī is reported to have appointed *'Aqīl* for management of his lawsuits; and when *'Aqīl* became old, he was replaced by another agent 'Abd Allāh ibn Ja'far.

Conditions of Agency

I. Conditions relating to the principal *(muwakkil/aṣīl)*

The conditions of the Principal are that he should have full authority of disposing of a matter, which he has entrusted to another person to perform it on his behalf. He, therefore, should be competent to undertake task himself for which he has appointed an agent. Thus, an insane, a minor, and the one placed

[2] Aḥmad ibn Ḥanbal, *Musnad Aḥmad,* Cairo: Dār al-Ma'ārif, vol. 1, pp.79, 143, 154, 112.

[3] Bukhārī, *Ṣaḥīḥ,* Kitāb al-Wakālah, no.230; Kitāb al-Daḥāya, no.5555.

[4] Muḥammad ibn Muḥammad, Fāsī, *Jam'al-Fawā'id,* Lahore:al-Maktabah al- Islāmiyyah, Ḥadīth no.4854.

under interdiction cannot enter into a contract of agency. They cannot make other peoples their agents for the performance of work on their behalf. A discerning minor (*sabī mumayyaz*) may, however, appoint agent for the performance of acts which are beneficial for the minor, but he is not allowed to appoint agent for transactions which entail loss for that minor.

II. Conditions relating to the agent (*wakīl*)

The condition of agent is that he should possess the capacity of execution that requires sanity and ability of understanding and discrimination in the agent. Thus, it is not requirement that the agent must necessarily be of age. A person having deficient capacity of execution can act as agent for another person. Ḥanbalī and Shāf'ī Jurists, however, postulate complete legal capacity for an agent. To them the general rule to be followed in this regard is that one, who does not have authority to dispose of a thing for him, is ineligible to be agent for disposition of that thing for others.[5] As such, *ṣabī mumayyaz* is not eligible to act as agent for others.

III. Conditions relating to subject-matter (*Muwakkal bihī*)

The subject matter of agency is the act for the performance of which the agent is appointed. Agency is permissible in each known disposition recognised by *Sharī'ah*. Some important conditions of the subject matter of agency are as follows:

1. It should be known to the agent to the extent that its performance is possible for him. Thus, if the agency is for the purchase of a thing, the genus, kind, quality and other necessary attributes of the commodity to be bought should be mentioned. The agency will be invalid where a person appoints another person as his agent to sell his property without defining and identifying that property.

[5] Ibn Qudāmah *al-Mughnī*, vol. 5, pp. 79-80.

2. It should be a lawful and permissible disposition. The agency is not permissible in acts of disobedience such as murder, theft, usurpation of property, and slander.

3. The disposition should be something that admits of representation. Hence, appointment of an agent for the act such as prayer, fasting, giving evidence, or for taking an oath is not permissible because these acts are to be performed by the principal himself. An eyewitness to an incident is required to give testimony himself. He is not allowed to delegate this task to another person. Similarly, an oath can be accepted only from the person concerned, not from his agent.[6]

Subject-Matter of an Agency

Some of the acts and dispositions for which agency is permissible are as follows:

- Sale and purchase
- Letting and hiring
- Borrowing and lending
- Bailment
- Making gifts
- Pledge
- Assignment of debts
- Suretyship and guarantee
- Deposits
- Litigation

---

[6] Zuḥaylī, *al-Fiqh al-Islāmī wa Adillahtu hū*, vol. 4, p.

- Marriage contracts
- Divorce
- Relinquishment of rights
- Admissions and acknowledgement of rights

Agent's duty towards his principal

The duties of an agent towards principal are:

1. To perform the undertaking according to instructions, i.e., to observe all the conditions and restrictions laid down by the principal.

2. To exercise due care and skill.

3. To carry out instructions personally, i.e., he is not allowed to `appoint another person to do an act delegated to him.

4. Not to permit a conflict of interest to arise, i.e., he is not allowed to purchase for himself property, which he is engaged to sell. The corollary to this case is that he must not sell his own property to the principal without fully disclosing the facts.

5. Not to make secret profit or misuse confidential information.

The effects and rights of the contract of *wakālah*

Muslim jurists are unanimous on the point that effects of a contract of agency revert to the principal because the agent only enforces orders and instructions of his principal. He derives authority from the principal. Hence, effects should revert to the principal, regardless of whether the agent attributed transaction to himself or to his principal. These jurists, however, differ among themselves regarding the mode of establishment of these effects. Ḥanafī jurists maintain that the *ḥukm* or effect is established first for agent and from him it passes on to the principal. The Shāfi'ī and Ḥanbalī jurists, on the other hand, hold that the effects of a contract revert directly to the principal.[7]The author of *al-Mughnī* says in this regard:

> "If an agent bought something for the principal with his permission, the ownership will stand transferred from the seller to the principal, without first entering into the ownership of agent".[8]

As regards secondary liabilities and rights with respect to a disposition, the Ḥanafī jurists maintain that these are attributable to the agent. For example, the effect of a contract of sale is the transfer of ownership in goods from seller to purchaser, whereas the liabilities and rights of contract are the delivery of the subject matter; claiming the price, exercise of the right of option of defect or inspection and returning goods in case of reclaiming. All these rights and liabilities are to be attributed to the agent not to the principal. This means that the agent is responsible for receiving goods from seller, handing over price to him, returning goods in case of defect to the seller. All these rights belong to the agent not to the principal. He alone will be sued for the price and not the principal.

This principle is applied to all such transactions and dispositions, which do not require attribution explicitly to the principal such as sale and purchase. In all such transactions the rights and liabilities are traceable to the agent. For example, in a contract of sale, it is agent alone who can demand price from purchaser. If the principal directs this claim against purchaser, he (purchaser) cannot be forced to make payment to him.

---

[7] Manṣūr ibn Yūnus, Bahūtī, *Kashshāf al-Qinā'*, Cairo: Maṭba'ah Anṣār al-Sunnah al-Muḥammadiyyah, 1366/1948 vol.2, p.228.
[8] Ibn Qudāmah, *Al-Mughnī*, vol. 5, p.130.

There are, however, certain other contracts, which must be attributed explicitly to the principal such as marriage, divorce, and settlement for murder. The rights in all these cases are traceable to the principal because the agent in these cases is merely an emissary carrying the consent of the principal to other party. Thus, if the agent concludes a marriage contract on behalf of husband, he (agent) will not be demanded to pay dower money. Similarly, the agent of wife cannot demand dower money from the husband. The Ḥanbalī jurists do not differentiate between the contract of sale and contract of marriage for this purpose. To them the effects as well as rights and liabilities in all the contracts are attributed to the principal.

Termination of Agency

Contract of agency is terminated under the following circumstances.

1. Mutual agreement of the parties to terminate the agency.

2. Unilateral termination by any of the two parties. Because of the consensual nature of principal/agent relationship, it is possible for either party to bring it to an end simply by giving notice of termination of agreement. All the acts and disposition of agent before receipts of notice will be considered valid and effective with respect to principal.

3. Discharge of obligation by the agent. When the agent performs the act with which he was entrusted through the contract of agency, the agency comes to an end.

4. Destruction of the subject matter. When the object of the agency becomes non-existent, the agency comes to an end. If the principal, for example, settled a disposition in which he appointed an agent, or its object perished, the agency will stand terminated.

5. Death or loss of legal capacity. When party ceases to possess legal capacity, i.e., he becomes insane or the court prohibits him from dispositions, the agency will be terminated.

6. Agency cannot be terminated when the right of a third party is attached to the contract. Thus, if a mortgager (debtor) appoints the mortgagee (creditor) as his agent for the sale of mortgaged property in order that the debt is cleared, then such agency cannot be terminated till the sale is affected.[9]

Acts of the unauthorized agent *(fuḍūlī)*

The word *fuḍūlī* is derived from *fuḍūlī*, which means meddling or the undertaking of affairs by a person that are not of his concern and *fuḍūlī* is one who intervenes in matter that does not concern him. Hence, *fuḍūlī* is a person who concludes a contract on behalf of another without proper authority. One who sells the goods of another or purchases something for him when he is neither the *walī* (guardian) of such person nor his duly appointed agent, he is acting as a *fudūlī* [10]

Legal Status of the acts of a *fuḍūlī*

There are two opinions of the Muslim jurists regarding the acts of the *fuḍūlī*. The first suggests that such acts are *bāṭil* and without any legal effects. According to the second opinion the acts by *fuḍūlī* are valid subject to ratification by the person on whose behalf the act has been undertaken.

---

[9] Zaydān, *al-Madkhal* p.348.

[10] Ḥassān, *al-Madkhal li Dirāsāt al-Islāmī*, p.393.

Opinion No.1: Acts of the *fuḍūlī* are *bāṭil* having no legal effects:

The Shāfi'īs and Ḥanbalīs are of the opinion that the contracts concluded on behalf of another are void and have no legal effects. The contracts are *bāṭil* (void) even if they are ratified by the person on whose behalf they are concluded, because a contract, which is *bāṭil*, cannot become *ṣaḥīḥ* on the basis of such permission. These jurists have based their opinion on the fact that the basic condition for undertaking such transaction is the proper authority and the *fuḍūlī* does not possess such authority. He is neither the owner of the goods nor does he possess the requisite authority and his acts are, therefore, without legal validity. The jurists holding this opinion rely on the tradition; "Do not sell that which is not with you". This is interpreted here to mean, "Don't sell what you do not own". The command here was issued by the Prophet (s.a.w.s) in the case of a companion who used to conclude a sale first and then buy the goods and deliver them later on. These jurists also maintain that a *fuḍūlī* does not have the capacity to deliver at the time of making a contract the thing, which he is selling. As such it resembles the sale of a bird in the air or fish in water, which is *bāṭil*.[11]

Opinion No.2: The acts of the *fuḍūlī* are *mawqūf* (suspended) till ratification:

The Ḥanafīs and Mālikīs are of the opinion that acts of a *fuḍūlī* are valid but can be assigned legal effects only when ratified by proper authority. If such ratification is awarded, such acts become valid taking their legal effects. If the ratification is refused the acts are void *ab initio*.[12]

---

[11] Ibn Qudāmah, *al-Mughnī*, vol. 4, p.155.

[12] Ḥssān, *al-Madkhal li Dirāsāt al-Islāmī*, p.396.

These jurists rely for their opinion on the tradition that the Holy Property (s.a.w.s) ratified the purchase and subsequent sale of a goat on his behalf by one of the companions. As regards the tradition prohibiting the sale of that which one does not possess, it is maintained by these jurists that it applies to sale on one's own behalf and not on behalf of another. It goes without saying that *fuḍūlī* acts on behalf of other people.

We may now distinguish between the legal effects assigned to a suspended contracts by a *fuḍūlī* in cases ratification is assigned and in cases where ratification is refused.. The Ḥanafīs consider sale and purchase separately for this purpose and we follow their method in this discussion.

a) Sale by a *fuḍūlī:* As already mentioned that Ḥanafīs and Mālikīs consider the sale of a *fuḍūlī* as valid but subject to ratification by the owner of the goods.

The suspension of the contracts concluded by a *fuḍūlī* implies that such contracts may be revoked by the purchaser or by the *fuḍūlī* before ratification. The result of this would be that even if the original owner or the person on whose behalf the *fuḍūlī* acted were to ratify the contract, it could still to be revoked. The reason is that in such a case the interest of the *fuḍūlī* would have priority. This is because the *fuḍūlī* becomes an agent hence all the rights of the contract revert to him. It is he who has to deliver the goods or price and exercise various options. All this may be injurious to him.[13]

The Mālikī jurists do not allow a *fuḍūlī* or a purchaser the right of revocation. This right belongs only to the owner who may revoke or ratify the contract, as he likes. If a *fuḍūlī* becomes the owner of the goods (through inheritance or gift etc.) that he sold without authority, such sale becomes void according to the Ḥanafīs and he would have to transact a new sale. Ratification

---

[13] Kāsānī, *Badā'i' al-sanā'i'*, vol. 2, p.233.

by the *fuḍūlī* in such a case is not possible. The rule according to the Ḥanafīs is that the cause of ownership must precede the sale and in this case the cause has come into existence after the sale.

The Mālikīs allow the *fuḍūlī* in such a case to revoke the sale if he inherits the property, as according to them, he inherits the right of ratification with it. If he becomes the owner due to other causes like purchase and charity, he has no right to revoke the contract and the sale will be implemented.[14]

b) Purchase by a *fuḍūlī:* The Mālikī jurists do not distinguish between sale and purchase by a *fuḍūlī.* According to them both are dependent on ratification by the person on whose behalf such a transaction was made. The same rule applies to a situation where a *fuḍūlī* attributes the contracts to himself or to the person on whose behalf he is acting. Hence, purchase by a *fuḍūlī* on behalf of another is valid but suspended till ratification. The seller does not have the right to revoke such a contract. If ratification is accorded, the *fuḍūlī* is considered as an agent but if ratification is denied, the *fuḍūlī* becomes the buyer.[15]

The Ḥanafī jurists distinguish between purchase and sale and also whether the *fuḍūlī* is attributing the sale to himself or to the person on whose behalf he is acting. Thus, if a *fuḍūlī* purchases on behalf of another but attributes the contract to himself then such a contract will be valid against him. It will not require buyer's ratification and ownership is transferred to him. Consequently, he will be obliged to pay the price. When *fuḍūlī* attributes the purchase to the person on whose behalf he is

---

[14] Kāsānī, *Kharashī,* vol. 5, p.18; *al-Sharḥ-al-Kabīr,* vol. 3, p.12. Cf. hassān, *al-Madkhal li Dirāsāt al-Islāmī,* p 400.

[15] Kāsānī, *Kharashī,* vol. 5, p.18 Cf. Ḥassān, *al-Madkhal.* p.402.

acting the sale is valid but is subject to ratification by such person.[16]

A necessary condition in cases of ratification is that the person on whose behalf he is acting must have legal capacity failing which it should be ratified by the *walī*.

Conditions of Ratification

There are certain conditions that have to be fully complied with before the principal can effectively adopt the contract. These are:

a. The subject matter of the contract must be in existence

Ratification is futile if the subject matter was destroyed before it was accorded. If the subject matter is destroyed in the hands of the *fuḍūlī* he is liable for its destruction. If it is destroyed at the hands of the buyer the real owner is at liberty either to claim compensation from *fuḍūlī* or from the buyer.

b. All three parties must be alive at the time of ratification

If ratification is accorded after the death of one of the parties, it shall have no legal effects.

c. Concerned parties must possess legal capacity at the time of the contract

If a *fuḍūlī* acts on behalf of a minor who accords ratification after attaining puberty, such ratification is without effect.[17]

---

[16] Zayn al-'Ābidīn, Ibn Nujaym, *al-Bahr al-Rā'iq*, Cairo: 1893, vol. 6, p.149. Ḥassān, *al-Madkhal*. p.403.

[17] 'Imrān Nyāzee, *Outlines of Islamic Jurisprudence*, Islamabad: ALSI p.140.

Mode of ratification

Ratification is either expressed or implied. Expressed ratification is by words or by way of delivery (of goods or price). Implied ratification is by way of *qarā'in* (context) like the owner of goods gifting away the price of the goods sold by the *fuḍūlī*. The Ḥanafīs maintain that mere silence on the part of the owner when knowledge of the sale has reached him, does not amount to ratification on his part.

Effects of ratification: If ratification is accorded in conformity with the conditions listed above, the *fuḍūlī* becomes the agent (*wakīl*) of owner. Such agency has retrospective effects from time of the act of the *fuḍūlī*. Thus, the *ḥukm* of the contract will pass to the owner while the *ḥuqūq* shall remain with the *fuḍūlī* who is now the agent.

Denial of ratification: If in case ratification is denied, the acts of the *fuḍūlī* become null and void having no existence. If ratification is denied when delivery of the goods sold has already been made to the buyer, the owner has the right to demand the return of such goods. If such property is destroyed in the hands of the *fuḍūlī* he alone is responsible, but after delivery both the *fuḍūlī* and the buyer are liable.

In case there is silence on part of the owner the Ḥanafīs keep the contract suspended without any limit of time. Mālikī jurists on the other hand limit it to a period of one year from the time when knowledge of the sale reached the owner after which performance of the contract becomes necessary. It is important to note here that through this opinion the Mālikīs have introduced the concept of limitation into Islamic Law.[18]

---

[18] Ḥassān, *al-Madkhal*, pp. 405, 406.

2. Guardianship *(wilāyah)*

Definition

It is an authority granted by the *Sharī'ah* to a person over the person and property of another person by virtue of which his dispositions in respect of such persons are assigned legal effects.[19] The legitimacy of guardianship has been established by the Qur'ān and the Sunnah. Verses 282 of Sūrat al-Baqarah provides that: "If the party liable is mentally deficient or unable himself to dictate, let his guardian dictate faithfully".[20] This shows that a minor has to be subjected to guardianship.

Kinds of Guardianship

There are two kinds of guardianship;

1. guardianship over the person, and
2. guardianship over the property.

The first kind implies the protection of the minor, the undertaking of his education and general bringing up. It also includes his marriage. The second kind implies safeguarding of the property of the minor, the lunatic and the insane.

Guardians and grades of guardianship

The following persons are entitled to be guardians of the property in Islamic Law;

- the father,
- the executor appointed by the father's will,
- the father's father,

[19] Zuḥaylī, *al-Fiqh al-Islāmī wa Adillatuhu*, vol. 4, p.139.
[20] Qur'ān 2: 282.

- the executor appointed by the will of father's father,
- the judge, and
- the executor appointed by the judge.

In default of the first four categories, the court may appoint a guardian from the following persons in the order of priority herein;

- full brother,
- consanguine brothers,
- full brother's son,
- consanguine brother's son,
- full paternal uncle,
- consanguine paternal uncle,
- full paternal uncle's son, and
- consanguine paternal uncle's son.

The jurists are unanimous on the point that guardianship of a minor is established for the father. But they differ among themselves regarding the one who follows the father in guardianships and comes next to him. According to Ḥanafī jurists executor appointed by father follows him. And if the father has not appointed executor in his life, it will shift to grandfather and from him to the executor appointed by grandfather. Thus, the executor appointed by the father will be given priority over grandfather.[21] The Mālikī and Ḥanbalī jurists acknowledge guardianship of minor for father and his executor first and then for judge or his nominee.

---

[21] Zuḥaylī, *al-Fiqh al-Islāmī*, vol.4, p.142.

The grandfather in their view is not entitled to guardianship of property because he is not like the father. He is more distant than him in degree and has less concern for minor's interest.[22]

The Shāfi'ī jurists give grandfather precedence over the executor. He is nearer to minor than executor appointed by father. In the absence of the father and grandfather, guardianship belongs to an executor to be appointed by any of them who died later. And after him it will be transferred to the judge or his nominee.[23]

Conditions of guardian: The jurists have laid down following three conditions for a person who assumes the position of guardian;

- He should be adult and sane,
- He must follow the sane religion as followed by his ward, and
- He should be capable of performing dispositions required by the guardianship.[24]

Rights and duties of guardian: It is a basic requirement of guardianship that all the actions and dispositions of the guardian should be directed towards realization of the interest of the ward. Thus, he is allowed to make any disposition, which may benefit him and augment his wealth. The Qur'ān says:

> "Come not nigh to the orphan's property except to improve it until he attains the age."[25]

This verse makes it imperative for the guardian of the orphan not to touch his property except for the purpose of improving

---

[22] Ibid.
[23] Zaydān, *al-Madkhal*, p.336.
[24] Ibid, pp. 337-338.
[25] Qur'ān,17:34.

it and the guardian should not take a personal advantage in the bargain made for the ward.

- It is not permissible for guardian to enter into any contract for ward, which may cause damage to him. Thus, he is not allowed to use his property for granting loans and giving gifts to people.

- A legal guardian of the property of a minor has power to sell or pledge the goods and chattels of the minor for the minor's imperative necessities suited to his life such as food, clothing, and medication.

- A legal guardian may enter into a transaction of exchange in respect of minor's property, if it has the effect of conserving it.

- He can also sell it if the property has been usurped, and the guardian has reason to fear that there is no chance of fair restitution.

- A guardian of the property of a minor appointed by the court is bound to deal with moveable property belonging to the minor as carefully as a man of ordinary prudence would deal in his own case.

- Where a minor upon attaining his majority claims to be fit to manage his financial affairs and the executor disputes such fitness, the latter cannot be compelled to deliver the minor's property until the minor has been declared by the judge to be capable of such management.

- If the executor refuses to deliver the property to the minor after the latter has been declared competent by the judge to administer his own property, and after the minor has duly called upon executor to make such delivery, the latter will be held liable for any loss associated to the property while it is in his hand.

Conclusion

- Delegated authority refers to the authority of the agent and the guardian.
- A contract of agency has three elements namely; principal, agent and Subject matter.
- The subject matter of agency is the act for the performance of which agent is appointed.
- The subject-matter of agency should fulfil the following conditions:
    - It should be known to the agent;
    - It should be lawful; and
    - It should admit of representation.
- The agent is required to perform the undertaking according to the instructions of the principal and exercise due care and skill.
- Agency comes to an end by a number of circumstances such as mutual agreement, unilateral termination, discharge of obligation, destruction of the subject matter and the death or loss of legal capacity.
- The dispositions of the *fuḍūlī* (self-imposed agent) are lawful subject to ratification by the principal in the opinion of Ḥanafī and Mālikī jurists.
- Guardianship is an authority granted by the *Sharī'ah* to a person over the person and property of another person by virtue of which his dispositions in respect of such persons are assigned legal effect.

- Islamic Law acknowledges guardianship for the father, the executor appointed by him, the father's father, the executor appointed by him and judge.

- It is a basic requirement of guardianship that all actions and dispositions of the guardian should be directed towards realization of the interest of the ward.

Chapter 7

Ṣaḥīḥ, *Fāsid* and *Bāṭil* Contracts

The Muslim jurists classify contracts into *ṣaḥīḥ* (valid), *bāṭil* (void) and *fāsid* (voidable or irregular) contracts with regard to their legal validity. A *ṣaḥīḥ* contract is the one whose *aṣl* (nature and essence) and *waṣf* (accessory circumstances or attributes) are in accordance with law. Thus, a contract will be deemed valid when:

- Its elements are complete;
- Conditions relating to elements have been met; and
- It is free from external prohibited attributes.

Thus, if any of the elements is missing or a condition is not met or the Lawgiver has prohibited it due to some attribute attached to it, the contract is *bāṭil* or *fāsid*.

A contract will, therefore, be *bāṭil* or *fāsid* if the acceptance is missing or it does not correspond with the offer or one of the parties does not possess legal capacity or the subject matter is non-existent or it cannot be delivered or the contract contains an element of *ribā* (interest) or *gharar* (indeterminacy). Thus, the contract is *bāṭil* as an element is missing or a condition has not been fulfilled or an attribute opposes the command of the Lawgiver and each of these results in the same effect according to the majority, i.e., the contract is *bāṭil*.[1]

The Ḥanafīs divided contracts into three kinds: *ṣaḥīḥ*, *fāsid* and *bāṭil*.

---

[1] Ḥassān, *al-Madkhal li Dirāsāh al-Fiqh al-Islāmī*, pp. 439-430.

Valid or *Ṣaḥīḥ* Contract

The *ṣaḥīḥ* contract is said to be concluded when all its element are found, the conditions of each element have been met and it also possesses such attributes of extrinsic nature which the law takes notice of. There is no disagreement among the Ḥanafīs and other jurists regarding this meaning of the *ṣaḥīḥ* contract.[2]

It has been mentioned earlier that according to majority there are three elements of contract namely, the *ṣīghah* (form) offer and acceptance; the subject-matter and contracting parties. The Lawgiver has assigned further conditions to these elements. The *ṣīghah* requires conformity between offer and acceptance, their issuance in the same session, existence of the *ījāb* till the issuance of *qabūl*. It also requires that a party to the contract must be sane, puberty and that the subject-matter must be legal, in existence, deliverable and known.

If the elements are present and the conditions are met the contract comes into existence in the eyes of the Lawgiver. However, it cannot be called *ṣaḥīḥ* or which is legally enforceable (*mun'aqid*) unless it is free from external prohibited attributes like *ribā* and *gharar*. If a contract contains any such attributes the Ḥanafīs consider such a contract as *fāsid*. The Ḥanafīs define the *ṣaḥīḥ* contract as that which is legal in its *asl* as well as *wasf*. The *asl* here stands for the elements and conditions and the *wasf* for the external attributes, or accessory circumstances or non-essential quality of contract. According to Ḥanafī jurists a contract, which contains the condition of *ribā*, is not a void contract because *ribā* occurs either in a loan contract or in a sale transaction, which are basically permissible. It is the vitiating condition of *ribā*, which invalidates such a contract. Thus, it is valid by virtue of the validity of loan or sale,

---

[2] Madkūr, *al-Madkhal li al-Fiqh al-Isalmī*, Cairo: Dār al-Nahḍah al-'Arabiyyah, 1380/1960, p. 601.

but not by virtue of invalidating accessory attribute of *ribā*. Such a contract, according to Ḥanafī jurists will not be declared void; instead it is an irregular contract that can be made lawful by removing the invalidating condition of *ribā*.[3]

Similarly, a contract that contains an element of uncertainty, indeterminacy or want of knowledge is not a void contract. The example of indeterminacy is where a seller tells a buyer, "I sell you one sheep out of these three sheep", or where a sale takes place without fixing the price of object. In both the cases the sale is *fāsid,* i.e., irregular according to Ḥanafī jurists which can be regularised by removing the cause of irregularity, i.e., by identifying the sheep and fixing the price.[4]

The *Hukm* of *Ṣaḥīḥ* Contract

A *ṣaḥīḥ* contract is one that give rise to its all assigned effects that Lawgiver has determined for it. These effects come into being on conclusion of the contract if it is enforced *(nāfidh)* and after the removal of the cause of suspension if it is *mawqūf* or suspended contract.[5]

Kinds of Valid Contract

A *ṣaḥīḥ* contract, as we have said, is one, which is legal both as regards its *asl* and the *wasf*. Such a contract must give rise to the effects assigned to it by the Lawgiver. Some jurists maintain, however, that there are *ṣaḥīḥ* contracts, the effects of which can be delayed till the happening of a future event. Such contracts are called *mawqūf* contracts, i.e., held up in suspense. This is the opinion of the Ḥanafīs, Mālikīs, and some Ḥanbalīs. The Shāfi'īs and some Ḥanbalīs do not admit delay in the effects of the contracts. According to them a *ṣaḥīḥ* contract must give rise to

---

[3] See Sanhūrī, *Maṣādir al-Ḥaqq,* vol. 2, pp. 147, 151.

[4] Ḥassān, *al-Madkhal li Dirāsāt al-Fiqh al-Islāmī* p. 432.

[5] Ibid, p. 431.

its effects immediately, i.e., it must be *nāfidh* (operative). *Mawqūf* or suspended contracts thus have no existence according to these jurists. Thus, a *mawqūf* contract is a kind of valid contract. It is a contract, which is not immediately enforceable. Dr. Sanḥūrī regards it a voidable contract.[6]

- The *nāfidh* (operative or immediate contract):

  The *nāfidh* contract is that in which:

  - the elements are found;
  - the conditions are met;
  - the external attributes are legal; and
  - the contract is not dependent upon ratification.

- The *mawqūf* contract is that in which:

  - the elements are found;
  - conditions are met;
  - *wasf* is legal; but
  - the effects are dependent upon ratification.

This contract, as we have noted, is not acceptable to the Shāfi'īs and some Ḥanbalīs.

Causes of suspension

The cause due to which the effects of a *ṣaḥīḥ* contract are suspended may be summarized as under:

a. Defective capacity: Contracts of minor possessed with discretion (*sabī mumayyaz)* or the one under interdiction (*ḥajr)*

---

[6] Sanhūrī, *Maṣādir al-Ḥaqq*, p.276.

due to *safah* (weakness of intellect) or *'atah* (lunacy or partial insanity)

b. Lack of proper authority: Contracts in which a person acts on behalf of another without proper authority are suspended. These are the contracts of a *fuḍūlī*, i.e., one who is neither guardian nor agent nor the owner or contracts of an agent who transgresses the limits prescribed by the principal.

c. Right of third party: If the owner sells the mortgaged property, it will be subject to the ratification of the mortgagee.

The cases of *maraḍ al mawt* (death illness) *ghaṣb* usurpation are also treated the same way. We may analyze the above causes in little more detail:

(a) Contracts suspended due to defective capacity: The *sabī mumayyaz* can be permitted to undertake certain kinds of transactions. Those, which are purely harmful, cannot be permitted. Those, which result in benefit only, are allowed. However, a transaction by such a minor in which there is a likelihood of both benefit and harm are valid but subject to ratification. The ratification may be accorded by the guardian after the transaction and before the minor attains puberty or by the minor himself after majority in case the guardian did not reject the contract before attaining majority.

The *ḥukm* of such a contract is that before ratification there are no effects and ownership is not transferred in goods or price. Once ratification is granted it acts retrospectively and the effects come into operation from the date of the contract. In case ratification is refused the contract becomes void.

(b) Suspension due to lack of proper authority: The rules relating to the *fuḍūlī* have already been studied and are applicable here. The contracts of the *fuḍūlī* are *ṣaḥīḥ* but *mawqūf*. If such contracts are ratified by one who possesses the authority, then the effects come into operation. Refusal to ratify shall make the contracts of the *fuḍūlī* void. In case the *fuḍūlī* has delivered the property, the *aḥkām* of *ghāṣb*, (usurpation) shall operate against him, i.e., he shall return the property or become liable for compensation. Ratification of course shall operate from the time of the contract.

c) **Suspension due to right of third parties**: There are cases where a person has the capacity and authority to act, i.e., he is the owner of the subject matter, but the rights of third parties are linked to it. The contract, thus, is suspended and needs to be ratified by such third party.[7]

Thus, if A, a mortgager decides to sell his property mortgaged with B from whom he has borrowed money, the right of B is likely to be endangered. B can claim that his loan be repaid first. This contract shall, therefore be suspended. In case B decided to forgo his claim upon the property he may ratify the contract, which shall be declared. In case he refuses to do so the contract shall become *bāṭil*. It may be mentioned here that before ratification by B, the buyer has a right to revoke the contract but A, the mortgager/seller, has no right to revoke the contact of sale made by him.

In the case of *maraḍ al mawt* (death illness) we know that any transaction, which is not at market value, will take the *ḥukm* of bequest and shall be valid up to one-third of the property. Beyond one-third of the property ratification shall be required from persons whose rights are affected namely the creditors and heirs.

---

[7] See Sanhūrī, *Maṣādir al-Ḥaqq*, pp.128-130; Ḥassān, *al-Madkhal*, pp. 449, 450; Zuhaylī, *al-Fiqh al-Islāmī wa adillatuhū*, vol. 4, pp. 229-230.

The *Lāzim* (Binding) and *Jā'iz* (Non-binding) Contract

A contract, which is *ṣaḥīḥ* and *nāfidh* is divisible into *lāzim* (binding) and *ghayr lāzim* also known as *Jā'iz.* (non-binding or terminable).

The *lāzim* contract

The *lāzim* contract is that in which none of the parties has a right to revoke the contract without the consent of the other, unless options have been granted to a party by virtue of which the right to revoke can be exercised.

The *jā'iz* or *ghayr lāzim* contract

It is that contract in which the right to revoke can be exercised by either party without the consent of the other party. The reason for a contract being *ghayr lāzim* or revocable are two:

(a) The nature of the contract, which allows independence to both parties as in *wakālah* (agency), *sharikah* (partnership), *wadī'ah* (deposit), *kafālah* (suretyship), and *'āriyah* (commodate loans). These contracts are *jā'iz* (terminable) or *ghayr lāzim* (non-binding) with respect to either party or one of them.

(b) An option is stipulated in the contract that prevents it from becoming *lāzim*. Thus, the party possessing the option can revoke the contract without the consent of the other party within the period of the option[8] (options have been discussed in detail under the title "Islamic Law of Options").

[8] See Ḥassān, *al-Madkhal,* pp. 452,453.

Fāsid (Irregular contract)

Definition

The *fāsid* (irregular) contract is the one whose elements are present (i.e., offer and acceptance) and all the essential conditions are complete, but an external attribute attached to the contract has been prohibited by the Lawgiver. The contract is legal as regards its *asl* but it is not proper as the *waṣf* is prohibited.[9]

Causes of Irregularity in *Fāsid* Contracts

Some important causes, which render a contract *fāsid are as follows:*

- defective consent, i.e., a consent obtained through coercion;
- want of knowledge leading to dispute (*gharar* and *jahl*);
- invalid condition or an ancillary condition not being collateral to the contract and not admitted by commercial usage and being one, which gives advantage to one of the contracting parties at the cost of the other; and
- Usury (*ribā* (usury) or undue enrichment.[10]

Discussion of the cause of irregularity in detail:

I. Defective consent due to coercion

The Majority of the Muslim jurists hold the view that a contract made under coercion is a void contract. The Ḥanafī jurists, on the other hand, view it as an irregular contract. To them such contract must be dissolved. However, if the coerced party after the removal of coercion ratifies the contract, it will become a

[9] Zaydān, *al-Madkhal li dirāsāt al-Sharī'ah al-Islāmiyyah*, p. 366.
[10] Sanhūrī, *Maṣādir al-Ḥaqq* vol. 2, p. 127.

valid contract. Thus, it can be regularized by ratification. According to Imām Zufar, a Ḥanafī jurist, it is a valid contract, however, it is suspended one, which is subject to ratification.[11] To him coercion is an impediment to enforcement of contract not to its validity. The ratification of irregular contract is possible before possession as well as after it.

II. Want of knowledge

Want of knowledge that invalidates contracts is the one that is likely to lead to dispute among the parties. For example, a person sold an unidentified sheep out of herd of sheep. This will certainly give rise to a dispute between the contracting parties because the buyer would naturally ask for the best sheep in the flock, whereas the seller would like to give the worst. It is, however, permissible to sell one item out of few identified items with the option of determination in favour of the purchaser.

Want of knowledge affecting the validity of contract is of the following types:

- want of knowledge relating to the subject-matter such as indeterminate object in a sale contract, or unidentified property in leasing contract;
- want of knowledge relating to consideration. It is where price of the sold article has not been fixed, and is left unspecified;
- want of knowledge relating to the time of performance. For example, A rented his house to B without fixing the hiring period, or A sold an object to B on credit without specifying the time of payment of price. Indeterminacy of period in a partnership contract does not invalidate it because

[11] Zuhaylī, *al-Fiqh al-Islāmī wa adillatuhū*, vol. 4, p. 380.

partnership is a non-binding contract in Ḥanafī jurisprudence. It can be terminated at any time.

- Want of knowledge relating to means of suretyship. Thus, if seller asked the purchaser to provide a guarantor or pledge some property as security for the deferred price of sale, it is necessary that the guarantor or pledged property be identified and made known to the creditor, otherwise the contract will be irregular on account of want of knowledge relating to means of suretyship.[12]

Gharar or uncertainty relating to necessary characteristics of a commodity also renders a contract irregular in the following manner:

- In sale contract: If a person sold a cow believing that it gives a particular quantity of milk, it will be an irregular sale because of uncertainty of milk yield or if he sold a cow believing that it bears a calf in its womb, again the sale is irregular on account of uncertainty.

- In partnership contracts: If the contracting parties agreed on particular amount of profit for one party, the contract is irregular because it is possible that partnership earns only that much profit which has been stipulated for one party or it does not earn anything. A contract of partnership with such a stipulation is regarded irregular.[13]

---

[12] Ibid, pp. 379-380.

[13] Muṣṭafā Aḥmad Zarqā, *al-Madkhal al-Fiqhī, al-'Amm*, Demascus: Maṭba'ah Tarbīn,1387/1968, vol. 2, pp. 699, 700.

III. Invalid condition or an ancillary condition not being collateral to the contract

Irregularity can also arise from the stipulation of an irregular condition. In Ḥanafī jurisprudence a condition is deemed to be irregular in the following cases:[14]

- When it is repugnant to the requisite of the contract such as to stipulate that the buyer will not sell the object he has purchased; or he will not rent it out, or to stipulate in a marriage contract that husband will not establish matrimonial relationship with his wife.
- When it is expressly prohibited by the Lawgiver, like selling an article on the condition that the purchaser will sell something else to the buyer or lend him some money or make him a gift. Such conditions are prohibited because Islamic Law expressly prohibits combination of two mutually inconsistent contracts - a loan and a sale.
- When it is against the commercial usage such as condition by the purchaser of corn that the seller will grind it, or a condition by a buyer of a piece of cloth that the seller will sew it.
- When it is advantageous to one party at the cost of other party. For example, where the seller reserves for himself an advantage from the sale such as the condition that he shall reside in the house sold for a period of two months after sale, or he will lend him some money.

Examples of such irregular conditions in a marriage contract is stipulations by a wife that husband will not marry another woman, or he will never divorce her, or he will divorce the existing wife. All such conditions render a contract irregular. It is pertinent to note here that these irregular conditions affect

[14] Zuhaylī, *al-Fiqh al-Islāmī wa adillatuhū*, vol. 4, pp. 381,382.

only the commutative contracts such as contract of sale, hiring, and cultivation, and do not affect gratuitous contracts such as gift, donation, *waqf* or the contracts of suretyship such as *kafālah*, mortgage, and *ḥawālah* (assignment of debt), or the contract of marriage. Irregular conditions in the aforesaid contracts do not invalidate them. Only the invalid condition is abrogated. The other part of the contract remains valid and effective. (Extrinsic conditions have been dealt with in detail in chapter entitled "Extrinsic conditions and their effect on contract").

IV. *Ribā*

Ribā occurs either in a loan transaction or in a barter contract. *Ribā* in a loan transaction means to stipulate excess over and above the principal sum to be paid by the debtor. It also takes place in a barter transaction. It is where a person exchanges two commodities of the same kind with excess such as two parties exchange 5 k.g. of wheat for 7 k.g. of wheat. According to Ḥanafī jurists a contract containing an element of *ribā* is an irregular contract. It can be made valid by removing the cause of irregularity. Thus, if the party, which has stipulated excess in its favour, annuls the condition of excess in the session of contract, the contract will become a valid contract. (The issue of *ribā* has been discussed in detail in a separate chapter).

The *ḥukm* of an irregular contract

Before possession

Legal effects are only assigned to the *ṣaḥīḥ* contract and not to an irregular contract. This rule has been applied by the Ḥanafīs to an irregular contract in which possession of the property has not been delivered. Such a contract must be revoked without the consent of either party. Thus, ownership in the property is not transferred and no rights and obligations have arisen. The seller cannot demand the price nor can the buyer force the seller to deliver the goods. The parties to such a contract have no option to permit an irregular contract or to relinquish the right of revocation. Each one of the parties can revoke the contract without the consent of the other.

The only way in which an irregular contract can become a valid or *ṣaḥīḥ* contract is by the removal of the cause of irregularity, i.e, the removal of the prohibited *waṣf.* Thus, if a contract declared irregular because of *ribā*, which is stipulated in the contract such irregularity can be removed if the party in whose favour *ribā* has been stipulated, decides to forgo it.

After possession

If the parties to the contract decide to implement it, e.g., the delivery of the goods by the seller to the buyer and delivery of the price to him by the buyer, then this contract, is strengthened somewhat as compared to the position before delivery. The result of this is that the right to revocation, which rested with, either party without the consent of the other now will rest with the party who had the benefit of the condition. This is so in cases like sale for an undetermined period or with the condition of extending credit to the seller. As regards cases like *ribā* or where the price is in form of wine, the right of revocation still rests with both parties.

When the buyer takes possession of property with the consent of the seller, then he can use it as the ownership passes to him by possession. In such a case, his obligation is to pay the value or market price of the goods purchased to the seller and not the price that was fixed in the agreement. Article 371 of the *Majallah* points to this fact. It reads: "In *bay' fāsid*, where the buyer has received a thing sold with the permission of the seller, he becomes the owner ".[15]

---

[15] *Majallat al-Aḥkām al-'Adliyyah*, Art. 371.

However, the parties can still revoke it if the buyer has not disposed it off. In such a case, if the seller wishes to resume the object, he must first pay the purchase-money to the buyer.[16] Until such restitution the goods are held by the purchaser as a pledge.[17] But if the buyer disposed of the property by resale or donation or added or subtracted from it, or changed it in such a way that it can no longer be regarded as the same object, then there is no right for either party to annul the contract.[18] Thus, where the buyer has sold the property, this second sale is valid and legally enforceable, it cannot be obstructed in Islamic Law by the fact that first sale was irregular.

Difference Between Valid and Irregular Contracts

Some differences between valid contract and irregular contracts are as follows:

- Ownership in a valid contract is transferred from the seller to the purchaser by mere offer and acceptance, whereas in irregular contract it is transferred to him by possession taken with the consent of the seller.
- In an irregular sale the value of the thing, i.e., its market price, is admissible whereas in a valid contract agreed price is paid. In an irregular hiring contract, the lesser is entitled to equitable and proper rent (according to market rate) and not to the specified rent. Similarly, in an irregular partnership, each partner gets the profit in proportion to his capital and not according to the agreement.

Revocation of irregular contract

Islamic Law does not approve of an irregular contract. Therefore, its revocation is necessary regardless of whether

---

[16] Ibid, Art. 373.

[17] Marghīnānī, *Hedāyah*, tr. Charls Hamilton, Sweden, 1891, p. 276.

[18] *Majallah*, Article 372.

delivery has been made or not. However, it cannot be revoked if the subject-matter has changed shape or is destroyed or has been disposed of by the buyer through sale or donation, and the second purchaser has sold it further. In all these cases the contract cannot be revoked.[19]

Forms of Irregular Contract

Some important forms of irregular transactions according to Ḥanafī jurists are as follows:

1. **Bayʻ al-Majhūl:** It refers to a sale in which the object of sale or its price or the time of its payment remains unknown and unspecified.

2. **Contingent contract:** It is a contract that is contingent upon an uncertain event. For example, A says to B, "I sell you my house if X sold me his house".

3. **Sale contract effective from future date:** It is a contract that comes into effect from future date:

4. **Bayʻ al ghā'ib:** It is a sale of what is not visible at the meeting of the parties. The seller in *bayʻ al-ghā'ib* has title over the subject matter but it is not available at the parties' meeting because it is elsewhere.

5. **Sale contract with unlawful consideration:** It refers to a sale whose consideration or price is something prohibited by Islamic law such as wine or pork.

6. **Bayʻal-ʻĪnah:** It is to sell a property on credit for a certain price and then to buy it back at a price less than the sale price on prompt payment, both transactions taking place simultaneously in the same session of the contract. According to Imām Abū Yūsuf, a Ḥanafī jurist, such sale is valid.

---

[19] Zarqā, *al-Madkhal al-Fiqhī al-ʻĀmm*, vol. 2, p. 703.

7. Two sales in one: Where a single contract relates to two sales. Such as to sell one commodity for two prices, one being cash and the other credit price, making contract binding against one of the two prices.[20]

The *Bāṭil* Contract

A *bāṭil* contract is defined by the Ḥanafīs as that which is illegal in its *aṣl* as well as its *wasf*.[21] The word *asl* refers to elements and essential conditions pertaining thereto while the *wasf* is the external attribute. The Ḥanafī say that there is only one element, i.e., *sīghah* (form). The *ṣīghah* has conditions that relate to *ījāb* and *qabūl* like conformity between them, their issuance in the same *majlis*, existence of the *ījāb* till the issuance of the *qabūl* or those, which relate to the capacity of the parties or the subject-matter. If any of these conditions is not fulfilled the contract becomes *bāṭil*. All this relates to the *aṣl*. As regards the *wasf* they maintain that it is an external attribute introduced into the contract by the parties, which is against Islamic Law.

The *bāṭil* contract does not give rise to any effect. Thus, no ownership is transferred nor is any kind of obligation found. The reason is that the contract in itself is prohibited and whatever is prohibited cannot give rise to rights. Performance of the contract is, therefore, not possible and none of the parties can enforce it.[22] If delivery of the goods has already been made then the property must be returned to the other party regardless of whether such illegality was known to the parties. If the buyer sells the goods to a third party after taking delivery, the original seller cannot be prevented from claiming the goods. The reason is that ownership cannot be transferred through a contract that

[20] See, Zuhaylī, *al-Fiqh al-Islāmī wa adillatuhū*, vol.4, pp.454-472.
[21] Zaydān, *al-Madkhal*, p. 366.
[22] Zuhaylī, *al-Fiqh al-Islāmī wa adillatuhū,* vol. 4, p. 237.

is *bāṭil*. This *ḥukm* is clearly different from that of a *fāsid* contract.

Ratification also has no role to play in a *bāṭil* contract. In case a *bāṭil* contract is concluded by a person suffering from death illness then the creditors or heirs have a right to claim restitution of property.

Causes of Invalidity

The causes which render a contract invalid, may be divided into two kinds:

(a) **Intrinsic causes:** These are the causes, which relate to *asl* or elements of contract such as the unlawfulness of subject-matter, non-existence of subject-matter, the absence of contractual capacity.

(b) **Extrinsic causes:** Extrinsic causes are the causes, that relate to *waṣf*, i.e., external attribute such as the contract contains element of *ribā* or *gharar*. It is pertinent to note that *ribā* and *gharar* are causes of irregularity of contract in Ḥanafī Law while in other schools they are causes of invalidity of contract. We will discuss here causes, which relate to first kind. (*ribā* and *gharar* have been discussed in the following chapters).

1. Unlawful object

It is a condition for the validity of a contract that the object of the contract be legal and lawful. It means that the object should be a thing in which transactions are permissible in the *Sharīʿah*. It should be ritually and legally clean. Any substance which is religiously and legally unclean, and the disposal of which have been restricted, cannot be a valid object of sale; e.g., wine, pig, intoxicants, blood and carcasses. The Ḥanafī jurists do not consider bones of dead animals, hair, skin as filth, so they allow their sale.[23] The rule to them is that anything not prone to death and decay is pure.

The legality of the object further requires that the purpose of the contract and its underlying cause should be recognized by the *Sharī'ah*. It should not be contrary to the objectives of the *Sharī'ah*. Therefore, a contract to run a brothel or a gambling house is void, because in the former case the contract is contrary to the preservation of the family unit, progeny and offspring which is an objective of the *Sharī'ah* and, in the letter case, the object is opposed to the preservation of property and amounts to devouring another person's properties wrongfully.[24]

The legality of the object also means that the act or service which is the subject-matter of contract must not be harmful for the contracting parties or the general public, e.g., hoarding commodities, growing of opium, a contract to kill a person, to usurp the property, or deprive a person of his property without compensation.[25]

Furthermore, if the object does not fulfill the intended objectives, again it will be held to be a void contract. Thus vegetables cannot be made the object of a pledge, because the purpose of a pledge is to retain pledged property and to sell it for satisfaction of the claim whereas vegetables are easily perishable. They, therefore, do not serve the intended purpose. Likewise public roads and public parks cannot be made the objects of sale, because they are meant for the benefit of the

---

[23] See Kāsānī, *Badā'i' al-sanā'i'*, vol. 5, p.140; *Mughnī al-Muhtāj*, vol. 2, p.11; Ibn Qudāmah , *al-Mughnī*, vol. 4, p.260.

[24] See Zuhaylī, *al-Fiqh al-Islāmī*, vol. 4, pp.185-186.

[25] Mushtaq Aḥmad, *Business Ethics in Islām*, Islamabad, International Institute of Islamic Thought and International Institute of Islamic Economics,1995, p.95.

public not for the benefit of an individual or a specific group of people.[26]

2. Absence of contractual capacity

As mentioned earlier, it is a requirement for a valid contract that the contracting parties be competent to conclude a contract. This means that they should be major and sane, and not prevented from transactions. Thus a contract will be deemed void if it is entered into:

(I) by an insane person.

(II) by a minor not possessed with discretion. (*ṣabī ghayr mumayyaz*).

(i) by a minor possessed with discretion if he made a transaction which is harmful to him or a transaction which may equally result in benefit and loss without permission of his guardian.

(ii) by a *ma'tūh* (partially insane) if it is a harmful contract for him.

(iii) by a *safīh* (weak of intellect) after he has been put under interdiction by the court.

(iv) by a *muflis* (bankrupt) whose debt exceed his earnings and the court, on the demand of his creditors has passed prohibitory orders. The disposal of property by such a person would be invalid and will produce no effects after such interdiction by the court.

(v) by a *fuḍūlī* (unauthorized agent) whose action has not been subsequently ratified by the principal.

---

[26] Zaydān, *al-Madkhal li Dirāsāt al-Sharī`ah al-Islāmiyyah*, p.308.

3. Non-existence of the subject-matter

Non-existence of the subject-matter is generally considered a cause of invalidity of contract. This principle applies to both commutative and gratuitous contracts. Mālikī jurists, however, allow donation or gift of a non-existent object.[27] Hence it is permissible in their opinion to donate a palm tree that will produce next year. According to other jurists the object of contract should exist at the time of contract regardless of whether the contract is commutative or gratuitous. Examples of non-existent objects are:

(a) sale of fruits before they have made appearance;

(b) sale of unborn animal; and

(c) sale of milk in the udders.

Contracts of *salam* and *istiṣnā‘* are approved by way of *‘istiḥsān* (juristic preference) despite absence of the object of contract.

4. Illegal purpose

It is a requirement of valid contract that its object and motivating cause should be lawful. Thus, any contract contrary to the intention of the Lawgiver and against the objectives of the *Sharī‘ah* is considered invalid in Islamic Law. Therefore, selling a weapon to a person who will use it to kill an innocent person, to enter a marriage contract in order to facilitate re-marriage between the divorced couple are invalid contracts.

In conclusion, we may say that a contract is valid according to the requirements of the *Sharī‘ah* with regard to its essence and external attributes while a void contract is contrary to Islamic

[27] See Ibn Rushd, *Bidāyat al-Mujtahid* vol.2, p.331, Qarāfi, *al-Furūq*, Beriut: al-Kutub al-‘Ilmiyyah, 1986, vol.1, p.150; Ibn Juzy, *al-Qawānīn al-Fiqhiyyah*, Beriut:Dār al-‘Ilm li al-Malāyīn, 1973, p.352.

Law both in its essence as well as external attributes; it does not give rise to any effect.

Conclusion

The above discussion may be summarized as follows:

- A *ṣaḥīḥ* (valid) contract is that whose basic elements, conditions and external attributes are in accordance with Islamic Law.
- A *bāṭil* (void) contract is contrary to Islamic Law both in its essence and external attributes. It does not give rise to any effect
- A *fāsid* (irregular) contract is one whose elements and essential conditions are valid according to the *Sharīʿah*, but an external attribute attached to the contract has been prohibited by Islamic Law.
- Important causes of irregularity are defective consent, want of knowledge, invalid condition and element of *ribā*.
- An irregular contract can become a valid contract by the removal of the cause of irregularity.
- Ownership in an irregular contract is transferred to the buyer by the possession taken with the consent of seller, not merely by the contract.
- In an irregular sale contract the value or the market price of the thing and not the agreed price is paid to the seller.

Chapter 8

Extrinsic Causes of Invalidity *Gharar* (Uncertainty)

Gharar is one of the major causes of the Invalidity of a contract. It is an external prohibited attribute that invalidates the contracts. Literally, *gharar* means risk or hazard. *Taghrīr* being the verbal noun of *gharar* is to unknowingly expose oneself or one's property to jeopardy.[1] It includes such elements as doubt, suspicion, uncertain conditions, the absolute lack of knowledge about and in determinability of the basic elements of the subject-matter.

Definitions of *Gharar*

- According to Sarakhsī: *Gharar* takes place where the consequences (of a transaction) remain unknown.[2]

- According to Ibn-Ḥazm: *Gharar* in sales occurs where the purchaser does not know what he has bought and the seller does not know what he has sold.[3]

- Ibn 'Ābidīn defines *gharar* in the following words: *Gharar* is uncertainty about the existence of the subject-matter of sale.[4]

---

[1] Mohammad Siddīq Darīr, *al-Gharar fī al-'Uqūd wa Āthāruhu fī al-Tatbīqāt al-Mu'āṣirah*, p.10.

[2] Sarakhsī, Abū Bakr Muhammad Ibn Aḥmad, *al-Mabsūt*, Beriut:Dār al-Ma'rif, 1978, vol.13, p.194.

[3] Ibn Ḥazm, *al-Muḥallah,* Dār al- Āfāq al-Jadīdah, vol. 8, pp. 343-389.

[4] Ibn 'Ābidīn, *Radd al-Muḥtār,* vol. 4, p.147.

- Ibn al-Qayyim has described *gharar* as being the subject matter, the vendor is not in position to hand over to the buyer whether the subject matter exists or not.[5]
- According to Ibn Rushd, *gharar* is to be found in contracts of sale when the seller suffers a disadvantage as a result of his ignorance, with regard to price of the article or the indispensable criteria relating to the contract or its object or quality or time of delivery.[6]
- *Sanhūrī*, an eminent modern jurist is of the view that lack of knowledge about the material terms of contract is the distinct feature of a *gharar* contract. He says that *gharar* takes place in the following circumstances:
  - (a) when it is not known whether the subject-matter exists;
  - (b) if it exists at all, whether it can be handed over to the buyer;
  - (c) when want of knowledge affects the identification of the genus or species of subject matter;
  - (d) when it affects its quantum, identity or necessary conditions; and
  - (e) when it relates to the date of a future performance.[7]

Forms of *gharar* according to Ibn Juzy

Ibn Juzay, a Mālikī jurist, has given a list of ten cases, which constitute in his view, a forbidden *gharar*:

---

[5] Ibn al-Qayyim, *I'lām al-Mu'qqi'īn,* vol. 1, p.357.
[6] Ibn Rush, *Bidāyat al-Mujtahid*, vol. 2, p.156.
[7] Sanhūrī, *Maṣādir al-Ḥaqq*, vol. 3, pp.31-41.

(i) Difficulty in putting the buyer in possession of subject-matter, such as sale of a stray animal or the unborn offspring when the mother is not part of the sale.

(ii) Want of knowledge with regard to the price or the subject matter, such as the vendor saying to buyer, "I sell you what is under my sleeve".

(iii) Want of knowledge with regard to the characteristics of the subject-matter such as the vendor saying to the potential buyer: "I sell you a piece of cloth which is in my home". Another example is the sale of an article without the buyer inspecting or the seller describing it.

(iv) Want of knowledge with regard to the quantum or the price or the quantity of the subject matter, such as an offer to sell "at today's price" or "at the market price".

(v) Want of knowledge regarding the date of future performance, such as an offer to sell when a particular person enters the room or when a particular person dies.

(vi) Two sales in one transaction, such as selling one article at two different prices, one for cash and the other for credit; or selling two different articles at one price: one for immediate remittance and the other for a deferred payment.

(vii) Sale of what is not expected to revive such as the sale of a sick animal.

(viii) *Bay' al-ḥasāt*, which is a type of sale whose outcome is determined by throw of a stone.

(ix) *Bay'al-munābadhah;* a sale performed by the vendor throwing a cloth at the buyer and achieving the sale transaction without giving the buyer the opportunity for properly examining the object of sale.

(x) *Bay' al-mulāmasah*, where the bargain is struck by touching the object of the sale without examining it.[8]

Forms of *gharar* transactions according to Siddīq al-Darīr

Siddīq al-Darīr an eminent modern scholar of *Sharī'ah* has given a detailed list of transactions that involve element of *gharar*. *Gharar*, in his view, sometimes relates to the form of contract and sometimes to its subject matter.[9]

I. *Gharar* or uncertainty relating to *ṣīghah* (form) of contract

The transactions belonging to this category are as follows:

1. **Two sales in one:** Two sales in one means that a single contract relates to two sales. It is where a seller says to a buyer: "I sell you this commodity for hundred (Rupees) on cash and hundred and fifty on credit", and the buyer accepts it without specifying the price at which he will buy the commodity. The *gharar* inherent in this contract is indeterminacy of the price. Thus the seller does not know at which price the buyer will buy the object.

2. **Earnest money (*'Arbūn*) sale:** It is a sale in which a person buys an item and pays a certain amount of money in advance to the seller on condition that if the transaction is completed the advance will be adjusted and if the bargain is cancelled the seller will not return the advance.

The majority of Muslim Jurists except Imām Aḥmad, hold that earnest money sale is invalid[10] because it amounts to taking of other's money without any compensation and also because it

[8] Ibn Juzy, *Qawanīn al-Ahkām al-Shar'iyyah*, pp. 282,283.

[9] *Darīr, al-Gharar fī al-'Uqūd*, pp. 13-30.

[10] See *Bidāyat al-Mujtahid*, vol.2, p.161, Ibn Qudāmah, *al-Sharḥ al-Kabīr*, vol3, p.63; Ibn Juzy, *al-Qawānīn al-fiqhiyyah*, p.258; Shirbīnī, *Mughnī al-Muhtāj*, vol.2, p.39.

involves uncertainty regarding the completion of transaction. *Darīr* is inclined to majority's view of invalidity.[11]

In our view earnest money is in the nature of an option contract. The money is being paid as a consideration to gain time from the selling party. The selling party is reciprocating by restraining himself in exercise of his legal right in respect of his property. However, the earnest money cannot be forfeited if the transaction cannot be completed because of the fault of selling party. The Accounting and Auditing Organization of Islamic Financial Institutions subscribes to the view of Ḥanbalī school and holds *'arbūn* valid.

3. **Contingent sale:** It is a contract that is contingent upon a condition e.g. "I sell you my house if A sold his house to me". The *gharar* at work behind this contract is that it is contingent upon the happening of an uncertain future event. Such sale is void in the opinion of the majority of Muslim Jurists. Imām Ibn Taymiyyah regards it valid.[12]

4. **Contract effective from future date:** It is a contract, which comes into effect at some future date e.g. the contract, shall be effective from such and such date. The *gharar* contained in such sale according to *Ḍarīr* is the possible change in price or other circumstances of the sale, which may affect real consent of the contracting parties when the time of performance approaches. But the fact is that there is no *gharar* in such sale. This sale is also valid in the opinion of Imām Ibn Taymiyyah.[13]

II. *Gharar* or uncertainty relating to subject-matter

This is of the following eight types:

---

[11] See Darīr, *al-Gharar fī al-'uqūd* , p.14.
[12] Ibid: p.16.
[13] Ibid: p.17.

1. Uncertainty regarding the genus of the object: It is where a person says to another. "I sell you an item for ten", and does not specify the object of sale.

2. Uncertainty regarding the kind of the object: Uncertainty and indeterminacy pertains to kind if the seller tells the buyer: "I sell you an animal at such and such price", without indicating the kind of animal."

3. Uncertainty regarding attributes of object: It is where the necessary attributes of the object of the sale are not described.

The opinion of Muslim Jurists is divided regarding the requirement of describing the subject-matter. Ḥanafī Jurists are of the view that the description of subject-matter is not necessary as long as it is present and visible for the buyer. But if the subject-matter is not visible, its description is necessary. Some Ḥanafī jurists disagree with this view and hold that description is not necessary as long as the right of inspection is established for the buyer. By exercising this right, he can reject the object if it does not correspond with description. But the proponents of description do not accept this argument. They say that right of inspection is given to buyer only to remove light uncertainty not the excessive one resulting from leaving a thing undescribed. An invisible object, therefore, should be described at the time of contract, and if some uncertainty still remains, it may be removed by exercise of right of inspection.[14]

Mālikī jurists regard description of subject-matter obligatory irrespective of the fact that it is present or absent, visible or invisible.[15]

Three opinions are attributed to Shāfi'ī jurists: **First**, sale is not valid until detailed description is given as in *salam* sale. **Second**,

---

[14] Ibn 'Ābdın *Radd al-Muḥtār*, vol. 4, p.29.

[15] Ibn Rushd, *Bidāyat al-Mujtahid*, vol. 2, p.148.

sale is not valid until relevant attributes are mentioned. **Third**, sale is valid even without mentioning attributes of object as long as the buyer has right of inspection.[16]

The Ḥanbalī jurists maintain that sale of an object with unknown attributes is not permissible.[17]

Some sales prohibited explicitly by the text due to uncertainty of the attributes are:

(i) sale of unborn calf without its mother;

(ii) sale of embryos; and

(iii) sale of bull's sperm etc.

As regard selling what is hidden in the ground such as carrot, onions, garlic, it is allowed by Ḥanafī jurists provided the buyer exercises the right of inspection when he uproots them. The sale of above mentioned things is invalid according to Imām Shāfi'ī and Imām Aḥmad as long as they are hidden in the ground.

To Imām Mālik it is permissible only when the buyer acquires complete knowledge about the object of sale.

4. Uncertainty regarding the quantity of the object: The knowledge of the quantity of object is necessary for validity of sale. Thus, to sell a heap of grain haphazardly without reference to its quantity is impermissible.

A traditional example of uncertainty regarding the quantity of object is *muzābanah*. It has been explained as sale of fresh dates on the palms against harvested dried dates. It implies buying something whose number, weight and measure is not known.

---

[16] Abū Zakariyyā Nawawī, *al-majmū'* Cairo: Maktabah al-'Āṣimah, 1966, vol.9, p.288.

[17] Abū Ishāq Shirāzī, *al-Muhaddab,* Cairo: Dār al-Naṣr vol.4, p.109.

5. Uncertainty regarding specification of object: *Gharar* relates to specification when things of different entities are sold without specifying one of them in particular such as in the sale of a piece of cloth out of bulk or a sheep out of a herd. Such sale is invalid according to Shāfi'ī and Ḥanbalī jurists on account of non-specification of object.[18] Ḥanafī jurists allow it to the extent of three items.[19] For example, the seller tells the buyer: "I sell you one sheep out of these three sheep." This sale is valid provided the buyer has the right to select one out of three later on. Mālikī jurists allow such sale with option of determination for the buyer, without fixing any number. Thus, it can be affected on small number as well as on large number.

6. Uncertainty regarding the time of performance: If the sale is on credit i.e. on deferred payment basis, the time of payment should be made known to the seller.

7. Uncertainty regarding the existence of object: This is another form of *gharar*, which relates to non-existent commodity such as sale of what this animal will produce.

Some jurists have reported *ijmā'*(consensus of opinion) of Muslim jurists on declaring sale of non-existent object invalid. They cite in support of this view a *hadīth* narrated by Abū Hurairah (r.a.t.a) that Holy Prophet (s.a.w.s.) prohibited *gharar* sale.[20] *Gharar* refers to a thing which is not known and whose outcome is concealed.

The fact is that the *ḥadīth* prevents only that non-existent which involves *gharar* such as sale of unborn calf but the things, whose existence is certain in future, are permissible objects of sale because they do not involve any *gharar*, which may lead to

[18] Ibid; vol.1, p.863; Ibn Qudāmah, *al-Mughnī*, vol.4, p.131.
[19] Kāsānī, *Badā'i' al-sanā'i'*, vol.5, p.158.
[20] Qarāfī, *al-Furūq*, vol.1, p.150; Ibn Rushd, *Bidāyat al-Mujtahid*, vol.2, p.331.

dispute and litigation among the parties. An example of this case is *salam* ((sale of future goods with advance) and *istiṣnā‘* (contract of manufacturing). Both are permissible in the *Sharī‘ah* although the subject-matter does not exist at the time of contract.

8. Uncertainty regarding delivery of object: Inability of seller to deliver the object of sale to the buyer also forms *gharar*, which invalidates the contract.

Examples:

- Sale of stray animal whose whereabouts are not known to the owner.
- Sale of a car which has been stolen by somebody and the vendor does not know where is it,
- Sale of goods yet to be acquired by the seller.

Effect of *Gharar* on Contracts

Gharar primarily affects commutative contracts meant for alienation of property for consideration such as sale and hire. The effect of *gharar* on hire is the same as on sale contract. Some points of similarity between the two contracts with regard to the effects of *gharar* are as follows:

(i) *'Arbūn* (earnest money) according to *Jmhūr* is impermissible in hire as it is unlawful in a sale contract. Modern *fuqahā'* consider it valid.

(ii) Both the sale and hiring contracts are not allowed to be made contingent upon some uncertain future event.

The rent and rented utility in a hiring contract should be known and specified in the same way as price and commodity should be known in sale contract.

(iii) It is a condition of valid sale that its subject-matter should be deliverable. The same rule applies to hiring contract. As such, the *ijārah* of stray animal is not permissible.

(iv) The time of *ijārah* should be fixed. In a deferred payment sale, the time of payment of price should also be fixed.

The Muslim jurists differ on the effects of *gharar* on gratuitous contracts. To Mālikī jurists, *gharar* has no effect on donations.[21] Thus, it is valid to donate escaped animal, fruits before they ripen. But according to Shāfi'ī, Ḥanafī and Ḥanbalī jurists, the subject matter of donation should be known and determined. They do not allow the donation of an unborn animal or milk in the udders.[22]

As regards will, all the jurists are unanimous that it is valid even if the subject matter is non-existent, undetermined and outside the control of testator or beneficiary. It is, therefore, permissible to make bequest of what an animal or a tree will produce. It is also valid to make bequest of an undetermined portion of property. This testament is treated valid and it is the duty of the heirs to specify that portion.

Insurance: A Modern Contract of *Gharar*

Definition

"A contract of Insurance is one whereby one party, i.e., Insurer promises in return for a money consideration, i.e., the premium to pay to the other party, i.e., the insured, a sum of money or

---

[21] Shirāzī, *al-Muhaddab* vol. 1, p.453.

[22] Kāsānī, *Badā'i' al-sanā'i'*, vol.6, p.188.

provide him with some corresponding benefit, upon the occurrence of an event specified in the contract".[23]

The premium is a price of an insurance policy. "It is the price at which the insurer i.e. the company is prepared to take risks and bear the burden of the probable loss involved in the contract of insurance. On the basis of law of averages and through experience the insurer finds a reasonable amount sufficient to cover his risk as well as other charges including his profit.[24] An insurance policy aims at providing compensation for potential loss or damages that are specified in the contract. For example, when a person insures his car with the insurance company he gets an undertaking from the company that it will undertake repairs of the damage, which is caused to the insured car as a result of an accident.

A contract of insurance is normally a contract of indemnity because it ensures a compensation for loss to the insured. The life insurance and personal accidents insurance, however, are not contracts of indemnity for in all such cases, the insurer has to pay compensation on the happening of an event without reference to loss.[25]

Types of Insurance

With regard to the subject matter of insurance and the risk covered by it, Insurance is of the following four types:[26]

---

[23] *Parkington and Anthony On Insurance Law*, London: O'Dowd Sweet & Maxwell 17th Edition, 1981, p.3.

[24] Liaquat Ali Khan Niazi, *Islamic Law of Contract*, p. 384.

[25] Ibid, p. 386.

[26] See M.A. Chishti, *Islam and Insurance: Alternative options,* paper presented at Senior Officers Training Programme held in Islamabad on Feb. 24, 1992.

1. Life insurance

This is insurance against the loss of life. The objective of life insurance is to provide financial help to the families of insured persons after their death so that in their absence the families do not become destitute and public charges.

2. Health insurance

Health insurance policy covers expenses of medical treatment of insured in case of his illness or bodily injury.

3. Property insurance

Property Insurance policy provides compensation to the insured who suffered some loss or damage consequent upon occurrence of a catastrophe or disaster inflicted upon his property, assets and other belongings.

4. Liability insurance

This is also called third party insurance. It refers to a situation where a person/institution incurs some liability towards a third person. These policies cover a variety of business and professional liability exposures. They protect people and organization against financial loss due to legal liability claim. In liability insurance the insurance company undertakes to compensate the effectee on behalf of insured person/institution.

Sharī'ah appraisal

A large number of contemporary Muslim jurists regard modern commercial insurance invalid and incompatible with the injunctions of Islamic Law.[27] Islamic Law does not allow *gharar*

---

[27] See Muftī Muhammad *Shāfi'ī*, *Bīmah Zindagī*, Karachi, Dār al-Isha'at;

Abul A'lā Mawdūdī, *Ma'āshiyāt-e- Islām*, Lahore: Islamic Publications, 1988; Ḥussain Ḥāmid, *Ḥukm al-sharī'ah al-Islāmiyyah*

transactions in which the seller does not know what he has sold and the purchaser does not know what he has purchased. In insurance, the buyer of insurance policy does not know what he has bought by his premium. The time of occurrence of event is also uncertain for the parties. As such, insurance is primarily a *gharar* contract.

Types of *Gharar* in Insurance

The element of *gharar* inherent in the insurance is of the following types:

1. Uncertainty about the payment of insurance amount

The opponents of insurance assert that there is uncertainty as to whether the insured person will be able to get amount of compensation. In other words, there is uncertainty about what the insured person buys with the premium.

For this purpose, one may take the example of car insurance. In this type of insurance, the insured person drives car throughout the year. If he does not come across any accident, he can make no claim against the company and thus his premium money is wasted without any material benefit occurring to him. On the other hand, if he comes across a serious accident which causes extensive damage to his car, in that case the company pays him several times greater than the premium he has paid. This shows that the insured does not know at the time of contract what he buys by the amount of premium. This mean that he gets nothing if the accident does not occur. On the other hand, he gets several times greater than the premium he paid, if he comes

---

fī 'uqūd al-Tāmīn, Cairo:1976 ; Muḥammad Siddīq Ḍarīr, *al-Gharar wa Atharuhū fī al-'Uqūd,* Cairo:1967; Zuhaylī, *al-Fiqh al-Islamī wa adillatuhū,* vol.4, p.671; Muṣlihuddīn, *Insurance and Islamic law,* Lahore: Islamic publications,1978. See *Majallah al-Buhūth al-Islamiyyah,* Riyadh, vols. 19-20, 1987, Pakistan: Council of Islamic Ideology, Report on Islamic Insurance system, 1992.

across serious accident. Both these situations are uncertain for him.

2. *Gharar* with regard to time of payment

Another form of *gharar* is uncertainty about the time of occurrence of event, and the time of the payment of compensation. The particular event against which insurance is required, is uncertain in nature. The parties to the contract do not know at the time of contract, whether the event will occur or not. If the event occurs it will bring pecuniary benefits in compensation for the insured and if it does not occur, he will get nothing. Thus, the acquisition of pecuniary benefits depends upon the occurrence of the event specified in the contract.

3. *Gharar* with regard to quantum

This means that the insured person does not know at the time of contract how much compensation he will get because it depends upon the magnitude of the unpleasant event which is the subject matter of contract.[28]

View Point of Proponents of Insurance Regarding *Gharar*

In opposition to the view as described above, another group of Muslim scholars hold the view that insurance is not contrary to the *Sharī'ah*. These scholars do not see an element of uncertainty in it. Some scholars of this group admit that there is an element of *gharar* in insurance but it is not too large to call for the invalidity of contract.

Their view point is discussed here in some detail:

---

[28] Ḥusain Ḥāmid, *Ḥukm al- Sharī'ah al-Islāmiyyah fī 'uqūd al-Tāmīn*, pp.84-86; Darīr, *al- Gharar wa Atharuhū fi al-'Uqūd*, p.65; *Majallah al-Buhūth al-Islāmiyyah*, Riyāḍ, vols. 19-20, 1987.

I. Insurance does not contain *gharar*

This view suggests that there is no uncertainty in the contract of insurance. In insurance what a person buys when he seeks insurance cover, is not the amount of compensation he receives when something happens to him or to his property. What he buys in fact is peace of mind. This is tangible return for the money he pays. This peace of mind is fair return on his investment. If something happens to him or to his property, he is compensated and his loss is redeemed. But if nothing happens he is happier, because he does not have to contend with any misfortune.

This assertion is factually incorrect. The buyer of the policy does not buy the peace or security by the premium he pays, instead, he buys the amount of insurance. This is clearly indicated in the contract. The contract specifies that the premium is price for amount of compensation. It does not refer to peace or security as consideration of premium. This goes without saying that human emotions are not tangible property which is sold or purchased. No one can promise the other that he will provide him pleasure, peace of mind or tranquility. This is an undertaking which the undertaker is unable to fulfill.

II. *Gharar* in insurance is of small degree

This suggests that the *gharar* contained in insurance is of small degree. Therefore, it does not call for the invalidity of contract. The reason is that insurance company can predict the chance of actual occurrence of event. It determines the risk through its past experience and scientific observation of certain incidents. The law of large number helps the company to calculate the number of likely happenings with some accuracy. This law points to the fact that some quantities which are uncertain and changing in individual cases, being different for each one, remain constant for a large group of similar persons. The gap between the probable and actual number of these accidents can also be determined. As such the element of *gharar* is negligible in the contract of insurance. [29]

Musṭafā Zarqā asserts that the prohibition of *gharar* is confined to the area of sale contracts when the outcome of a sale is not certain but depends upon chance. Forbidden *gharar* occurs only when uncertainty exceed acceptable limits.[30] An insurer can by the simple use of the law of average know and determine the amount received from and given to the insured person.

If we consider this particular aspect, we find that the assertion that the element of uncertainty in insurance is negligible, is not correct. Insurance by its nature is a contract of uncertainty. *Gharar* and uncertainty always remain distinct features of this contract. But if we suppose for a while that it is not a contract of uncertainty because the company has the ability to predict the event with some accuracy, this remain an undeniable fact that the event is always uncertain for the insured person. He does not know whether it will happen or not. Thus, it is an uncertain contract for him.

Conclusion

The preceding discussion may be summarized as follows:

- *Gharar* refers to lack of knowledge about the material terms of contract.

---

[29] See Musṭafā Zarqā , *'Aqd al-Ta'mīn wa Mawqif al-Sharī'ah Minhu*, Damascus: University Press, 1381/1962. Muhammad Nejatullah siddīqī, *Insurance in an Islamic Economy*, Leicester: The Islamic Foundation 1984. M.A. Chishtī, *Islam and Insurance Alternative options*, Islamabad: International Institute of Islamic Economics, 1992.

[30] See Musṭafā Zarqā, *Niẓām al-Ta'mīn wa Mawqif al-Sharī'ah Minhu*, Paper presented at first International Conference on Islamic Economics, Makkah, 1976.

- *Gharar* takes place when it is not known whether the subject-matter exists or not, or if it exists, whether it can be handed over to the buyer or not.

- Following are some forms of *gharar* contract:
  - Uncertainty regarding the existence of the subject-matter
  - Inability to deliver the object of sale.
  - Lack of knowledge with regard to necessary characteristics of the subject-matter.
  - Want of knowledge with regard to the time of performance of contract.

- Some traditional types of *gharar* are:
  - Two sales in one transaction
  - Earnest money sale
  - *Bay'al-munabadhah* (Throw sale)
  - *Bay'al-mulāmasah* (Touch sale)
  - *Bay'al-ḥaṣāt* (Sale taking place through pebbles)
  - Contingent contract.

- *Gharar* affects commutative contracts, meant for alienation of property for consideration such as sale and hire. It does not affect gratuitous contracts such as *waqf*, donation and gift.

- The Modern insurance contract is a contract of *gharar*. The element of uncertainty and lack of knowledge inherent in the insurance relates to the occurrence of the event, i.e., the subject matter of contract, the acquisition of amount of insurance, its quantity and time of payment.

Chapter 9

Extrinsic Causes of Invalidity

Ribā also forms a major cause of the invalidity of contracts. It operates mainly in the contracts of loan and *ṣarf* (money barter).

Literal Meaning of *Ribā*

Ribā literally means increase, addition, and augmentation. The Qur'ān has used the word *ribā* in its literal meaning in *Surat al-Rum*, which says:

وَمَا آتَيْتُم مِّن رِّبًا لِّيَرْبُوَ فِي أَمْوَالِ النَّاسِ فَلَا يَرْبُو عِندَ اللَّهِ وَمَا آتَيْتُم مِّن زَكَاةٍ
تُرِيدُونَ وَجْهَ اللَّهِ فَأُوْلَئِكَ هُمُ الْمُضْعِفُونَ

> "That which you give in usury in order that it may increase on other people's property has no increase with Allah, but that which you give in charity seeking Allah's pleasure, has increase manifold.[1]

Technical Meaning of *Ribā*

Technically, *ribā* means an increase in the principal, stipulated in loan transaction. So, anything chargeable in addition to the principal amount as a contractual obligation falls under the purview of *ribā* and is, therefore, prohibited.

Abū Bakr Jaṣṣās has defined *ribā* in the following words:

> "It is a loan given for stipulated period with stipulated increased on the principal payable by the loanee.[2]

The above definition carries the following ingredients:

---

[1] Qur'ān, 30:39.
[2] Jaṣṣaṣ, *Ahkam al-*Qur'ān, Lahore: Suhail Academy

- *Ribā* is an increase over and above the principal sum.
- It is an excess which is payable as a contractual obligation.
- It is excess, which is against a specified period of deferment.

It is evident from this explanation that the above definitions only cover that *ribā* which occurs in loan transactions, i.e. *ribā al-nasai'ah* or the *ribā al-jāhiliyyah* (*ribā* of time of ignorance). It does not touch upon the *ribā*, which occurs in barter transactions dealt with by the Sunnah of the Prophet (s.a.w.s.).

An eminent scholar, Muhammad 'Alā Thanwi, author of *Kashshāf Iṣṭilāḥāt al-Funūn*, has defined *ribā* in the following words:

> "*Ribā* is an increase without any corresponding consideration which has been stipulated in favour of one of the two parties, in a contract of exchange."[3]

Ingredients of the definition

The following are the ingredients of definition:

- *ribā* is an increase (actual or constructive),
- it is without corresponding consideration, i.e., without risk, labour and capital;
- the increase is stipulated in favour of one party,
- it is stipulated in an exchange of property for property.

The distinct feature of this definition is that it embraces in its ambit all forms of *ribā* and does not restrict *ribā* to loan transaction referred to in the definition of Abu Bakr al-Jassas. It describes *ribā* in a comprehensive sense to include the *ribā* of

---

[3] Muhammad A'la Thanwi, *Kashshaf Iṣtilahat al-Funun*, Beirut: Sharikat al-Khayyat le al-Kutub, n.d., vol. 3, p.592.

loan transactions as well as *ribā* of barter transactions. It encompasses very return and all excess arising from exchange of property for property regardless of whether exchange takes the form of loan or sale of money for money or barter transaction between two homogeneous articles or transaction between two different commodities.

Other Meanings and Definitions of *Ribā*

1. *Ribā* is the stipulated excess without a counter-value in sale.[4]

2. *Ribā* is an excess according to a legal standard of measurement or weight in one or two homogenous articles opposed to each other in a contract of exchange and in which such excess is stipulated as an obligatory condition on one party without any return.[5]

3. *Ribā* is an increase in one of the homogenous equivalents exchanged without this increase being accompanied by a return.[6]

4. *Ribā* is an illicit profit or gain resulting from non-equivalence in the counter value of the reciprocal benefits during an exchange of two articles of the same species and genus governed by the same efficient cause.[7]

5. It is undue profit not in the way of legitimate trade out of the loan of gold and silver and necessary articles of food.[8]

---

[4] Sarakhsī, *al-Mubsūt*, vol. 12, p. 105

[5] Muhammad 'Ala al-Din Ḥaṣkafi, *Tanwīr al-Abṣār*, Cairo: Matba'ah al-Wa'iz, vol. 2, p.255.

[6] 'Abd al-Raḥmān, *Kitāb al-Fiq 'Ālā al-Madhāhib al-Arba'ah*, vol. 2, p.246.

[7] Nabil salih, *Unlawful Gain and Legitimate Profit in Islamic Law*, p.16.

[8] Abdullah Yusuf 'Ali, *The Holy* Qur'ān*: Translation and Commentary*, p. 15.

Ribā in the Qur'ān

The Qur'ān has dealt with the issue of *ribā* in the following verses: These are produced below in order of their revelation.

Frist Revelation (5 years before *Hijrah*) *Sūrat al-Rūm,* verse: 39

وَمَا آتَيْتُم مِّن رِّبًا لِّيَرْبُوَ فِي أَمْوَالِ النَّاسِ فَلَا يَرْبُو عِندَ اللَّهِ وَمَا آتَيْتُم مِّن زَكَاةٍ
تُرِيدُونَ وَجْهَ اللَّهِ فَأُوْلَئِكَ هُمُ الْمُضْعِفُونَ

"That which you give in usury in order that it may increase on other people's property has no increase with Allah: But that which you give in charity seeking Allah's pleasure, has increase manifold."

In this verse Allah has expressed His disapproval of *ribā* and stated that *ribā* does not carry a reward from Allah in the hereafter. The wealth acquired through *ribā* is deprived of the blessing of Allah. Charity on the other hand, brings Allah's blessing and favour.

Second Revelation (Early Madinah period) *Sūrat al-Nisā* Verse, 161.

وَأَخْذِهِمُ الرِّبَا وَقَدْ نُهُواْ عَنْهُ وَأَكْلِهِمْ أَمْوَالَ النَّاسِ بِالْبَاطِلِ وَأَعْتَدْنَا لِلْكَافِرِينَ
مِنْهُمْ عَذَابًا أَلِيمًا

"That they took usury though they were forbidden and that they devoured man's substance wrongfully, we have prepared for those among them who reject faith a grievous punishment."

In this verse the Qur'ān tells us that *ribā* was prohibited for Jews and that they incurred the wrath of Allah for taking *ribā*.

Third revelation (After Ghazwah Uḥud) *Surat Al-'Īmrān*, verse 130.

يَا أَيُّهَا الَّذِينَ آمَنُواْ لاَ تَأْكُلُواْ الرِّبَا أَضْعَافًا مُّضَاعَفَةً وَاتَّقُواْ اللّهَ لَعَلَّكُمْ تُفْلِحُونَ

"O Believers! Take not doubled and redoubled interest and fear God so that you may prosper."

In this verse the Qur'ān has pointed out the heinous practice of taking double and multiplied interest prevalent amongst Arabs. The believers have been enjoined to refrain from such act.

Fourth Revelation (shortly after *Āl-'Īmrān) Surat al-Baqarah* verse 275-277

الَّذِينَ يَأْكُلُونَ الرِّبَا لاَ يَقُومُونَ إِلاَّ كَمَا يَقُومُ الَّذِي يَتَخَبَّطُهُ الشَّيْطَانُ مِنَ الْمَسِّ
ذَلِكَ بِأَنَّهُمْ قَالُواْ إِنَّمَا الْبَيْعُ مِثْلُ الرِّبَا وَأَحَلَّ اللّهُ الْبَيْعَ وَحَرَّمَ الرِّبَا فَمَن جَاءهُ
مَوْعِظَةٌ مِّن رَّبِّهِ فَانتَهَىَ فَلَهُ مَا سَلَفَ وَأَمْرُهُ إِلَى اللّهِ وَمَنْ عَادَ فَأُوْلَئِكَ
أَصْحَابُ النَّارِ هُمْ فِيهَا خَالِدُونَ {275/2} يَمْحَقُ اللّهُ الْرِّبَا وَيُرْبِي الصَّدَقَاتِ
وَاللّهُ لاَ يُحِبُّ كُلَّ كَفَّارٍ أَثِيمٍ {276/2} إِنَّ الَّذِينَ آمَنُواْ وَعَمِلُواْ الصَّالِحَاتِ
وَأَقَامُواْ الصَّلاَةَ وَآتَوُاْ الزَّكَاةَ لَهُمْ أَجْرُهُمْ عِندَ رَبِّهِمْ وَلاَ خَوْفٌ عَلَيْهِمْ وَلاَ هُمْ
يَحْزَنُونَ

"Those who devour usury will not stand except as stands one whom the evil one by his touch has driven to madness. That is because they say: "Trade is like usury". But God has permitted trade and forbidden usury. Those who after receiving direction from their lord, desist shall be pardoned for their past. Their case is for God to judge. But those who repeat (the offence) are the companions of the fire; they will abide there forever. God will deprive usury of all blessings, but will give increase for deeds of charity, for He loves not creatures ungrateful and wicked. Those who believe and do deeds of righteousness and establish regular, prayers and regular charity will have their reward with their lord. On them shall be no fear, nor shall they grieve."

The fourth revelation severally censured those who take *ribā* and established clear distinction between trade and *ribā*.

Fifth Revelation (9 or 10 A.H. Farewell Pilgrimage) *Surat al-Baqarah* verse 278-280.

يَا أَيُّهَا الَّذِينَ آمَنُواْ اتَّقُواْ اللّهَ وَذَرُواْ مَا بَقِيَ مِنَ الرِّبَا إِن كُنتُم مُّؤْمِنِينَ {278/2} فَإِن لَّمْ تَفْعَلُواْ فَأْذَنُواْ بِحَرْبٍ مِّنَ اللّهِ وَرَسُولِهِ وَإِن تُبْتُمْ فَلَكُمْ رُؤُوسُ أَمْوَالِكُمْ لاَ تَظْلِمُونَ وَلاَ تُظْلَمُونَ {279} وَإِن كَانَ ذُو عُسْرَةٍ فَنَظِرَةٌ إِلَى مَيْسَرَةٍ وَأَن تَصَدَّقُواْ خَيْرٌ لَّكُمْ إِن كُنتُمْ تَعْلَمُونَ.

> "O you who believe! Fear God and give up what remains of your demand for usury, if you are indeed believers. If you do it not, take notice of war from God and His apostle, but if you turn back you shall have your capital sums. Deal not unjustly and you shall not be dealt with unjustly. If the debtor is in difficulty, grant him time, till the time of ease, but if you remit it by way of charity, that is best for you if you only know *(al-Baqarah 278-280).*

Inferences drawn from these verses:

1. There is a sharp contrast between charity and usury. Usury creates conflict, hatred, jealousy and economic warfare among individuals whereas charity promotes harmony, cooperation and collaboration in the society.

2. There is distinct difference between legitimate trade and usury. Not every surplus in transaction is forbidden. The surplus, which is a result of selling and purchasing, is legitimate and lawful. The surplus which one earns without exertion and bearing risk and liability is prohibited.

3. The believers have been asked to give the remaining amount of *ribā* and permitted to receive their principal amounts. This gives Quranic definition of *ribā*, that is, any addition to the capital in a transaction of loan is *ribā*.

4. No distinction has been made between an addition in the capital sum of the loan based on simple interest and an addition based on compound interest.

5. No distinction has been made between a loan contracted for the purpose of consumption and that contracted for production.

6. The creditors have right to their capital sums only.

7. To demand excess in the capital is injustice to the debtor and to deny the creditor his principal amount is an injustice to him.

8. Continuing any further dealings in *ribā* will amount to inviting war from Allah and His Messenger.

9. Creditors have been asked to give time to debtors for repayment of capital, if necessary.

10. To write off a debt altogether is an act of charity.

Forms of *Ribā* al-Qur'ān, i.e. *Ribā al-Jahiliyyah*

The *ribā* mentioned in the Qur'ān was practiced by the Arabs in the pre-Islamic period in the following three forms.

1. They advanced loan by stipulating excess over and above the principal sum of loan contract. Thus, the increase was stipulated in the beginning of the contract i.e. at the time of advancing a loan. Abu Bakr al-Jassās, writes in *Ahkām al-Qur'ān:*

   "The *ribā* which was known to and practiced by the Arabs was that they used to advance loan in the form of *dirham* and *dinār* for a fixed term with an agreed excess over and above the amount of loan.[9]

2. They used to advance loan on the condition that they would take a fixed amount each month, while the principal amount still remained. Thereafter, when it was time for the repayment of the debt, they demanded the principal from the debtor. If he was unable to pay, they increased the term and payable amount.

3. They used to sell a commodity on deferred payment basis, when the time of payment approached, the seller used to increase the amount due and give him more time. Suyuṭi explains this practice in the following words: "They used to purchase a commodity on the basis of deferred payment, then on the date of maturity the seller used to increase the amount due in lieu of further delay".[10] Thus, the increase of amount was not stipulated at the time of concluding contract of debt, but at the time of maturity of contract.

Ribā in Sunnah

The *ahādith* dealing with *ribā* are of two categories: First, those, which reaffirm the type of *ribā*, mentioned in the Qur'ān. The second categories are those that introduce a new form of *ribā*, not mentioned in the Qur'ān. This latter form of *ribā* is known as *Ribā al-faḍl*.

A few of the *ahādith* relating to either category are reproduced below:

---

[9] Abū Bakr al-Jaṣṣaṣ, *Aḥkām ul-* Qur'ān, Beirut: Dar al-Kitab al-'Arabī, vol. 1, p. 465.

[10] Suyuṭi, *al-Durr al-Manthur*, Beirut: vol. 2, p. 72

The first category of *ahādith* on *ribā*

1. The Prophet (s.a.w.s.) is reported to have said in his last *hajj* sermon (the farewell address).

   "Beware, all *ribā* outstanding from the *ribā* prevalent during the pre-Islamic era is void. You are entitled to your principal money. Neither shall you oppress nor shall you be oppressed.[11]

2. "Beware! All *ribā* of pre-Islamic era is annulled and the first claim of *ribā* which I cancel is that of my uncle."[12]

3. From Jābir, who said: "The Messenger of Allah (s.a.w.s.) cursed the one who charges *ribā*; he who gives it; the one who records it; and the two witnesses; saying that "they are all equal".[13]

The second category of *ahādith*

1. From Abu Sa'īd al-Khudri, who said: "the Messenger of Allah (s.a.w.s.) said: "Do not sell gold for gold except when it is like for like; nor misappropriate one through the other; nor sell silver for silver except like for like; nor misappropriate one through the other, nor sell things that are absent for those that are present".[14]

2. From 'Ubādah Ibn Ṣāmit who said; "The Messenger of Allah (s.a.w.s.) said: Gold for gold, silver for silver, wheat for wheat, barley for barley, dates for dates, salt for salt, like for like, in equal weights, from hand to hand. If those

---

[11] Muslim, *ṣaḥīḥ,* Chapter of hajj

[12] Muslim, *ṣaḥīḥ,* Chapter of hajj

[13] Bukhārī, *ṣaḥīḥ, Kitāb al-Buyū'* Muslim, *ṣaḥīḥ,* Chapter on *Ribā*

[14] Muḥammad ibn Isma'īl Ṣan'āni, *Subul al-Salām,* Beirut: Dar al-Fikr, 1938, vol. 3, p.37

> species differ, then sell as you like as long as it is from hand to hand".[15]

These two *ahādith* provide that the following three transactions are usurious transactions.

(i) a transaction of money for money of the same denomination where the quantity on both sides is not equal, either in a spot transaction or in a transaction based on deferred payment.

(ii) A barter transaction between two weighable or measurable commodities of the same kind, where the quantity on both sides is not equal or where delivery from any one side is deferred.

(iii) A barter transaction between two different weighable or measurable commodities when delivery from one side is deferred.[16]

Kinds of *Ribā*

There are two main kinds of *ribā*: *ribā al-duyūn* and *ribā al-buyu'* (*ribā* of debt transactions and *ribā* of sale transactions) *ribā al-buyu'* is further divided into two kinds, i.e., *ribā al-faḍl* and *ribā al nasā.*

I. Ribā al-faḍl (*Ribā* by way of excess)

It is the excess revealed through a *Sharī'ah* criterion stipulated in one of the two counter-values, in transaction of exchange.[17]

The *Sharī'ah* criterion in this definition refers to weight or measure of capacity or count. Thus, if two persons were

---

[15] Ibid., vol. 3, p. 37.

[16] Order of the Supreme Court's Appellate Bench on Ribā. *The News*, December 24, 1999

[17] Kasani, *Bada' al-sana'i'*, vol. 5, p.183

exchanging wheat with each other, the quantity must be equal on both sides; if there is excess on one side, which would amount to *ribā al-faḍl* (*ribā* by way of excess). *Ribā al-faḍl* takes place in a homogenous exchange with increase from one side in terms of weight or measurement. In the above example if 5 kg wheat is exchanged for 6 kg wheat, that would amount to *ribā al-faḍl.*

II. Ribā al-nasā' (Ribā of delay)

It is *ribā* by way of deferment of completion of an exchange *ribā al-nasā'* (*ribā* by way of deferment) takes place when articles of the same genera or different genera, whether measured or weighed, are exchanged with deferment on one side, whether or not there is real excess in favour of either side. Thus, if 5 kg gold is exchanged for 5 kg gold with a delay of one year, it will amount to *ribā al-nasā'* because the price has risen from a period of delay.

Rationale underlying the prohibition of *ribā al-faḍl*

The rationale underlying the prohibition of *ribā al-faḍl* can be summarized in the following points:

1. In barter transaction, if the same commodity is exchanged it is likely that a party with ability to judge difference in quality will exploit the ignorance of less knowledgeable party in giving him less than the real value of the commodity. Therefore, the lawgiver has safeguarded him against injustice and exploitation by stipulating that the exchange should be equal on both sides.

2. An unequal exchange of the same commodity gives way to hoarding, monopoly and profiteering. The rich man, for example, gives 1 kg of superior dates for 5 kg inferior dates. What actually happens that all the inferior dates are

transferred to the rich man at the cost of 1/5 amount of the superior dates with him, with the following results:

(i) A huge amount of dates has been stored with the rich man. He starts hoarding them.

(ii) The small quantity of the superior dates in the hands of a large number of poor persons will soon be finished. Only the inferior quality of dates will be left in the market.

iii) The rich man will monopolize the inferior dates and sell them in the market at very high rates, even higher than the normal market rates of the superior dates.[18]

3. By prohibiting *ribā al-faḍl*, i.e., unequal exchange of the same commodity, Islam has in fact encouraged the use of cash money. The Prophet (s.a.w.s.) had instructed Bilāl (r.a.t.a.) to sell two measures of dates for money and then purchase superior ones with that money. Thus, the *aḥādith* relating to *ribā* seek to promote money as medium of exchange in the economy.

4. Deferred delivery brings undue benefit for one party. For example, Mr. A sells $100 to Mr. B for Rs. 5500 to be delivered next year. By next year the exchange rate in the market has changed from 1 $ 55 Rs. To 1 $ 65 Rs. But Mr. B will deliver Rs. 5500 only not Rs. 6500. This shows that benefit of change in exchange rate over the year went to one party, in this case Mr. B. If exchange rate moved in other direction, Mr. A, would have been the gainer. In short one party will gain while the other will lose.

[18] Ghulam Murtaza, *Socio-Economic System of Islam*, Lahore: Malik Sons Publishers, 1990, pp. 34, 35.

5. The restriction levied in the *ahādith* of *ribā al-faḍl* and *ribā al-nasā'*, seeks to forestall the entry of real *ribā* through the back door.

Underlying cause (*'illah*) of the prohibition of *ribā al-faḍl* and *ribā al-nasā'*

The Muslim Jurists are unanimous on the point that prohibition of *ribā al-faḍl* and *ribā al-nasā'* is not restricted to six commodities mentioned in the *ḥadith*. The prohibition is extendable to other commodities, which resemble the six commodities with regard to the *'illah* (underlying cause).

The Jurists employ the method of analogical reasoning in extending the prohibition to other commodities besides the six commodities contained in the *ḥadīth* of 'Ubādah ibn Ṣāmit.

It is generally agreed that analogical reasoning is valid when the following conditions are met:

1. Te *'illah* should represent the compelling factor which has motivated or is intended by the legal rule; it should be plain and consistent.

2. The same *illah* should appear in both elements of analogy, object as well as subject. A mere resemblance between attributes is not sufficient.

3. The general rule governing the object of the analogy should be of general application and not restricted to a specific case.

   The Jurists while agreeing on the application of the rule of prohibition to other commodities disagree on the underlying cause.

We now take up the viewpoints of the jurists regarding the underlying cause which is at work behind the prohibition of *ribā al-faḍl* and *ribā al-nasā'*.

Ḥanafī viewpoint

The Ḥanafī jurists consider the underlying cause to be similarity of species, i.e. the exchanged articles belong to the same genus and the similarity of the method of estimation, i.e., both articles, besides being of the same genus, are weighed or measured when they change hands.[19] According to this interpretation, all weighable articles such as iron and cotton if exchanged with each other, must fulfill the requirement of equality or sameness in quantity and simultaneous exchange. If the transaction fails to meet the first condition, it will amount to *ribā al-faḍl* and should the transaction fall of meeting second requirement that would rise to *ribā al-nasā'*. *Ribā* according to this viewpoint does not run in eggs because they are neither weighed nor measured, rather, they are sold by count.

Shāfi'i viewpoint

Shāfi'ī jurists hold that the *'illah* for gold and silver is their being prices of the things or the currency-value *(thamaniyyah)* and for wheat, barley, dates and salt is food-value *(ṭu'm)*. Thus, *ribā* runs in vegetables if two vegetables of the same kind are exchanged with each other either with excess or delay, since they belong to the class of foodstuff.[20]

Māliki viewpoint

The Māliki jurists determine the *'illah* for gold and silver by their currency-value *(thamaniyah)*, and for the remaining four articles by their food-value provided they can be stored for a reasonable time without perishing. Thus, *ribā* does not run in vegetables and fruits because these are perishable.

---

[19] Kāsānī, *Bada'i al-Sana'i'*, vol. 5, p. 183.

[20] Khatib Baghdadi, *Mughni al-Muhtaj*, vol. 2, p.23.

As regards Mālikis, *'illah* for gold and silver can be extended to any modern currency. Imām Mālik is reported to have said:

"If the people of an age make currency out of the skins of camels, and that becomes prevalent among the people, I view its exchange with gold or silver with delay unlawful".[21]

This means that Imām Mālik applies the rules relating to *ṣarf* (money exchange) and *ribā* to all such articles, which assume the status of currency.

The difference between the viewpoints of Imām Shāfi'ī and Mālik on the *'illah* of gold and silver is that Imām Shāfi'i while considering both metals as currencies, restricts this attribute of price-worthiness to these two metals. He regards these metals money by creation. To him, no other thing can assume this role. Thus the attribute operating in gold and silver, to Imām Shāfi'i is not of general application. Imām Mālik, on the other hand, considers this rule, of general application and not restricted to a specific case. So a homogeneous exchange of currency should fulfill the requirements of equality in quantity and prompt delivery from both sides. In case of heterogeneous exchange (dollars with Rupees) the equality is not a requirement; however, it is necessary that both currencies be exchanged in the same session of contract. Delay or deferment in delivery by either party would make it a contract of *ribā al-nasā'*.

Ḥanbalī viewpoint

Different versions relating to *'illah* are attributed to Imām Aḥmad ibn Ḥanbal.

(i) the *'illah* for gold and silver is twofold: the exchanged articles belong to the same genus and they change hands by way of weight. As for the other four articles quoted in the Ḥadith,

---

[21] Sahnun, *al-Mudawwanah al-Kubra*, Beirut: Dar Sadir, n.d. vol. 8, pp.395, 396.

the *'illah* is again two fold; the exchanged articles belong to the same genus and they change hands by way of measure. This viewpoint is similar to that of the Ḥanafi School.

(ii) the *'illah* for gold and silver is their currency-value *(thamaniyyah)*, and for the remaining four articles, their food-value *(ṭu'm)*. This version is close to that expressed by the Shāfi'i and Mālki jurists.

(iii) the *'illah* for the four commodities is their being foodstuffs which are weighable and measurable; thus there is no *ribā* when the exchanged foodstuffs are neither measurable nor weighable, or when the exchanged counter-values are not foodstuffs.[22]

Ribā al-Faḍl, Ṣarf and *Qarḍ* (Loan)

Some *Sharī'ah* scholars hold the view that the *aḥkām* of *ribā al-faḍl*, not only apply to the sale of gold for gold or silver for silver or money for money but also apply to *qarḍ* transaction. They argue that loan is basically a form of exchange transaction in which money is exchanged for money. According to this view, a loan of amount Rs. X is an exchange of Rs. X today with Rs. X tomorrow, which is prohibited according to *aḥadıth* of *riba al-faḍl*. Thus, a loan of Rs. 1000 for instance, will be impermissible if the return of this amount form the borrower is not on spot even if the borrower returns the same amount of loan i.e Rs.1000. The reason being that according to *ḥadīth*, exchange of gold for gold must be on spot. The above loan transaction violates this requirement, and amounts to *ribā al-faḍl*. They contend that as a matter of principle both the loans i.e loan with interest and loan without interest are prohibited in view of the prohibition of *ribā al-faḍl*. The only exception to this fundamental rule of prohibition is where the loan is granted by way of benevolence, for consumption purposes provided the time for repayment is not fixed. The issue of similarity between

[22] Ibn Qudamah, *al-Mughni*, vol. 6, pp.54-57

Ṣarf (exchange of money for money) and *qarḍ* (loan transaction) and the prohibition of *qarḍ* (loan) was raised by some scholars before the *Sharī'ah* Appellate Bench of Supreme Court of Pakistan in *ribā* case in 1999. Dr. Riaz ul-Hassan Gilani, a prominent lawyer contended that *qarḍ* (loan) is covered under *ribā al-faḍl*. Thus, a loan transaction whereby the repayment of principal money (which stands for gold or silver) is delayed form one side is *ribā al-fadl*, hence *makrūh* even though it is returned without any addition, because the transaction of gold for gold or money for money is permissible only when two conditions are fulfilled:

a) That the quantity on both sides is equal,

b) That the exchange is effected on spot.

In interest free loan, the condition (b) is lacking, while in interest-based loan both conditions are missing, but both kinds of loan fall within definition of *ribā al-faḍl*. (Moulana Taqi Usmani's judgement on *Ribā* 1999, para 108,109). Maulana Muhammad Taqi Usmani has disagreed with this view. In his opinion *qarḍ* (loan) and *ṣarf* (exchange of money for money) are two different contracts. The rules of *ṣarf* cannot be applied to *qarḍ* transactions. He writes in his judgement:

> "This submission of the learned counsel is not tenable at all, because it is based on a major confusion between the transaction of sale and transaction of loan. The learned counsel has equated the transaction of loan with the transaction of sale. The *ḥadīth* dealing with *ribā al-fadl* refers to a sale transaction, and not to a loan. The exact words of *ḥadīth* are:
>
> "Do not sell gold for gold, except in equal quantities...and do not sell the deferred (gold or silver) for the (gold or silver) delivered on the spot."

Here the words "Do not sell" are clear to show that the *ḥadīth* is speaking of a transaction of sale and not of a loan. There are many points of difference between the two transactions. The contention of the learned counsel that even an interest-free loan is covered by *ribā-al-faḍl* is, therefore, fallacious on the face of it, because the Holy Prophet (s.w.a.s), himself has not only allowed the transactions of interest-free loan but has also practiced them while he never allowed a sale of gold for gold on deferred payment basis. The learned counsel has referred to the *aḥādīth* in which the Holy Prophet (s.w.a.s) has condemned borrowing loans without genuine need and refused to pray *janazah* of a person who died indebted. But here again, the learned counsel has confused two different issues. The Holy Prophet (s.w.a.s), did not condemn borrowing loans because the transaction itself was prohibited, but he did so for the simple reason that it is not at all advisable for a person to incur the liability of a loan without a genuine need. Had it been on the basis of the prohibition of the transaction of loan itself, it would have been prohibited for both the lender and the borrower, but obviously advancing a loan has never been held as prohibited. The learned counsel himself referred to a *ḥadīth* reported by Ibn Majah to the effect that advancing a loan is more meritorious than spending in charity (*ṣadaqah*). It clearly indicates that the transaction of loan in itself is not prohibited as a transaction, however, the people are advised not to incur the liability of a loan without a genuine need. Conversely, a sale of gold for gold or silver for silver on deferred payment basis is a prohibited transaction in itself, and this prohibition is applicable to both the parties, and has never been allowed for any one of them in any case.

"To sum-up, the *aḥādīth* of *ribā al-faḍl* are meant to cover the transactions of sale only, and have nothing to do with

> the transaction of loan which are covered by the rules of *rib al- Qur'ān* or *ribā al-jāhiliyyah* and where it is clearly mentioned that the creditor in a transaction of loan is entitled to claim only his principal amount, and if he does so, it has never been prohibited. It is, therefore, not correct to say that a transaction of interest-bearing loan, fixing an amount as interest right from the beginning of the transaction, is covered by the prohibition of *ribā al-fadl* rather than the *ribā al-* Qur'ān and that the banking interest being a transaction of *ribā al-faḍl* is not *ḥarām*."[23]

Some other flaws in the above proposition of similarity between *qarḍ* and *ṣarf* (sale of money for money) are as follows:

1. *Ṣarf* (sale of money for money) and *qarḍ* are two different contracts. *Ṣarf* is a commutative transaction (*mu'āwaḍ'ah*), while loan is gratuitous transaction (*tabarru'*). The lender does not take any consideration for the amount he has lent.

2. It is also an established fact that *qarḍ* in the period of Holy Prophet (s.a.w.s) was extended with both fixation of time and without fixation of time for repayment. Imām Bukhārī in his *Ṣaḥīḥ* has narrated a *ḥadīth* under the title "fixation of time in *qarḍ*". He has concluded that time fixation in *qarḍ* is allowed. Same is the opinion of Ḥaḍrat 'Abdullah Ibn 'Abbās (r.a). From amongst the *fuqahā'*, the Mālikī jurists recommend fixation of time of repayment in loan transaction. They categorize loan as debt contract which is recommended to be concluded for a fixed period. The Qur'ān in *Sūrat al-Baqarah*, verse 282, instructs that debt transactions contracted for specified period be recorded. The verse

[23] Supreme Court's Judgement on Ribā, Judgement of Maulana Taqi Usmani, Paras 110, 111, 112

says: O ye who believe; when ye contract a debt for a fixed period, record it in writing...: (2:282). This instruction implies that *qarḍ* being a sub-category of debt, is allowed with time fixation. According to Ḥanbalī jurists, if time is fixed for the repayment of loan, then a Muslim is duty bound to fulfill his commitment. According to Ḥanafī and *Shāfi'ī* jurists, observance of stipulated period is only a moral obligation on part of borrower. The lender may demand the payment of loan even before that period. It is pertinent to note that Ḥanafī jurists also acknowledge many exceptions to their stated rule. Ibn 'Ābidīn has identified many situations in which observance of stipulated time becomes obligatory upon the borrower. The *Sharī'ah* scholars at AAOFI subscribe to the view of Malikī jurists. The *Sharī'ah* Standard no. 19 on loan provides:

> "It is perimissble to state a period in *qarḍ*. The borrower is, therefore, under no obligation to return it prior to the termination of contract, nor can the lender demand it back prior to end of the period. If, however, no period is stipulated, it is binding upon the borrower to return its substitute (*badl*) on demand.[24]

3. Another argument to prove that *qarḍ* (loan) does not fall under the rules of *ṣarf* (exchange of gold for gold, or silver for silver or money for money) is that the subject matter of *ṣarf* is gold, silver or money while *qarḍ* is affected on every fungible thing that has its substitute available in the market. According to Ḥanbalī jurists, *qarḍ* can be affected even on non-fungible good, such as

[24] AAOIFI, *Sharī'ah* Standerd no. 19, loan(Qard), Article 6.

animals. The permissibility of concluding loan on animals is established by the following *ḥadīth*:

> "It is narrated by Hadrat Rāfi' that Holy Prophet (s.a.w.s) borrowed a young camel, and then received charity of camels and ordered Rāfi' to give camel to him. Ḥaḍrat Rāfi'(r.t.a) informed the Prophet (s.a.w.s) that closest (to the borrowed camel) he could find, was a six-year camel. Then, the Prophet (s.a.w.s) ordered him to give it to him and added: 'the best among you is the best in repaying his debt."[25]

5- The Holy Prophet (s.a.w.s) has prohibited from combining *bay'* (sale) and *qarḍ* (loan) in one transaction. Haḍrat 'Abdullah Ibn 'Amr Ibn Al 'Āṣ (r.a) narrates the Holy Prophet (s.a.w.s) said:

> "A *salaf* (loan) and *bay'* (sale) in one contract are not perimitted, nor are two conditions in a sale, nor the profit from a thing for which the liability for loss is not borne, nor the sale of what you do not have."[26]

> Here we observe that the *ḥadīth* has treated *qard* and sale as two different and independent contracts.

The conclusion of this discussion is that the *qarḍ* and *ṣarf* are two separate and independent contracts. The *aḥkām* of *ṣarf* and *ribā al-faḍl* cannot be applied to *qarḍ* transaction. A *qarḍ* transaction with fixation of time, does not convert loan contract into *ribā* transaction, unless the lender demands increase on the principal amount.

---

[25] Muslim, *Ṣaḥīḥ,* kitāb al-Musāqāt, Ḥadīth no. 1600

[26] Abu Dawūd, *Sunan,* Kitāb al Buyū', Ḥadith no. 3504

Other Forms of *Ribā*

Under this title we will deal with some other forms of *ribā*, which are doubtful contracts from the *Sharī'ah* point of view. The contracts falling under this category conform to the requirement of the *Sharī'ah* with regard to *ṣīghah* (form of contract) but their objectives oppose the intention of the lawgiver, as they provide a legal device and subterfuge to circumvent the obstacles posed by *ribā* prohibitions. A majority of Muslim jurists, therefore, regards such forms of contract invalid.

The following are some of these contracts.

1. *Bay' al-'īnah*

Under this contract a person sells some object on credit for a certain price and then buys it back at a price less than the sale price on prompt payment, both transactions taking place simultaneously in the same session of contract. We can understand this from the following illustration.

A, sells a commodity to B for Rs. 100/- on one-year's credit. A, then buys the commodity back for Rs. 80/- from B on immediate payment. In the above case, A is a creditor and B is a debtor. A has advanced loan of Rs. 80/- under the cover of sale transaction in which he earns a surplus of 20 rupees. Another form of *bay'al-'īnah* is to sell commodity on cash and then buy it back at a higher price to be paid at some specified time in future. In this case, the prospective debtor sells an object for cash to the prospective creditors. The debtor immediately repurchases the object for a higher amount payable at a future date. Thus the transaction amounts to a loan with object as security. The difference between the two prices represents the interest. It is called *'īnah* because the *'ayn* (substance) in this case returns to its owner. Financing under buy-back arrangement in some countries resembles this contract.

The majority of Muslim jurists consider this transaction invalid because the intended objective of the transaction opposes the objectives laid down by the Lawgiver. This form of transaction, in their view, is nothing more than a legal device aimed at circumventing the obstacle posed by the prohibition of *ribā*.[27] These jurists establish the prohibition of this transaction by a tradition of *'Ā'ishah* (r.a)when Umm Mahabbah informed her that she had a slave girl whom she sold on credit to Zayd ibn Arqam for eight hundred dirhams. Zayd soon decided to sell the salve, so Umm Mahabbah bought her back for six hundred on immediate payment. *'Ā'ishah* (r.a) said, "what you sold was bad, and bad was what you bought. Make it known to Zayd that his *jihād* alongside Messenger of Allah has been nullified, unless he repents." Umm Muhabbah asked her, "What if I should just take my capital from him". She replied, "Those who after receiving direction from their Lord desist, shall be pardoned for the past." Imām Shāfi'i maintains that *bay' al-'īnah* is permissible. The *ḥadīth* of *Ā'ishah* is not established in his view.[28]

2. *Bay' al-wafā'*

This is a transaction in which a person in need of money sells a commodity to a lender on the condition that whenever the seller wishes, the lender (the buyer) would return the purchased commodity to him upon surrender of the price. The reason for its designation as *wafā* is the promise to abide by the condition of returning the subject matter to the seller if he too surrenders the price to the buyer.[29] Like *bay' al-'īnah,* this too is legal device for *ribā.* The purchaser in this case is a creditor who benefits from the object held in his custody as pledge till the debtor pays

[27] Zaki Badawi, *Nazariyyat al-Ribā al-Muḥarram*, Cairo: al-Majlis al-'Alā le Ri'āyah al-Funūn, 1940, p. 203.

[28] Qurṭubī, *al-Jām'i li Aḥkām al- Qur'ān*, Cairo: 1353/1935, vol. 3, pp. 359, 360.

[29] Ibn Rushd, *Bidayat al-Mujtahid*, vol. 2, p.118.

him back his amount and retrieves his object. Islamic injunctions on pledge clearly provide that the creditor is not entitled to make profit out of the pledged property. Any profit drawn from it is interest.

3. Ḥaṭṭ wa ta'jjal

Under this transaction the lender hastens the repayment of his delayed debt by taking an amount that is less than the value of the debt.[30] He accepts his money ahead of the time of maturity in lieu of discount on his principal amount. This is similar to present day practice of discounting of trade bills in the banks.

Viewpoints of Muslim jurists regarding *Ḥaṭṭ wa ta'ajjal*

The opinions of Muslim Jurists are divided on the legitimacy of *haṭṭ wa ta'jjall.*

First opinion

Discounting for hastening the payment is permissible. This opinion is attributed to Ibn 'Abbās, Nakh'ī, Abū Thawr and Zufar. They assert that the Holy Prophet (s.a.w.s.) had instructed Bani Naḍir to reduce the amount owed to them and receive immediate payment. It is reported that when Banī Naḍīr were evicted from Madinah, a group of them came to the Holy Prophet (s.a.w.s.) with a complaint that they had been evicted at a time when people owed them money, whose payments were not yet matured. The Holy Prophet (s.a.w.s.) advised them to reduce the amount owed to them and demand prompt payment.

Second opinion

This opinion suggests that the practice of discounting for hastening the payment is not lawful. The majority of Muslim

[30] Badawī, *Nazaryyat al-Ribā al-Muḥarram*, p. 205.

Jurists subscribe to this opinion. They put forward following arguments in favour of their standpoint:

1. A discount on the original amount for hastening the payment is similar to taking excess on the original amount. This is because in both the cases time is assigned to monetary value. Imām Sarakhsi said:

> "If a person is in debt of one thousand dirham for a specified period and he agrees with the creditor that he will pay him five hundred dirhams and will make payment to him ahead of time of maturity, it is not permissible, because the debtor has forfeited his right in time for five hundred and the creditor has also forfeited his right in five hundred in lieu of time, Hence it is an exchange of time for money, which is not lawful in our view.[31]

The real significance *haṭṭ wa ta'jjal* (reduce and hasten payment) referred to in the *ḥadīth* is that the Holy Prophet (s.a.w.s.) had instructed the Jews to give up their claims of interest or excess over and above the principal amount and take back original amounts only before the time of maturity. In other words, the Holy Prophet (s.a.w.s.) allowed them to receive their delayed debts before the time of maturity on the condition that they will reduce the amount of debt. The *ḥadīth* according to this interpretation does not suggest reduction in the original amount in return for immediate payment.

2. The *ḥadīth* of *haṭṭ wa ta'jjal* (discounting) came before the prohibition of *ribā*. The event of Bani Naḍir took place in fourth year after *Hijrah*, then in the sixth year after *Ghazwah Khayber* came the prohibition of *ribā al-faḍl*. Thereafter, in the year ten after *hijrah* the verses relating to *ribā* were revealed which contain final and conclusive prohibition of *ribā*. Thus,

---

[31] Sarakhsī, *al-Mabsūt*, vol. 21, p. 31.

the *ḥadīth* of discounting is abrogated by the subsequent revelations on *ribā*.[32]

Third opinion

This opinion suggests that discounting is permissible if it is affected without the condition of immediate payment. This means that if the debtor repaid his deferred debt before time of maturity and the creditor reduced some amount without its being a contractual obligation, then it is permissible, because former is not condition for latter.

Indexation of Loans and *Ribā*

Inflation and the consequent erosion in the purchasing power of money is an important contemporary issue confronting Muslim jurists, which has led to considerable debate and discussion. Inflation essentially harms the interests of the lender since he receives, at the time of its return, less money in terms of its purchasing power that he had originally lent. Suppose one borrows one thousand rupees from another for a period of one year. After the year the rupees is devalued by 10 per cent. If the borrower pays the lender one thousand rupees as per agreement, then he is actually paying him 900 rupees only. This means that in terms of purchasing power of money, he is paying him less than what he has borrowed.

As a solution to this problem some Muslim scholars suggest that the borrower should try to compensate lender for the loss of the value of money by giving such an extra amount, which at least offsets the drop that results from inflation. For this purpose, they have suggested that loans should be indexed to the rate of inflation in the economy.

[32] Ibid.

In view of the above, indexation is characterized as "a scheme to link the nominal value of deferred payment to a suitable index of the purchasing power of money."[33]

A number of schemes of indexation have been proposed by economists, of which three are especially noteworthy. The first consists of linking indexation with general price level in the economy, represented through a basket of commodities known as the consumer goods basket. The second scheme consists of linking indexation with the price of some specific commodity, which has a stable value. In other words, it suggests that the loan should be presumed to have been offered in that commodity itself. The third scheme suggests that the loan should be offered and repaid in terms of specially introduced financial instruments, which have fixed value.

Muslim scholars are sharply divided regarding the validity and legitimacy of indexation of loans. A group of scholars favour indexation and do not see anything contrary to the injunctions of the *Sharī'ah* in it, rather these scholars find it in conformity with the principles of justice and fairness laid down in the Qur'ān and the *Sunnah*. Those who hold indexation of loans to be valid and legitimate in *Sharī'ah* include scholars like Rafīq al-Miṣrī, Sulṭān Abū 'Alī, M.A. Mannān, Ziauddin Aḥmad, Salim Qureshi, 'Umar Zubayr, Gul Muḥammad, Mawlānā Muḥammad Ṭāsīn and several other scholars.

As against this, there is yet another group that maintains that the idea of indexation does not conform to the teachings of Islam. It involves an assumed positive return on loans. Those who maintain this viewpoint are:

---

[33] Munawar Iqbal, *"Inflation, Indexation and role of Money"*, Paper presented in the workshop on *Sharī'ah* Position on Indexation, Jeddah, 1987.

Muhammad 'Umar Chappra, Monzer Kahf, M. Nejatullah Ṣiddiqi, Muhammad Ḥasanuz Zaman, Mawlānā Taqi Usmāni, 'Ali Aḥmad Salus, and some other prominent scholars. The council of Islamic Ideology of Pakistan has also expressed its opposition to indexation. The same view has been upheld by the Federal Shari'at Court of Pakistan.

In the following lines an attempt will be made to explain the position of the *Sharī'ah* on the question and to analyse the arguments of the proponents as well as the opponents of indexation in the light of the general objectives of the *Sharī'ah* and the relevant texts of *fiqh* relating to the repayments of debts and the exchange of currency.

Arguments of Proponents

The arguments of proponents of indexation are summarized as follows:

1. Justice and fairness: The Justice and fairness in mutual dealings are corner stones of the Islamic economic system. Qur'ān repeatedly enjoins upon believers to be just and fair in their dealings. It says, "God commands justice, the doing of good and liberality to kith."[34] It also says, "Be just, that is nearest to piety".[35] It further says, "You shall inflict no injustice and shall suffer none."[36] It is undoubtedly true that inflation causes both injustice and unfairness to the lender.

2. Principle of redress of harm: It is an accepted principal of the Islamic *Sharī'ah* that no damage should be borne nor should any be caused. Inflation causes a loss in the real value of monetary receipts while indexation provides redress against such damage.

---

[34] Qur'ān, 16:90

[35] Qur'ān, 5:8

[36] Qur'ān, 2:279

3. Giving full measures: Islam has strictly forbidden the practice of diminution in weights and measures, thereby depriving others of their due rights. In this regards the Qur'ān says, "and give full measure and weight with justice".[37]

This Quranic instruction of giving full measures is not limited to conventional weights and measures. It encompasses all measures of value. In modern economies, money is the biggest measure of value. Now in the period of inflation, the recipient does not receive what is really due to him. Indexation corrects this situation.[38]

Arguments of the Opponents of Indexation

The most serious objection raised by the opponents of indexation is that indexation involves an assumed positive return on loans. Hence it is a form of *ribā*. They do not favour the idea of compensating lender for the loss he suffers as a result of inflation. They find following demerits and flaws in the scheme of indexation, from the islamic point of view.

1. *Gharar* and *Jahl* (Uncertainty and lack of knowledge): It is a requirement of the *Sharī'ah* that both the values in an exchange contract *('uqud al-mu'awaḍāt)* should be clearly determined. Muslim jurists are unanimous on the point that in a sale on deferred payment, if the price to be paid by the buyer is not fixed, it will render the contract void. Ibn 'Ābidin says: "Fixation of price is a requisite for the validity of a contract of sale. If the price is left unspecified or market value is made the price of commodity then the contract will be invalid."[39] This shows that the obligation of the buyer in the contract of deferred payment should be fixed at the time of making the

---

[37] Qur'ān, 6:152.

[38] Munawar Iqbal, Inflation, Indexation and role of Money.

[39] Ibn 'Abidīn, *Radd al-Muḥtār*, vol. 5, p.60.

contract. In the case of indexation, however, the liability of the debtor is known only on the date it is due.

2. Injustice and unfairness: The element of injustice and unfairness is inherent in the indexation will be evident from the following:

(i) In the Islamic Law of Indemnity the one who has caused wrong to someone is responsible for redressing or compensating that wrong. Inflation and the consequent damage to the money of lender is never an act of the borrower. This loss would have happened even if the lender had not lent his money. Hence, why should the borrower be held responsible for the loss and be asked to pay any compensation? Such a scheme obviously causes harm to the borrower.

(ii) The basket of consumers' goods which is the most popular method of indexation does not provide a just and fair standard for determining the purchasing power of money. To quote the words of Ḥasanuz Zamān:

> "This basket represents the consumption habits of an average person, which does not necessarily represent the habits of actual men and women living in a society. This average will be fair for some but an unjustifiable favour for some others."[40]

To explain this point further, it needs to be pointed out that a large majority of our population does not consume most of the goods contained in the basket. Their basket is generally restricted to a few things only such as cooking oil, soap, pulses, and flour. The consumer's basket, on the other hand, consists of about forty items, which are hardly consumed by the

---

[40] S.M. Hasanuz Zaman, Indexation of Financial Assets, an Islamic Evaluation, Islamabad, International Institute of Islamic Thought, 1993, p.40.

majority. If such a basket were adopted as a standard to determine the purchasing power of money, it would be unjust and unfair to many people.

The Element of *Ribā al-Faḍl*

Indexation also contains the element of *ribā al-faḍl*. It involves an excess in one counter value in the exchange of two commodities of the same genus and conflicts with the *ḥadīth* which requires that a fungible good is to be returned by its like, and good quality and bad quality have no relevance for such a contract. Thus, darkened silver has the same value in weight as polished silver. There is a consensus among the *fuqahā'* that the sameness in the tradition mentioned above, means sameness in kind and quantity, not in value.

Rules for exchange of fungible goods

The *fuqahā'* are so emphatic about "sameness" that they have ruled out all considerations of value or quality. In order to realize this objective, they have laid down very clear rules so as to ensure the sameness of quantity. Ibn Qudāmah has mentioned some of these rules:

(1) The loan of the *dirham* of unknown weight is not permissible.

(2) If *dirhams* are lent by weight, they should be returned by weight.

(3) If *dirhams* are lent by counting their repayment must be by counting.

(4) The borrower will be required to return the same quantity, which he borrowed regardless of any change in price.[41]

---

[41] Ibn Qudāmah, al-Mughnī, vol. 4, p.210.

It is due to this requirement of sameness that the Shāfi'i Jurists invalidate the loan of non-fungible goods because sameness cannot be realized in it. The workshop on indexation organized by the Islamic Development Bank in Jeddah in 1987 emphasized this point in the following words:

> "In the context of indexation, the scholars attending the workshop emphasized that the work "*mithl*" referred to in the tradition of the Prophet Muhammad (s.a.w.s.) on *ribā* means sameness in kind and quantity according to the *Sharī'ah*. Sameness in quantity means sameness in weight, measure or number, not sameness in value. This is in adherence to what the *Sunnah* has indicated and it is in compliance with what the *ummah* has agreed upon unanimously and what it has been practicing."[42]

It is evident from the above that the *Sharī'ah* disallows any excess over and above the principal sum in all circumstances. The additional amount received by the lender through indexation falls under the purview of the *ḥadīth* which declares that each loan that entails some monetary benefit is a kind of *ribā*. In fact, indexation is an attempt to provide justification for banking interest. A bank may claim that the excess paid to the depositor is compensation for the loss suffered by the latter during the period money remained in custody of bank, and it is not *ribā*. As such, this device opens the back door for interest.

No doubt constant rise in prices inflicts great harm on the majority of people. It especially harms people with limited and fixed incomes and prevents the equitable distribution of wealth in the society. Inflation is a social evil that adversely affects

---

[42] Recommendations of workshop on *Sharī'ah* Position on Indexation (April 25-28, 1987) Organized by Islamic Development Bank, Jeddah, 1987.

almost all the members of the society. Thus, it is not merely an individual's problem. It would be unjust as well as irrational to hold only one party of the contract, namely the borrower, responsible for this phenomenon and ask him for compensation. Such an attitude will only further widen the area of injustice instead of narrowing it down. It is the obligation of the state to control prices and adopt measures that would reduce the level of inflation.

Conclusion

- *Ribā* is defined as an increase in the principal, stipulated in loan transaction.
- The Qur'ān has dealt with the issue of *ribā* in *Sūrah al-Rum* (Verse 39), *Sūrah al-Nisā'* (Verse 161), *Sūrat al-'Imrān,* (Verse 130) and *Sūrah al-Baqarah* (Verses 275-281)
- The *ahādith* dealing with *ribā* are of two categories:
  - Those, which reaffirm the type of *ribā* mentioned in the Qur'ān.
  - Those that introduce new forms of *ribā*, i.e., *ribā al-faḍl* and *ribā al-nasā'*
- *Ribā al-faḍl* takes place in a homogeneous exchange with increase from one side in terms of weight or measurement.
- *Ribā al-nasā'* takes place when articles of the same genera or different genera are exchanged with deferment from one party.
- The prohibition of *ribā al-faḍl* and *ribā al-nasā'* seeks to forestall the entry of real *ribā* through the back door.
- The prohibition of *ribā al-faḍl* is not restricted to six commodities. It is extendable to commodities, which

resemble the six *ribawī* commodities with regard to underlying cause.

- The Muslim jurists have provided different underlying causes of the prohibition of *Ribā al-faḍl* and *Ribā al-nasā'*.
- Other forms of *ribā* are: *bay' al-'inah* (buy-back agreements), *bay' al-wafā* and *haṭṭ wa ta'jjal* (discounting for hastening the payment).

Chapter 10

Defect of Consent and its Effect on Contract

As mentioned earlier, consent of the parties forms the basis of a contract. A contract is considered valid only when it is concluded by a free consent. A defect of consent leading to nullity of contract arises when a party gives his consent as a result of mistake, fraud and duress or coercion. In these circumstances the contract becomes voidable at the option of the party whose consent was so obtained.

In the following lines we will discuss mistake, fraud and coercion and their effect on the validity of contract.

I. Mistake *(Khaṭā')*

Mistake is generally defined as a "belief that is not in accord with the facts".[1] Mistake conceived by Muslim jurists relates either to genus (substance) of the object or its substantial quality. An example of the former is sale of corundum (*yaqūt*). If a stone is sold as being corundum but turns out to be only glass the sale is void, the reason being the difference between glass and corundum.[2] An example of a mistake in the substantial quality is where a person purchases a piece of cotton as Egyptian cotton, which turns out to be Japanese cotton.[3] Similarly, when a person purchases a book believing that it is from a particular author and it turns out to be of another author, he suffers from mistake of substantial quality.

---

[1] Sanhūrī, *Masṣādir al-haq*, vol.2, p.104.

[2] Sarakhaṣī, *al-Mabsūṭ*, vol. 13, pp. 12-13.

[3] Zaydān, *al-Madkhal li dirāsah al-Sharī'ah al-Islamiyyah*, p.353.

Effect of contract with mistake

The Muslim jurists are unanimous on the point that a mistake bearing on genus renders a contract invalid as in the case of corundum.[4] As for mistake that relates to substantial quality, they hold that it makes contract voidable at the option of the party that suffered from mistake.[5]

The distinction between the categories of substantial and non-substantial has been made mainly with regard to usufruct of the object–the use to which it is intended to be put; and principally to the object the contracting party has in mind when he forms the contract. The quality must, therefore, be material in the mind of contracting party who is claiming the mistake: this is so whether it is clearly stated or merely implied. An instance is the buying of an animal for its meat, which the purchaser later discovers to be blind. Here, the purchaser cannot avoid the contract, because the defect of blindness is hardly pertinent to the intended use of the subject matter of the transaction, that is, to obtain meat.[6]

If the species of the object is the same, but an appreciable difference exists between the thing contracted for and the usufruct of the intended object, then the contract is again voidable by virtue of mistake as to meaning (substance). For instance a cloth is sold in a different colour or pattern to the one intended and it is not in accordance with the purpose of the contract.[7]

The mistake with regard to substantial quality affects those contracts only which admit of revocation such as commutative

---

[4] Zayla'ī, *Tabyīn al-ḥaqā'iq*, vol.4, p.52.

[5] Zuḥaylī, *al-Fiqh al-Islāmi wa Adillahtuhū*, vol. 4, p.217; Madkūr, *al-Madkhal*, p.646.

[6] Rayner, *Islamic Law of Contract*, p.180.

[7] Ibid. p.181.

contracts. It, however, does not affect the contracts, which do not accept revocation such as contract of marriage. Thus, a marriage contract cannot be revoked on the grounds of absence of required quality in the wife in the opinion of Ḥanafī jurists. Imām Aḥmad, on the other hand, holds that the husband has right to revoke the contract if he entered the contract relying on the words of guardian that she is beautiful but she appeared ugly, or she is virgin but it appeared that it is her second marriage.[8]

The mistake concerns non-substantial quality where the object is of the same substance as that contracted for, and the representation made by the seller as to its quality is false. For instance, a seller presents an object as a ruby, which is later found to be yellow. Here, the sale is valid but not binding on the purchaser because the mistake is not about the substance of the object nor is it deemed to have affected the usufruct intended by the purchaser and the true sale.[9]

A reference to the Egyptian civil code would be quite relevant to know as to which mistake affects a contract. This law determines that a mistake is essential when:

- It has bearing on the quality of goods, which the parties have considered essential or which must be deemed essential, taking into consideration the circumstances surrounding the contract and the good faith that should prevail in business relationship.
- It has a bearing on the identity, or on one of the qualities of the person with whom the contract is entered into, if

[8] Ibn Qudāmā, *al-Mughnī*, vol. 6, p.526.
[9] Rayner, *Islamic Law of contract,* p.182

this identity or this quality was the principle factor in the conclusion of the contract."[10]

II. Fraud *(Tadlīs, Taghrīr, Khilābah)*

Fraud is another cause of nullity of an agreement. It occurs when the conduct of one of the parties is such that without it the other party would not have contracted.

"Fraud is to induce a person by some deceptive means with a view to obtain his consent to a contract without which he would not have consented to the contract".[11] If what is so represented by words or conduct, be false, that is, not in agreement with the facts and the person making such representation is aware of it, the representer is said to be guilty of fraud.

Fraud in Islamic Law includes the misrepresentation of Western Law, which is defined as "a false statement of fact, made by one party before or at the time of the contract which induces the other party to enter into the contract".[12] The act of fraud which gives innocent party right to revoke the contract, must fulfill following conditions:

(i) Misrepresentation of a material fact must occur,

(ii) There must be an intent to deceive,

(iii) The innocent party must rely on misrepresentation,

(iv) The innocent party must suffer an injury. Thus, fraud alone does not cause the annulment of contract.

---

[10] *Egyptian Civil Code*, Article 121 (a) & (b).

[11] *The Law of Business contracts*, p.102.

[12] Zarqā, *al-Madkhal al-Fiqhī al-'Āmm*, vol. 1, p.374.

Traditional Forms of Fraud in Islamic Juristic Literature

The Muslim Jurists have discussed various forms of fraud, some of them are as follows:

1. *Taṣriyah*

It is to tie the udder of a she-camel or sheep to allow the animal's milk to accumulate in her udder so as to give a false impression to the intending buyer of a very productive milk-yield. In this respect the Holy Prophet (s.a.w.s) says:

> "Do not tie up the udder of she-camels and sheep. If anyone among you buys a she-camel or sheep whose udder have been tied up, has option (of annulment) after milking it; either to retain it or to return along with a measure of dates (in lieu of the milk consumed by the purchaser).[13]

The act of *Taṣriyah* renders the contract voidable at the option of the buyer, who has suffered lesion from this fraud. This is the viewpoint of the majority. Ḥanafī jurists do not approve annulment of contract. They allow the defrauded party to claim undue increase from the seller.[14]

2. *Najash or Tanājush* (False bidding to raise price)

It is to offer a high price for a commodity without any intention to buy it, the sole aim being to cheat somebody else who really wanted to buy the commodity. The Holy Prophet (s.a.w.s) has prohibited this practice. It is related on the authority of Abū Hurayrah (r.a.t.a) that the Prophet (s.a.w.s) said: 'O people! With a view to bargaining with the people who come with their animals laden with commodities for sale, do not go to meet

---

[13] San'ānī, *Subul al-Salām*, vol.3, p.26.
[14] Ibn 'Ābidīn, *al-Radd al-Muḥtār*, vol.4, p.101.

them (outside the town) and if a person is bargaining with another, do not interfere by bidding higher.[15]

Najash or *tanājush* is a vitiating factor of contract and renders the contract voidable. *Tanājush* gives a buyer right to revoke the contract. This is the viewpoint of majority of Muslim jurists. Shāfi'ī jurists do not acknowledge this right for the buyer.[16]

3. *Ghabn fāḥish*

Ghabn fāḥish means excessive loss suffered by a party to the contract as a result of concealment or misrepresentation, or deception or fraud practiced by the other.

Explanation: Whether the loss is excessive/exorbitant or not is to be ascertained in view of the market value of the subject matter. Article 146 of Jordanian Civil Code States: "Evaluation concerning *Ghabn fāḥish* in real estate or other property is a matter for the estimators alone".

Ghabn is regarded light (*yasīr*) if the difference between the price at which goods were sold and their real market value is so small that the merchants do not generally take it into account in their dealings. For instance, a book worth Rs. 100/- is sold for Rs. 110, it will not be a *ghabn fāḥish* but if it if sold for Rs. 150/- it will amount to *ghabn fāḥish*.

Effects of *Ghabn Fāḥish*

Ḥanafī viewpoint

The Ḥanafī jurists are of the view that excessive loss suffered by a party alone is not a cause of nullity of contract. It annuls the contract only when it is caused by a fraud, or misrepresentation. For example, A sells a watch worth Rs. 300/- for Rs. 600/- to B claiming that market value of such watch is 700/- rupees. B

[15] Ṣan'ānī, *Subul al-Salām*, vol. 3, p.18.

[16] Zuhaylī, *al-Fiqh al-Islāmī*, vol. 4, p.223.

relying upon the words of A purchases it for Rs. 600/-. B has suffered from *ghabn fāḥish*, which is a result of fraud. Such *ghabn fāḥish* gives him right to revoke the contract.[17] In this respect the *Majallah* states:

> "If there is an excessive lesion without fraud in the sale, the person who has suffered loss cannot annul the sale."[18]

There are, however, certain cases in which excessive loss of a party alone without fraud affects the contracts such as the sale of *waqf* property or the property of *bayt al-māl* or the property of minor or insane. If the property of these people and institutions is sold with *ghabn fāḥish*, i.e., at a much lower price as compared to its market value, the sale will be revoked.[19]

Ḥanbalī viewpoint

Ghabn fāḥish affects the contracts and makes it voidable at the option of the party which suffered lesion irrespective of the fact that it is a result of fraud or otherwise.[20]

Shāfi'ī viewpoint

The Shāfi'ī jurists do not admit the right of revocation for the buyer. They say that the lesion has occurred because of the negligence of buyer. Thus, he alone is responsible for the loss.[21]

4. *Talaqqī al-rukbān*

It is another form of fraud and misrepresentation. It is a transaction where a city-dweller takes advantage of the ignorance of a bedouin carrying objects of prime and general

---

[17] Ibn 'Ābidīn , *Radd al-Muḥtār*, vol.4, p.166.
[18] *Majallah*, Article 356.
[19] Ibid, Article 356.
[20] Ibn Qudāmā, *al-Mughnī*, vol. 4, pp.212-218.
[21] Shirbīnī, *Mughnī al-Muḥtāj*, vol. 2, p.36.

necessity for sale and cheats him in the course of the sale. The shrewd city-dweller goes out of town to meet the bedouin merchant and buys his goods at a cheap rate, depriving the latter of the opportunity of first surveying the market to acquaint himself of the current market rate. The Holy Prophet (s.a.w.s.) said:

> "It is forbidden to meet the riders (i.e. the traders) on the road (for the purpose of taking undue advantage). Whosoever meets a trader on road and buys goods from this trader, the vendor has the right of option and cancellation of such deal when he arrives at the market."[22]

5. Inflated price in trust sale

Another form of fraud is where the seller in a trust sale, sells goods at an inflated price to buyer. The buyer bases himself on the price the seller claims to have himself paid in order to suggest to him a purchase price.[23]

In trust sale the buyer takes the declaration of the person selling on trust. The latter's declaration may, of course be a lie, for he may in fact have acquired the article at a much lower price than the one he claims in order to make a large profit.[24]

Following are kinds of trust sale:

- *Tawliyyah*: Resale at cost price.
- *Murābaḥah*: Resale with profit increase.
- *Waḍʿīah*: Resale with loss.

The fraud in trust sale renders the contract voidable at the option of buyer. He may either revoke the contract or claim

---

[22] Ṣanʿānī, *Subul al-Salām,*vol. 3, p.21.

[23] Zuḥaylī, *al-Fiqh al-Islāmī wa Addillatuhū*, vol. 4, pp.710-711.

[24] Sanhūrī, *Maṣādir al-haq* vol. 2, p.158.

reimbursement of undue increase from the seller. Ibn 'Ābidīn states that if the amount of deception is one-fourth of the original, the buyer has the right to devalue one-fourth of profit from the stated price.[25]

Some Jurists suggest that the swindled purchaser should either cancel the sale completely or retain the goods at stated price. He does not have the option of devaluation of undue increase.

6. *Tadlīs bi al-'ayb* (Fraud with defect)

Soundness of the object is an implied condition of the contract. It is not permitted for a person to sell a defective object knowingly. Whatever may be the cause of diminishing the price amongst merchants is considered as a defect. A buyer discovering a defect in the article purchased is at liberty to return it to the seller, unless he was aware of the defect beforehand.

A purchaser is entitled to compensation for a defect in an article where it has sustained a further blemish in his hands, but he cannot in this case return it to the seller. He is also entitled to compensation if the return be rendered impracticable by any change in the subject.

Coercion *(Ikrāh)*

Sarakhsī defines coercion in the following words: "By coercion one designates the action of one person against another suppressing the consent of this latter person or vitiating his consent".[26] Zayla'ī defines *ikrāh* as: "An action directed against a person, which suppresses his true consent".[27] According to the

---

[25] Ibn 'Ābidīn , *Radd al-Muḥtār*, vol. 4, p.155.

[26] Sarakhsī, *al-Mabsūt*, vol. 14, p.39.

[27] Fakhr al-Dīn 'Uthmān ibn 'Alī Zayla'ī, ,*Tabyīn al-Ḥaqā'iq*, Būlāq: al-Maktabah al-Kubrā al-Amīriyyah, 1313-1315, vol. 5, p.181.

Majallah, "*ikrāh* is to compel, without right, a person to do a thing without his consent or by fear".[28]

In modern Law coercion is some element of force, either physical or economic used to suppress one party's consent to choose whether or not to enter into a particular contract. Under such circumstances the contract is voidable at the instance of the innocent party.[29]

Conditions of Effective Coercion

Following are conditions, which give rise to annulment of contract under coercion:

- Coercion should be legally unjustified.
- It should emanate from a party who has the power to execute his threat, that is, it must be realistically practicable.
- It must be of such a nature as to intimidate the victim: that is, it must be of significant and imminent danger.
- The compelled person must believe that if he does not comply with the compeller's demands, the harm promised by the compeller will be inflicted upon him.

Kinds of Coercion

Coercion is divided into two kinds:

1. Perfect coercion *(Ikrāh tāmm)*

It leads to destruction of life, or loss of limb or one of them. It annuls the juridical act done under constraint.

---

[28] *Majallah*, Art. 948.

[29] *Business Law*, p.116.

2. Imperfect coercion *(Ikrāh nāqiṣ)*

This causes only grief and pain. It is compulsion, which is by things like a blow or imprisonment. Imperfect or minor coercion also annuals consent, but supposes that the contracting party who suffered this coercion could still exercise his free will. Such would be the case if he was threatened with blows not liable to cause his death or to cripple him.[30]

Effects

The opinion of Jurists is divided on the validity of contract with coercion. Ḥanafī jurists maintain that contract concluded under coercion is valid because it has been agreed to by intention of the party, even though the consent was not freely given. In the opinion of these jurists, coercion does not render the contract void but merely voidable. It gives rise to effects, which are assigned to voidable contracts. The party whose consent was obtained through coercion has the right either to ratify it in which case it will become binding or to annual it.[31] Imām Zufar considers such contract suspended (*mawqūf*) subject to ratification.

The viewpoint of the Mālikī jurists on the effect of a contract concluded under coercion is similar to that of the Ḥanafī school of law. They regard it a valid contract but non-binding. The party, who has been coerced, has the right to revoke it. The Shāfi'ī and Ḥanbalī jurists regard the act under coercion non-existent since the essential condition of the juridical act, i.e., the will, is vitiated.[32] The Shāfi'īs argue that *khiyār* and consent are interdependent concepts and cannot operate independently in the intention to create legal relations.[33]

---

[30] Zaydān, *al-Madkhal*, p.361.
[31] Zarqā, *al-Madkhal*, vol. 1, p.371.
[32] Zahaylī, *al-Fiqh al-Islāmī,* vol.4, p.216.
[33] Ibid.

Conclusion

- A defect of consent leading to nullity of contract arises when a party gives his consent as a result of mistake, fraud and coercion.
- Mistake is a belief, which is not in accord with the facts. It relates either to genus of the object or its substantial quality.
- The mistake bearing on genus renders the contract invalid while the mistake relating to substantial quality makes contracts voidable.
- Fraud is to induce a person by some defective means with a view to obtain his consent to a contract without which he would have not consented to the contract.
- Traditional forms of fraud include;
  - *Taṣriyah*
  - *Najash* (false bidding to raise price)
  - *Ghabn fāḥish*
  - *Talaqqī al-rukbān*
  - Inflated price in trust sale
  - *Tadlīs bi al-'ayb*
- Coercion refers to an action of one person against another suppressing the consent of the latter. It is a cause of nullity of contract.

Chapter 11

Extrinsic Conditions and their Effect on the Contract

The opinion of Muslim jurists is divided on the extent of freedom enjoyed by the contracting parties to insert extrinsic or ancillary conditions in the contract. The reason for emphasising this issue is that the Lawgiver has assigned certain legal effects to contracts while the extrinsic conditions remove or modify these effects. For example, the effect of sale is to transfer ownership of the goods sold and their usufruct to the buyer immediately. Now if a person sells a car to another on the condition that he (seller) reserves right to use it for a month. This condition has direct bearing on the effects of the contract because it delays the effects of the contract. Is such condition valid? In other words can contracting parties by their mutual consent agree to a condition, which may change and modify the effects, which the *Sharīʿah* accords to contract?

The jurists have differed among themselves on this point. One school, which emphasises the supremacy of the autonomy of the will of contracting parties, holds that the parties are free to insert any condition. They deem every clause or condition in the contract valid provided it does not contradict any text of the Qur'ān and the *Sunnah*. Another school has adopted a very rigid and extreme position. This school holds that conditions are generally not valid except where the text provides for them.

A third school while favouring the position held by the second school that the contracting parties do not have the right to modify the effects of contracts, allows for some conditions, which either confirm the effects or are normally recognised, in the commercial usage. Unlike the first school, this school is rather restrictive which does not accept conditions except those, which conform to the principles laid down by this school for admissibility of conditions. Now we discuss these viewpoints and their arguments in detail.

Viewpoint of Ẓāhirī Jurists

Ẓāhiī jurists impose total ban on ancillary conditions except the conditions, which are approved by the text. To these jurists basic presumption of law is that all contracts and conditions are prohibited except that which is established by the text or *ijmā'* (consensus of opinion).[1]

Their arguments

- Holy Prophet (s.a.w.a) said, "He who performs an act we have not ordered him, his act is null and void."[2]
- Holy Prophet (s.a.w.a) said: "A loan made at the same time as a sale is illicit. Two conditions in a sale are not allowed nor is profit without corresponding liability and sale of what is not possible."[3]

Thus, the Ẓāhirī Jurists invalidate all such conditions, which do not figure in the Qur'ān and the *Sunnah,* or they introduce modification to the effects of a juridical act.

Ḥanbalī viewpoint

The Ḥanbalī viewpoint represents a very liberal approach as it acknowledges complete autonomy of will in contracts and transactions.[4] To Ḥanbalī jurists general rule with regard to

---

[1] Ibn Ḥazm, *al-Muḥallāh, vol.* 2, p. 412.

[2] *Iḥkām fī Uṣūl al-Aḥkām,* vol. 5, p.32; *Taysīr al-Wuṣūl ilā Jāmi' al-Uṣūl.* vol. 1, p.63.

[3] *Nayl al-Awṭār,* vol. 5, p.190.

[4] For Ḥanbalī Viewpoint, See Ibn Taymiyyah, *Naẓriyyat al-'Aqd,* p.15,16; and *Fatāwā 'ibn Taymiyyah* vol. 3, p.323.

contracts and conditions is permissible unless a text from the Qur'ān or the *Sunnah* or a valid consensus makes them invalid. They do not demand a text providing for permissibility, as it is demanded by the Ẓāhirī scholars. Thus, to combine two contracts in one or to sell with the condition of loan from buyer are not valid conditions because the text has explicitly prohibited it. Apart from it all other conditions are permissible. It is, therefore, permissible for a woman to stipulate in marriage contract that her husband will not compel her to leave her hometown. It is also permissible to stipulate that he will not marry another woman. Such condition would be binding upon husband and give her right to revoke contract if he does not honour it. They also allow the seller of a house to stay in the house sold for some specified time as a part of contractual condition.

Their arguments

- The Qur'ān says: "O you who believe: fulfill your contracts".[5] It also says: "And fulfil every promise, because every promise will be inquired into".[6] In these verses Allah has ordered believers to fulfill their obligations and undertakings towards each other and prohibited from violating them. This includes conditions the parties insert in the contract by their free will.

- The Holy Prophet (s.a.w.s) said: "Muslims are bound by their stipulations unless it be a condition which turns *ḥarām* into *ḥalāl* or *ḥalāl* into *ḥarām*."[7]

  This *ḥadīth* allows inserting conditions in contract, and the parties are bound to abide by it. The only limitation imposed on the parties is that they should not insert a

---

[5] Qur'ān, 5:1.
[6] Qur'ān, 17 :34.
[7] Shawkānī, *Nayl al-Awṭār*, vol. 5, p.255.

condition, which is inconsistent with the injunctions of Islam.

- As regards the *hadīth* which declares all such conditions void, which do not exist in the Book of Allah, these jurists, argue that prohibition contained in it is applicable to those conditions only which are against the Book of Allah, i.e., against its injunctions. The meaning of *hadīth* in the light of this interpretation would be that if someone stipulated for a thing which is not recommend in His book, this act on his part will be regarded null and void.
- The Ḥanbalīs differentiate between *'ibādāt* and *mu'āmlāt*. *'ibādāt* are established by the explicit injunctions of the *Sharī'ah*. As for *Muāmlāt* (transactions) the governing principle is permissibility and absence of prohibition.[8]

Viewpoint of Ḥanafī, Shāfi'ī and Mālikī Jurists

The jurists of these schools divide the condition into three kinds.[9]

(a) Valid conditions

Valid conditions are further divided into four categories:[10]

(i) Conditions, which confirm the effects, attributed to juridical act by the *Sharī'ah*. Such conditions strengthen the purpose of contract. The condition, for example, to sell on the condition that the seller will not hand over good to buyer unless he pays the price is a valid condition because

---

[8] Ibn Taymiyyah, *Fatāwā*, vol. 29, pp. 16-18; *Naẓriyyat al-'Aqd*, p. 314.

[9] Madkūr, *al-Madkhal li al- Fiqh al-Islāmī*, p. 664. See for details: Sarakhsī, *al-Mabsūṭ* vol. 13, pp. 14-28; Ibn al-Humām, *Fatḥ al-Qadīr*, vol. 5, p.314; Ibn 'Ābidīn, *Radd al-Muḥtār*, vol. 4, p.126

[10] See 'Ādil Muṣṭafā Basyūnī, *Al-Tashrī' al-Islāmī wa al-Nuẓum al-Qānūniyyah al-Waḍ' iyyah*, p.152,153

it stresses and confirms the effects of contract and realizes its objective.

(ii) Condition, which is admitted explicitly by the *Sharī'ah,* such as the option of stipulation, reserved for a party to revoke or ratify a contract within three days. Such condition is valid because the *Sharī'ah* has sanctioned the option of stipulation *(khiyār al-sharṭ)* and option of inspection *(khiyar al-ru'yah).*

(iii) A condition, which is intimately, connected with the contract such a pledge of security in a contract of surety.

(iv) The Ḥanafī jurists also allow a condition, which has been established by custom. A modern example of such condition is to purchase air-conditioner with the condition that the company will be responsible for its repair for two years.

b) Irregular condition

A condition is regarded irregular if:

- it is repugnant to requisites of the contract;
- it is irreconcilable with the purpose and effects of contract;
- it is not allowed by the *Sharī'ah;*
- it is not allowed by custom and usage; and
- it gives undue advantage to one of the contracting parties

The *ḥukm* of such condition is that it renders the entire juridical act invalid. It especially affects commutative contracts. The condition by an owner of a house to stay in the house sold for one year is an irregular condition, which affects whole contract and renders it invalid. But it does not affect gratuitous contracts.

The contract containing such condition remains valid, the condition alone is regarded null and void. The reason for the difference between commutative contracts and gratuitous contracts is that in the former case the condition disturbs balance of benefits involved in the contract. It gives one of the parties an advantage that is not balanced by a corresponding gain or benefit of the other. On the other hand, gratuitous contracts do not involve bilateral benefits, so no question of the disruption of equilibrium arises. An irregular condition in gratuitous contract, therefore, does not nullify whole juridical act.

c) Void conditions

It is a condition, which directly infringes any rule of the *Sharīʿah,* or inflicts harm on one of the two contracting parties or derogates from completion of contract, such as the condition imposed by the seller that the purchaser will not sell it further to any party. The condition, which brings benefit for one of the two contracting parties and disturbs the equivalence of benefits, is, in fact, a kind of *ribā* and is, thus, considered null and void.[11]

The *ḥukm* of a contract with a void condition is that the condition is severable from the contract, it does not nullify the whole contract. The condition alone will be regarded null and void.

Meaning of two conditions in sale and two transactions in one

The tradition prohibiting the two conditions and two transactions referred to above has been interpreted by the jurists in a number of ways. Sarakhsī, a Ḥanafī jurist, commenting on the tradition says:

> "The description of the two conditions in sale is to say (So much for cash and so much for delay). The

[11] Zaydān, *al-Madkhal,* p.398.

> contract here is *fāsid* because the buyer did not specify the price at which he has agreed to purchase goods. Thus, the cause of irregularity of this contract is indeterminacy with regard to price of goods."[12]

Regarding the legal status of two transactions in one, Imam Shāfi'ī is reported to have stated his opinion in the following words:

> "It carries two interpretations: first, I sold you this commodity for two thousand on credit and one thousand in cash and sale is binding and irrevocable at one of the two prices. The sale is void because contract is contingent upon an unspecified thing. Second: I sell you my house on the condition that you sell your horse to me. This is invalid because it involves exploitation of buyer who is compelled to purchase a thing, which he does not want. It also contains *gharar* because the seller does not know whether the second sale will take place or not."[13]

This sale is invalid in the Ḥanbalī School as well because of the element of *gharar*.[14]

Conclusion

- The opinion of Muslim jurists is divided on the legality of extrinsic conditions in a contract.
- The Ḥanbalī jurists emphasise the supremacy of the will of contracting parties and allow every condition and stipulation in a contract as long as it does not contradict any text from the Qur'ān or the *Sunnah*.

---

[12] Sarakhsī, *al-Mabsūṭ*. vol. 14, p.36
[13] Shīrāzī, *al-Muhadhdhab*, vol. 1, p.267
[14] Ibn Qudāmā, *al-Mughnī*, vol. 4, p.234.

- The Ẓāhirī jurists impose total ban on extrinsic conditions. They accept only those conditions, which are approved by the explicit texts of the Qur'ān and the *Sunnah*.
- The Ḥanafī, Shāfi'ī and Mālikī Jurists divide conditions into valid, irregular and void.
- Valid conditions are those, which confirm the effects, attributed to juridical act by the *Sharī'ah* and which are admitted explicitly by it, such as the option of stipulation.
- A condition is regarded irregular if:
    - It is repugnant to requisites of the contract
    - It is irreconcilable with the purpose and effects of contract
    - It is not allowed by the *Sharī'ah*
    - It is not allowed by custom and usage
    - And it gives undue advantage to one of the contracting parties
- Void condition is a condition, which directly infringes any rule of the *Sharī'ah*, or inflicts harm on one of the two contracting parties or derogates from completion of contract.

Chapter 12

Islamic Law of Options *(Khayārāt)*

Muslim jurists have suggested number of devices to safeguard contracting parties against hasty undertaking. These devices give a party, who signed contract unwisely and then regretted his haste on seeing some lesion or fraud, an opportunity to ponder over his transaction and revoke the contract. These devices are called *khayārāt* (plural of word *khiyār),* i.e., options in Islamic Law. They have been designed to maintain balance in transactions and to protect a weaker party from being harmed. They constitute preventive measure against error, defect in goods, want of knowledge concerning quality of things and lack of desired quality. The meaning of *khiyār* is that a contractor has right to ratify the contract or to annual within the period of option.

Kinds of Options

The options allowed in Islamic Law are as under:

- *Khiyār al-Sharṭ* (Option of condition)
- *Khiyār al-Ta'yīn* (Option of determination)
- *Khiyār al-'Āyb* (Option of defect)
- *Khiyār al-Ru'yah* (Option of inspection)
- *Khiyār al-Waṣf* (Option of description)[1]

These options are established either through the rule of the *Sharī'ah* or the agreement between the parties. Options of defect and option of inspection have been granted by the *Sharī'ah*

---

[1] Zuhaylī, *al-Fiqh al-Islāmī wa Adillatuhū,* vol. 4, p.250

while the option of stipulation, option of determination, and option of description are established by agreement.[2] Some modern authors class option of condition under first category.

1. *Khiyār al-Sharṭ* (Option of condition)

Khiyār al-Sharṭ is that option through which one party or both of them stipulate for themselves or for someone else the right to revoke the contract within a determined period.[3] For instance, the purchaser says to the seller "I purchased this thing from you but I have the right to return it within three days". As soon as the period is over, the right to revoke, derived through this option, lapses. The result of this option is that contract which is binding initially becomes non-binding with the stipulation of this option.

Legality of *khiyār al-sharṭ*

It is reported that the Holy Prophet (s.a.w.s) granted this option to Ḥibbān ibn Munzir who complained that he was defrauded each time he made a purchase. He was directed by the Holy Prophet (s.a.w.s) to say whenever he made a purchase "No cheating, and I reserve option for three days.[4] The purpose of option is to give chance to a person who suffered some loss in transaction to revoke contract within stipulated time. The option is stipulated normally at the time of the contract. According to Imām Shāfi'ī and Imām Aḥmad it should be stipulated at the time of contract. Other jurists allow it even after the contract has been concluded, as long as the parties are in the same session of contract.

[2] Ḥassan *al-Madkhal*, p.455.

[3] Zuḥaylī, *al-Fiqh al Islāmī wa Adillatuhū,* vol. 4, p.254; See also Zaydān, *al-Madkhal*, p.377.

[4] Shawkānī, *Nayl al-Awṭār* vol. 5, p.182.

Contract in which *khiyār al-sharṭ* is permitted

Khiyār al sharṭ is permitted in those contracts, which accept revocation like sale, hire, *muzāra'ah* (crop sharing). It cannot be stipulated in those contracts, which do not accept revocation such as divorce, manumission etc.

As regard those contracts, which are revocable by nature like agency, and partnership, the stipulation of *khiyār al-sharṭ* would be futile as they can be revoked at the will of either party. It is also not permitted in contracts of *salam* (sale of future goods)[5] and *sarf* (money exchange) .

For whom the option is stipulated

The option can be stipulated by one of the parties for himself or for a third party. The third party then becomes the *wakīl* of the party for purpose of exercising the option but it does not prevent the party from exercising the option himself.

Maximum period of *khiyār al-sharṭ*

There is agreement amongst the jurists that *khiyār al-sharṭ* can be stipulated for a period of three days or less. This agreement is based on the tradition quoted above.

The jurists disagree as regards any period over three days. Imām Abū Yūsuf and Mohammad and the Ḥanbalīs are of the opinion that it is permitted to lay down a period of more than three days without any restriction of the maximum period.[6] Imām Abū Ḥanīfah and Shāfi'ī do not allow it for more than three days. The reason is that *qiyās,* i.e. general rule prohibits the stipulation of *khiyār* altogether, which is then permitted as an exception from the tradition. The necessity has been

[5] Abū Zahrah, *al-Milkiyyah wa Nazariyyat al-'Aqd* p. 393.

[6] Ibn Qudāma, *al-Mughnī* vol. 3, p.585, Kāsānī, *Badā'i' al-Ṣanā'ī'* vol. 5, p.174 .

acknowledged as three days by the tradition and cannot, therefore, be extended beyond such period.[7] According to the Mālikīs the period of *khiyār* varies from case to case. Thus, it may be one day when a piece of cloth has been purchased and may be one or two months when a house has been purchased.[8]

Effect of the contract with *khiyār al-sharṭ*

The difference between the jurists as regards the *ḥukm* of the contract can be reduced to two opinions.

First opinion: The effects do not come into operation during the period of the option. The contract remains suspended *(mawqūf)* during the period of the option or till such option is exercised. Thus right in the property is not transferred to one in whose favour the option has been stipulated.

Second opinion: The effects come into operation but the contract is now not binding or *ghayr lāzim* and can be revoked during the period of the option by the one in whose favour the option has been stipulated.

The option may be exercised expressly or impliedly. Revocation does not require the *ḥukm* of the court to become effective. Ratification may also be expressed or implied.[9]

Termination of the option

The option ceases to be applicable in the following cases:

i) Death of one in whose favour the option was operating

In such case the option becomes extinct and the contract is now binding as regards the representative of the deceased.

---

[7] Shirbīnī, *Muhgnī al-Muḥtāj,* vol. 2, p. 47; Kāsānī, *Badā'i'al-Sanā'i'*, *vol.* 5, p.174.

[8] Ibn Rushd, *Bidāyah al-Mujtahid,* vol. 2, p.208.

[9] Hassān, *al-Madkhal*, pp.456,457.

The exercise of the option is a personal right and cannot pass to the heirs. According to the Mālikīs and Shāfi'īs on the other hand, it is right which can be inherited and the heirs can exercise the option within the stipulated period.

ii) Termination of the period

On termination of the period the contract becomes binding and irrevocable.

iii) Destruction of the subject matter

In this case also the contract becomes binding.

2. *Khiyār al-ṭa'yīn* (Option of designation)

Option of designation is the right of buyer to choose, designate or determine within a pre-stated time one object out of two or more which are proposed to him. The basic rule is that the subject matter must be known, i.e., ascertained at the time of contract. There is, however, a genuine need of the people to buy an unascertained thing out of a number of ascertained things with a right to ascertain the exact thing later. For example, one buying a car out of three vehicles offered for fixed price, gets opportunity through this option to have cars examined by a specialist and choose one of them. Reserving the right to ascertain the bought item later is known as the *Khiyār al-ṭa'yīn* or the option of ascertainment.

This option is imposed by the buyer only and it results in making a binding contract non-binding in favour of the buyer.

Effects of the option

The general rule is that the goods being purchased must be ascertained at the time of the contract. On the basis of this rule the Shāfi'īs and the Ḥanbalīs do not permit the stipulation of the option of ascertainment. The option if stipulated would make the contract *bāṭil*. The Ḥanafīs and Mālikīs allow this option because one may be in need of consulting other or for pondering over the purchase and at the same time he does not wish to lose the bargain also. It may also happen that he is the agent of someone and wants to refer the matter to his principal.[10]

The option is allowed as an exception through *'istihsān* (juristic preference) against *qiyās* (general rule) and its operation is very narrow being permitted mainly in the contract of sale. Again it is permitted to the buyer only as the necessity on which it is based cannot be established for the seller according to the majority of the Ḥanafīs.

Duration of *khiyār al-ṭa'yīn*

Those who maintain that *khiyār al-ṭa'yīn* is a condition, which operates within *khiyār al-sharṭ*, or is a kind of *khiyār al-sharṭ* grant the same period as stipulated for the *khiyār al-sharṭ*. Thus the maximum period is three days according to Imām Abū Ḥanīfah and unlimited according to Imām Abū Yusuf and Muhammad. Another opinion within the Ḥanafī School is that *khiyār al-ṭa'yīn* is independent of *khiyār al-sharṭ* and thus has no fixed period.[11]

Conditions of *Khiyār al-ṭa'yīn*

- The number of unascertained items should not exceed three i.e., those out of which one has to be ascertained. The reason is that necessity does not go beyond three.
- There should be a difference in value between the three items and the price of each must be known.

---

[10] See Kāsānī, *Badā'i'al-Sanā'i'*, vol. 5, P.158; *Dasūqī 'Alā al-Sharh al-Kabīr*, vol. 3, p. 91.

[11] Kāsānī, *Badā'i'al-sanā'i'*, op. cit. vol. 5, p. 158.

- The period of the option should be determined within the confines of the *khiyār al-sharṭ* (majority opinion).[12]

Effects of the *khiyār al-ṭa'yīn*

A contract with this option is binding for the seller and non-binding for the buyer. As the *khiyār al-ṭa'yīn* operates within the *khiyār al- sharṭ,* it is possible for the buyer to revoke the purchase in all three items.

On the termination of the period, the contract becomes binding and it is now necessary for the buyer to ascertain one of them. This is the opinion of the Ḥanafīs. The Mālikīs maintain that on termination of the period, the sale is void in all items. In other words, the option must be exercised within the period otherwise, the contract is void. Some of the Ḥanafīs who maintain that *khiyār al -ṭa'yīn* in not a part of *khiyār al-sharṭ,* are of the opinion that the contract cannot be revoked in all items and one item must be ascertained.

Factors terminating the option

- Exercise of the option whether express or implied.
- Destruction of one of the items.
    a) In possession of the buyer: The goods destroyed become ascertained and the buyer is liable for the price.
    b) In possession of the seller: Buyer has a choice to accept what remains or to call off the contract.

[12] Madkūr, *al-Madkhal li al-Fiqh al-Islāmī,* p.680; See also Zaydān, *al-Madkhal li Dirāsāt al-Sharī'ah,* p.381.

- Death of one who possessed the option. The contract becomes non-binding for the heirs and right of revocation lapses. The heirs must ascertain one item.

3. *Khiyār al-Ru'yah* (Option of examination)

Option of examination is the right accorded to a person buying or brings anything not yet present at the moment of the signature of the contract to confirm or cancel the said contract after inspecting the object.

Knowledge of the subject matter at the time of contract is an essential condition. Such knowledge is possible through an examination of the subject at the time of the contract or by description in a manner, which removes all kinds of *jahālah* (want of knowledge).

Some of the jurists consider examination at the time of contract essential and any condition permitting examination later would make the contract *bāṭil.* The Ḥanafīs allow the sale of things, which have not been seen or examined at the time of the contract and grant an option to the buyer to examine the goods later. If he finds the goods or property to his liking, he may accept them and in the alternate he may revoke the contract. This is known as the option of examination or *khiyār al- ru'yah.*

Opinions of *fuqahā'* regarding option of examination

There are two opinions relating to the *khiyār al- ru'yah* which are summarised below:

Option 1

The Shāfi'īs are of the view that the contract in which the subject matter has not been examined is not valid.[13] Thus they

[13] Shīrāzī, *al-Muhadhdhab* vol. 1, p. 263.

reject the validity of *khiyār al-ru'yah*. They argue on the basis of the tradition, "do not sell what you do not have".[14]

The Mālikīs agree with the Shāfi'īs in general but when examination at the time of the contract becomes impossible or is likely to result in grave loss (e.g. exposure of a very expensive piece of cloth time and again for buyers) they allow sale by minute description. In such case the buyer may exercise option of inspection and reject the object if it does not conform to description.[15]

The Ḥanbalīs maintain that sale must be through examination at the time of the contract and if this is difficult, sale may be by description. Thus they reject *khiyār al-ru'yah* also.

Option 2

The Ḥanafīs differing with the other schools maintain that the contract in which the buyer has not seen the goods is a contract which is valid and enforceable but is non-binding and the buyer has the option to revoke it upon examination. This is known as the *khiyār al -ru'yah.* It is very important to note here that through this option the buyer can reject the goods upon examination even if the goods were described minutely and are found to conform to the description upon examination. This option can be stipulated for the buyer only.

The Ḥanafīs argue that the tradition, "Do not sell what you do not possess" applies to one who does not own the goods and has not capacity to deliver. It does not apply to the goods, which cannot be seen at the time of the contract. They also quote in support a tradition to the effect that: "He who buys a thing which he has not seen has an option upon seeing it."[16]

---

[14] Shawkānī, *Nayl al-Awṭār*,vol.5,p.164.

[15] Ibn Rushd, *Bidāyat al-Mujtahid* vol. 2, p. 155.

[16] Madkūr, *al-Madkhal li al- Fiqh al-Islāmī,* p.686.

They also base its legality on a judgement against Ḥaḍrat 'Uthmān (r.a.) who had sold land to Ḥaḍrat Ṭalhah. Either had not seen the land. Someone said to Ṭalhah "you have made a bad bargain". He replied", I have not seen the land and thus have an option". Jubayr ibn Muṭ'am arbitrated the dispute and allowed Ṭalhah right of option. The course taken by this litigation without any objection on the part of the companions is said to have established right of option of examination for buyer. [17]

Conditions related to the option

(i) The buyer must not have seen the goods, which are the subject matter of contract.

(ii) The contract must be in property, which is specified, and not in that which is sold by description. Things specified are like houses, land horses, etc. which possess their own individuality.

Effects of the option of examination

The option makes the contract non-binding. The seller cannot revoke such a contract, which is binding for him even if he has not seen his own property. The property passes to the buyer and the contract is non-binding.

Facts terminating the option

- The option ends with the examination of the subject matter. There is no fixed period for the option, however, once the goods have been examined, the option is terminated.
- The option lapses if the subject matter is destroyed. The contract becomes irrevocable upon destruction of the subject matter.

---

[17] Abū Zahrā, *al-Milkiyyah wa Nazariyyat al-'Aqd* p.398.

- The death of the buyer makes the contract binding for the heirs of the buyer.
- If the buyer examines the property and disposes it off, the contract becomes irrevocable.

4. *Khiyār al-'ayb* (Option of defect)

It is a right given to a purchaser in a sale to cancel the contract if he discovers that the object acquired has in it some defect diminishing its value.[18] The option has been imposed by the law itself and the parties do not have to stipulate it. It is thus a necessary condition of the contract. The goods are liable to be rejected if undeclared defects are discovered. When the seller specifically states that he is not responsible for any defects then the buyer acts at his own risk and goods cannot be rejected.

This option is based on the traditions:

- "He who defrauds another is not from amongst us."[19]
- "It is not permitted for seller to sell things which are defective unless he points it out to him."[20]

The option operates in favour of one buying or hiring property. The option is valid in case of goods, which need to be specified like a house, land or any room, which has its own individuality.

Conditions for exercising option of defect

- The defect should be such which causes decrease in the sale of the property. The defect may be obvious or hidden.

---

[18] Kāsānī, *Badā'i' al-sanā'ī'* vol, 5, p. 247.
[19] Bukhārī, *sahīh,* quoted from *Jam' al-Fawā'id.* hadīth no. 4668.
[20] Shawkānī, *Nayl al-Awṭār,* vol. 5, p. 224.

- The defect should have existed prior to the contract. A defect appearing later after delivery is not valid for purpose of the option.
- The defect should continue after delivering till the time of the exercise of the option. If the defect disappears before this, there is no option.
- The buyer should have no knowledge of the defect at the time of the contract or at the time of delivering.
- There should not be any agreement of non-guarantee. If the purchaser who by an agreement of non-guarantee expressly exonerated the seller of any responsibility for defect in the article sold, then he cannot in future avail himself of the option of defect.

Effects of option of defect

The contract with the option of defect is revocable. The purchaser of an object with defect has the choice to confirm the sale or to cancel it. This is the majority opinion. The Mālikī jurists distinguish between the minor (*yasīr*) defect and major (*fāhish*) defect and propose that if the defect is minor, the buyer may confirm the sale while being returned part of the price paid in proportion to the extent of the defect. In case the defect is major, he has the choice either to cancel it or confirm it without compensatory restitution. The Ḥanbalī jurists hold that the buyer of an object with defect whether minor or major, may confirm the sale while being paid the difference between the price of the article in perfect condition and its price with defect.

Factors terminating the option

(i) Acceptance of object with defect by the buyer

(ii) Destruction of the object in the hands of buyer.

The death of buyer does not terminate the option. The right in such case is inherited by the heirs.

Conclusion

- Islamic law of option provides a device to safeguard contracting parties against hasty undertakings.
- The options allowed in Islamic law are:
    - Option of condition
    - Option of determination
    - Option of defect
    - Option of inspection
    - Option of description
- The option of inspection and option of defect are granted by the *Sharī'ah* whereas the options of condition, determination and description are established by the mutual agreement.

Chapter 13

Classification of Contracts

The modern Muslim jurists have classified contracts from various perspectives to facilitate understanding. One classification is according to their function and purpose and the other is according to their time of completion.

A. Classification According to Function of Contract

Contracts from this perspective are divided into the following seven categories:

1. *Tamlīkāt* (Contract for alienation of property)

The contract falling under this category aims to make a person owner of a thing or its usufructs. They may be for consideration and without consideration. In the former case, they are designated as *'uqūd al-mu'āwaḍāt* (commutative contracts) such as sale, hiring, *ṣarf* (money changing), *ṣulḥ* (composition), *istiṣnā'* (manufacturing contract), *muzāra'ah* (cultivation) and *musāqāh*, in the latter case, they are called *'udūd al-tabarru'āt* (gratuitous contracts) such as gift, bequest, *waqf* (religious endowment) *'āriyah* (commodate loans) and *ḥawālah* (assignment of debt). Sometimes a contract begins with donation and ends up with exchange. Thus at the final stages it becomes a commutative contract such as contract of loan and surety by the orders of debtor.

2. *Isqāṭāt* (Contracts extinguishing rights)

The object of such acts and contracts is to extinguish established rights. They may be with consideration and without consideration. The examples of first kind are divorce without consideration, manumission, remission of debt, withdrawal of the right of *shufa'ah* (pre-emption), whereas the divorce for consideration and accepting blood money instead of *qiṣāṣ* are the examples of second kind.

3. *'Iṭlāqāt* and *Tafwīḍh* (Contracts of authorisation)

The purpose of these contracts is to delegate power and authority to a party to carry out a transaction which was not permissible for him before this delegation, like agency, permission to a person placed under interdiction person for dispositions.

4. *Taqyīdāt* (Contracts restrictive of the rights of others)

The principle feature of these contracts is to restrict the liberty of a person and prevent him from the right of disposal and use of property such as preventing insane, lunatic, minor and insolvent person from dispositions.

5. *Tawthīqāt* (Contracts of guarantee)

The purpose of such contract is to secure the debt of creditors. The contracts which serve this purpose are: *kafālah* (suretyship), *hāwālah* (assignment of debt) and *rahn* (pledge).

6. *Ishtirāk* (Partnership)

The purpose of contracts falling in this category is to share the profit of a business such as *mushārakah, mudhārabah, muzāra'ah*.

7. *'Uqūd al-Ḥifz* (Deposits and bailments)

These contracts aim at safeguarding the property of a person like deposit and bailment.[1]

[1] Zuhaylī, *al-Fiqh al-Islāmī wa adillatuhū*, vol. 4, pp. 244, 245. Zaydān, *al-Madkhal*, pp. 375, 376.

A contemporary scholar Muhammad Salām Madkūr has treated *'uqūd al-mu'awaḍāt* and *'uqūd al-tabarru'āt* separately instead of classing them under *tamlīkāt*.[2] The contracts according to his scheme are as follows:

I. *'Uqūd al-Mu'āwaḍāt* (Commutative contracts)

These contracts contain exchange of counter values from both the contracting parties such as contract of sale, and *iājrah* (hiring). *'Uqūd al- mu'āwaḍāt* includes the following contracts:

- Contract of Sale: Contracts of sale are further classified as under:
  - a) Classification according to object:
    - *Muqāyaḍah* (barter)
    - *Ṣarf* (money changing)
    - *Salam* (sale with immediate payment and deferred delivery)
    - *Bay' Mu'ajjal* (deferred payment sale)
    - *Bay' Muṭlaq* (sale of object for money)
  - b) Classification according to price:
    - *Tawliyah* (resale at cost price)
    - *Murābḥah* (resale at cost price plus some profit)
    - *Waḍī'ah* (resale with loss)
    - *Musāwamah* (resale with agreement that no reference be made to the original cost price).
- Contract of hiring: This may be divided into:

---

[2] Madkūr, *al-Madkhal*, pp. 595, 596.

- *Ijārat al-Ashkhāṣ* (rendering services)
- *Ijārat al-Ashyā'* (letting things)

- Loan contract
- *Istisnā'* (contract of manufacturing)

II. *'Uqūd al-Tabarrū'āt* (Gratuitous contracts)

The main feature of these contracts is donation of property. The donor transfers ownership of that property to a party without consideration. Following contracts fall under this category.

- *Hibah* (gift)
- *Waṣiyyah* (bequest)
- *Waqf* (endowment)
- *Kafālāh* (guarantee)
- *'Āriyah* (commodate loan)

III. *'Uqūd al-Isqaṭāt* (Relinquishment of rights) such as:

- Remission of debt
- Relinquishment of right of pre-emption.

IV. *'Uqūd al-Iṭlāqāt* (Authorization) such as:

- *Wakālah* (agency)
- *'Īsā'* (making a person guardian)
- Removal of interdiction from discerning minor.
- Manumission

V. *'Uqūd al-Taqyīdāt* (Contracts restrictive of the rights of others) such as:

- Dismissal of agent.
- Dismissal of guardian and superintendent of *waqf* from their offices.
- Interdiction of minor from disposition
- Interdiction of insane, lunatic, insolvent etc.

VI. *'Uqūd al-Sharikāt* (Contracts of partnership)

They include:

- *Sharikat al-mufāwaḍah*
- *Sharikat al-'inān*
- *Sharikat al-wujūh*
- *Sharikat al-a'māl*
- *Sharikat al-muḍarabah*

VII. *'Uqūd al-ḍamanāt* (Contracts of suretyship)

They include:

- *Kafālah*
- *Ḥawālah*
- *Rahn*

VIII. *'Uqūd al-Istiḥfazāt* (Contract of depositing)

Sir Abdur Rahim has rather followed legalistic approach and classified Islamic contracts as follows.[3]

1. Alienation of property for exchange, namely
   - sale
   - without exchange, namely *ribā* or simple gift
   - by way of dedication, namely *waqf.*
   - to create succession, namely bequest.
2. Alienation of usufruct
   - In exchange for property namely *ijārah* which includes letting things movable and immovable for hire, contracts for rendering services such as for carriage of goods, safe custody of property, domestic and professional services.
   - Not being in exchange of property, for example; commodate loans and deposits.
3. Contracts for securing the discharge of an obligation, namely; pledge and suretyship.
4. Contracts for representation namely; agency and partnership.

B. Classification of Contracts with Regard to Time of Completion

Having regard to time of completion, the Muslim jurists have divided contracts in to the following three kinds.[4]

---

[3] Sir Abdur Rahim *'Muhammadan Jurisprudence*, Lahore: All Pakistan Legal Decisions, 1977, pp. 227, 228.

[4] Madkūr, *al-Madkhal*, p. 611.

1. *Al-'Aqd al-Munjaz* (Contract immediately enforceable)

It is a contract, which unconditionally becomes complete after the offer is accepted and its consequences in the form of obligation ensue immediately. Thus a contract will be regarded *'aqd munjaz* if:

- It is free from any option reserved for a party like option of the buyer to revoke contract within three days.
- It does not depend upon ratification by the party concerned. For example, the contract concluded by a discerning minor or the one placed under interdiction due to idiocy and lunacy, is suspended till it is ratified by their respective guardians. Similarly the contract made by a *fuḍūlī* (unauthorized agent) is also a suspended contract, which is enforceable only on ratification by the principal. The sale of mortgaged property also remains suspended till the mortgagee forgoes his claim upon the property and ratifies the contract.
- It is not contingent upon a condition or happening of an uncertain event in future i.e. I sell you my house if A sold his house to me. As general principle, Muslim jurists hold that a valid contract should give rise to the effects assigned to it by the Lawgiver immediately. It is for this reason that majority of jurists do not admit of suspended contracts because such contracts cause delay in the enforcement of contracts.[5] Ibn al-Qayyim and Ibn

---

[5] See Ibn Humām, *Fath al-Qadīr* Vol. 5, P. 195; Nawawī, *al-Majmū'* vol. 9, p. 340; hajawaī, *al'Iqnā'*, vol. 3, P. 157; Ibn Qudāmā, *al-Mughnī,* vol. 6, p. 599.

Taymiyyah, however, approve contingent contracts and regard them valid.[6]

2. ***Al'Aqd al-Muḍāf li al-Mustaqbal* (Contract effective from future date)**

Such contract is not valid according to majority of the jurists since they hold that the effects should ensue immediately without any delay.[7] They, however, allow the contracts made on usufructs to be effective from future date like the contract of leasing, manufacturing because a person does not own usufructs immediately as he does in the case of sale contract, but he owns them gradually, so the future time is considered in such contracts. *kafālah* (suretyship) and *ḥawālah* (assignment of debt) are also considered to be the contracts of above-mentioned category. A *kafīl* (surety) is not required to pay debt immediately when the contract is concluded. So it is valid if the surety were to say to the creditor "if your debtor did not pay off his debt to you by the beginning of next month, then I will make this payment". Similarly, the agency, divorce and *waqf* are valid from future date. Contract of bequest also by its nature admits of delay, as it cannot be enforced in the life of legator. The contract of *ijāra* partakes the attributes of both the *'aqd munjaz* and *gayr munjaz.*

The contract of sale in the opinion of all the jurists is immediately enforceable contract, thus it is not permissible to say "I sell you this house of mine in the beginning of next year." The jurists see in this postponement and delay an element of *gharar* (uncertainty). It is like a contract which is contingent upon an uncertain event which the parties do not know whether it will occur or not or it is dependent upon condition

---

[6] Ibn al-Qayyim, *I'lām al-Muwaqqi'īn* vol. 3, p. 237.

[7] Darīr, *al-Gharar fi al-'Uqūd*, pp. 4-5.

about which the parties do not know whether it will be fulfilled or not.[8]

But the fact is that there is substantial difference between *'aqd muḍāf* (effective from future date) and *'aqd mu'allaq* (contingent upon event or condition), in the former case the parties clearly know the time of performance of obligation whereas in latter case they do not know as to when it will be performed and whether or not it will be performed. Commenting on the viewpoint of jurists, Dr. Muhammad Ṣiddīq observes: " Indeed the only *gharar* in a future contract lies in the possible lapse of interest of either party which may affect his consent when the time set therein comes. If someone buys something by '*aqd muḍāf* and his circumstances change or the market changes bringing its price down at the time set for fulfillment of contract, he will undoubtedly be averse to its fulfillment and will regret entering into it. Indeed the object may itself change and the two parties may dispute over it".[9]

It is pertinent to note that Ibn al-Qayyim and Ibn Taymiyyah do not subscribe to majority's viewpoint. They maintain that '*aqd muḍāf* is permissible, without distinction between sale contract and leasing contract.

3. *Al-'Aqd al-Mu'allaq* (Contingent contract)

It is a contract, which is contingent upon happening of an uncertain event. Such contract takes effect on the happening of contingency. According to the majority, the contingent contracts are void especially when they belong to the class of commutative contracts such as sale and leasing. The reason is that the contracting parties do not know whether the event will occur or not, and whether the contract will be subsequently enforced or not. It is also possible that one of the contracting

---

[8] Madkūr, *al-Madkhal*, p.614.

[9] Darīr, *al-Gharar fī al-'Uqūd*, p.19.

parties may change his mind when the event occurs. According to Hanfi jurists even the gratuitous contracts are not permissible if made to take effect on the happening of contingency. Thus, it is not permissible to make a gift dependent on entrance of Zayd or the arrival of Khalid. Similarly, in *waqf*, it is essential that the appropriation should not be made to depend on contingency. There are, however, some contracts, which are allowed to be made contingent upon uncertain event such as agency, bequest, and suretyship assignment of debt, manumission and divorce. Thus it is allowed to say to wife, "if you leave my house, then you are divorced" or to say to prospective agent, "if I traveled abroad, then you will be my agent". Ibn al-Qayyim diverging from the majority position held that the contingent contracts are valid. He does not see any *gharar* in them.[10]

Conclusion

- The contracts with regard to the object, principal features of contract have been classified as follows:
  - contracts for alienation of property;
  - contracts extinguishing the established right;
  - contracts of authorization;
  - contracts of partnership;
  - contracts of guarantee; and
  - contracts for safeguarding the property of a person.
- According to some scholars they are classified as under:
  - commutative contracts such as sale, hiring;
  - gratuitous contracts such as *waqf*, gift;

[10] Ibn Taymiyyah, *Naẓariyyat al-'Aqd*, p.227.

- contracts of trust such as agency depositing;
- contracts of partnership such as *sharikah, muḍārabah, muzāra'ah* ; and
- contracts of suretyship such as guarantee, assignment of debt and pledge.

◙ Contracts with regard to time of completion are divided into the following three kinds:

- *'Aqd munjaz* (contract immediately enforceable);
- *'Aqd muḍāf li al- mustaqbal* (contract effective from further date); and
- *'Aqd mu'allaq* (contingent contract).

Part II
Specific Contracts

Chapter 14

Contract of Sale

The contract of sale is one of the most important contracts for the exchange of goods. It is defined as "an exchange of a useful and desirable thing for similar thing by mutual consent in a specific manner.[1] The word "useful" excludes from the purview of definition of unuseful transactions such as the sale of one rupee for one rupee. While the word "desirable" excludes things such as carrion and dust from being valid objects of sale, as these things are not desired by the people. The words "in a specific manner" signify the modes of conveying consent such as offer and acceptance, and conduct.

Some jurists have added the words "for the alienation of property"[2] to the above mentioned definition to denote that the purpose of such a contract is to transfer property in goods to the buyer, and in price to the seller. Thus, the complete definition of sale will be as follows: "Exchange of useful and desirable thing for a similar thing by mutual consent for the alienation of property". It can also be defined as "exchange of property for property with mutual consent."

Definition of *Māl* (Subject-matter)

According to the Ḥanafī school, *māl* is that which is desired by the people and stored for use at a time of need.[3] It does not treat benefits and incorporable rights as *māl*. The Shāfi'ī jurists on

---

[1] Kāsānī, *Badā'i' al-sanā'i'*, vol. 5, p. 133: Ibn al-Humām *Fatḥ al-Qadīr* vol. 5, p.73.

[2] Shirbīnī, *Mughni al-Muḥtāj* vol.2:2, Ibn Qudāmā, *al-Mughnī* vol. 3, 559.

[3] Ibn 'Abidīn, *Radd al-Muhtār* vol.4. p.3.

the other hand include benefits in the definition of *māl*. To them the sale contract contains both transfer of ownership in goods and transfer of ownership in benefits.[4] The Mālikī jurists, like Ḥanafī jurists do not regard benefits and incorporeal rights as *māl* and consequently do not allow their sale.

Dissatisfied with the definitions of *māl* in early jurisprudence, Musṭafā Zarqā, a renowned scholar, has applied *māl* to everything that has legal and material value among the people.[5] The property in this sense refers to any tangible or intangible thing that gives determinate capacity to a person to use it to the exclusion of whole world. It includes both abstract and unreal rights. It applies equally to the objects, which have perceptible existence in the outside world as well as to intangible property such as trademarks and intellectual property.

Classification of *Māl*

Property has been classified in different ways:

I. Movable and immovable

There are two principal classes of property movable (*manqūl*) and immovable (*ghayr-manqūl*). By immovable is primarily meant land and along with it all permanent fixtures, such as buildings. The characteristic of movable property is that it may be removed from one place to another place. Movable property is classified as follows:

(a) *Makīlāt* or things, which are ordinarily sold by measurement of capacity.

(b) *Mawzūnāt* or things, which are sold by, weight.

---

[4] Shirbīnī, *Mughnī al-Muhtāj* vol.2, p.3.

[5] Muṣṭafā Aḥmad Zarqā, *al-Madkhal al-Fiqhī al-'Am*, Demascus: Matba'ah Tarbīn, 1968, Vol.3, P.122.

(c) *Madhru'āt* or things which are estimated by linear measurement.

(d) *'Adadiyyāt* or things which are estimated by linear measurement.

All articles of the nature of *makīlāt, mawzūnat, 'adadiyyāt*, and *madhrū'at* are comprehensively called *muqaddarāt*.

II. Fungible or similar *(Mithlī)* and non-fungible or dissimilar *(Qīmī)*

An article is said to belong to the class of similar *(mithlī)* if the like of it can be had in the market without there being such difference between the two as people are apt to take into account in their dealings. A thing belongs to the class of dissimilar if the like of it is not available in the market or if it be available, it is with such difference that people will not take it into account in fixing the price.[6]

III. Determinate *('Āyn)* and indeterminate *(Dayn)* property

Connected with the division of things into similar and dissimilar is the division of property into *'ayn* that is, specific or determinate and *dayn* or non-specific or indeterminate property. The chief distinguishing test is when a man is to get certain property from another who either borrowed it from him or took it by force, whether he is entitled to recover it in species or not. If he is, then it is called specific or determinate and if he is not, it is called non-specific or indeterminate.

Articles of the class of similar cannot, as a rule, be recovered specifically, and are thus regarded as *dayn* or indeterminate property. Hence, gold and silver in the shape of coins or otherwise, grain, oil and the like are *dayn* or indeterminate property. Therefore, if a man sells an article for one hundred

---

[6] See 'Abd al-Rahīm *Muhammadan Jurisprudence.* p. 211.

dirhams out of a bag of money pointed out to him by the buyer, he does not become entitled to be paid out of the identical bag but his claim will be satisfied on being paid an equivalent amount. Generally speaking, all indeterminate property rests on the mere responsibility or obligation of the person from whom it is recoverable.[7]

Conditions for Validity of Sale

1. Contracting parties should possess legal capacity necessary for concluding contract, i.e., they should be competent to conclude the contract.
2. The commodity should be anything in which transactions are permissible in the *Sharīʿah.* This means that it should be a pure substance ritually and legally clean. Therefore, any substance, which is religiously and legally unclean and upon whose disposal there are restrictions cannot serve as an object of sale: e.g. wine, pig, intoxicants, blood, and the carcasses of an animal are not valid objects of sale.
3. The merchandise must be either in actual existence or it should be capable of being acquired and delivered to a buyer in the future.
4. The transactions, which involve an element of uncertainty and risk with regard to the existence and acquisition of subject matter, are forbidden in Islamic Law. Examples are as follows:
    - The sale of fish in water
    - Sale of a foetus in the womb
    - Sale of milk in the udder of an animal

---

[7] Ibid, p. 212.

- Sale of fruits on tree at the beginning of season when their quality cannot be established.

From this it may be concluded that only that non-existent thing is excluded from the purview of a valid transaction, which involves an element of uncertainty. Things, which can be produced and manufactured in future, are the valid objects of sale as they are free from the attribute of uncertainty.

5. Goods should be owned by someone. If one sells something before acquiring ownership, such sale is invalid. Things in which no real ownership can be established, e.g., pious endowment (*waqf*) or public property are also excluded from being the subject matter of sale contract.

6. The item should be possessed by the owner. It is a necessary condition so that he is able to deliver it to the purchaser in the event of the sale contract. Things, that are not in actual possession, such as a thing lost or usurped, cannot be made the subject matter of a contract. Besides, the Holy Prophet (s.a.w.s) has prohibited the sale of foodstuffs before taking their possession. Other things can be validly sold before taking their possession if the vendor can subsequently deliver them to the purchaser.

7. The item of sale should be known to the contracting parties. This requires that their subject-matter should be ascertained. It can be realized through examination of the object if it is present in the session of contract or through a precise description if it is not available at the time of the contract. The description should be detailed enough to do away with all vagueness and uncertainty. The majority of the jurists allow it. The Shāfi'īs do not allow sale by description and stipulate actual examination at the time of the contract as a necessary condition. Sale by description

confers the "option of description" upon the buyer, whereby he can reject the goods if they do not conform to the description.

8. The conditions of property have been discussed in detail in Chapter-3 under the title Elements of Contract: Subject-matter.
9. Consideration may be deferred to a fixed future period but it cannot be suspended on an event the time of the occurrence of which is uncertain. Thus, it is not lawful to suspend payment until the wind shall blow, or until it shall rain; nor is it lawful even though the uncertainty be so inconsiderable as almost to amount to a fixed term. Thus, it is not lawful to suspend payment until the sowing or reaping time.
10. The sale contract should be absolute and not contingent upon a future event. For example, A says to B, "If X wins election, my car stands sold to you". Such a contract is invalid.
11. The sale must be instant. The majority of the jurists are of view that sale contract must come into effect immediately on the conclusion of the contract. Its effects cannot be postponed to a future date. Thus, it is not valid to make contract effective from some specified date in future.

Expressly Prohibited Sale Contracts of Islamic law

1. *Bay' al-Mukhāḍarah*

It refers to sale of fruits on tree before their benefit is evident since they are not free from being spoiled. It is narrated by Anas ibn Mālik that God's Messenger (s.a.w.s) forbade the sale of fruit till they were almost ripe. Allah's Messenger further said: "If Allah spoiled the fruits what right would one have to take money of one's brother?"[8] *Mukhāḍarah* also refers to the sale of grain or vegetables before they are ripe.

2. *Bay'al-Juzāf*

This applies to sale of foodstuffs at random or haphazardly. It is a sale of goods, which are not determined as to their quantity.

3. *Bay' al-munābadhah* (Throw sale)[9]

- Such a sale is affected simply by two parties mutually exchanging their goods without any examination by either side.
- Sale is completed when the seller throws down the goods with no opportunity for the purchaser to see it.

4. *Bay'al-mulāmasah*[10]

This is to buy an object by merely touching it, without examining it. It is a sale of a piece of cloth already folded, that is bought by merely touching it, and renouncing in advance the right to revoke on inspection.

5. *Bay'al-muḥāqalah*[11]

Sale of wheat in exchange of wheat in ear to be estimated by conjecture.

---

[8] Bukhārī, *sahīh* as quoted in Shawkānī, *Nayl al-Awṭār*, vol. 5, p.183.

[9] Ibid, vol. 5, p. 159.

[10] Ibid.

[11] Ibid

6. *Bay'al-uzābanah*[12]

Sale of fresh fruits in exchange of dry fruits in a way that the quantity of dry fruit is measured while the quantity of fresh fruits is uncertain.

7. *Bay' al-Ḥaml*

Sale of what a female animal bears in the womb.

8. *Bay' al-Ḥasāt*[13]

In this form a sale is affected by saying: "of these pieces of cloth, I sell you the one upon which falls pebble thrown in the air".

9. *Mu'āwamah*[14]

The selling of fruits on tree in advance for two or three years.

10. *Ḍarbat al-ghā'iṣ*[15]

Such a transaction is affected by saying: "I dive into the sea, if I have anything (pearl), it will be yours at such and such price".

11. *'Asb al-faḥl*

This refers to renting service of a male animal to cover female animal. The Holy Prophet (s.a.w.s) is reported to have prohibited such contract and disallowed receiving price or cost of this service.[16]

---

[12] Ibid

[13] Shawkānī, *Nayl al-Awṭār* vol.5, p. 156.

[14] Ibid., vol. 5, p. 186.

[15] Ibid., vol. 5, p.158.

[16] Ibid., vol. 5, p.155.

12. Sale of fish in water

This type of sale was commonly practiced by Arabs in pre-Islamic period. Holy Prophet (s.a.w.s) forbade such contracts.[17]

13. *Bay'Ḥabl al-Ḥablah*

This refers to sale of younglings to be brought later from the foetus of an animal.[18]

14. *Bay' al-kāli' bi al-kāli'*[19]

This means exchange of credit for credit. What is prohibited by this contract is the purchase by a man of a commodity on credit for a fixed period, and when the period of payment comes and he finds himself unable to pay the debt, he says, "Sell it to me on credit for further period, for something additional. Where upon he sells it to him. The Prophet (s.a.w.s) has prohibited such a sale.[20]

15. *Bay' wa salaf* (Selling and lending)[21]

The explanation of this practice is that one man says to other "I shall take your goods for such and such if you lend me such and such. In a tradition the Holy Prophet (s.a.w.s) asked 'Attah Ibn Asīd, his representative to the people of Makkah, to stop the people of Makkah from making a selling and lending contract concurrently.[22]

---

[17] Ibid., vol. 5, p. 156.

[18] Ibid., vol. 5, p. 156.

[19] Ibid., vol. 5, p. 165.

[20] 'Abd Allah 'Alwī Ḥājī Ḥassān, *Sale and Contracts, in Early Islamic Commercial Law*, Islamabad: Islamic Research Institute, 1994, p.65.

[21] Ibid., p.66.

[22] Shawkānī, *Nayl al-Awṭār*, vol. 5, p. 190.

16. Sale of milk in the udder of animals

The Prophet (s.a.w.s) is reported to have prohibited this transaction except when the milk was measured after milking.[23]

17. Sale of food before possession

The Holy Prophet (s.a.w.s) has prohibited the resale of food before possession. From Ibn 'Umar, (may Allah be pleased with him) said, "I bought oil in the market and was about to take it when I met a man who offered me a good profit. I decided to strike a bargain with him and at that time someone took hold of my elbow from behind. I turned behind and saw that it was Zayd ibn Thābit. He said, 'Do not sell it at the spot you bought it from, not until you have moved it to you camel-pack. The Messenger of Allah (s.a.w.s) forbade the sale of goods on the spot they are bought, not until the traders move them to their camel-packs".[24] The purpose of this *hadīth* is to emphasize the principle of liability, which means that food bought, should not be sold unless it has moved into the liability of buyer. This is realized either through delivery of possession or identification of a particular lot of food sold.

It also aims at discouraging over-trading and involvement of middleman. An example is when a person purchases grain lying in an agricultural farm and without removing it from the farm sells it to another person for a higher price than the price at which he had purchased it. This new middleman sells it further at a relatively higher price than his purchase price. This process continues and everybody keeps on earning thousands of rupees without investing anything while the commodity remains where it was at the first place during its first transaction, only its price keeps on increasing and till it actually reaches the market in front of real consumer its price is increased many

---

[23] Ibid., vol. 5, p. 158.

[24] Ibid., vol. 5, p. 167.

times. Hence, this *hadīth* represents an indirect order to end the profession of middleman.[25]

Kinds of Sale Transactions

Following are important kinds of sale in Islamic Law.

1. *Muqāyaḍah:* The sale of goods for goods, or barter trade.
2. *Bay' Muṭlaq:* The sale of goods for money.
3. *Ṣarf*: The sale of money for money or money changing.
4. *Salam:* This is a sale in which the price is paid in advance and the articles are delivered on a future date.
5. *Istiṣnā'*: A Contract of manufacturing
6. *Murābaḥah:* In such a transaction the vendor sells an article for the cost price in addition to a certain stated profit.
7. *Bay'al-mu'ajjal*: Credit sale or sale on deferred payment basis.

I. *Muqāyaḍah*

Barter trade is permissible. If the commodities to be bartered belong to the class of *ribā* commodities, then the requirement of the Lawgiver is as follows:

a) If both the commodities are of the same genus, then immediate delivery and equality has to be observed.

b) If they differ in kind, then they should be exchanged in the same session of contract.

c) In case of exchange of homogeneous commodities, the quality has to be ignored. The Prophet (s.a.w.s) had,

[25] See Ghulām Murtazā, *Socio-Economic System of Islam*, pp. 38-39.

reportedly rejected the transaction in which Bilāl (r.a.t.a) had exchanged two measures of inferior dates for one measure of superior ones.[26]

II. *Bay' Muṭlaq*

This is sale of goods for money. Although barters trade is permitted with some qualifications, use of cash money is preferred and encouraged by Islam. This preference of cash money comes almost close the requirement when barter of the same commodity is involved. The purpose is to avoid any occurrence of *ribā*. The Prophet (s.a.w.s) had instructed Bilāl (r.a.t.a) to sale two measures of inferior dates for money and then purchase superior ones with that money. This shows the importance of money as an instrument of just and equitable exchange. The *hadīth* in question is indicative not only of the importance attached to money but also of the consideration of current market rates with regard to the exchange of produced goods. Needless to stress that money provides a standard for real and just exchange of value of various commodities.

III. *Ṣarf*

Sale of absolute price for absolute price is known as *ṣarf* contract. The main conditions of *ṣarf* contract are as follows:

1. The condition that is specific to the contract of *ṣarf* and distinguishes it from all other contracts is that the counter values must be delivered and taken possession of within the session of the contract. In other words, a condition for delay cannot be stipulated.

2. No option can be stipulated in this contract. The reason is that an option delays the transfer of ownership and this violates the first condition of spot delivery and possession.

[26] Bukhārī , *sahīh as quoted in Nayl al-Awṭār*, vol. 5, p. 207.

3. Equality or sameness in weight is must if gold is exchanged for gold, but if gold is exchanged for silver, then equality is not the requirement of the *Sharī'ah*. In this case the counter-values must be exchanged simultaneously.

4. Good and bad quality of exchanged counter-values is not relevant in this contract.

The rules of *ṣarf* contract have been mentioned in a large number of *aḥādīth* The best known of these *aḥādīth* are the two that have been narrated by 'Ubādah ibn al-Ṣāmit and Abū Sa'īd al-Khudrī:

(i) From 'Ubādah Ibn al-Ṣāmit, who said, The Messenger of Allah (s.a.w.s) said: "Gold for gold, silver for silver, wheat for wheat, barley for barley, dates for dates, salt for salt, like for like in equal weights, from hand to hand. If the species differ, then sell as you like, as long as it is from hand to hand."[27]

(ii) From Abū Sa'īd al-Khudrī, who said: "The Messenger of Allah (s.a.w.s) said, "Do not sell gold for gold, except when it is like for like, and do not misappropriate one through the other, and do not sell silver for silver except like for like and do not misappropriate one through the other, and do not sell things absent for those that are present".[28]

The rules mentioned earlier are not specific with gold and silver or *dīnār* and *dirham* alone, but are applicable to every commodity or thing that performs the functions of money namely; a medium of exchange, unit of value, and standard of deferred payment.

---

[27] Shawkānī, *Nayl al-Awṭār*, vol. 5, p. 201.

[28] Ibid.

It is worth mentioning that gold and silver are considered as species of price in Islamic Law. It makes no difference whether gold and silver is sold in the shape of coins or ornaments or otherwise. They are treated always as price because it is the very nature of these metals. When gold is sold for silver or vice versa, there is no requirement of equality in bargain but the delivery of both articles is a must. Thus, two parties exchanging dollars with rupees must have to exchange them in the same session of contract without any delay.

Some modern Scholars claim that gold and silver are real money whereas paper currency is merely a token money. They infer from this that the rules involving the exchange of gold and silver and other fungible goods cannot be strictly applied to paper currency.

In the following lines we will discuss the position of paper currency according to the *Sharī'ah.* The discussion on the legal position of paper currency in Islamic Law requires to define first what is money and what functions it performs in the economy of our time.

Definition of Money

Money has been defined as a "thing that serves as a commonly accepted medium of exchange or means of payment"[29] Another famous and comprehensive definition of money is that "Money is any generally acceptable means of payment in exchange for goods and services and in settling debts."[30] Money performs four main functions. It is (i) a medium of exchange or means of

[29] Paul A. Samuelson and William Nordhaus *Economics*, New York: McGraw Hill Book Company, 1993 p. 226.

[30] Fischer, Dornbusch and Schmalensee, *Economics*, Singapore: McGraw Hill Book Company, 1993, p. 623.

payment, (ii) a measure of value or a unit of account, (iii) a standard of deferred payment, and (iv) a store of value.

Money is classified under two categories: (1) commodity money and (2) token money. The former functions as a medium of exchange and is bought and sold as ordinary goods. Token money, however, is considered to be a means of payments whose value or purchasing power as money exceeds the cost of its production and its value in alternative uses. Modern monies are accepted because the law requires them to be accepted. These are fiat monies or legal tender. Legal tender is the money that a government has declared acceptable in exchange and as a lawful way of paying debts.[31]

Historically, many commodities including precious metals have performed these functions, but only those metals were picked up for this purpose that were scarce and had a worldwide demand. The principal forms of money are now coinage, notes and credit instruments. But since coins are now very rarely made of precious metals, they perform the token function, being almost worthless in content when compared with its face value.[32] At present, paper money is the most widely used form of money and is a pure token because its intrinsic price has no relevance to its face value.

The position of gold and silver in the *Sharī'ah*

A study of *fiqh* literature on the issue reveals that Muslim jurists treated *dinār* and *dirham* as money, not because they were made of gold and silver, but because they possessed the characteristics of money; that is, they served as a unit of account, a medium of exchange and measure of value. To them the *'illah* (underlying

---

[31] Ibid., pp. 626-27.

[32] Ziauddīn Aḥmad,*Currency Notes and Indexation,* Islamic Studies, 28.1(1980) p.52.

cause) in gold and silver in the context of the contract of *ṣarf* is currency-value or price-worthiness (*thamaniyyah).*[33]

Gold and silver have been *thaman* or money since early ages because they were capable of effectively functioning as a medium of exchange and a common measure of value.

The legal position of paper money

If we consider the matter carefully, it is evident that there is no essential difference between the old metallic money and the paper money of our time since both serve as a measure to determine the value of other commodities. Paper money, therefore, is real money for all the practical purposes. This fact has been established and emphasized in the writings of several eminent Muslim Scholars. Yūsuf al-Qardāwī, for instance writes:

> We pay price of goods, wages to workers, dower to wives, *diyat* in *qatl al-khaṭā* in this paper money. If someone steals it, he is subjected to the punishment of theft in all codes of criminal law. Then why should we deny it the status of legal money?[34]

Keeping all these facts in view the Fiqh Academy of Makkah in its meeting held in October, 1986 maintained that paper money has all the characteristics of gold and silver. It is *thaman* from the point of view of the *Sharī'ah* and consequently it is subject to all the rules of the *Sharī'ah* pertaining to *ribā, zakāh, salam,* and other contracts which are applicable to gold and silver.[35]

---

[33] Kāsānī, *Badā'i'sanā'i'*, vol.5, p.183.

[34] Atiq al-Zafar, *Ribā aur Bank Kā Sūd* translation of Yūsuf Qardāwī's, *Fawā'id al-Bunūk hiya al-Ribā al-Muharam* pp. 40, 41..

[35] Rābiṭah al-'Ālam al-Islāmī, *Qarārāt Majlis al-Majma', al-Fiqh al-Islāmī,* pp. 96,97.

The workshop held under the auspices of the Islamic Development Bank in Jeddah in April, 1987 on indexation also concluded that: "Paper money assumes the functions of gold and silver money from the point of view of the applicability of the rules of *ribā* and *zakāh* as well as being the principle of *salam* contracts, a capital of *muḍārabah* or investment in a partnership.[36]

IV. *Salam* Contract

In Arabic, the word *salam* means to advance. This is a contract whereby the purchaser pays the price in advance and the delivery of subject matter is postponed to a specified time in future.

Thus, *bay' salam* is a sale in which advance payment is made to the seller for deferred supply of goods. *Salam* was also prevalent even before the advent of the Holy Prophet (s.a.w.s) perhaps with a different nomenclature. When the Holy Prophet (s.a.w.s) migrated to Madinah, his Madinan companions brought this mode of sale to his notice for seeking his guidance. He termed it as *salam* and allowed it to them with some conditions.

As a matter of principle the sale of a commodity, which is not in possession of the seller, is unlawful. This is what the Holy Prophet (s.a.w.s) is stated to have laid down as a general rule. Thus the practice of *bay'salam* is legalized as an exception. According to some jurists the legality of *bay' salam* is established from the Qur'ān.

> "O ye who believe; when ye contract a debt for a fixed term, record it in writing."[37]

---

[36] Recommendations of the Workshop on *Sharī'ah* position on Indexation. (25-26 April 1987) organized by Islamic Development Bank, Jeddah.

[37] Qur'ān: 2, 282.

The reason why the Holy Prophet (s.a.w.s) permitted it with some conditions is necessity faced by growers and traders. It is stated that the practice as qualified by Holy Prophet (s.a.w.s) continued during his lifetime and the following period. The later jurists unanimously treated it to be a permissible mode of business. The jurists have not confined the application of this mode of sale to those agricultural products, which as the *hadīth* suggests, could be weighed or measured. But have expanded the list of salamable items to all the commodities that could be precisely determined in terms of quality and quantity.

Difference Between *Salam* Sale and Ordinary Sale

All the basic conditions of a contract of ordinary sale remain the same in *bay' salam*. Yet there are some points of difference between the two. For example:

(a) In *salam* sale it is necessary to fix a period for the delivery of goods, in ordinary sale it is not necessary.

(b) In *salam* sale commodity not in possession of the seller can be sold; in ordinary sale, it cannot be

(c) In *salam* sale only those commodities, which can be precisely determined in terms of quality and quantity, can be sold; in ordinary sale everything that can be owned is saleable, unless the Qur'ān or the *hadīth* prohibits it.

(d) A *salam* sale cannot take place between identical goods, for example; wheat for wheat or potato for potato; in ordinary sale it is permissible to sell identical goods.

(e) In the *salam* sale, payment must be made at the time of contract; in ordinary sale payment may be deferred or may be made at the time of the delivery of goods.

The Conditions of a Valid *Salam*

A valid contract of *salam* sale requires the fulfillment of the following conditions, which are over and above the conditions of an ordinary sale:

1. It is necessary that the buyer pay the price of the object in full to the seller in advance. If the price is not paid at the time of the contract, it will amount to sale of a debt for debt, which has been prohibited by the Holy Prophet (s.a.w.s).[38]

2. An outstanding loan due on the seller cannot be fully or partially fixed as price nor a loan outstanding on a third party can be transferred to the seller in future adjustment towards price.

3. A single amount for payment of different commodities or of the same commodity in different periods or at different places is not approved because in the former case it may lead to a dispute on pricing in the event of the seller's failure in delivering some of the contracted items and in the latter case price fluctuation over the period may become a point of dispute if the seller fails to supply the item on some fixed period. It is, therefore, necessary that the amount for each item and for each period of delivery be separately fixed.

4. The object of *salam* should be defined by description. It requires a precise and minute description of the commodity, which removes all vagueness and uncertainty. Identification of object should include genus, species, colour, and country of origin and any other feature, which has an effect on the price.

---

[38] Shawkānī ,*Nayl al-Awṭār*, vol. 5, p.165.

5. *Salamable* articles include fungible things, i.e., weighable, measurable, and accountable by number. Non-fungible things such as precious stone cannot be sold on the basis of *salam* because every piece is normally different from the other rendering their exact specification impossible. To some jurists any article determinable by description, can be the object of *salam* contract. Thus, domestic animals are valid object of *salam* subject to identification.

6. The commodity should be well defined but not particularised to a particular unit of farm, tree or garden, because there is possibility that crop of that farm is destroyed before delivery.

7. The object of *salam* should be in existence from the time of contract until the time of delivery. This is the Ḥanafi viewpoint. Other jurists hold that it should be habitually available at the time of delivery.

8. A *salam* contract cannot be applied on things which must be delivered on spot. So, gold cannot be sold for gold by way of *salam*. Similarly, wheat cannot be sold for barley because they cannot be exchanged with delay. It is necessary that the exchange of gold for gold or wheat for barley should take place simultaneously in the same session of contract.

9. About the minimum period of delivery, the jurists have the following opinions:

   a) Ḥanafī jurists fix this period at one month. To some Ḥanafī jurists minimum delay should be three days. But, if vendor dies before the delay has elapsed, the *salam* reaches maturity.

   b) According to the Shāfiʿī jurists *salam* can be immediate and delayed.

c) According to the Malikī jurists, delay should not be less than 15-days.

10. The time of the subject-matter of *salam* should be fixed at the time of the contract.

11. As regards delivery before time, the opinion of the majority of Muslim jurists is that seller can discharge his obligation before the agreed term and the purchaser will be forced to accept the delivery if an early delivery does not harm him. But if he apprehends that he will suffer damage by early delivery i.e. fruits, which may be consumed or need storing, then he will not be forced to accept early delivery. Mālikī jurists, on the other hand, maintain that he is entitled to refuse it even if it does not harm him.

12. Fixing the place of delivery is requisite if it entails extra expenses, or the place of contract is not a suitable place for delivery.

13. It is not permitted to exchange goods other than those specified while the contract of *salam* still exists because it results in the sale of awaited goods before they have been received. Besides, this falls under the prohibition of selling foods before possession. The Holy Prophet (s.a.w.s) said, "Whoever buys foodstuff should not sell it before he receives "or possesses it".[39]

14. The buyer is not allowed to take back anything in *salam* except the sum of money or goods themselves.

15. In order to ensure that the seller honours his commitment given to the buyer to supply the agreed quantity of the specified goods on the due date or at the agreed time, the

[39] Ibid., vol. 5, p. 167.

buyer has a right to claim surety or pledge or both. This is generally agreed upon by the jurists.

16 The buyer is not allowed to enjoy ownership rights over the purchased goods before taking them into his possession. Thus, he cannot sell them or make them a partnership capital, unless he takes over the goods.[40]

Revocation of the contract

As stated above a seller is bound to deliver the goods as stipulated. There may, however, be situations when it is not possible for him to honour his commitment; the examples are death, or damage to the goods while lying with the supplier for delivery. In the event of death of the seller the contract of *bay' salam* will be deemed to be rescinded and the buyer will claim the return of his money from the heirs.

In the event of the death of the buyer, however, the contract will remain operative. Damage to the goods will nullify the contract only when it exceeds the normal extent of damage. In the event of revocation of the contract, the buyer will receive back his advance. Ordinarily the buyer has no right to change the conditions of the contract in respect of the quality or quantity or the period of delivery of the contracted goods after payment is made to the seller. Both parties, however, have the right to rescind the contract in full or in part. The buyer will thus have a right to receive back the amount advanced by him, but not more or less than it.

[40] See for detailed explanation of these conditions. Zuhaylī, *al-Fiqh al-Islāmī wa Adillatuhū*, vol. 4, pp. 599-624. and hasanuz Zaman, *Bay' Salam, Principles and their applications* paper presented in the seminar on Islamic Financing Techniques, Islamabad Dec. 1984.

Modern Applications of the *Salam* Contract

Islamic banks and financial institutions use *salam* as a mode of financing. They finance the needs of farmers who need money to grow their crops. They enter into an agreement with them for advance purchase of agriculture produce, specifying complete details of the commodity, its quality, price and time of delivery and make payment of the amount at the time of entering into the agreement. When the commodity is produced and supplied to the bank on the appointed date, they sell it at profit in the market.

Steps of transactions

- Request by the client to provide cash against certain goods.
- Bank buys defined goods in advance.
- Price is generally cheaper than the market price.
- Bank makes payment to client.
- Bank takes security against his performance.
- On delivery, the bank sells the goods through the agent with profit.
- Buy-back is not allowed in *salam*.

Disposal of *Salam* commodity

Sale through agency

- On receipt of *salam* goods, bank signs agency agreement with the client.
- The client as agent of the bank sells the goods.
- Amount taken over the desired price is commission of the agent.
- Risk of price and destruction of goods before sale, is borne by the bank.
- Actual sale should be concluded and documents of sale be provided to the bank.

Through *murābaḥah* contract

- Bank at the time of contact of *salam* with farmer, may enter into a promise with a third party to sell certain goods to him.
- Third party undertakes to buy goods.
- On delivery, actual *murābaḥah* is executed

The banks may also sell the commodity through a parallel contract of *salam*. The period in the second contract is shorter while the price is fixed a little higher than the price of first transaction. Thus, they earn profit by the difference between two prices. There may be another way of benefiting from *salam*. The bank may obtain a promise to purchase from a third party. This promise should be unilateral from the prospective buyer. Being merely a promise, and not an actual sale, the buyer will not have to pay the price in advance. Therefore, a higher price may be fixed and as soon as the commodity is received by the institution, it will be sold to the third party at a pre-agreed price according to the terms of the promise.[41]

While resorting to parallel *salam* contract, two conditions must be observed by the banks:

1. In an arrangement of *salam*, the bank enters into two different contracts. In one of them the bank is the buyer and in the second one the bank is the seller. Each one of these contracts must be independent of the other. For example, if A has purchased from B 1000 bags of wheat by way of *salam* to be delivered on 31st December, A can contract a parallel *salam* with C to deliver to him 1000 bags of wheat on 31st December. But while contracting parallel *salam* with C, the delivery of wheat to C cannot be conditioned with taking delivery from B. Therefore, even if B did not deliver wheat on 31st December, A is duty

[41] Taqī 'Usmānī, *An Introduction to Islamic Finance*, p. 194.

bound to deliver 1000 bags of wheat to C. Similarly, if B has delivered defective goods which do not conform with the agreed specifications, A is still obligated to deliver the goods to C according to the specifications agreed with him.

2. Parallel *salam* is allowed with a third party only. The seller in the first contract cannot be made the purchaser in a parallel contract of *salam*, because it will be a buy-back contract, which is not permissible in the *Sharī'ah*.[42]

V. *Istisnā'*

Istisnā' consists in ordering an artisan or manufacturer to make certain goods answering a given description. By *istisnā'* one may engage for example, a cobbler to make a pair of shoes for a fixed price or ask a tailor to make a suit to be delivered later.[43]

According to Imām Kāsānī the material of object must be from the manufacturer. If it is provided by the customer, and the manufacturer has used his labour and skill only, it will not be a contract of *istisnā'*, instead it would be a contract of *ijārah*, i.e., a contract to hire services of a person to undertake a specific work. Thus, if a person gives a piece of iron to an ironsmith to make a specific vessel for a known consideration, it is permissible but it will not be *istiṣnā'*, rather it will be called a contract of hiring.[44]

The legality of this from of contract is based on a custom, which prevailed from the time of the Holy Prophet (s.a.w.s) and is also justified having regard to the need of people.

---

[42] Ibid., *p.* 195.

[43] *Badā'i'sanā'i'*, vol. 5, p. 3.

[44] Ibid.

Difference Between *Istisnā'* and Other Allied Contracts

The contract of *istisnā'* resembles the contract of *salam* and *ijārah.* It has also similarity with the "promise to sell". Here we will highlight some differences between *istisnā'* and the above-mentioned contracts for a better understanding of the contract of *istiṣnā'*.

Difference between *istiṣnā'* and the "promise to sell"

Istiṣnā' resembles "promise to sell" in that it constitutes a promise on part of manufacturer to make an object, which is non-existent at the time of contract

Ḥākim al-Shahīd from amongst the Ḥanafī jurists is of the view that *istiṣnā'* is a promise to sell. The majority of Aḥnāf, on the other hand, hold the opinion that it is a sale not a promise to sell. Their opinion is based on the following arguments.

1. All the Jurists are unanimous on the point that legality of *istisnā'* is established by *istiḥsān* (juristic preference) and there is no denying the fact that this principle is invoked in the contracts not in the promises.

2. The jurists allow option of inspection (*khiyār al-ru'yah*) in *istisnā'*, which is an evidence of the fact that it is a sale because options are valid in contracts only.

3. In *istisnā'* the parties have right to resort to court in case of dispute arising from some default or breach of contract. This is a proof of its being a contract because litigation is permissible in contracts which are binding on parties not in simple promises.[45]

[45] See Zayla'ī, *Tabyīn al-haqā'iq* vol. 4, p.124.

Difference between *istiṣnā'* and contract of personal services

Istiṣnā' is similar to *ijārah* of professional services, because services of a manufacturer are hired to manufacture a thing as in the case of *ijārah*. But the difference between the two is that the subject matter in the former case is the object, which is required to be made while the subject matter in latter case is the work to be done, or the performance to be made by the manufacturer. So, if A, a customer asks B, a cobbler, to make a shoe out of the material provided to him by A, then the subject matter in such case would be the act of making shoe, not the shoe itself and the contract would be that of *ijārah*. If A, a customer asks B, a manufacturer to make a shoe from his own material, then the subject matter in such case is the shoe.

What strengthens this conclusion is the fact that if the manufacturer provided the object, which he had made before the contract and the customer accepted it, the contract would be valid. This shows that the subject-matter of the contract is the object itself not the work. On the other hand, contract for work or service requires that it should be done after the contract is concluded. The contract of *istiṣnā'*, however, resembles the contract of personal services in the following two points.

(a) It lapses on death of one of the parties just like a contract of personal services.

(b) The man who has ordered the goods is entitled to refuse or accept it if he finds that they are not according to order.[46]

---

[46] See Kāsanī, *Badā'i' al-sanā'i'*, vol. 5, p.4.

Difference between *istiṣnāʿ* and *salam*

Following are some points of difference between *istisnāʿ* and *salam*.

1. The commodity in *salam* rests on responsibility (*dimmah*). It is considered a debt (*dayn).* It is normally a weighable, measurable or countable thing, while the commodity in *istisnāʿ* is treated as determinate thing (*ʿayn)* such as furniture or shoe or tailoring cloth.

2. The subject matter of *istiṣnāʿ* is always a thing, which needs manufacturing while *salam* can be affected on everything whether it needs manufacturing or not.

3. The price in *salam* is paid in advance, while in *istiṣnāʿ* contract the price can be paid any time during the contract.

4. The time of delivery in *salam* is specified, whereas it is not required in *istiṣnāʿ* that the time of delivery be fixed. According to Imām Abū Ḥanīfah if time is fixed in *istisnāʿ*, the contract will be a *salam* contract, and will no longer be an *istiṣnāʿ* contract.

5. *Salam* is a binding and irrevocable contract while the *istiṣnāʿ* can be revoked unilaterally.[47]

Conditions of *istiṣnāʿ*

Ḥanafī jurists acknowledge three conditions for a valid contract of *istisnāʿ*, they are:

1. The subject of *istiṣnāʿ*, should be precisely mentioned in terms of its kind, quality and quantity.

2. There should be some work or performance involved in the commodity.

[47] See: Ahmd Yūsuf, '*Uqud al-Muʿmalāt' al-Maliyyah,* p. 216.

3. The time of the completion of work and delivery should not be fixed. This is the view of Imām Abū Ḥanīfah. His two disciples disagree with his teacher and hold that time should be fixed.

4. The price or consideration should also be specified.[48]

Termination of *istiṣnāʿ*

The contract of *istiṣnāʿ* is terminated in the following circumstances:

1. By completion of work and handing over the object to the purchaser.

2. By the death of manufacturer.

   It is pertinent to note that death causes termination of contract only when the contract is for specific performance and the heirs of deceased manufacturer do not have ability to carry out the work in required manner.

Modern Applications of *Istiṣnāʿ*

Islamic banks and financial institutions use *istisnāʿ* as a mode of financing. They finance the construction of houses factories on a piece of land belonging to client. The house or factory is constructed either by the financer himself or by a construction company. In this latter case, the bank enters a sub-contract with that construction company. But if the contract concluded between the bank, i.e, the financer, and the client provides specifically that the work will be carried out by the financer himself, then the sub-contract is not valid. In such a case, it is necessary that the bank should have its own construction company and expert contractors to discharge the task.

---

[48] See Kāsib 'Abd al Karīm, *'Aqd al-Istiṣnā' fī al-Fiqh al-Islāmī*, pp. 133,134.

The financer in the contract of *istiṣnāʿ* for the purpose of construction is under obligation to construct house in conformity with the specifications detailed in the agreement. Some agreements provide that the financer will be liable for any defect in construction and destruction of the building during the period specified in the contract. In case the financer assigns the task of construction to a third party, it is necessary that it should supervise construction work in a regular manner. The price of construction may be paid by the client at the time of agreement and may be postponed till the time of delivery or any other time agreed upon between the parties. The payment may be in lump sum or in installments. In order to secure the payment of installments, the title deeds of the house or land may be kept by the bank as security till the last installment is paid by the client.

The mode of *istiṣnāʿ* is used also for digging wells and water canals. Islamic banks finance the agricultural sector through this mode and play an effective role in activating this important sector of the economy.

VI. *Murābaḥah*

Murābaḥah is a sale of goods at a price covering the purchase price plus profit margin agreed upon between the contracting parties. In *murābaḥah*, the seller discloses the cost of the sold commodity. He tells the purchaser that he has purchased commodity, say, for hundred rupees and that he will charge ten rupees as profit over and above the original price. It is also permissible to fix the profit in percentage i.e. 5% 10% of the cost.

Murābaḥah is basically a trust sale (*bayʿ al-amānah)* in which the buyer depends and relies upon the integrity of the purchaser as regards the cost he mentions to buyer. Thus, it is the moral and legal obligation of the seller to be honest and truthful in stating the price at which he purchased the goods, and if he succeeded in obtaining a discount or rebate, it should also be acknowledged and accounted for the benefit of the purchaser. In Islamic Law, the contract of sale with regard to the cost of the sale's object to the seller, is divided into three kinds:

(i) *Tawliyah*: resale at the stated original cost with no profit or loss to the seller.

(ii) *Wadī'ah*: resale at a discount from the original cost.

(iii) *Murābaḥah*: the resale at fixed surcharge or rate of profit on the stated original cost.

The main purpose of these sales is to "protect the innocent general consumer lacking expertise in the various items of trade from the wiles and stratagems of sharp traders."[49]

Commenting on the economic function of trust sales (*wadī'ah, tawliyah, murābaḥah)* Abraham Udouitch writes:

> The chief concern is to avoid any fraud on the part of the seller by setting out detailed guidelines regarding the considerations that are to enter into determining the cost of any item. Foremost among these is the price paid by the seller for the goods in question. In addition, a variety of expenses connected with the maintenance, improvement and transport of the goods may be included in the cost, which forms the basis of the *murābaḥah* sale. The custom of the merchants served as the criterion for determining exactly which expenses were to be included. The general rule emerging from the numerous cases discussed is that money expended directly on the goods or on services indispensable to their sale (e.g., brokerage fee) may be included, whereas the personal expenses of the merchant and other expenses not directly involved

[49] Marghīnānī, *al-Hidāyah,* vol. 3, p. 56.

with the goods are not to be figured into the stated original cost. As an additional protection to the consumer, the seller should avoid any misleading statement.[50]

Remedies for swindled purchaser

In the event of *murābaḥah* purchaser discovering that the price he has paid to the vendor was unduly inflated, Islamic Law provides relief to the deceived purchaser. The remedies suggested by different schools of law are as follows:

Opinion of the Ḥanafī jurists

In such a case the purchaser would have to make up his mind either to accept the sale at the stated price or rescind it and take his money. But if the subject matter is destroyed in the hands of purchaser or he consumes it, he would lose his right to revoke contract. According to Imām Abū Yūsuf the *murābaḥah* purchaser has no choice except to devalue undue increase.[51]

Opinion of the Malikī jurists

The purchaser would have right either to keep the *murābaḥah* object in consideration of its real or to relinquish the object of the transaction unless the *murābaḥah* vendor forces him to keep it at the real price.[52]

Opinion of the Shāfi'ī jurists

Two opinions are attributed to Imām Shāfi'ī:

(i) He has the option either to revoke contract or to take undue increase and keep the object.

---

[50] Udovitch, the *Partnership and Profit in Medieval Islam*, p. 220.

[51] Sarakhsī *al-Mabsūṭ*, vol. 13, p. 86.

[52] Ibn Rushd, *Bidāyat al-Mujtahid*, vol. 2, p.162.

(ii) He has no option other than to keep it at real price after devaluation of undue increase. [53]

Conditions of *Murābaḥah*

The conditions of *murābaḥah* contract are as follows:[54]

1. Disclosure of original price

It is necessary for the validity of the *murābaḥah* transaction that the second purchaser (*murābaḥah* purchaser) should have knowledge of the original price. This means that the seller should disclose price of the commodity. If the price is not disclosed in the session of contract, and contracting parties leave the *majlis*, the contract will be invalid.

2. Fixation of profit

The profit should be fixed and added to the cost price and be mentioned in the contract.

3. Ascertainment of price

Murābaḥah is valid only where the exact cost price can be ascertained. If the exact cost is not known, the commodity cannot be sold on *murābaḥah*. Instead it will be sold without reference to the cost. This is applicable to cases where a person has purchased two or more things in a single transaction, and he does not know the price of each object separately.

4. Validity of first contract

The first contract should be a valid contract. But if the first contract is *fāsid*, i.e., irregular, then the second sale is not permitted on the basis of *murābaḥah* because the *murābaḥah* is resale of a thing for similar to its first price with the addition of

---

[53] Ibid.

[54] See Zuhaylī, *al-Fiqh al-Islāmī*, vol. 4, pp. 704-706.

profit, and the irregular sale is not allowed with the stated price. It is allowed only with the legal value, i.e., the market price.

Expenses in relation to *murābaḥah*

The opinion of Muslim jurists is divided as to what expenses can be added to the price and constitutes a basis for the calculation of profit.[55]

The Mālikī school

Expenses that can be added to the price are those that have affected the commodity such as dying or tailoring. The expenses incurred on services such as the fare for the transporting or storing the commodities in a warehouse rented for this purpose can be added to the price but cannot be considered for the purpose of calculating profit.[56]

The Ḥanafī school

All the expenses which are accepted normally by commercial practice can be added to the cost price whether such expenses have affected the commodity itself (e.g. dyeing or tailoring) or were incurred on account of such commodity (e.g. transporting goods or paying commission to a middleman).[57]

The Ḥanbalī and Shāfi'ī schools

All actual expenses incurred as regards the commodity can be added to capital provided that the *murābaḥah* purchaser is made aware of the amount of these expenses and their origin.[58]

---

[55] Nabīl sālih, *Unlawful Gain and Legitimate Profit in Islamic Law*, p.118.

[56] Ibn Rushd, *Bidāyat al-Mujtahid*, vol. 2, p. 161.

[57] Kāsānī, *Badā'i' al-Ṣanā'i'*, vol. 5, p. 223.

[58] Ibn Rushd, *Bidāyat al-Mujtahid*, vol. 2, p. 161.

Modern Applications of *Murābaḥah*

The Islamic banks use this technique to finance projects. They buy commodities for cash and then sell them to a potential client on cost plus profit principle on deferred payment basis. In Islamic banks *murābaḥah* is practiced in the following way:

(i) The client approaches the bank with the request to purchase certain goods for him. He also provides the description of the required goods.

(ii) In case the bank agrees to his request, it asks the client to give an undertaking to purchase the goods with a stated profit margin. The banks can enter into an actual sale agreement with the client if the commodity is owned by the bank.

(iii) After signing the "undertaking for purchase", the bank makes purchase of required goods. The original principle is that the bank itself purchases the item directly from the supplier. It is, however, also permissible to carry out the purchase by authorizing an agent to execute the purchase.

(iv) After the bank has purchased goods and taken possession of them, it enters into a *murābaḥah* contract with its client. The contract includes certain increase (profit) over the cost of goods and the schedule of payment. The bank hands over goods to the client in lieu of cheques bearing future dates according to the payment schedule.

(v) In order to secure the payment of price, the bank may ask the buyer to furnish a security in the form of mortgage.

(vi) In case of defect in the commodity discovered later on, the buyer can return it to the bank and claim re-imbursement of what he has paid.[59] It is however, permissible for the bank to stipulate in the contract of *murabaḥah* that the bank is free from responsibility for all or some defects of the commodity. In such case, the customer cannot exercise option of defect.

In order to avoid any *ribā* element, the bank provides that the agreement of the bank and the actual execution of buying do not contribute any legal obligation on the partner to buy. Hence the risk is still that of the bank. Until the partner fulfills his original promise of re-buying the commodity, the risk remains with the bank, which justifies the profit.

Status of promise in Islamic law

Here a question arises as to whether such undertaking or promise to purchase is binding on the client. Muslim jurists have provided different answers to this question:

1. Shāfi'ī and Ḥanbalī jurists are of the view that promises are not mandatory. They represent just a moral obligation on the promisor to fulfill his promise.

2. The Mālikī jurists regard promises as binding. This view is attributed to Ibn al-'Arabī and Ibn Shubramah.

3. The Ḥanafī jurists acknowledge the validity of *bay' al-wafā'* which establishes the fact that the Ḥanafīs also favour the concept of the binding nature of promises. In *bay'al-wafā'* the purchaser of an immovable property undertakes that

[59] Shanqīṭī, *'Uqūd Mustaḥdathah* Madinah: Maṭba'ah al-'Ulūm wa al-ḥikam, 1992, p.381.

he will return it to the seller if he (the seller) returns price to him. Such a promise is binding on the purchaser[60].

The Islamic Fiqh Academy has made the promises in commercial dealings binding on the promisor with the following conditions:

(a) It should be one-sided promise.

(b) The promise must have caused the promisee to incur some liabilities.

c) If the promise is to purchase something, the actual sale must take place at the appointed time by the exchange of offer and acceptance. Mere promise itself should not be taken as the concluded sale.

(d) If the promisor backs out of his promise, the court may force him either to purchase the commodity or pay actual damages.[61]

Islamic banks deal with this issue in two different ways. In Dār al-Māl al-Islāmī the customer requests the bank to purchase the goods and submits intent to buy same on arrival, this promise is binding. In the Kuwait Finance House, the customer gives a non-binding promise to buy the commodities that were purchased by the Kuwait Finance House.

Conclusion

- Sale is an exchange of a useful and desirable thing for a similar thing by mutual consent for the alienation of property.

---

[60] Ibn Juzy, *al-Qawānīn al-Fiqhiyyah*, p. 258, Ibn Qudāmah, *al-Mughnī*, vol. 4, pp. 17-195.

[61] Resolution no. 2 and 3, Islamic Fiqh Academy, See Academy's Journal no.5, vol. 2, p. 1509.

- In Islamic law property is divided into movable and immovable, fungible and non-fungible, and finally into determinate and indeterminate property.

- Islamic law has prohibited all sale contracts, which contain the element of *gharar* (uncertainty) such as *mukhāḍarah, muhāqalah,* and *mulāmasah.*

- Important kinds of sale are:

  - *Salam*
  - *Ṣarf*
  - *Murabaḥah*
  - *Bay' mu'ajjal*
  - *Istiṣnā'*

- Salam is a sale in which the price is paid in advance and articles are delivered on future date. It is affected on the commodities, which can be precisely determined in terms of quality and quantity.

- *Ṣarf* refers to sale of money for money. The counter values in this contract must be delivered and taken possession of in the session of contract.

- Islamic law treats todays paper currency as real money for all the practical purposes.

- *Istiṣnā'* consists in ordering an artisan or manufacturer to make certain goods answering a given description.

- *Murābaḥah* is a transaction in which a vendor sells an article for the cost price in addition to a certain stated profit.

- *Murābaḥah* is a trust sale in which the buyer depends and relies upon the integrity of the purchaser as regards the cost he mentions to the buyer.

Chapter 15

Contract of *Ijārah* (Leasing)

Definition

The word *ijārah* literally means to give something on rent. In the language of law, it means lending of some object to somebody in return for some rental against a specified period. It can also be described as sale of usufruct for consideration. It includes letting things moveable and immovable for hire and rendering services such as custody of property and professional services.

The word *ijārah* is used for two different situations. In the first place, it means to employ the services of a person on wages given to him as consideration for his hired services. The employer is called *musta'jir* while the employee is called *ajīr*. The second type of *ijārah* relates to the usufructs of asset and properties, and not to services of human beings. *ijārah* in this sense means to transfer the usufruct of a particular property to another person in exchange for a rent claimed from him. In this case, the term *ijārah* is analogous to the English term leasing. Here the lessor is called *mu'jir*, the lessee is called *musta'jir* and the rent payable to the lessor is called *ujrah*.[1]

The jurists have formulated various definitions of *ijārah* regarding its principle features.

The definition of *ijārah* in different schools is as follows:

[1] Taqī 'Usmānī, *An Introduction to Islamic Finance*, pp. 156, 157.

Ḥanafī school

It is contract on usufructs for a known consideration.[2]

Shāfi'ī school

It is a contract on a known and permissible benefit in exchange of a known return.[3]

Mālikī school

It is an alienation of lawful usufructs for a fixed charge for a fix period. For the Mālikī Ibn Rushd says; *ijārah* resembles a sale contract whereby price and use are exchanged.[4]

Ḥanbalī school

Ijārah is contract for the lawful and defined use of a lawful and determined corporeal object for a specific period of time. It is also defined as providing a defined work for a fixed price.[5]

Features of *Ijārah*

1. The preceding definitions set the following features of *ijārah*. The purpose of *ijārah* contract is alienation of usufructs unlike contract of sale, which aims at alienation of property.
2. The benefits to be derived should be known and specified.
3. The benefits, which are the subject matter of contact, should be permissible in the *Sharī'ah*. Thus, the hiring of a house for manufacturing wine is not permissible. Similarly,

---

[2] Kāsānī, *badā'i' al-ṣanā'i'*, vol. 4, p.174; Zayla'ī, *Tabyīn al-Ḥaqā'iq* vol. 5, p.105.

[3] Shirbīnī, *Mughnī al-Muḥtāj*, vol. 2, p.332.

[4] Ibn Qudāmah, *al-Sharḥ al-Kabīr*, vol.4, p.2; Ibn Qudāmah, *al-Mughnī* vol. 5, p. 398. Ibn Rushd, *Bidāyat al-Mujtahid*, vol. 2, pp.219-220.

[5] Bahutī, *al-Rawḍ al-Murbi'*, p. 214.

hiring a woman for the purpose of singing would also be against Islamic law.

4. The rent or compensation should be specifically fixed.

5. The period of contract should also be specified in the contract.

Legitimacy of *Ijārah*

The legality of *ijārah* is established by the Qur'ān, the *Sunnah* and *ijmā'*.

Qur'ān

(i) Allah says: "And if they suckle your (offspring) give them their `recompense."[6]

(ii) "Said one of the (damsels): "O my father: engage him on wages. `Truly the best of men for thee to employ is the man who is strong and trusty."[7]

Sunnah

(i) Said the Holy Prophet (s.a.w.s), "Give wages of the person hired before his sweat dries up."[8]

(ii) "If someone hires a person, let him inform him about the wages he is to receive."[9]

(iii) Haḍrat Sa'd ibn Abī Waqās reported that in the age of the Holy Prophet (s.a.w.s) the owners of the land used to let their lands on rent.[10]

---

[6] Qur'ān,65: 6.

[7] Qur'ān,28: 26.

[8] san'ānī, *al-Salām*, vol. 3. p. 81.

[9] Shawkānī, *Nayl al-Awṭār*, vol. 5, p. 292.

[10] Nasā'ī, *Sunan* (Urdu) Karachi: Qur'ān Mahal, n.d. vol.3, p.60.

Ijmāʿ

All the companions of the Holy Prophet (s.a.w.s) unanimously held that *ijārah* is a lawful contract. They themselves practiced all lawful forms of this contract. In the *Sharīʿah* permissibility of *ijārah* has been constructed on *istiḥsān*, which is a departure from a rule of precedent. According to a general rule of Islamic law of contract, an object, which does not exist at the time of contract, may not be sold. However, *ijārah* is valid despite its being sale of the usufructs, which are non-existent at the time of contract. Analogy would thus invalidate *ijārah*, but *istiḥsān* exceptionally validates it on the authority of the *Sunnah* and *ijmāʿ*.

Imām Sarakhsī stating the lawfulness of this contract writes:

The contract and dealings practiced before Islam are valid practices for us also in the absence of any text disapproving them. The Holy Prophet (s.a.w.s) was sent as Prophet and he saw the people practising *ijārah* and he approved that practice.[11]

Kinds of *Ijārah*

There are two main kinds of *ijārah*, namely *ijārat al-ashyā' and ijārah al- ashkhāṣ.*

1. *Ijārah al-ashyā'* refers to hiring of things such as houses, shops, lands, animals and beasts etc. This is also known as *ijārah al-ʿayn.*

2. *Ijārat al-ashkhās* refers to hiring of services, such as to hire a painter to paint a house. This kind is also called *ijārah al-dhimmah.*[12]

---

[11] Al-Sarakhsī, *al-Mabsūṭ,* vol. 15, p.74.

[12] Al-Jazīrī, *Kitāb al-Fiqh ʿalā al-Madhāhib al-Arbaʿah*, Beriut: vol. 3, p.110.

The person hired for rendering services is called *ajīr* who is either *ajīr khāṣ*, the employee or *ajīr mushtarak,* i.e., independent contractor. *ajīr khās* renders service for one person for a fixed period while *ajīr mushtrak* works for a large number of people like tailor, laundryman, and ironsmith.

Conditions of *ijārat al-ashyā'*

1. The subject of *ijārah* must have a valuable use. Therefore, things having no usufruct at all cannot be leased.

2. It is necessary for a valid contract of lease that the corpus of the leased property remains in the ownership of the seller, and only its usufruct is transferred to the lessee. Therefore, the lease cannot be affected in respect of money, eatables, fuel and ammunition, because their use is not possible unless they are consumed. If anything of this nature is leased out, it will be deemed to be a loan and all the rules concerning the transaction of loan shall accordingly apply. Any rent charged on lease shall be treated as an interest charged on a loan.[13]

3. As the corpus of the leased property remains in the ownership of the lessor, all the liabilities emerging from the ownership shall be borne by the lessor, but the liabilities referable to the use of the property shall be borne by the lessee.

Example

A has leased his house to B. The taxes referable to the property shall be borne by A, while electricity bills and all expenses referable to the use of the house shall be borne by B, the lessee.[14]

---

[13] Taqī 'Usmānī, *an Introduction to Islamic Finance*, p.157.
[14] Ibid.

4. The subject-matter of *ijārah,* namely, the usufruct should be known, and `identified. There should not be any uncertainty and vagueness about the usufructs, which may lead to discord and dispute among the parties. The lessor should specifically mention the subject-matter. It is not permissible to lease an unspecified thing. Thus if a person says: "I rented you one of these two houses", the contract would be invalid because the subject-matter in this case is unknown and unidentified.[15]

5. The leasing period should be fixed, whether, it is long or short. It is the viewpoint of the majority of the *fuqahā'*. Imām Mālik, on the other hand maintains that a long period for the use of usufructs is not advisable, because it may cause dispute and tussle.[16] As regards property of orphans and *waqf,* the Ḥanafī jurists hold that long period of lease of these properties is not permissible so that the lessee may not claim his ownership over them because of long possession. They propose that it should not be hired out for more than three years.[17]

6. The subject-matter should be something that can be actually delivered. Thus, the renting out of a stray animal is not permitted.

7. The object and purpose of the contract should be lawful. Thus, it is not permissible to hire a house for the purpose of gambling or manufacturing wine.

8. The article to be hired should be physically fit for hire.

---

[15] Kāsānī, *Badā'i' al-sanā'i'*, vol. 4, p. 180.

[16] See Shirbīnī, *Mughnī al-Muhtāj* vol. 2, p. 349; Ibn Qudāmah, *al-Mughnī,* vol. 5, p. 401.

[17] Ibn 'Ābidīn, *Radd al-Muhtār,* vol. 5, p. 2-3.

9. In the contract of hiring a land, the use of land should be specified whether it is for cultivation or construction of building.

10. If a beast of burden is hired for carrying a burden, the quantity and quality of burden, the destination and the period for which it is required should be stated. If the lessee loads with the burden more than the specified, he will be called to compensate. Similarly, if he uses the animal in an unusual manner, which causes its death, he will be regarded *ghāṣib* (usurper) and called for indemnification.[18]

11. The lessee cannot use the leased asset for any purpose other than the purpose specified in the lease agreement. If no such purpose is specified in the agreement, the lessee can use it for whatever purpose it is used in the normal course. However, if he wishes to use if for an abnormal purpose, he cannot do so unless the lessor allows him in express terms.

12. The lessee is liable to compensate the lessor for every harm to the leased asset caused by any misuse or negligence on the part of the lessee.

13. The leased asset shall remain in the risk of the lessor throughout the lease period in the sense that any harm or loss caused by the factors beyond the control of the lessee shall be borne by the lessor.

14. A property jointly owned by two or more persons can be leased out, and the rental shall be distributed between or among all the joint owners according to the proportion of their respective shares in the property.

---

[18] Zayla'ī, *Tabyīn al-haqā'iq*, vol. 5, p. 113.

15. A joint-owner of a property can lease his proportionate share to his co-sharer only and not to any other person.

16. Rent to be paid should be a lawful thing and known.

17. Rent should not be paid in the same genus or specifics. Thus, a house cannot be rented in exchange of house. This condition is peculiar to the Ḥanafī school.[19]

Conditions of *ijārat al-ashkhās*

1. In the contract of hiring services, the work required to be performed should be specifically fixed such as the carriage of goods, or building house etc.

2. Performance or work should not be prohibited in the *Sharī'ah.* Thus, it is not permitted to hire a magician to teach magic, or a singer for the purpose of singing. Similarly, it is not permissible to hire the services of a person to kill another person or torture him, because they are acts of sin and disobedience, hence prohibited in the *Sharī'ah.*

3. The service required to be rendered should not be a mandatory duty. It is, therefore, not allowed for a person to hire a person to pray, to perform *hajj*, to lead prayer, to teach the Qur'ān because they are mandatory duties, so the worker is not entitled to wages if he is hired for any of them.

   As regards charging fee for teaching the Qur'ān or the principles of faith, accepted rule of the Ḥanafī School is that no one is allowed to charge any fee for teaching these subjects because it is held to be a form of worship (*ibādah*). This was the ruling of early jurists. The jurists of subsequent ages, when they saw that the people were

---

[19] Kāsānī, *Badā'i' al-sanā'i'*, vol. 4, p. 194.

reluctant to teach the Qur'ān gave a *fatwā* in favour of charging fee for teaching the Qur'ān. They considered it necessary in order to encourage the teaching of Islam.[20]

4. The contract of *ijārah* should not comprise any condition according to which the rent or wages might be paid from the article manufactured, or wrought upon the rental goods.

Some other rules concerning *ijārah*

1. The property hired is a trust in the hands of the lessee. Thus, if it is destroyed without any negligence on the part of the lessee, he will not be responsible for that loss or damage.

2. The lessee is required to exercise maximum care of property and use it properly. An improper and unusual use of the property will change his status from trustee to usurper, and in case any destruction takes place, he will be liable for compensation.

3. Rent of hired property becomes due:

   i) on the attainment of usufruct of the hired property or goods, and

   ii) ability of the lessee to use the usufruct of hired goods.

4. *Ijārah* is a binding and irrevocable contract. Thus, it cannot be revoked unilaterally.

5. Unlike the sale contract, *ijārah* can be enforced from some specified future date. Thus, it is permissible to say that this contract will be effective from January 1, 2021.

---

[20] Zayla'ī, *Tabyīn al-ḥaqā'iq,* vol. 5, p. 124.

6. *Ajīr mushtarak* (Independent contractor) such as tailor or shoemaker will be held accountable for the loss of goods in his custody regardless of whether they are destroyed by his fault or without his fault. This ruling has been given by the *fuqahā'* on the grounds of public interest so that trustees and tradesmen exercise greater care in safeguarding people's properties.[21]

Modern Applications of *Ijārah*

There are two main types of *ijārah* (leasing) practiced by the modern banks namely finance lease and operating lease.

1. Finance lease

The finance lease is based on a contract between the lessor and the lessee for hire of a specific asset selected from a manufacturer or vendor of such assets by the lessee. The lessor retains the ownership of the asset and the lessee has possession and use of asset on payment of specified rentals over a period. Though the lessor is the legal owner, the lessee is given the exclusive rights to the use of the asset for the duration of the contract. The rentals during the fixed primary period are sufficient to amortize the capital outlay of the leasing company and provide an element of profit. The primary period is closely related to the estimated useful life of the asset and the lessee is normally responsible for all operating costs such as maintenance and insurance. The lessee has also the options for a secondary period of lease in which the rentals are reduced to nominal amount.

[21] Kāsānī, *Badā'i' al-sanā'i'*, vol. 4, p. 210, Ramlī, *Mughnī al-Muhtāj*, vol. 2, p. 35, Ibn Qudāmah, *al-Mughnī*, vol. 5, p.487.

The period of lease usually ranges from 5 to 15 years depending on the useful life of the asset.[22]

Since all the risk is borne by the lessee, instead of lessor in finance lease, it makes the contract objectionable from the *Sharī'ah* point of view. In *Sharī'ah,* risks of damage and obsolescence is exclusively borne by the lessor. Besides, the leased item or equipment cannot be returned to the lessor during the primary period of lease. The lessee cannot cancel the contract even if he finds the item unuseful during the term. The fact that the rent is related to the approximate useful life of the item and that the lessor recovers the entire cost of equipment plus some profit, make this contract doubtful from Islamic point of view.

2. Operating lease

This is "non-full payment" lease as rentals are insufficient to enable the lessor to recover fully the initial capital outlay. The residual value is recovered through disposal or re-leasing the equipment to other users. In this lease major consideration is given to the use of equipment. Unlike the finance lease system, the lessee can cancel the contract before it expires without paying any penalty. Under this arrangement the risk of damage and depreciation is borne by the lessor.

Ijārah in Islamic Banks

1. *Ijārah muntahiyah bittamlīk*

It is a leasing of movable or immovable property with eventually transferring the title in the leased asset to the lessee. It may also be defined as an agreement combined with an

---

[22] Council of Islamic Ideology, *Elimination of Ribā from the Economy and Islamic Modes of Financing*, 1991, p. 13.

undertaking by the lessee to purchase the asset during the lease or at the termination of the lease.

The financial institution on the request of client purchases a movable or immovable property and rent it to him who pays an agreed sum in installments over an agreed period. He gives an undertaking that he will buy the property at the termination of lease period. By virtue of this undertaking, he buys the asset and becomes owner of the asset.

Steps of lease transaction in Islamic Banks

- Bank buys a car, say, worth 12 lac rupees.
- Bank pays ownership related cost i.e. registration, *takāful* cost.
- Leases it to customer for agreed monthly rentals, say, Rs.37, 762/-. Rentals cover cost price plus some profit.
- Lease period is 3 years, for instance
- Bank takes an undertaking from the client that he will buy car on the expiry of lease period.
- Bank takes 15% security deposits amounting to Rs.1,80000/-
- After 3 years, bank sells it to customer against security deposit.

Difference between conventional lease and *ijārah*

- Conventional lease combines sale and lease in one contract, (Hire-purchase) not allowed in *Sharī'ah*.
- In *ijārah*, lease and sale are two independent contracts.
- In conventional lease rentals start with lease contract.
- In *ijārah*, rental start with delivery of asset.
- In conventional leasing, customer is responsible for all loss and damage.
- Islamic bank, bears all ownership related risks.
- If asset is destroyed or stolen, conventional leasing company continues charging rental.

- Islamic bank does not charge any rental.
- In conventional lease, asset is automatically transferred to customer.
- Extra amount is charged, if rent is not paid in time.
- Islamic bank does not charge increase.

2. Direct lease

This is a mode whereby the Islamic banks allow the customer to use the capital assets owned by the banks for a limited period of time ranging from few days to few months depending upon the type of asset in question. In return the lessee pays a monthly or annual rental fee.

Conclusion

- *Ijārah* is a contract for usufruct for a known consideration.
- *Ijārah* includes letting things for hire and rendering services.
- The subject-matter of *ijārah* should be permissible thing or act.
- It should be known and identified.
- The rent or compensation should be specified/fixed.
- The property hired is held to be a trust in the hands of lessee. Thus, if it is destroyed without any negligence on his part, he will not be held responsible for that loss or damage.
- *Ajīr mushtarak* (Independent contractor) is held accountable for the loss of goods in his custody regardless of whether they are destroyed by his fault or without his fault.

- There are two main types of *ijārah* (leasing) practiced by the modern banks namely, finance lease and operating lease. Finance lease is objectionable from the *Sharī'ah* point of view because in this form of lease all the risk is borne by the lessee.

- *Ijārah* Muntahiyah Bittamleek is a combination of leasing property and granting the lessee an option of eventually acquiring the object of lease. It is permissible in the *Sharī'ah*.

Chapter 16

Contract of *Mushārakah* (Partnership)

The word *sharikah* is used in the literal sense to mean mixing or mingling. *Sharikah* or partnership implies an underlying idea of mixing shares in such a way that one of them cannot be distinguished from the other. In its technical sense, *sharikah* signifies a particular relationship that exists between two contracting parties, although there may be no actual mixing or mingling of shares.

Definition

The Muslim jurists have offered various definitions of partnerships with regard to its important features.

Mālikī definition

"It is a permission from each of the partners to the other for appropriation and disposition while retaining the right to transact personally (in such wealth)."[1]

Ḥanbalī definition

"*Sharikah* is the participation of two or more persons in the entitlement of a thing and disposition."[2]

Shāfi'ī definition

"*Sharikah* is an establishment of a right in a single thing held in common between two or more persons".[3]

---

[1] Ibn Qudāmah, *al-Sharh al-Kabīr* vol. 3, p.348.
[2] Ibn Qudāmah, *al-Mughnī* vol 5, p.1.
[3] Shirbīnī, *Mughnī al-Muḥtāj*, vol.3, p.211.

Ḥanafī definition

"*Sharikah* is a contract between two or more people for participation in capital and its profit."[4]

Of all the preceding definitions, the last one may be said to be the most comprehensive, as it encompasses all the necessary ingredients of a partnership namely; agreement, business involving investment from the partners and sharing of expected profit.

Definition of Partnership in Law

The Pakistan Partnership Act, 1932 defines partnership as:

> "A relationship between persons who agree to share the profits of a business carried on by all or any of them acting for all."[5]

Following are the main features of modern partnership.

a) Agreement: There must be an agreement between the parties concerned. Without agreement, partnership cannot be formed. The agreement may be express or implied. It is however, preferable to reduce it to writing so that any future dispute may be settled in accordance with the provisions of the agreement.

b) Number: There should be more than one person to form a partnership. However, there is a restriction on the maximum number of the partners. In case of ordinary business, the partners must not exceed 20 partners and in case of banking contracts it must not exceed 10 partners.

---

[4] Ibn 'Abidīn, *radd al-Muhtār*, vol.3, p.364.

[5] *Partnership Act 1932,* Section 34.

c) Business: The object of the formation of partnership is to carry on any type of business as long as it is lawful.

d) Profit-sharing: The basic purpose of the formation of partnership is to earn profit. The profit is to be shared as agreed between the partners. If there is no such agreement they will share profits equally. The contribution towards the losses will be in the same proportion as the sharing of profits unless there is contract to the contrary.[6]

e) Conducted by all or on behalf of all: The business of partnership is conducted by all the partners or any of them acting for all. But each partner is allowed to participate in the management by law.

f) Unlimited liability: Each partner is liable to the full satisfaction of the liability of partnership jointly and severally. However, one or some of the partners with the agreement of other partners may have limited liability. However, all the partners in a firm cannot be with limited liability.

g) Investment: Each partner contributes his share in the capital according to the agreement. Some persons may become partners without investing any capital to the business. They devote their time, energy, skill, judgement and ability to the business instead of capital and receive profit.

h) Transferability of share: The interest of a partner in a firm cannot be transferred and assigned to a third person without the consent of other partners.

i) Position of partners: Every partner is an agent as well as principal to the other partner. In this capacity he can bind the other partners by his acts as well as will be bound by

6.

the acts of other partners if they were carried out during the normal conduct of business by his act. In the position of an agent he can enter into a contract with another person or parties on behalf of his partner or partners.[7]

j) Duration: Partnership may be for an indefinite period of time. It may also be for a definite period. Some partnerships are formed for completion of a single venture.[8]

Concept of Company in Modern Law

Definition of company

Company is a voluntary association of different persons created by law as a separate body for specific purposes. It possesses a common capital contributed by its members, such capital being divided into transferable shares. The liability of each such member is limited to the extent of value of the shares he holds.[9]

Characteristics of a company

The following are the main characteristics of a joint-stock company.

a) Legal entity: A company is an artificial person, which is created by law. It is a separate legal entity apart from its members. It can purchase property or transfer the title of property or sue in a court of law in its own name.

b) Perpetual existence: The company is a creation of law and it continues to exist until it is wound up by the legal procedure. The death or retirement of any member does

---

[7] *Partnership Act 1932* Section 22.

[8] *Partnership Act 1932,* Section 18 & 19.

[9] See *Company Law in Pakistan,* 1986. (p.22)

not affect the life and existence of the company. Its life is distinct from that of its members.

c) Limited liability: The liability of each shareholder is limited to the extent of his share. Other assets of the members cannot be taken into consideration for the liabilities of the company.

d) Constitutional status: A company is person under the law, but it is not to be considered citizen in the eyes of law.

e) Number of members: In case of public limited company, the minimum number of members is seven. There is, however, no restriction on the maximum number of members. In case of private limited company, the minimum number of members is two while the maximum is fifty.

f) Transferability of shares: The shares of a public company are transferable. This type of share may easily be purchased or sold in the stock exchange market.

g) Management: The management of company is centralized in a 'Board of Directors' who are elected by the general shareholders. But the shareholders, who are the actual owners of the company, are not allowed to participate directly in the management.

h) Nature of business and management: The nature of business is mentioned in the object clause of the 'Memorandum of Association', which cannot be changed except by the sanction of the court. The procedure of management, on the other hand, is laid down in the 'Articles of Association'.[10]

---

[10] Ibid, pp. 22, 23.

Legitimacy of *Sharikah*

The legitimacy of *sharikah* as a valid mode of business is established by the Qur'ān, the Sunnah and *ijmā'*. Some of the relevant verses of the Holy Qur'ān and traditions of the Holy Prophet are cited in the following lines.

The Qur'ān Says:

وَإِنَّ كَثِيرًا مِّنَ الْخُلَطَاءِ لَيَبْغِي بَعْضُهُمْ عَلَى بَعْضٍ إِلَّا الَّذِينَ آمَنُوا وَعَمِلُوا الصَّالِحَاتِ وَقَلِيلٌ مَّا هُمْ

"And verily, many partners oppress one another, except those who believe and do righteous deeds, and they are few."[11]

(i) The Holy Prophet (s.a.w.s.) said that Allah says:

I am the third of the two partners as long as they do not cheat one another. But when one of them cheats the other, I leave them[12] (i.e., they are deprived of the blessing and favour of Almighty Allah)."

ii) The Holy Prophet (s.a.w.s) also said: "Allah Almighty is with the two partners unless they defraud each other."[13]

(iii) *Sharikah* business was prevalent in the Arabian Peninsula at the advent of Islam. The Holy Prophet (s.a.w.s.) accorded his tacit approval to this practice. He himself carried on business on the basis of partnership before his declaration of prophethood.

---

[11] Qur'ān, 38: 24.

[12] Abū Da'ūd, *Sunan*, Kitāb al-Buyū', Bāb al-Sharikah.

[13] Ibn Qudāmah, *al-Mughnī*, vol.5, p.3.

The validity of *sharikah* is proved by the consensus of the Muslim Ummah too. The entire Muslim scholars in all ages had been in agreement in regard to the validity of *sharikah* form of business.

Kinds of *Sharikah*

There are two main kinds of *sharikah*:

1. *Sharikat al-Milk* (Proprietary partnership).
2. *Sharikat al-'Aqd* (Contractual partnership).[14]

1. *Sharikat al-milk*

Sharikat al-milk is defined by the *majallah*, as "the existence of a thing in the exclusive joint-ownership of two or more persons due to any reason of ownership, or it is the joint claim of two or more persons for a debt that is due from another individual arising from a single cause". [15]

In this type of *sharikah* each and every one has ownership in every smallest part of the capital. The property, which is difficult to divide and distinguish, forms the subject matter of a proprietary partnership. It is of two kinds:

(a) Compulsory partnership: It is a partnership, which becomes effective without any action on the part of the partners, such as inheritance.

(b) Optional partnership: It is a partnership which becomes effective through the act of parties e.g. joint-purchase or joint-acceptance of gift or a bequest, joint seizure of an article in enemy's country in the course of war or where they unite their respective properties in such a way that

---

[14] *Majallah,* Article 1045.

[15] Ibid., article 1060.

one is not distinguishable from the other, such as mixture of wheat with barley.[16]

Rules Relating to *Sharikat al-milk*

1. Each partner is a stranger with respect to the share of the others.
2. The partners are not allowed to undertake any act of disposal with respect to the other's share except with the latter's permission.
3. Each partner can sell his own share without the other partners' consent, except in cases where share of one partner cannot be distinguished from the other.
4. The share of one partner in the possession of another co-owner is governed by the rules of *wadī'ah* (deposit). If one co-owner further deposits such property with a third party without the permission of his partner, he is liable for compensation *(ḍamān)* if the property is destroyed.
5. Right to demand the recovery of a debt belongs to each co-owner jointly and severally. A debt possessed by one partner is governed by the rules of *sharikat al-milk*. Further, postponement of the recovery of a debt cannot be granted by one co-owner without the permission of the other.[17]

---

[16] Ibid, articles 1063, 1064.

[17] See Nyazee, Imran Ahsan, *Islamic Law of Business organization-Partnerships*, Islamabad, The International Institute of Islamic Thought and Islamic Research Institute, 1997, pp. 36-37.

2. *Sharikat al-'aqd*

It is a partnership, which comes into being as a result of agreement between two or more persons in order to share the profits.[18]

Kinds of *Sharikat al-'aqd*

According to the Ḥanafī jurists, *sharikah* is of three types:

1. *Sharikah al-Amwāl*
2. *Sharikah al-A'māl*
3. *Sharikah al-Wujūh*

Each of the above kinds is further divided into *'inān* (limited) or *mufāwaḍah* (unlimited). Thus, they are of the following six categories:

1. *Sharikat al-Amwāl* by way of *mufāwaḍah.*
2. *Sharikat al-Amwāl* by way of *'inān.*
3. *Sharikat al-A'māl* by way of *mufāwaḍah.*
4. *Sharikat al-A'māl* by way of *'inān.*
5. *Sharikat al-Wujūh* by way of *mufāwaḍah.*
6. *Sharikat al-Wujūh* by way of *'inān.*[19]

Conditions for contractual partnership

The following are the basic conditions common to every type of contractual partnership (*Sharikah al-'aqd)*

Basic elements

A contractual partnership should include all the basic elements of a valid contract, i.e.,

(i) Offer and acceptance;

---

[18] *Majallah,* article 1329.

[19] Zayla'ī, *Tabyīn al-haqā'iq,* vol 3, p.313.

(ii) Competence of parties: Only legally competent person capable of disposing property and conferring mandate can be a party to a contractual partnership

(iii) Subject matter: It is also necessary that the subject matter of partnership be a lawful trade. Thus, a partnership for trade in wine and other illicit things is invalid.

Agency

Each kind of contractual partnership should contain a contract of agency. Each partner is an agent of the other partners in all dispositions made by him, in trading and in accepting work.

Division of profit

It should be declared in what way the profit is to be divided between the partners.

Known portion of profit

Shares of profit to be divided between the shareholders must be known by division, for instance, one half (1/2) one third (1/3) or one fourth (1/4). No fixed amount or portion of the profit can be stipulated for any of the partners. The loss is to be borne in proportion to the respective capitals of the partners.

Entitlement to profit

According to the Ḥanafī jurists a partner in a contractual partnership becomes entitled to the profit in one of three ways.

i) By capital
ii) By work
iii) By the liability incurred by the partner. [20]

---

[20] Kāsanī, *Badā'i' al-Ṣanā'i'*, vol.6, p.62; Ibn al-Hamām, *Fatḥ al Qadīr*, vol.5, p.21.

According to the majority of Muslim jurists, however, a partner becomes entitled to the profit by capital and labour only. According to the Ḥanafī jurists, it is lawful that the capital of each[21] partner be equal and yet the profit be shared unequally. Zufar, Shāfi'ī, and Mālik do not subscribe to this view because according to them the share in the larger portion of profit is earned without any responsibility since the responsibility is in proportion to capital which one advances. The arguments of the Ḥanafī scholars on this issue are twofold:

First: The Prophet (s.a.w.s) has said "The profit between partners should follow the agreement between them and the loss should be borne in proportion to their investments."[22] In this precept of the Holy Prophet (s.a.w.s), no distinction is made between the equality or inequality of their properties.

Second: In the same manner as a person is entitled to profit by virtue of capital, he is also entitled to it by virtue of labour as in the case of *muḍārabah*. It may happen sometime that one of the partners is more skillful and expert in business than the other, consequently he will not agree to the other sharing equally with him in the profit.

Now we take up the kinds of *shariat al-'aqd* (contractual partnership) in detail.

Sharikat al-amwāl (Investment partnership)

Definition

It is an agreement between two or more persons to invest a sum of money in a business and share its profits according to agreement. The investment of this partnership consists of

---

[21] Ibn Juzy, *al-Qawānīn al-Fiqhiyyah*, p.284.

[22] Jamāl al-Dīn 'Abd Allah Zayla'ī, *Naṣb al-Rāyah*, Cairo: Dār al-hadīth, 1st ed. 1938, vol.3, p.478.

capital contributed by the partner. It is divided into two kinds, i.e., '*inān* and *mufāwaḍah.*

Specified conditions for *sharikat al-amwāl*

There are certain conditions of *sharikat al-amwāl* which are applicable to both *'inān sharikat al-amwāl* and *mufāwaḍah sharikat al-amwāl.*[23] These conditions are as follows:

a. Present capital

The Ḥanafīs stipulate that the capital of the *sharikah* must be an ascertained commodity (*'ayn'*) and not *dayn*, i.e., wealth that is absent. Present wealth, in their view, is wealth available for transactions, and not necessarily present physically on the spot. Hence, in the opinion of the Ḥanafī jurists, the absence of capital, at the time the contract is negotiated, does not invalidate the partnership as long as the capital is in hand, when the joint purchase is made. Kāsānī says:

> Among these conditions is the availability of the wealth in the form of an *'ayn* (ascertained commodity). It should neither be a receivable (*dayn)* nor absent wealth, otherwise, the partnership will not be permissible, either as *'inān* or as *mufāwaḍah.* The reason is that the purpose of the partnership is profit and this is achievable through transactions in the capital. Such transactions are not possible in a *dayn* nor in wealth that is absent. The purpose cannot be achieved. The presence (availability of the goods), however, is stipulated at the time of the transaction and not at the time of the contract. The contract of *sharikah* is completed with the purchase transaction.

[23] See Kāsānī, *Badā'i' al-sanā'i'*, vol.6, p.59.

> The availability of the goods comes into operation then.[24]

According to Imām Mālīk the capital should be present at the time the contract is concluded. The jurists are also unanimous that *mufāwaḍah* or *'inān* partnership cannot be concluded on debt.[25]

b. Intermingling of capitals

The majority of Muslims do not stipulate mixing of capitals (*khalṭ)* prior to the conclusion of the contract. In this regard Imām Sarakhsī says:

> In our view, *'inān* does not require the intermingling of investment. However, according to Zufar and Shāfi'ī, mingling is pre-requisite for a valid partnership. In the Shāfi'īs view, proprietary partnership (*sharikat al-milk)* is the underlying principle of all partnerships and that contractual partnership must be based on it.[26]

Shāfi'ī holds that the meaning of the word *sharikah* is intermingling and it is realized only through ownership. If the two investments are mingled in a manner that makes them indistinguishable from each other, then the partnership becomes effective through ownership and a contractual partnership can be built upon it. If one of the investments is lost before they are intermingled, the loss is borne exclusively by its owner and any projected contractual partnership cannot become effective because the capital did not undergo the process of intermingling.[27]

---

[24] Ibid., vol. 6, p.60.

[25] Ibn Rushd, *Bidāyat al-Mujtahid* vol.2, p.250.

[26] Sarakhsī, *al-Mabsūṭ*, vol.11, p.177 .

[27] Nawawī, *Minhāj*, vol.2, p.213.

The condition of intermingling in Shāfiʻī Law requires that the capital advanced by the parties be uniform, i.e., the currency should be of the same denomination and quality.

c. Absolute currency

It is also a condition for a valid *sharikat al-amwāl* that its investment is in the form of money. Assets in the form of merchandise are unsuitable for partnership investment. According to the majority of legal scholars, a partnership in which the investment consists of goods is invalid. Imām Mālik holds that capital in the form of currency is not a pre-requisite and that partnership in goods is permissible if their value is determined on the day the contract is concluded.

According to the majority, agency is the necessary attribute of partnership and agency is unrealisable in goods as investment. Kāsānī says;

> It is not permissible for one person to say to another: "Sell your goods so that we may share its price." Since agency, which is one of the indispensable features of partnership, is not permissible, partnership also is not permissible. It is, however, permissible for one to say to another: "Buy goods with the hundred *dirhams* belonging to you on the condition that what you buy be shared between us." [28]

He further writes:

> Partnership in goods is not permissible because it leads to ignorance regarding the profit at the time of division. For the amount of the investment will consist of the value that will not be known except with conjecture and estimation. The amount of profit

[28] Kāsānī, *Badā'iʻ al-Sanā'i*, vol.6, p.59.

will, therefore, be unknown and this will lead to dispute at the time of division. [29]

Kinds of *Sharikat al-Amwāl*

As mentioned earlier, *shariakt al-amwal* is divided into two kinds, i.e., *'inān sharikat al-amwal* or *sharikah al-amwāl* by way of *'inān* and *mufāwaḍah amwal* partnership or *sharikat al-amwāl* by way of *mufāwaḍah.*

Following is detailed description of both these kinds.

'Inān sharikat al-amwāl

Meaning of 'inān

It is derived from the word *'inān*, i.e., reins of riding animal. The rider holds the reins with one hand, while doing something with the other. Similarly, each one of the partners in this partnership hands over the reins (right) of transaction in some wealth to the other and not in the rest. Further, the animal has two reins, one longer and the other one shorter. Similarly, this partnership is permissible both with equal and unequal capital and labour.

The definition of *'inān*

It is a contract between two or more persons to work in any particular trade with determined capital and to share profit and loss with determined rates. All the Muslim jurists are unanimous on its validity.

Types of *sharikat al-'inān*

The *'inān* partnership on the basis of its scope is divided into two general categories:

---

[29] Ibid.

1. General *'inān* or ordinary *'inān* partnership.

2. Specific *'inān* or restricted *'inān* partnership.

General *'inān*

It is a partnership formed for the purpose of general trade with no restrictions with respect to the commodities that could be dealt with or the transactions that could be negotiated. Any legitimate trading activity designated to bring the profit comes within its purview.

Specific *'inān*

In this type of partnership, partners are confined to the trade with a certain category of goods defined in the partnership agreement. This agreement could be continuing one, spread over a considerable period of time and involving numerous transactions, or it could be limited to a single venture, i.e., the purchase of the desired merchandise and its subsequent sale. The mutual agency of the associates in the specific *'inān* extends only to the commodities or areas of trade agreed upon and no further.

General rules regarding the *'inān* partnership

Following are the general rules regarding the *'inān* partnership:[30]

a) Management: It is lawful that the partnership is carried out by both the partners or either of them.

b) Mutual agency and not surety: Each partner in *sharikat al-'inān* is the agent of the other partner, so he possesses all the rights of the agent. He is not required to be surety for the other.

[30] Zuhaylī, *al-Fiqh al-'Islāmī wa Addillatuhū,* vol.4, pp.415-416.

c) Equal or unequal capital: The *'inān* does not require equality, so the capital of one of the partners may be more than that of the other.

d) Equal or unequal distribution of profits: Profits may be divided equally or unequally. Thus, it is lawful that capital of each partner be equal and yet the profits be unequally distributed. It is permissible according to the Ḥanāfīs that profit be distributed unequally with the equality of capital provided the partner getting larger share of profit contributes extra labour for the extra amount because according to them the person is entitled to profit by capital labour and responsibility (*ḍamān*) and in the present case labour is causing profit. Thus, if one of them stipulates for himself a share in the profit proportionally larger than that of his colleague, this is permissible. Imām Zufar from amongst the Ḥanafīs does not agree with this opinion. Ḥanbalī and Zaidī jurists favour Ḥanafī viewpoint that profit follows the agreement, while the loss is according to the capital. According to Mālikī, Shāfi'ī and Zāhirī jurists and Zufar both profit and loss should be strictly in accordance with the capital as the profit is an increase in the capital and loss in the decrease so both should be governed by the capital.

Rights of partners in *'inān* partnership

The rights, duties and obligations of the *inān* partners pertain only to that portion of their respective property invested in the joint undertaking. In all matters that are not of their partnership, each of them is a stranger in relation to his other partner. Following are some important rights of partners in an *'inān* partnership:[31]

a) Right to sell goods for cash and credit: Each partner has the right to sell the goods of the *sharikah* for cash as well as for

[31] Ibid. vol.4, pp.415-416.

credit. Likewise, he has right to purchase for cash or for credit. He enjoys this right without any restriction and limitation on him. The right is conferred upon him by virtue of the contract and he does not need special permission from the other partners for doing so.

He cannot, however, purchase on credit in excess of the capital of the *sharikah*. This would amount to *istidānāh* for which special permission is required from the other partners. If other partners expressly authorize him he may incur debts in excess of the amount of partnership fund. *Istidānāh* means to purchase on credit for the partnership in excess of the capital. It is in fact a mode of enhancing financial liability of the investors.

b) Right to *ibḍā'*: *Ibḍā'* means to hand over the property and capital of partnership to a merchant, who is not partner in partnership business, to trade with it without receiving any remuneration or commission and to return it with profit to the partnership. The *'inān* partner has right to enter into an *ibḍā'* even if the partner does not expressly permit him to do so, because it is the practice among the businessmen. The reason for its permission is that he has a right to employ a person for the business in which he has to pay wages, while in *ibḍā'* he is not required to pay remuneration to the merchant, so it is more beneficial for business than to hire services of somebody for remuneration.

c) Right to *muḍārabah*: Each partner is also at liberty to give his capital in the way of *muḍārabah*, because the partnership is designed for profit and *muḍārabah* is a mode of earning profit.

d) Right to appoint agent: A partner in the *sharikat al-'inān* is at liberty to appoint a person as his agent for the business transactions. The businessmen cannot undertake all the business activities themselves so they often appoint others as their agents. This being requirement of business is permissible in *'inān* as well.

e) Right to mortgage or pledge: A partner in this *sharikah* can pledge or mortgage the assets of the partnership and also accept such pledges but only with the permission of the partners.

f) Right to deposit: The partner has the right to deposit goods belonging to the partnership; for depositing is one of the customary practices of merchants.

g) Contractual obligations of a partner: According to the Ḥanafīs all the obligations and rights arising from a contract made by a partner will revert to him. Thus if one of them has purchased something, or hired services, he alone will be sued with respect to claims arising from such transactions. Likewise, it is he who has right to sue third parties for all claims connected with the contract he concluded, and his other partners will be considered strangers as far as these claims are concerned.

h) Right to travel: According to majority of the Muslim jurists, a partner can also travel to another place with the *sharikah* property if there is no specification of place in the agreement, but according to Abū Yūsuf and Shāfi'ī the partner has no such right except by the explicit permission of his other partners.

i) Right to extend gift and *qarḍ*: A partner does not have right to gift the property of the partnership. Similarly, he does not have right to grant loan from the common funds.

Liability of partners in the *'inān* partnership

An *'inān* partnership comprehends mutual agency but not mutual surety. By virtue of this mutual agency but no mutual surety, each of them does not become liable for that which is owed by his colleague. Thus, liability towards third party is several but not joint.

Formation of the *'inān* partnership

Partnership in an *'inān* partnership is open to any person meeting the minimum standards of legal competence. There are no restrictions with respect to personal status, which is peculiar to *mufāwaḍah*. Any person of either sex who is of age and of sound mind may legitimately contract an *'inān* partnership.

Similarly, a difference in personal status between prospective partners does not constitute a barrier to the formation of a valid *'inān* partnership. An *'inān* partnership negotiated between two minors with the explicit approval of their guardians is valid, as is a partnership between Muslim and *dhimmī*.

Dissolution of the *'inān* partnership

The circumstances affecting the termination of all contractual partnerships including *'inān* partnership are as follows:

a) Recession of the contract by either party

Partnership can be terminated by the unilateral recession of one of its members. In this case the dissolution of partnership does not become effective until the other partners become aware of their partner's action. According to Section 43 of the Partnership Act 1932, in case of partnership at will any partner may dissolve the firm by serving notice in writing to all the existing partners of his intention to dissolve the firm.

b) Death of one partner

The death of one of the partners results in the immediate termination of the partnership because the underlying contract of *wakālah* becomes void (*bāṭil)* upon death and the *sharikah* is structured upon *wakālah*. As each of them is also the agent of the other and the death automatically discharges the agent, whether the latter knows about it or not. Any transaction conducted by the surviving partner after his colleague's demise and ignorance of the fact, will be strictly on his own account. Heirs of the deceased partner have no claim to the profits nor they are liable for any obligation, which might arise from any such transaction. There is no provision in Islamic law by means of which a partnership can remain intact after the death of one of its members. If the heirs wish to continue the association with the surviving partner, they must negotiate completely a new agreement.

c) Apostasy and emigration to enemy lands

If both the partners are Muslim, the apostasy of one of them and his emigration to non-Muslim territory *(dār al-harb)* results in the termination of partnership.

d) Insanity of one of the partners

The loss of mental competence by one of the partners also results in the termination of partnership, provided the insanity is continuous. The Muslim jurists disagree about the period of insanity. According to Abū Yūsuf, the period is one month, but according to Muhammad it is a full year. Thus *sharikah* will not stand dissolved before the expiry of this period.

e) Expiration of period

If the *sharikah* was established for a limited period, it will stand terminated by the expiration of that period. The same position has been taken by the law, as explained in Section 40 of the Partnership Act 1932.

f) Completion of venture

When the undertaking or venture is completed the partnership may be dissolved. Section-42 (b) of the Partnership Act 1932 also confirms this position.

g) Mutual consent

The partnership can also be terminated by the mutual consent of the whole capital or of the stock of each partner.

h) Loss of capital

(i) Loss of capital before purchase: If the whole partnership capital or the capital of either partner perishes before any purchase is made, the contract of partnership is annulled.

(ii) Loss of capital after intermingling: Where capital perishes after the mixture, the loss falls upon the partnership, because property of each is no longer distinguishable from other. So the loss must be borne by both parties.

(iii) Loss of capital after purchase by one partner: A purchase made by one partner where the capital of the other perishes afterwards is also shared by the both.

(iv) Loss of one capital before purchase of the other partner: If one partner makes a purchase with his own capital and the capital of the other afterwards perishes before he has made any purchase the purchased goods will be considered joint property of the parties and will be shared by them according to agreement.

Mufāwaḍhah sharikat al-amwāl

Mufāwaḍah literally means the participation in each thing with equality, but technically it has a narrower meaning, because it applies to equality in real estate and goods".[32]
The author of *Hidāyah* defines it in the following words:

> It is a contract of participation between two or more persons, with the condition of complete equality with respect to capital, profit and status, for working with

[32] Ibn 'Ābidīn, *Radd al-Muhtār*, vol.4, p.402.

> their own wealth, or with their labour in another's wealth, or on the basis of their credit-worthiness, so that each partner is a surety for the other.[33] This shows that in this partnership each partner enjoys complete equality in the areas of capital, management and right of disposition.

According to the Ḥanafīs *mufāwaḍah* contains the following elements.

i) Equality in wealth (capital), profit and loss and participation in the affairs of the partnership.

ii) Equality in contractual capacity and religion.

iii) Each partner is an agent of other partners.

iv) Each partner is also responsible on behalf of other partners of their acts and deeds, i.e., he is surety for his partner.

Sharikat al-a`māl: Work partnership

Definition

It is a partnership in which the partners contribute investment in the form of labour and skill. It is also called *sharikat al-abdān* because the partners perform manual labour, like tailors, butchers and so on. It is also known as *sharikat al-Ṣanā'i'* because the capital of the partners is their skill.

Through this *mushārakah* the artisans, technician and others skilled and unskilled labour join together in one or different places, without any capital to produce some commodity or perform some work, on the condition that they will divide between them the profits arising from it. The type of labour

---

[33] Marghinānī, *al-Hidāyah*, vol.3, p.3.

envisaged is usually a skill in some kind of manufacture such as tailoring, dyeing, or weaving.

The work partnership can take the form of limited partnership or unlimited partnership namely;

(i) *'Inān* work partnership

ii) *Mufāwaḍah* work partnership

'Inān work partnership

'Inān work partnership is based on the concept of agency and not on suretyship. Thus, each partner is liable only for the obligation personally incurred by himself.

Condition for Acceptance and Performance of Work

a. Right of accepting work and performing it

Each partner has the right to accept work and then to perform it himself on behalf of the *sharikah*. It is also permitted that one of them accepts work, while the other performs it. In a business that requires mixed labour, the work may be accepted by one and then performed jointly by both. For example, in the tailoring business, it is permitted that one person accepts work, cuts the cloth and then hands it over to his partner for stitching and completion.

b. Right to delegate the work accepted

No partner can be forced for personal performance of the work that he accepted. He is at liberty to do the work personally or to delegate it to another. If the customer stipulates performance of the work by a particular partner, in that case the partner has to perform it.

c. Performance of work is liability of each partner

The general rule in the contracts of personal services is that performance can be demanded from the person making the contract alone. As such, the Partner accepting the work should be sued for its performance. This rule, however, is given up in *'inān* work partnership on the basis of *istihsān*. Thus, either of the partners may be required to perform the work, which is accepted by his other partner. Similarly, each partner has right to demand remuneration from the customer.

The *Majallah* has explained this point in some detail;

> Each Partner is the agent of the other in the acceptance of work. For the work that is accepted by one of them, performance is binding upon him as well as his partner. *'Inān* by way of *sharikat al-a'māl* has the same *ḥukm* as *mufāwaḍah* with respect to *ḍamān al-'amal* (liability of work). Thus, the work accepted by one of the partners may be demanded by the customer from any partner he chooses. Each partner is (legally) bound for the performance of such work. He does not have the right to say: "This work was accepted by my partner and I have nothing to do with it." [34]

Section 1388 of the Majallah states that: *'Inān* by way of *sharikat al-a'māl* takes the *ḥukm* of *mufāwaḍah,* in the demand for compensation from the customer and for full satisfaction of the claim for wages. The customer is absolved of this liability by paying to one of them.

Division of profit

The profit in *'inān* work partnership is divided according to liability of work. It is not linked with the actual work

---

[34] *Majallah*, Article, 1387. See also Nyazee, *Islamic Law of Business Organization: Partnerships*, pp.150, 151.

undertaken by either of partners. The loss is also divided in proportion to liability borne. For example, if a partner becomes liable for one-third of the whole work accepted by the partnership, he would be entitled to 1/3 of the total profit earned by the partnership. In regard to the division of profit in *'inān* work partnership Imām Sarakhsī expounds his opinion in the following words:

> In the case of partners in work, if one of them is absent or is ill, or does not work, while the other is working, the profit is still to be shared by them according to what they have agreed upon. This is due to the tradition from the Messenger of Allah (s.a.w.s) that a person came to him and said: "I work in the market and I have a partner who prays in the mosque." The Messenger of Allah said: "Perhaps your work is blessed because of him." The meaning here is that claim to reward derives from acceptance of work and not necessarily from its direct execution. The acceptance is (presumed to be) from both, even if one of them works.[35]

The ratio fixed for the liability for performance is what will determine the ratio for sharing profits. It is obvious that if such a ratio for *ḍamān al-amal* is not fixed, it will be presumed to be equal.[36]

Mufāwaḍah work partnership

This partnership requires equal share of liability undertaken by each partner, and equal share of profit and loss. The compensation received for the work is shared equally by all the partners, irrespective of the fact that the work is done in the partnership or outside the business. In the *'inān* partnership

---

[35] Sarakhasī, *al-Mabsūṭ*, vol. 11, pp. 152-158.

[36] Ibid., vol. 11, p.154.

wages for work done by a partner outside the business belong to the partner alone.

Mālikī work partnership

Mālikī work partnership resembles the Ḥanafī work partnership closely, but in some aspects it is more restrictive than Ḥanafī partnership. For example, it requires that all its members should follow the same trade or profession.

The Following are some distinct features of the Mālikī work partnership:

1. Similarity of trade and uniformity of place

The partners should follow the same trade or profession like partnership between two tailors. The Mālikī jurists also prefer that both the partners should work in the same place, i.e., in the same stall.

2. Actual participation in work

All the partners should participate in actual work. A partnership in which all the work is assigned to one partner while the other provides some equipment but not work is invalid partnership. The non-working party would be entitled to some equitable rental fee for use of equipment. It is also not permissible that one accepts the work and the other undertakes the work.

3. Division of profit according to work

The division of profit and loss in this partnership follows each partner's work, which he contributes. No premium is placed on the quality of each partner's labour.[37]

---

[37] For Mālikī work partnership see Ibn Rushd, *Bidāyat al-Mujtahid*, vol.2, p.192.

Sharikat al-wujūh (Credit partnership)

According to Sarakhsī it is a partnership of two people without capital upon the condition that they will buy on credit and sell for cash. It has been called by this name on the grounds that they employ their credit-worthiness, because credit is extended only to those who have good reputation among the people (traders).[38] *Sharikat al-wujūh* or credit partnership can be of two types according to the Ḥanafīs:

(i) '*Inān* credit partnership

(ii) *Mufāwaḍah* credit partnership.

Conditions for sharing profit and loss in the *'inān* credit partnership

According to the Ḥanafī jurists the conditions for sharing of profit and loss in this type of partnership are as follows:

1. Specified share in the goods purchased

The primary condition for this type of partnership is that the share of the partners in the goods purchased must be specified. The remaining stipulations are based on this condition.

2. Entitlement to profit based upon liability

The type of liability mentioned in the *'inān* work partnership was called *ḍamān al-a'māl*. The type of liability involved here is the liability for the price of the purchased goods, and is based upon the share of ownership in the property purchased. Once something is purchased, it becomes the asset of the partnership and its value is based upon its price. The ratio in which this asset is owed by the partners is the basis and not the ratio of the debt owned. Thus, if the share of a partner is one-half in the purchased goods, he is liable for half the price owned for these

[38] Sarakhsī, *al-Mabsūt*, vol. II, pp.152-158.

goods. He is, therefore, entitled to half the profits. This shows that the profit in this partnership must correspond with the liability.

3. Unequal ownership in the purchased goods

Equality of ownership in the purchased goods is not a requirement. The partners may agree on any ratio of ownership they want, and the profit between them has to be distributed according to that ratio.

4. Stipulation of profits contrary to ownership

The stipulation of profits contrary to ownership is of no consequence. If an additional profit is stipulated for any partner, it means that the ratio of ownership is violated. The condition will, therefore, be ignored, if the liability for the price is equal. The reason appears to be that the skills, reputation and good work of one partner are already linked with the amount of credit a partner can raise. The ratio of ownership in the price has already taken all those things into account

5. Excess work

Excess work in this partnership is of no consequence for entitlement to profit. Sarakhsī says:

> In this contract a stipulation of profits in excess (over the ratio of ownership) is not valid when there is equality of ownership in the thing purchased. The reason is that this excess is not linked either to the share of the partner in wealth or to his work or to *ḍamān*. Stipulating such a part of the profits will amount to something that is not supported by liability to bear loss. If an excess of the profits is desired, it is necessary to stipulate corresponding excess in ownership of the purchased goods (and thus in the liability to bear loss). This way, it may be, that one

third is for one partner and two-third for the other, and thereafter the other profits may be shared in proportion to the ownership.[39]

Conditions for mufāwaḍah credit partnership according to the Ḥanafī jurists

The conditions of *mufāwaḍah* credit partnership differ from those of *'inān* in the following respects:

1. It is not necessary in this partnership to specify the share of a partner in the goods purchased on credit, because the contract of *mufāwaḍah* requires equality, and all the shares are equal. This makes equality of shares in goods purchased, a condition for this partnership. In *'inān*, the shares have to be specified.

2. Any partner may be sued for the price of the goods purchased, because he is an agent as well as surety for his partner(s). In *'inān,* the *ḥuqūq* (rights of performance) revert to the dealing partner, and the other partner cannot be sued.

3. Each thing purchased on credit by a partner for business purposes is bought for the joint business. This stipulation does not apply to goods purchased on cash for his personal business as the business transactions are entirely on a cash basis and should not be a part of the credit *sharikah*, because business on credit-worthiness is based upon credit purchased alone. The employment of cash payments would convert it to a *mufāwaḍah* based on *mal* (*sharikat al-amwāl* by way of *mufāwaḍah*).[40]

---

[39] Nyazee, *Islamic Law of Busines Organization: Partnerships*. p.155,156.

[40] Ibid. p.173.

Modern Forms of Partnership

The Islamic financial institutions frequently use *mushārakah* as a mode of financing which is considered also a real alternative to interest under an Islamic economic system. Following are some forms of *mushārakah* financing.

1. Project financing

Islamic Banks provide project finance on the basis of *mushārakah* One or two or more entrepreneurs approach the bank for finance and the bank along with other partners provides complete finance. All the partners, including the bank, have the right to participate in the management of the project. Any one or all of them also have right to waive this right. The profits are distributed according to agreed ratios, which need not be the same as capital proportion but loss has to be shared exactly in the same proportion in which different partners provided finance.

Since the finance in the above mentioned case is provided completely by the bank and its partners, they jointly assume the role of *arbāb al-māl* (financers) and the entrepreneurs, the *muḍāribūn*. Thus, it is a type of *muḍārabah* partnership. But if the investment is provided by both the parties, i.e., the bank and entrepreneurs or the businessmen then it is a *mushārakah* arrangement. The bank before financing any project gets it evaluated by its experts. If it is found feasible and is expected to be profitable, and there is satisfaction on the part of bank that the entrepreneurs have sufficient experience to handle the project, then the partnership is negotiated. Profits are allocated according to an agreed proportion, allowing for managerial skills to be remunerated. This type of *mushārakah* terminates with the project's completion.

2. Financing of a single transaction

Islamic banks also provide finances in order to meet day to- day needs of small traders. The traders approach the bank requesting it to finance purchase of certain goods. Now if the bank considers transaction profitable, it finances purchase of required goods on the basis of *mushārakah*. Then the goods are sold in the market and both the parties share profit in proportion to their investment.

This instrument can also be employed for financing of imports and exports. If the letter of credit has been opened without any margin, the form of *murābaḥah* is adopted, and if the L/C is opened with some margin, the form of *mushārakah* is observed. After the import goods are cleared from the port, their sale proceeds are shared by the importer and the financer according to a pre-agreed ratio. In this case the ownership of the imported goods remains with the financer, to the extent of the ratio of his investment.

3. Redeemable *mushārakah*

In this category, the bank participates in the capital of a company, or a business venture or agricultural project on the condition that it will recapture its initial investment along with its agreed share in the profit. The other partner or partners also promise at the time of contract that they will purchase the share of bank in the investment and will gradually become the sole owners of that project. Suppose A, a client, owns a piece of land worth 100,000/- rupees. He does not have money to construct house. So he approaches B, a bank for finances. B agrees to provide required finance on the condition that it will share the rent of that house and will also get back its initial investment of Rs. 100000. They also agree that on the return of B's capital, A, the client will become the sole owner of that house. On the completion of house, rent is fixed, say, at Rs. 1000/- per month, which is to be shared by the parties in proportion to their share in the investment. It is also agreed between the parties that A, the client will pay to the bank after every six months a sum of Rs. 20000 worth capital of bank B. The client A pays first instalment of the capital to A on stipulated date. This payment increases the share of A in the investment from Rs. 100000 to Rs. 120000 i.e. from 50% to 60%, and consequently his share in the rent is also increased from Rs. 500 to Rs. 600. After the payment of second instalment share of A in investment goes up to Rs. 140000 raising his ratio of capital also to 70% while the share of B, the bank is reduced to Rs. 60000/- and consequently its share in rent is also reduced to that proportion. This process goes on until after the payment of all instalments in a period of two years and half, the client becomes the sole owner of that house.[41]

Diminishing Partnership in Islamic Banks

DM defined

"A partnership in which a party after participation in ownership of an asset can redeem his capital along with some profit gradually".

DM contract

- DM consists of three contracts i.e, co-ownership, *ijārah* and sale in the following manner:
- A contract between bank and client partner to create a joint ownership.
- Promise by client partner to purchase the share of bank.
- Bank gives units of his share to the clients on lease.
- Client partner goes on purchasing the units of ownership of bank and the rent goes on decreasing.
- After the purchase of shares of bank, client partner becomes the sole owner of asset.

[41] See Taqī 'Usmānī, *Introduction to Islamic Finance*, p.61.

Application of DM for house financing

- A, a client and B, a bank buy a house for one lac rupees with contribution of Rs.20000/- and Rs.80000/- respectively.
- A, owns two units and B owns eight units of ownership. Value of each unit is Rs.10000/-.
- B, promises to buy one unit of A's share quarterly.
- A, gives his share (Eight units) to B on lease of Rs.1000/- per month.
- A's share in rent is Rs.200/- and B's share is Rs.800/-.
- After three months A buys one unit by paying Rs.10000/-.
- Now share of bank's ownership is decreased from eight units to seven units.
- Share of bank in rent is decreased from Rs.800/- to Rs.700/-.
- After the purchase of all units the house becomes the sole property of the client.
- Bank's share of Rs.80000/- may be divided into 20 or 40 units depending on the capacity of client to pay back bank's share.

Diminishing *musharakah* for construction

- DM may be used for construction of house.
- A, a client owns land worth 10 million rupees and needs 8 million from B, an Islamic bank for construction.
- B, Islamic bank buys part of plot for 8 million (buys 8 units).
- Pays this amount in four equal installments.
- When the house is complete, bank leases its part of ownership to the client, at agreed rentals.
- One year after the disbursement of last installment, the bank would start selling its units.

- Up to one year, client will only pay rent on the bank's part of house.
- On purchase of unit, by the client, ownership of bank in house will decrease and its share in rent will also decrease.
- On the purchase of last unit, the client will become sole owner of house.

Conclusion

- *Mushārakah* is a relationship between persons to share profit of a business.
- *Mushārakah* is based on the principle of agency.
- There are two main kinds of *mushārakah,* i.e., proprietary partnership and contractual partnership.
- Contractual partnership is further divided into three kinds:
    - *Sharikat al-amwāl* (investment partnership.
    - *Sharikat al-a'māl* (work partnership).
    - *Sharikat al-wujūh* (credit partnership)
- According to Ḥanbalī jurists *muḍārabah* is also a kind of contractual partnership.
- In *sharikat al-amwāl* and *muḍārabah* it is necessary that the capital should be in the form of money, present at the time of contract. In case of *muḍārabah* the additional requirement is that it should be handed over to the *muḍārabah*
- Entitlement to profit: A partner is entitled to profit in a contractual partnership by capital, work and liability.
- *Sharikat al-amwāl* may be concluded either in the form of *'inān* or *mufāwaḍah.* In case of *'inān* partnership, the

partners may contribute amounts and may share profits at different rate while in *mufāwaḍah* they contribute equal capital and get equal share of profit.

- In *mufāwaḍah* each partner provides surety for the other partner because it is based on the idea of mutual surety.
- In all partnerships, the liability towards third party is several but not joint, while in *mufāwaḍah* liability towards third parties is several and joint.
- *Sharikat al-a'māl* (work partnership) is a partnership on work and labour as the capital of partnership. According to the Mālikī jurists the partners must belong to the same trade, and they should work in one place. Besides, all he partners should participate in actual work and should get profit according to their work.
- In *sharikat al-wujūh* (credit partnership) profit flows from the responsibility undertaken to provide capital from loans raised by the partners on account of their goodwill or influence.

Chapter 17

Contract of *Muḍārabah*

Muḍārabah, *qirāḍ*, and *muqāraḍah'* are different terms used to express special type of the business arrangement in which the capital is from one side while the labour or work is from the other side.

The word *muḍārabah'* is derived from the phrase *"al-ḍarb fīl arḍ"* which means to make journey. It is called so because the worker strives and toils in course of business. Likewise, the words *qirāḍ* and *muqāraḍah* are derived from the word *qaraḍa'* that means to cut off. It is so called because the investor cuts off the disposition of his sum of money from himself and transfers its disposition to the agent.

Various Definitions of *Muḍārabah*

The following are the definitions of *muḍārabah* in different schools of law.

Ḥanafī school

"It is a partnership *(sharikah)* for participation in profit in which capital is from one side, whereas labour or skill *(ʿamal)* is from the other side."[1]

Mālikī school

"*Qirāḍ* is an agency for trading in delivered cash for a part of profits if their extent is known"[2]

---

[1] Ibn 'Ābidīn, *Radd al-Muhtār*, 5:645.

[2] *Kharshī* 6:2

Shāfi'ī school

It is an agreement whereby an owner hands over the capital to a worker who trades with it and the profit is shared by the parties.[3]

Ḥanbalī school

It is where a person gives his capital to another person for business in order to share the profit according to stipulation.[4]

Modern definitions of *muḍārabah*

A renowned scholar 'Alī al-Khafīf has defined *muḍārbah* as "contract for sharing the profit of a business in which one party contributes with capital and other with his labour."[5]

Dr. Rashād Khalīl, another scholar, has defined that it is a contract whereby a legally competent person hands over a known and defined capital to a person possessed with reason and discretion to trade with it for a part of profit defined in proportion.[6]

It is important to note here that Islamic Law, unlike English Law does not differentiate between a company and partnership firm. Therefore, *muḍārabah* can be a partnership firm as well as a company. This difference has given rise to a controversy between State Bank of Pakistan (SBP), Corporate Law Authority (CLA), and the Finance Ministry as to which category of business organization a *muḍārabah* will be referred to, and what rules of taxation, tariffs and revenue will be activated against it. The stance of CLA is that it is a financial

[3] Shirbīnī, *Mughnī al-Muḥtāj*, vol. 2, p.309.

[4] Ibn Qudāmah, *al-Mughnī*, vol. I5, p.134.

[5] Alı al-Khafīf, *al-Sharikāt fī al-Fiqh al-Islāmī*, Cairo:1941, p.65.

[6] Rashād Khalīl, *al-Sharikāt fī al-Fiqh al-Islāmī*, Maktabah Tawfīqiyyah, Cario:1399/1979, p.154.

institution like House Building Finance Corporation (HBFC), whereas SBP is arguing that it is a bank.

Legitimacy of *Muḍārabah*

The legitimacy of *muḍārbah* is established by the Qur'ān, the *Sunnah* and *'ijmā'*.

Qur'ān

The Qur'ān says, "And others who journey through the earth seeking the bounty".[7] Abū Bakr Jassas explains that they seek bounty of Allah through trade and disposition.[8]

Sunnah

1. The Holy Prophet (s.a.w.s.) is reported to have said: "There is great blessing in three things: The credit sale, the *muḍārabah* and mixing wheat and barley for domestic consumption, not for sale."
2. The Holy Prophet (s.a.w.s) gave his tacit approval to the conditions imposed by Ibn 'Abbās (r.a.t.a.) who used to give money on the basis of *muḍārabah.*
3. The aforesaid tacit approval has also been reported in the case of Ibn Ḥizām (r.a.t.a).
4. The Holy Prophet (s.a.w.s.) himself acted as *muḍārib* (agent/manager) for Khadījah (r.a.t.a.) prior to his marriage.

Ijmā'

Many instances have been cited to prove that *'mudārabah'* was a lawful business and was frequently employed by companions

---

[7] Qur'ān 73:20.

[8] Jaṣṣāṣ, *Ahkām al-Qur'ān* 3:45.

of Holy Prophet (s.a.w.s.). Some of the examples are the following:

Abū Mūsā, the Governor of Kūfā wanted to remit public money to the *bayt-al-māl*. He gave the amount to Abd Allah (r.a.t.a.) and 'Ubayd Allah (r.a.t.a.) sons of caliph `Umar (r.a.t.a.). They traded with it. The Caliph's assembly that comprised of many companions of the Holy Prophet (s.a.w.s.) treated it to be an ex-post facto *muḍarabah* and took half of the profits earned by two brothers, in addition to the public money.[9]

It is also reported that Caliph 'Umar (r.a.t.a.) used to invest orphan's property on the basis of *muḍārabah'*.

Qiyās

As for as analogy is concerned, diverse views of scholars are found. This diversity is because some say that *muḍārabah* defies analogy while others allow analogy.

According to Imām Sarakhsī *muḍārabah* is proved by way of juristic preference *(istiḥsān)* and not by analogy. He writes: Analogy is not permissible, because it is hiring for unknown wages, in fact for non-existent wages. The work too is unknown. It is permissible on the basis of *istiḥsān*.

He adds:

> It is also allowed because people have a need for this contract. The owner of capital may not find his way to profitable trading activity, and the person who can find his way to such activity, may not have the capital. And profit cannot be attained except by means of both

[9] Shawkānī, *Nayl al-Awṭār* 5:236; Kāsānī, *Badā'i'* vol.6, p.79, Mālik ibn Anas, *al-Muwaṭṭa* , vol.2, p.987.

> of these, that is capital and trading. By permitting this, the goal of both parties is attained.[10]

Elements of *Muḍarabah*

According to the Ḥanafīs, *muḍārabah* consists of only one element, i.e. forms (offer and acceptance). This is provided in *Majallah*, in the following words:

> The essence of a *muḍārabah* is an offer and acceptance. For example: If the owner of capital says to the person who provides the labour "Take this capital and do the work and labour in return, on the terms that the profits are to be divided between us, half and half, or, as two to one," or if he says anything else which represents the meaning of a *muḍarabah* like, "Take this money and make it capital and let the profit be in common between us in this proportion," and the *muḍārib* (working partner) accepts, a contract of *muḍārabah'* is concluded.[11]

Shāfi'īs acknowledge five elements for a *muḍārabah* contract namely:

(a) Parties to '*muḍārabah* contract *('āqidān)*

(b) Work/labour. *('amal)*

(c) Profit

(d) Capital

(e) The form (offer and acceptance)

In the opinion of the majority or *jamhūr*, *muḍārabah* has three elements:

---

[10] Sarakhsī, *al-Mabsūṭ*, vol.22, p.19.

[11] *Majallah*, Article 1405.

(a) Parties to *muḍārabah* contract. *('Āqidān)*

(b) Subject matter *(ma'qūd 'alayh)*

(c) The form (offer and acceptance)[12]

Conditions of *Muḍārabah*

Conditions relating to *muḍārabah* are of three kinds:

a) Conditions concerning partners

The partners must have legal capacity to enter into a contract of *muḍārabah*. This legal capacity includes competence to develop a 'Principal'-'Agent' relationship. This requires that none of the parties should be insane or minor or placed under interdiction because of insolvency or weakness of intellect *(safah)*. The competency of a partner is codified in the *Majallah* as under:

> It is a condition that the owner of property should be competent to appoint an agent, and that the *muḍārib* should be competent to be his agent.[13]

b) Conditions relating to capital

The capital used in *muḍārabah* must fulfill the following conditions;

(1) Capital must be in absolute currency. It must be in absolute currency or in financial form or must contain money properties (as economists call it). Merchandised form' or goods are prohibited. However, Ḥanafīs and Ḥanbalīs allow it in the case, financing partner first sells them out and then gives money for business to his working partner. Some details about it are given in the *Majallah* which are as follows: "It is a condition that the capital be some kind of

---

[12] See Kāsānī, *Badā'i' al-sanā'i'*, vol. 6, p.87; *Hāshiyat al-Dusūqī* vol.3, p.517.

[13] *Majallah,* Article 1408.

silver or gold money."[14] "Brass coins which pass current are by custom considered to be like silver or gold".[15]

Goods and commodities are not regarded eligible capital in *muḍārabah* partnership, because they render the amount of profit uncertain which may lead to dispute and litigation among the parties. Kāsānī Says:

> The *muḍārabah* in goods leads to uncertainty concerning the amount of the profit at the time of division. This is so because the value of the goods is known only by estimation, chance and conjecture and will differ with the difference of those who do the estimating. An uncertainty in turn leads to dispute and, consequently, to discord.[16]

They may also lead to inequitable advantage and undue enrichment for one of the parties and converse disadvantage to the other, because of the fluctuation of price of goods between the date they are remitted to the agent-manager and the date of their conversion into ready money. Writes Sarakhsī;

> Since the profit in *muḍārabah* emerges only after the investment has been returned, in fact to the investor, any marked rise in the market value of goods serving as the basis for the *muḍārabah* would cancel out any profit for the agent. Any drop in the market value would put the investor at a disadvantage and provide the agent with unjustified and, in a sense, unearned profit.[17]

---

[14] Ibid., Article 1338.

[15] Ibid., Article 1339.

[16] Kāsānī, *Badā'i' al-Sanā'i'*, vol.6, p.82.

[17] Sarakhsī, *al-Mabsūt*, vol. 22, p.23.

2. It should be known and defined in terms of quality and quantity. An uncertainty and indeterminacy concerning the amount of capital renders the contract invalid.

3. It should be ready cash, and not absent money in the form of debt, or money usurped by someone. But it is permissible to authorise a person to collect the debt and make it a capital of *muḍārabah*. It is also lawful to the majority of jurists to start *muḍārabah* with a capital lying as deposit with the agent *(muḍārib)* or someone else. The investor in this case may instruct the agent to collect the money from the depositor and use it as capital of *muḍārabah*, or he may directly arrange with the depositee to change the status of his capital from that of a deposit to that of *muḍārabah* investment.[18]

The Mālikī jurists do not permit the shifting of capital in the form of debt into *muḍarabah* capital. Udovitich explains the position of Maliki Law on this point in the following words:

> For a creditor to ask the debtor to use the amount of money owed as a *muḍārabah* investment is not permissible because a *muḍārabah*' cannot be formed with liable money, i.e., money for which the agent has some liability. Undoubtedly another reason for excluding this type of arrangement, although not stated in the sources, is the easy abuse to which it could be put in concealing a usurious loan.[19]

4. It should be handed over to the agent. All the Muslim jurists are unanimous on the point that the transfer of control over the money to the agent is pre-requisite for the

---

[18] Ibid.; Shirbīnī, *Mughni al-Muḥtāj* 2:31; Dusūqī, *Hāshiyat al-Dusūqi* 3:518, Ibn Qudāmah, *al-Mughnī* 5:68

[19] Uduvitch, *Partnership and profit in Medieval Islam*, p.187.

validity of *muḍārabah*. This is necessary so that agent is able to trade with it.

c) Conditions relating to profit

The conditions of profit are as follows:

1. Both the parties should know it. It is not valid to leave profit unsettled at the time of agreement.

2. Division of profit should be on proportional basis such as one-half, one-third, one-fourth. It is, therefore, not permissible to fix a specific amount as profit for one of the contracting parties. In case all the profit is stipulated for *muḍārib,* then it is no longer a contract of *muḍārabah* instead; it is a contract of loan. This is the viewpoint of the Ḥanafi and Ḥanbalī jurists.[20] According to the Shāfi'ī *fuqahā* the contract of *muḍārabah* will become invalid because *muḍārabah* requires proportional division of profit, which is non-existent in this case. It cannot be called loan contract also, because the contract was not concluded for that purpose.[21] If all the profit is stipulated for investor, then the contract is no longer a contract of *muḍārabah,* rather it will become an *ibḍā'* activity.[22] It is necessary that profit should not be stipulated for one party, as also it is necessary that it should be proportional. Any violation of proportional division rule renders the *muḍārabah* invalid and in such case it is treated as a regular hire *('ijārah)* with the agent entitled to an equitable remuneration *(ajr mithl)* for his work, but thereby disqualified from any share in the profit. On the other hand, in case of loss, the agent is free

[20] Kāsānī, *Badā'i' al-sanā'i'*, Vol. 6, p. 86., Ibn Qudīmah, *al-Sharh al-Kabīr* vol.5, p.131.

[21] Shirbīnī, *Mughnī al-Muhtāj*, vol. 2, p.313.

[22] Kāsānī, *Badā'i' al-sanā'i'*, Vol. 6, P. 86.

of responsibility because in this matter he is a trusted person.[23]

Types of *Muḍārabah*

Muḍārabah is of two types: absolute or unrestricted *muḍārabah* and restricted *muḍārabah*. The absolute type is the one in which the capital is handed over without determination of the type of work that is to be done, the location, the time, the quality of work and the person with whom the *muḍārib* has to trade.

Unrestricted *muḍārabah*

It is also called unlimited mandate or perpetual or absolute *muḍārabah*. The *Majallah* defines it in the following words:

> Unrestricted *muḍārabah* is a *muḍārabah*, which is not restricted in terms of time, place, kind of trade, or person from whom he is to buy and to whom he is to sell. But if it is restricted with one of these, it is a restricted *muḍārabah*. For example: If one says, "Buy and sell at such a time or in such a place, or sell such a kind of property, or, trade with such person or with the inhabitants of such a town," It is a restricted *muḍārabah*.[24]

The above mentioned definition imparts that if a *muḍārabah* is free from restrictions regarding time, place, trade policy, and person with whom business is to be done, it is called absolute or unrestricted *muḍārabah*. The working partner in all such cases is left exclusively on his own prudence and discretion. His authority may extend from very minor issue to major issues in investing the capital money for earning profit. Thus, the working partner has every right to use money in the manner he

---

[23] Udovitch, *Partnership and profit in Medieval Islam*, p.191.

[24] *Majallah*, Article 1407,

deems fit. In such case he is permitted to undertake all such transactions, which are allowed in commercial usage.

Permissible dispositions in absolute *muḍarabah*

The Following are transactions and dispositions, which are allowed for *muḍārib;*

1. To buy and sell all types of merchandise as he sees fit.
2. To buy and sell for cash and credit.
3. To give goods as *biḍā'ah.*
4. To keep them as deposit or pledge.
5. To hire helpers as needed.
6. To rent or buy animals and equipment.
7. To travel with the capital.
8. To mingle it with his own resources
9. To give it as *muḍārabah* to a third party.
10. To invest it in a partnership with a third party.[25]

Summarizing the permissible dispositions of *muḍārabah* Sarakhsī Writes:

> If the investor says to the agent, "act with it as you see fit", then he may practice all of these things except the loan. For the investor has consigned the control of his capital to the agent's discretion in a comprehensive way; and we know that his intention is the inclusion of all that is the customary practice of merchants. The agent, thereby, has the right to engage in *muḍārabah,*

[25] Uduvitch, *Partnership and profit in Medieval Islam*, p.204.

> a partnership and to mingle the capital with his own capital because this is a practice of the merchants.[26]

From this, we may conclude that the validity of agent's action will be determined by comparing his questioned action with the customary practice of the merchants. If such action conforms to the practice, then it is legitimate and binding upon the investor. He, however, is not allowed to commit *muḍārabah* partnership to any sum greater than the capital in hand without the investor's specific authorization. Similarly, he is not permitted to borrow money on behalf of *muḍārabah* unless he is specifically authorized to do so.

Restricted *muḍārabah*

Muḍārabah is restricted when the liberty of action of agent *(muḍārib)* is restricted in terms of kind of trade, time, and place. The restrictions allowed to be imposed by the investor are not a matter of agreement among the jurists. For example, the restriction to purchase from a particular person is permissible to Ḥanfīs and Ḥanbalīs but not permissible to according to Shāfi'īs and Mālikīs.[27]

The restriction to purchase goods from a particular place is valid according to the Ḥanafī, Ḥanbalī jurists but not valid to Malikis and Shāfi'īs. The condition to trade in particular merchandise such as books, gold and silver is valid to all the jurists. The Mālikī and Shāfi'ī jurists, however, suggest additional condition that such merchandise should be habitually available in the market.[28] As regards restricting *muḍārabah* with a

---

[26] Sarakhsī, *al-Mabsūṭ* vol.22, p.39.

[27] Sarakhsī, *al-Mabsūt* vol. 22, p.42; Ibn Qudāma, *al-Muhgnī* vol.5, p.69, Ibn Rushd, *Bidāyah al-Mujtahid*, vol. 2, p.213, Shīrāzī, *al-Muhadhdab* vol.1, p.392.

[28] Dusūqī, *Hāshiyat al-Dusūqī* Vol.3, p.53, Shirbīnī, *Mughnī al-Muhtāj*, vol. 2, p.311.

predetermined duration, the Mālikīs and Shāfi'îs refuse to recognize the validity of such condition whereas Ḥanbalīs and Ḥanafis regard it to be valid.

It is worth noting that when a *muḍārabah* is of predetermined duration, this does not mean that the investor and the agent-manager are precluded from making use of their basic right, that of withdrawing from *muḍārabah* at will. It only means that the agent- manager is not entitled, after the elapse of the pre-agreed duration to continue performing act of commerce on behalf of *muḍārabah,* if we accept the liquidation.[29]

From preceding discussion we may conclude that imposing restriction on the activity of agent is permissible, provided these do not grossly hamper and frustrate the purpose of *muḍarabah,* which is to get profit.

Dissolution of *muḍarabah*

The *muḍārabah* contract is dissolved under the following circumstances:

1. Unilateral termination

Since the contract of *muḍārabah* is a non-binding contract, any partner can terminate it unilaterally provided the other partner is made known of this decision and the capital is in the cash form. However, if the capital is in the form of goods, the termination of contract and the disengagement of agent by investor is not allowed. In such case the agent has right to sell the goods in order to reconvert them to cash.

2. By expiry of fixed time

If the *muḍārabah* was for a fixed time, it will be terminated on the expiry of that period. This is provided in *Majallah* in the

[29] Nabīl salih, *Unlawful gain and Legitimate Profit in Islamic Law*, pp.140-141

following words: "When the owner of the capital has fixed the duration of *muḍārabah*, the *muḍārabah* is dissolved when the prescribed time elapses".[30]

3. By death of any of the partners

If any of the partners in a *muḍārabah* dies, *muḍārabah* comes to an end. *Majalla* puts it in the following words: "If the owner of the capital, or the *muḍārib* (working partner) dies, the *muḍārabah* is dissolved."[31]

4. By insanity of any of the partners

In case any of the partners becomes insane the *muḍārabah* will come to an end.

"If the owner of the capital, or the *muḍārib*, dies, or becomes continuously mad the *muḍārabah* is dissolved."[32]

5. By disregard of express direction

The working partner is under the obligation to abide by direction of financing partner in a restricted *muḍārabah*. Thus, if he does not comply with these instructions the *muḍārabah* will be dissolved by virtue of the breach of trust on which *muḍārabah* stands.[33]

Majallah explains this point in the following words: "If the *muḍārib* (working partner) goes beyond what he is permitted, or acts contrary to the condition, he becomes a wrongdoer (*ghāṣib).* In case he has done so, the profit and loss from the

---

[30] *Majallah,* Article 1423.
[31] Ibid., Article 1429.
[32] *Majallah*, Article 1429.
[33] Ibid., Article 1422.

trading falls on him, and if property of the partnership is lost, he is responsible."[34]

6. By destruction of capital

The *muḍārabah* is also dissolved by the destruction of capital before initial purchase has taken place. The agent will not be held liable for this destruction if he exercised maximum care. But if it is destroyed due to his negligence or by some action on his part, then he is responsible. However, the *muḍārabah* in all such cases will stand dissolved.

Conclusion

- *Muḍarabah* is a partnership in which capital is from one side whereas labour or skill is from the other side.
- The capital in this partnership must be in absolute currency, it should be ready cash not in the form of debt and should be handed over to the *muḍārib*.
- The division of profit should be on proportional basis such as one-half, one third etc.
- *Muḍārabah* is of two types i.e. restricted and unrestricted.
- *Muḍārabah* is dissolved by unilateral termination, expiry of fixed time, death and insanity of a partner and the destruction of capital.

---

[34] Ibid., Article 1421.

Chapter 18

Contract of *Kafālah* (Suretyship or Guarantee)

Definition

Literally the word *kafālah* means joining and merging. Technically it is defined as merging of one liability with another in respect of demand for performance of an obligation.[1] Thus, the liability of principal obligor is merged with that of the surety for the discharge of a pecuniary obligation or debt or the delivery of property. According to this definition the claim or demand may be addressed to both the surety and principal debtor. The creditor or oblige can call upon either the original debtor or the surety to perform the obligation. As regards debt the principal debtor remains primarily liable for his debt.

Elements of *Kafālah*

According to majority viewpoint, contract of *kafālah* has five elements:

(i) *Kafīl* or *ḍāmin (surety)*
(ii) *Makfūl bihī* or *maḍmūn* (subject matter of *kafālah)*
(iii) *Makfūl 'anhu* or *maḍmūn 'anhu* (obligor)
(iv) *Sīghah* i.e., offer and acceptance (form of contract)
(v) *Makfūl lahū* (oblige or creditor)

Legitimacy of *Kafālah*

Kafālah is established by the Qur'ān, the Sunnah and *ijmā'* (consensus of opinion).

---

[1] Marghinānī, *al-Hidāyah*, pp. 317, 318.

Qur'ān

In *Sūrah Yūsuf*, the prophet Yūsuf (s.a.w.s) guaranteed to give a camel-load to the one who would restore the missing drinking cup of the king. The Qur'ān: says "He who restores it, shall have a camel-load, and I guarantee it."[2]

Sunnah

(i) Holy Prophet (s.a.w.s) said, "The guarantor is responsible."[3]

(ii) It is narrated in Ṣaḥīḥ Bukhārī that the Holy Prophet (s.a.w.s) once refused to lead the funeral prayer of a person because he had not paid off his debts. On that Abū Qatādah, a companion of the Holy Prophet (s.a.w.s) undertook to pay his debt, so the Prophet (s.a.w.s) accepted his guarantee and led the prayer.[4]

Ijmā'

Besides, there is a consensus of opinion among all Muslim jurists that *kafālah* is a valid contract because it serves the need of the people. It secures the right of the creditor and repels harm from the debtor.

Kinds of Suretyship

Suretyship is of two kinds:

(1) *Kafālah bi al-nafs*, i.e., suretyship for the person.

(2) *Kafālah bi al-māl*, i.e., suretyship for the property or the surety for the discharge of claim.

---

[2] Qur'ān 12:72.
[3] Ibid., vol. 5, p. 314.
[4] Shawkānī, *Nayl al-Awṭār*, vol. 5, p. 251.

1. *Kafālah bi al-nafs*

This is a contract whereby the surety undertakes to produce the person. This is generally required when a person becomes surety to produce an accused person before the court of law. The *kafālah* for person is lawful in the opinion of all jurists except Imam Shāfi'ī who is of the view that surety for the production of person cannot exercise authority over the accused person and as such it is not valid.[5]

2. *Kafālah bi al-māl*

It is the suretyship for the satisfaction of claim whereby the surety may be called upon to perform the obligation of the principal debtor if he makes default in the payment of his debt. *Kafālah bi al-māl* is further divided into following kinds:

(i) *Kafalah bi al-dayn* (suretyship for debt): It means to guarantee the payment of debt to the creditor owed by the principal debtor.

(ii) *Kafālah bi al-Taslīm* (Suretyship for possession): It is to be surety to deliver property to its owner such as to be surety on behalf of a lessee to transfer possession of leased property to the lessor or his agent on expiry of the lease period.

(iii) *Kafālah bi al-dark*: *Kafālah bi al -dark* is a guarantee by a seller that he will return the price of object if it is taken over by somebody else in exercise of his better right. It is also defined as a "guarantee in favour of seller that if the title of the seller is defective, the surety will make good the loss suffered by the purchaser on that account".

---

[5] Shirbīnī, *Mughnī al-Muhtāj*, vol. 2, p. 203; Shīrāzī, *al-Muhadhdhab*, vol. 1, p. 342.

Contract of Guarantee in English Law

Contract Act 1872 describes a contract of guarantee and its related terms in the following words:

> A Contract of guarantee is a contract to perform the promise, or discharge the liability of a third person in case of his default. The person who gives the guarantee is called "surety", the person in respect of whose default the guarantee is given is called the "principal debtor" and the person to whom the guarantee is given is called the creditor.[6]

This definition suggests that a surety can undertake to perform the promise, i.e., to discharge the liability on behalf of the principal. The Pakistani Law relating to guarantee provides the following three types of guarantee:

1. General Guarantee: It is a guarantee, which is given for all acts and obligations of a person(s). It is usually without any condition and restriction.
2. Specific Guarantee: When a guarantee is given for a specific transaction only, it is called specific guarantee.
3. Continuing Guarantee: It is provided in Sec-129 in the following words: "A guarantee, which extends to a series of transactions is called continuing guarantee".[7].

Rules of *Kafālah*

Following are some important rules of the contract of *kafālah*. They relate to *makfūl 'anhu* (principal debtor or obligor), *kafīl* (surety) *makfūl lahū* (creditor or obligee) and *makfūl bihī* (subject-matter)

[6] *Contract Act*, 1872, Section; 126.
[7] *Contract Act*, 1872, Art 129.

Kafālah for principal debtor who dies insolvent

According to Imam Abū-Ḥanīfah a suretyship for a principal debtor who dies in a state of insolvency is not valid, because he is unable to perform his obligation. It is a debt, which stands discharged after his death. However, if a person dies solvent, he will be considered capable of performing his obligation. Imām Abū Ḥanīfah interprets the suretyship of Abū Qatādah as an acknowledgement of an old suretyship concluded between him and the deceased (principal debtor) during his lifetime. In opposition to this view, Imām Abū Yūsuf and Muhammad hold that *Kafālah* for an insolvent deceased is valid, because death does not discharge the liability of an insolvent debtor. Commenting on the *hadīth* of Abū Qatādah they say that the Holy Prophet (s.a.w.s) had urged his companions to become surety for the debt of deceased person. He had asked them to undertake the payment of debt at the time of funeral prayer. The undertaking and suretyship of Abū Qatādah was in response to that appeal. It was not an old suretyship concluded during lifetime of debtor, as understood by the other jurists. This is an evidence of the fact that the debt existed and was not annulled by the death of the principal debtor.[8]

Another proof of the existence of debt is that if a person accepts the payment of debt voluntarily on behalf of deceased, it is lawful for creditor to demand from him. This also proves that the deceased is not released from his liability in any manner.

The possibility of there being an old suretyship in the *hadīth* of Abū Qatādah has been ruled out by the majority. They say that another *hadīth* makes manifest that it was creation of new suretyship. *Ḥadīth* discloses that Abū Qatādah voluntarily

---

[8] Kāsānī *Badā'i'al-sanā'i'*, vol.6, p.6; Ibn Rushd, *Bidāyat al-Mujathid*, vol.2, p.294.

became surety for the undischarged liability of the deceased debtor.[9]

The stand point of Imām Abū Ḥanīfah has been explained by the author of "*I'lā al-Sunan*" in the following words: "If the purpose of *kafālah* of deceased is to safeguard and secure creditor's right and to provide him a right to claim his debt from surety, then such *kafālah* is invalid because obligation of *kafālah* is to share the responsibility of the principal debtor regarding the repayment of debt while in case of the death of the principal debtor, his liabilities die with him. But if *kafālah* of deceased means to discharge principal debtor from the accountability in the hereinafter without acknowledgement of right of creditor to claim his debt, then such *kafālah* is lawful."[10]

Ibn Qudāmah, a Ḥanbalī jurist has concluded from the *hadīth* of Abū Qatādah that *kafālah* is valid for everyone who is under some obligation regardless of whether he is alive or dead, solvent or insolvent because *hadīth* is absolute and does not make any distinction between solvent debtor and insolvent debtor.[11]

The conclusion of this discussion is that in the opinion of Imām Abū Ḥanīfah *kafālah* for insolvent deceased is not valid while according to majority it is valid for every debtor. In former case surety cannot claim its reimbursement of what he paid, and in the latter case he is entitled to claim.

Imām ibn Ḥazm is of the view that if the debtor dies insolvent, there is no need for *kafālah* on his behalf and he will not be accountable in hereinafter because he was not able to discharge obligation during his life time. So far as the rights of creditors

---

[9] Shawkānī, *Nayl al-Awṭār*, vol. 5, p. 251.

[10] Zafar Aḥmad 'Usmānī, *I'lā al-Sunan*, Karachi: Idārah al-'Ulūm al-Islāmiyyah, vol.14, p. 496.

[11] Ibn Qudāmah, *al-Mughnī*, vol. 4, p. 593.

are concerned, their debts are payable from *zakāt* property as the payment of debt from *zakāt* property is also permissible.[12]

Rules Relating to Surety

Since the contract of suretyship creates a liability for surety, it is necessary that he should be legally competent to enter a contract. Legal competence in the context of suretyship is defined as sanity, puberty and capacity to wisely handle financial matters. Following persons are considered to be incompetent for the purpose of suretyship.

1. A Minor insane, idiot and all other persons suffering from any legal disability

A minor insane, idiot and all other persons suffering from any legal disability with regard to incurring of financial obligation cannot become sureties for any person. A suretyship by a minor is invalid regardless of whether he is authorized for business by his guardian. He cannot undertake any guarantee even with the permission of his guardian because the guardian is not authorized to approve of any action of the minor that involves any financial loss to him. Such suretyship would be invalid even if the surety on attaining puberty acknowledges the existence of suretyship because such suretyship does not exist in the eyes of law. If a guardian borrowed something for providing necessities of life to an orphan and asked that orphan to be surety for this debt, this is lawful. Likewise, if a father purchased something on credit for his minor child who also owns property and instructed him to undertake the payment of debt as his surety, it is valid because he has undertaken a liability which existed even before this suretyship on account of being owner of some

[12] Ibn hazm, *al-Muhallā*, vol. 5, p.164.

property and the guardian or father was entitled to recover what he spent on him from his property.

2. **A person on deathbed**

A person on deathbed can be a surety but such suretyship is enforceable only to the extent of one third of the property. If such a person declared that he had undertaken this liability while legally competent, then the suretyship can extend to whole of his property.

3. **A person placed under interdiction**

According to Imām Aḥmad ibn Ḥanbal a person who is suffering from a legal disability on account of being spendthrift is not competent to be surety because by this contract he undertakes a financial liability, which is harmful to him. On the other hand, an insolvent person can be a surety because insolvency by itself is no bar to the contract of suretyship. He can be pursued after the removal of insolvency.[13]

Rules related to the *makfūl lahū* (Creditor)

1. The oblige or creditor should be known to the *kafīl*, because without this the objective of suretyship i.e. the security of right cannot be realized. This purpose can be attained only when the person whose right is secured through the contract of suretyship is known to *kafīl.*

2. According to Imām Abū Ḥanīfah and Imām Muhammad, *makfūl lahū* should be present in the session of contract. In this respect they hold that if creditor is not present in the session there must be someone to approve the contract on his behalf. The reason is that *kafālah* involves a contract, which entitles creditor to claim his debt from the surety.

[13] Ibn Qudāmah, *al-Mughnī*, vol. 5, p. 598.

This necessitates offer from the surety and acceptance from the creditor. But according to Imam Abū Yūsuf *kafālah* does not require acceptance by the creditor. *Kafālah* only conveys the meaning of junction, which is realisable by the unilateral declaration of *kafīl*. Therefore, his offer alone is valid for the completion of suretyship and the presence of the creditor is not necessary.[14]

Rules related to *makfūl bihī* (Subject-matter)

1. *Kafālah* or suretyship is permissible in respect of all pecuniary claims related to the enforceable rights of the creditors such as the amount of loan, price of a commodity in credit sale, rent of leased property, commodity in *bay'al salam,* amount of dower, blood-money, value of usurped property, remuneration or wages of a worker.

2. Suretyship for the property held by somebody in a fiduciary capacity is not permissible such as:

   - Deposits
   - Capital of *muḍārbah* and partnership
   - Loan for use or commodate loans
   - Hired property
   - Property of the seller taken by a person with an intention to purchase it before the price is mentioned to him.

3. *Kafālah bi al-taslīm* (suretyship for possession), suretyship for giving possession is valid, and the surety will be bound to ensure the delivery of possession. In the case of surety for the production of a person, the surety is released from his responsibility by the death of the person. In the same

[14] Ibn Humām, *Fatḥ al-Qadīr*, vol. 5, p. 390.

way, the suretyship for possession comes to an end when the reversionary claim expires.

4. It should be an established debt. A debt, which has not been established, yet in the *dhimmah* of a person, cannot be the subject matter of suretyship. Therefore, suretyship for maintenance of wife before it is fixed by the court or mutual agreement is not valid because it becomes an established debt only when it is decided by court or by mutual agreement between husband and wife. On the other hand, suretyship for dower (*mahr*), price of sold property, debt of *salam* is valid as these are the established debts and there is genuine need to secure them.

5. It is not a condition that the extent of debt be known to the surety. The suretyship is lawful for an unascertained amount. The reason is that suretyship rests upon a broad foundation and a small degree of uncertainty does not vitiate it.

   The author of *Badā'i' al-Sanā'i'* constructs his arguments in favour of suretyship for unknown and undefined property on the saying of God: "He who restores it shall have a camel load". Here God has permitted *kafālah* for camel load, which is unspecified. He also takes its validity from a *hadīth* of the Holy Prophet (s.a.w.s) in which he declared, "He who died and left any debt unpaid, I am responsible for its paymen.t" Here the Holy Prophet (s.a.w.s) guaranteed payment of an unascertained debt.[15]

6. Suretyship in crimes is not valid. The suretyship for any right, the fulfillment of which is impracticable by means of suretyship, is not valid, as in cases of *ḥadd* punishments or retaliation because substitution and proxies are not admitted in case of corporeal punishment. Guarantee for

[15] Kāsānī, *Badā'i' al-sanā'i'*, vol. 6, p. 6.

the production of persons of criminals under the sentence of such punishment is lawful.

Legal Effects of Suretyship

The effects of suretyship are as follows:

1. Right of creditor to claim his debt from surety is established. However, he is at liberty to demand payment either from principal debtor or from his surety.
2. In case of suretyship for production, the right of court of law is established to demand the production of accused person in the court.
3. In case of suretyship for possession, surety is required to give possession of property to its owner.

Contract of suretyship does not imply the release of the principal debtor from his liability. If the release of the principal debtor is stipulated in the contract, in such case the contract will become a contract of *ḥawālah*. Imām Shāfi'ī does not validate such a stipulation as it is inconsistent with the purpose of suretyship. The majority also does not favour the release of the principal debtor. This viewpoint is founded upon a tradition of the Holy Prophet (s.a.w.a.) in which he said, "the soul of a believer does not rest until his debts are paid."[16] From this it is established that the principal debtor is not released as a result of the contract of suretyship and the creditor can claim his debt from any of the two persons, i.e., surety and principal debtor.

1. In the case of suretyship for production of a person, if that person dies, the surety is released from his responsibility.

[16] Abd al-Laṭīf Āmir, *al-Duyūn wa Ṭuruq Tawthīquhā fī al-Fiqh al-Islāmī*, *p. 212.

2. The death of the surety also terminates the contract of *kafālah bi al- nafs.* (suretyship for production of person).

3. In the case of suretyship for property if the surety dies, the suretyship is not terminated. The debt can be collected from his property. If the creditor dies his heirs or executors may demand the discharge of the obligation.

4. The surety in the contract of suretyship for production is released by producing the accused person in the court of law. The effect is also the same in case that person himself appears before the court.

5. In case of suretyship for property, the surety is released from his liability by the payment of the debt regardless of whether the payment is made by the principal debtor or the surety.

6. He is also released when the creditor absolves the surety or the principal debtor from the liability of payment of debt, and forgoes his claim against the debtor.

7. In case of suretyship for giving possession the surety is released from his liability by handing over the property to its owner.

Right of surety to claim reimbursement of what he paid, is established. However, claim is established only after the payment of debt, not before.

Contract of Guarantee in Islamic Banks

A bank guarantee is an irrevocable obligation by the bank to pay an agreed sum in case of the failure or default of its client in fulfilling particular obligation. As a result of this guarantee, bank becomes liable to pay out against guarantee in the event of default. Before issuing guarantee, bank assesses client's financial position and credit worthiness. It may take necessary security to minimize its risk. This may be against cash collateral or some other security such as mortgage.

Fee for letter of guarantee

Conventional banks charge percentage based fee, keeping in view guaranteed amount and period of guarantee. It is not permissible in Islamic law, to take fee for guarantee. Guarantee is an act of benevolence, and goodness. In case, letter of guarantee is without cover then fee is a form of *ribā*, because it is a loan from the bank, and any increase charged on it is *ribā*. In case the letter of guarantee is with cover, it is not lawful to charge fee because guarantee is an act of benevolence. It is pertinent to note that Islamic banks take actual administrative expenses or service charge on issuance of guarantee. In case guarantee is called, conventional bank charges interest for the period during which it remained out of pocket, while Islamic bank does not charge any interest on it.

Types of Bank Guarantee

Bid bond

A bid bond is issued by a bank on behalf of client bidding to secure a contract or project. It guarantees to project owner that a bidder has capacity to take on job (construction for instance) if selected. and will enter into a contract. This guarantee gives the employer/contract owner compensation for additional costs if the party submitting the tender does not take up the contract and it is awarded to another party. This is issued for an amount equal to between 1 and 2 percent of contract value.

Performance bond

It guarantees satisfactory completion of a project by a contractor. It is issued to a party which needs bond, i.e. owner of project, or government entity.

Advance payment guarantee

An advance payment guarantee is used when the contract provides for advance payment to be made to the seller, and it guarantees that the advance amount will be returned to the buyer, if the seller does not fulfill its obligations on delivery of goods or service. Here the beneficiary of guarantee is buyer. It is intended to bind the supplier (the bank's customer) to use the advance payment for the purpose stated in the contract between the customer (supplier) and principal (buyer).

Guarantee securing credit line

This surety is given to a creditor on claims against the debtor in case a loan is not repaid as per the terms of the agreement. This guarantee is generally issued for those who are not generally eligible for loan like students. For disbursing loan to them the bank may require a guarantee of class 1 officer.

Conclusion

- Islamic Law has introduced a number of contracts to safeguard the right of creditor and to ensure the safe return of his amount of capital. These contracts are:
    - *Kafālah* (suretyship)
    - *Ḥawālah* (assignment of debt)
    - *Rahn* (pledge)
- *Kafālah* means merging of one liability with another in respect of a demand for performance of an obligation.
- *Kafālah* is of two types i.e. suretyship for production of person and suretyship for property.

- *Kafālah* for principal who dies insolvent is not valid in the opinion of Imām Abū Ḥanīfah. According to other jurists such *kafālah* is permissible.

- *Kafālah* is permissible for the pecuniary obligations and debts due on the principal, not for the property held on trust.

Chapter 19

Contract of *Ḥawālah* (Assignment of Debt)

Ḥawālah is an effective mode for the security of debts. The word *ḥawālah* is derived from *taḥwīl*, which conveys the meaning of shifting a thing from one place to another. In the language of law it means "the shifting or assignment of debt from the liability of the original debtor to the liability of another person".[1] It can also be defined as substitution of one obligor for another with the agreement of the creditor. The purpose of *ḥawālah* is the payment of debt through the assignment of a claim. The meaning of *ḥawālah* can be understood by the following illustrations:

(i) A is indebted to B and has a claim against C. He can settle his debt by transferring his claim against C to the benefit of B.

(ii) A has debt owing to him from B and owes debt to C. C, instead of realizing from A and A taking his debt from B, can realize it from B through the contract of *ḥawālah*. In this case debtor B is substituted for debtor A with the agreement of C. A is discharged.

The debtor who transfers debt is called *muḥīl* (debtor-assignor), the creditor *muḥāl* (creditor-assignee) and new debtor to whom transfer is made, *muḥāl ʿālayh* (payer/substituted debtor).

Lane provides three forms of transfer while discussing the nature and scope of *ḥawālah*. These forms are as follows:

---

[1] Zaylaʿī, *Tabyīn al-ḥaqāʾiq*, vol. 4, p. 1717.

(1) The transfer of a claim of debt by shifting the liability from one person to another.

(2) The transfer of a debt by shifting the liability of him who transfers it to whom it is transferred.

(3) An order for the payment of debt or of a sum of money, given by one person, upon another, to a person.[2]

Validity of *Ḥawālah*

Following are some traditions, which establish the validity of transfer of debt, i.e., *hawālah*.

It is related by Abū Hurayrah (r.a.t.a.) that the Holy Prophet (s.a.w.s) said: "To evade and defer (payment of loan) on the part of a person who is rich, is tyranny. If loan is transferred to a rich person he (the transferee of liability) should be pursued (for its payment)".[3]

It is narrated by Ibn 'Umar (r.a.t.a.): "To evade and defer (payment of loan) on the part of rich person is cruelty. And if it (liability) is transferred to a rich person, he should be followed".[4]

Several inferences can be drawn from these traditions:

1. It is lawful to transfer one's debt from one to another.
2. In case of transfer of loan from the debtor to the transferee, the latter should be asked to pay as he substitutes the debtor.

---

[2] Edward William Lane, *Arabic-English Lexicon, S,v. "hAWĀLAH".*

[3] San'ānī, *Subul al-Salām* , vol. 3, p.61.

[4] Shawkānī, *Nayl al-Awṭār,* vol. 5, p. 250.

3. After the transfer is made, the original debtor may be discharged from his liability towards creditor whose interest is safeguarded by the transfer of debt.

4. The transfer of loan from the debtor to the transferee requires consent of all, i.e. debtor, creditor and transferee.

5. The creditor should accept the assignment of debt and pursue the new debtor for collection of his debt as long as the assignment is to a solvent person.

The negotiability or assignability of debt in the history of Islam is as old as Islam itself. It started with the undertaking by a man of means to pay the debt of another in straitened circumstances and developed into a medium of commercial transactions. In this age also negotiability of instruments of loan is of utmost importance in all commercial-cum-banking transactions. *Ḥawālah* has the ingredients of guarantee. An instrument is also negotiated for the purpose of guaranteeing or securing the payment of the loan due on a promissory note, a cheque or a bill of exchange. As such, when A, a drawer, draws a bill upon B ordering him to pay C, he in fact guarantees him, i.e., C the payment of his debt due on A. Similarly, when A, a holder of instrument negotiates it to B, he secures the payment of debt due on the bill. An acceptor of an instrument after accepting it becomes primarily liable while a drawer's liability becomes secondary and conditional. In the same way a substituted debtor/payer in a contract of *ḥawālah* becomes primarily liable.

Imām Abū Ḥanīfah's viewpoint regarding *ḥawālah*

Imām Abū Ḥanīfah defines *ḥawālah* as a transfer of debt, transfering the liability of the original debtor, to a third person.[5] This definition implies that after the conclusion of *ḥawālah* the

[5] Kāsānī, *Badā'i' al-sanā'i'*, vol.6, p.17.

principal debtor will be relieved from the liability. He argues that the term *ḥawālah* is derived from the word *taḥwīl*, which necessitates the transfer of debt to the third person and the exemption of the transferor.

Imām Muḥammad's viewpoint

Imām Muḥammad is of the opinion that *ḥawālah* is the transfer of demand only while the actual burden of payment rests with the principal debtor.[6]

Imām Zufar also maintains that the transferor is not exempted because of the analogy that subsists between his case and that of suretyship or bail, for both are contracts of suretyship or bail. The person who is bailed is not exempted from the debt so neither should the transferor.[7]

In fact, *ḥawālah* is different from suretyship in the sense that in the contract of guarantee or suretyship or bailment if the creditor releases the original debtor from his liability, the same will be applicable to his surety and as such he will automatically be released from his liability towards his principal debtor. On the other hand, in a contract of *ḥawālah* if the creditor releases the original debtor from debt, this release may not necessarily extend to the substituted debtor. He remains under obligation to pay the debt until he is also released expressly by the creditor.

Effects of *Ḥawālah*

Normally the effect of *ḥawālah* is to discharge the debtor (*muhīl*) from the debts he owes to the creditor/assignee (*muhāl lahū*). *Ḥawālah* can also occur with the condition that the debtor/assignor (*muhīl*) shall remain liable for the debt, in such case *hawālah* is similar to a guarantee. Thus, the

[6] Ibn Nujaym, *Bahr al-Rā'iq*, vol. 6, p.344.

[7] Kāsānī, *Badā'i' al-sanā'i'*, vol. 6, p.18; Ibn Nujaym, *al-Bahr al-Rā'iq*, vol. 6, p.344.

creditor/assignee has the right to claim settlement from either debtor/assignor or the substituted debtor.

According to Imām Aḥmad ibn Ḥanbal and Imām Shāfi'ī, when the new debtor is solvent, the creditor/assignee has no recourse what so ever against the creditor/assignor in the event that the debt is not settled by the substituted debtor. Thus, the discharge of the debtor/ assignor is total and irrevocable unless his guarantee was obtained especially for the case of non-payment by the substituted debtor. This is substantially the opinion of the Mālik, with the difference that, for Mālik the creditor/assignee has the right of recourse against the debtor/assignor in the case of misrepresentation in assignment to the new debtor who was already bankrupt before the *ḥawālah* was concluded.[8]

For the Ḥanafīs, *hawālah*, in principle, discharges the debtor-assignor with the exception that the creditor/assignee (*muhāl lahū*) has a right of recourse against him in the event that his claim is in danger of failing either for the reason that the new debtor is insolvent or because he renounces the existence of *hawālah* and the creditor has no proof thereof.[9]

Kinds of *Ḥawālah*

Ḥawālah is either absolute *(muṭlaq)* or conditional (*muqayyad*). Absolute *hawālah* refers to that contract where payment is not restricted to the property of the transferor in the hands of substituted debtor.

Ḥawālah is conditional when it contains a stipulation that the creditor's debt may be paid up from the debt of the debtor due from the substituted debtor or anything belonging to the

---

[8] Khattāb, *Mawāhib al-Jalīl*, vol.5, p.95.

[9] Nabīl Sālih, *Unlawful Gain and Legitimate Profit in Islamic Law*, p.105.

debtor, which is in possession as a security with the substituted debtor. All other forms of *hawālah* are unrestricted and absolute.[10]

This distinction is the creation of Ḥanafī fiqh but the other three Schools do not subscribe to *ḥawālah muṭlaq* as *ḥawālah*. The effect of the two categories determine the validity of other classification i.e. *ḥawālah al-ḥaq* and *ḥawālah al-dayn* because *ḥawālah al-haq* is a form of *hawālat muṭlaq*.

It is to be noted here that in *ḥawālah al-ḥaq*, the right of creditor in the debt due from the debtor is transferred to a new party. It is against *hawālah al-dayn* in which the liability is transferred to a new party. While discussing the subject our primary concern will be the *ḥawālah al-dayn,* i.e., the assignment of liability or debt.

Rights and duties of parties

1. In an absolute *ḥawālah*, the substituted debtor, after making payment to the creditor steps in the shoes of the creditor as against the original debtor.

2. In a restricted *ḥawālah* the right of the debtor to property in possession of substituted debtor, ceases. Thus, if the substituted debtor after accepting the liability returns the property to debtor, he will remain liable to perform his obligation towards the creditor. However, after making payment to him, he can claim his money from the debtor.

3. The jurists differ among themselves regarding a *ḥawālah* which is with condition that creditor's debt may be paid up from the debt of the debtor due from substituted debtor or from the property belonging to the debtor in the hands of transferee, and the debtor died before the payment. The question here is as to who has the superior right to this

[10] *Majallah*, Article 678 - 679.

property - the creditor of *ḥawālah* or other creditors of the debtor?

Majority of the Ḥanafī jurists hold that all creditors are equal as far as this right is concerned. Thus, if this property is distributed and the creditor gets some portion of it, he cannot demand the remaining from the transferee, as the *hawālah* was restricted with that property only.[11]

On the other hand, Imām Zufar is of the view that the right of creditor of *ḥawālah* is superior to other creditors, as the right of creditor was attached to property, and the property in question is no more his property because he isolated himself from it in his life. The same situation continues to exist after his death. Moreover, the right of the creditor of *hawālah* was attached to it in the debtor's life, while the right of other creditors was attached after his death. As such former's right is superior to latter's right like the right of pledgee over the pledged property.[12]

4. If *ḥawālah* was with a condition that the substituted debtor would make payment from the amount realised from purchaser in a credit sale. Then the subject matter is destroyed before delivery to the purchaser or it is returned by him exercising his option of inspection or defect, in such case, the *ḥawālah* is still valid and the substituted debtor is liable to pay. However, after the payment he can claim it from the transferor. This means that the substituted debtor is liable to honour his commitment even if the cause of his obligation ceases to exist.

How is *ḥawālah* concluded?

The different modes of concluding *hawālah* are as follows;

---

[11] Kāsānī, *Badā'i' al-sanā'i'*, vol. 6, p.16.

[12] Ibid.

(a) *hawālah* with consent of all the parties: By concerned parties is meant the debtor/assignor (*muḥīl*), the creditor/assignee (*muḥāl lahu)* and the substituted debtor/payer. This is in principle an ideal situation where all concerned parties' consent to the substitution of a new debtor for the original debtor.

(b) *hawālah* by agreement of the creditor and the new debto/payer: The original debtor does not participate in this sort of *hawālah*. This is lawful according to Ḥanafī jurists.

(c) *hawālah* by agreement of debtor/assignor (*muhīl*) and the creditor/assignee (*muhāl lahū*): For the Ḥanafīs this is contingent upon the new debtor's agreement. To others his consent is not necessary, especially when he is solvent.

(d) *hawālah* by agreement of the debtor/assignor (*Muhīl*) and the new debtor /payer (*muḥāl 'alayh*): This *hawālah* is contingent upon the creditor's agreement according to Ḥanafī, Shāfi'ī and Mālikī jurists. Ḥanbalī jurists hold that when the new debtor is solvent, his consent is not necessary.[13]

Circumstances under which absolute *ḥawālah* is terminated

According to Imām Abū Ḥanīfah, contract of *ḥawālah* is terminated and debt reverts to the principal debtor in the following circumstances:

(i) Where the transferee denies the existence of the contract upon oath, and the creditor cannot produce witnesses to prove it.

[13] Nabīl sālih, *Unlawful Gain and Legitimate Profit in Islam*, pp. 103, 104.

(ii) Where the substituted dies poor and insolvent. In either case the debt is destroyed, since in neither case is it practicable for the creditor to receive payment from the substituted debtor.[14]

Termination of restricted *ḥawālah*

1. If *ḥawālah* was with condition that payment is to be made from property of the debtor-assignor in possession of the substituted debtor, and then a person who was the rightful owner of that property turned up and took its possession, the *ḥawālah* is void and the debt is returned to the debtor who made the *ḥawālah*. In other words, restricted *ḥawālah* is terminated when the property in the hand of substituted debtor does not belong to the assignor and is taken possession of by its owner.

2. It is terminated, if the property held by the substituted debtor in fiduciary capacity is destroyed without any negligence on part of substituted debtor.

3. It is not terminated in the following two cases:

   (a) If the property was held in trust, and destroyed by negligence.

   (b) It was a property of assignor usurped by transferee.

Comparison between *Ḥawālah* and Negotiable Instruments

1. In Islamic law *ḥawālah* is introduced to guarantee the payment of debt on behalf of the original debtor. An instrument is also negotiated for the purpose of guaranteeing or securing the payment of loan due on a bill of exchange or promissory note.

---

[14] Marghinānī, *al-Hidāyah*, vol. 3, p. 99.

2. In the opinion of majority the valid form of *ḥawālah* is the one in which the substituted debtor of liability is the debtor of the original debtor. In other words, the *ḥawālah* must be with consideration. The same is the position in the negotiable instruments. It is presumed that every negotiable instrument when it has been accepted, endorsed, drawn or made was accepted, endorsed, drawn or made for consideration.[15]

3. In Ḥanafī law it is not necessary that the substituted debtor be the debtor of the original debtor. He may accept the liability voluntarily. The section relating to acceptance for honour and payment for honour with reference to promissory note and bill of exchange conveys the same sense.[16]

4. In Islamic law a thing for which a *hawālah* is made must be a debt. Negotiable instruments are also restricted to dealing in money only.

5. The drawing of a bill or instrument by one bank on another for the benefit of a third person would be *ḥawālah*. According to the Ḥanafīs and those who agree with them it is immaterial whether the drawee is a debtor of the drawer or not because for them it is not a condition that the substituted debtor should be debtor of the transferor but the acceptance by a drawee is a condition precedent for implementation of *ḥawālah*. The majority of the jurists do not treat acceptance by the drawee as essential if he is indebted to the transferor or drawer in the same amount. According to this view it becomes a *ḥawālah* only if the person in whose name the bill of exchange is made payable, is a creditor of the drawer. In case he is not a creditor, the

---

15 ʻAbd al-Laṭīf ʻĀmir, *al-Duyūn wa Tawthīquhā fī al-Fiqh al-Islāmī*, Cairo: pp. 160, 161.

16 *Negotiable Instruments Act*, Section 108 (a).

bill creates an agency in which the drawer shall be the principal and the payee shall be his agent. In this case it will be possible to call the instrument as a bill of exchange.

6. About the right of a third party the position of the Act is the same as that of Islamic law. If the obligation of the drawer towards the first payee terminates or becomes void and the payee then endorses the cheque or any other negotiable instrument in favour of a holder in due course and the latter demands its payment or reimbursement from the drawer, the drawer is stopped from pleading termination of his liability as the right of the third person has accrued in this case. Thus, if A draws a bill on C. Later on the obligation of the A towards C becomes void, and C then endorses it in favour of D, who is holder in due course. A's liability towards D is not terminated.[17]

In Islamic law, also, the substituted debtor of liability of the debtor is not competent to defend against the claim of the creditor by pleas with which he could defend the action of the debtor unless the debt of the debtor due against him be factually non-existent. If the creditor transfers to a third person his right against the purchaser for a sum of one thousand *dirham* and thereafter the purchaser exercises his option for defect and cancels the sale, the transfer is not terminated, because it now involves the right and interest of persons who were not party to contract.

The general rule is that contracts without consideration and those that are fictitious or forged are void. The following sections form an exception to the rule on account of the provision of negotiability, which may involve the interest of a number of third parties who in their turn may have paid consideration for it under a bonafide belief about the document

[17] *Negotiable Instruments Act,* Section 9.

being genuine and legal. The Act protects the interest of such holders in due course of the negotiable instruments. The presumption of the law is that an innocent party should not be made to suffer.

Section 41 provides that an acceptor of a bill of exchange already endorsed is not relieved from liability, by reasons that such endorsement is forged, if he knew or had reason to believe the endorsement to be forged when he accepted the bill.[18]

Section 42 states that an acceptor of a bill of exchange drawn in a fictitious name and payable to the drawer's order is not, by reason that such name is fictitious, relieved from liability to any holder in due course claiming under an endorsement by the same hand as the drawer's signature, and purporting to be made by the drawer.[19]

Section 43 declares that negotiable instrument made, drawn, accepted, endorsed or transferred without consideration or for a consideration, which fails, creates no obligation of payment between the parties to the transaction. But if any such party has transferred the instrument with or without endorsement to a holder for consideration, such holder, and every subsequent holder deriving title from him may recover the amount due on such instrument from the transferor for consideration or any prior party thereto.[20]

Ḥawālah and the concept of assignment in English Law

The concept of assignment and transfer in the legal history of Islam is as old as Islam itself. The *hawālah* was followed not only as a guarantee for the payment of debt to the creditor but also as a medium of commercial transactions. *Ḥawālah* in its later

[18] *Negotiable Instruments Act,* Section 14.
[19] *Negotiable Instruments Act,* Section 42.
[20] *Negotiable Instruments Act,* Section 43.

form was known as *saftajah* (bill) which is infact precursor of today's negotiable instruments. A deep study of the subject reveals that from the 1st or 2nd century Hijrah it was used not only in commercial transactions but also in transfer of money from one place to another so as to avoid dangers of road a practice which is also prevalent in contemporary banking system. Ibn Zubayr used to take money from some persons in Mecca and would give them a letter addressed to Mus'ab ibn Zubayr in Iraq, instructing him to pay that money, to those persons in Iraq. Ibn Abbās and Ḥaḍhrat 'Alī were questioned about the legality of the transactions and they found no harm in it.

For centuries, the concept of assignment remained alien for Europe. It was in early eighteenth century when the concept started creeping into its legal system. In the French Law, the term "*avel*" is used for a special guarantee of indemnity on negotiable instruments, whether used in favour of stranger or any person signing it. The word "*avel*" is not therefore used in the sense of *hawālah,* rather the term *kafālah* is nearer to it. Whatever be the sense of "*avel*", there is no doubt that the concept traveled to Europe from Islamic *fiqh*.

As regard the assignment or transfer of the contractual rights and liability, the basic presumption of the law was that, all such rights being personal to the parties concerned, cannot be transferred to a third person who is not party to the contract, as such act might encourage multiplying litigation or maintenance of the suit. But with the passage of time the growing needs compelled the jurists to accept some modification in the harsh rule. The first thing which was subjected to such modification, was the question of the assignment of debt, after this the area of assignability was widened to cover the other rights and liabilities.

Modern Forms of *Ḥawālah*

1. Withdrawal from a current account

If current account holder issues a cheque in favor of his creditor then such transaction is a *ḥawālah* transaction, because he is transferring his debt to the bank. Bank in this case is substituted debtor. Issuer assign the principal debtor.

2. Bills of exchange

A bill of exchange is a form of *ḥawālah* if the beneficiary is creditor to the drawer. The drawer is, in this case, the transferor who gives orders for the paying bank to pay a certain sum of money at a specified date to the defined beneficiary. The party executing payment of such amount of money is the payer whereas the beneficiary, i.e. the holder of the bill, is the substituted debtor.

3. Endorsement of a negotiable instrument

An endorsement of a negotiable instrument in a manner that transfers title to its value to the beneficiary is form of *ḥawālah* if the beneficiary is a creditor to the endorser.

4. Transfer of money (Remittances)

The request of a customer for the institution to transfer a certain amount of money in the same currency from his current account to particular beneficiary is a transfer of debt if the applicant is a debtor to such a beneficiary.

Conclusion

- *Ḥawālah* means shifting or assignment of debt from the liability of original debtor to the liability of another person.
- After the transfer of debt, the original debtor is discharged from his liability.

- In absolute *ḥawālah,* the transferee after making payment to the creditor can claim its reimbursement from the debtor. In restricted *hawālah* the right of debtor to property with the transferee, ceases.
- The absolute *hawālah* is terminated when the transferee dies poor and insolvent.
- Restricted *hawālah* is terminated when the property of transfer in the hand of substituted debtor is taken by the one who is entitled to it, or when it was a trust in his hand and was destroyed without any fault or negligence on his part.
- *Ḥawālah* resembles negotiable instruments in that its purpose is to guarantee the payment of debt to the creditor. An instrument is also negotiated for the purpose of guaranteeing or securing the payment of loan due on a bill of exchange.

Chapter 20

Contract of *Rahn* (Pledge/Mortgage)

Definition

1. According to the Majallah, *rahn* is the security that can be lawfully employed for satisfaction of a claim in respect of a debt.[1]

2. According to Lane, "*Rahn* means to pledge or lodge a real or corporeal property of material value in accordance with the law, as security for a debt or pecuniary obligation."[2]

Legitimacy

The legitimacy of *rahn* is established by a number of texts from the Qur'ān and the *Sunnah*. Some of such texts are as follows:

Qur'ān

"If you are on journey and cannot find a person to write (your debt), then pledge in hand (shall suffice)."[3]

It is to be mentioned here that it is not necessary that a pledge may be held on security only on a journey. The fact is that pledge has been mentioned in the context of journey because such situation generally arises when a person is on journey. In such state it is likely that he may not find a scribe to write down the debt. The jurists are unanimous on the point that the principle regarding loan against security as laid down in the verse will also apply when the parties, even though at home,

---

[1] *Majallah*, Art. 701.

[2] E.W. Lane, Arabic English Lexicon, letter, S.V. "R".

[3] Qur'ān 2:282.

agree to lend and borrow money against security. This will also apply to cases where the lender does not trust borrower.

Sunnah

1. Ḥaḍrat Qatādah narrated that Ḥaḍrat Anas (r.a.t.a.) went to the Prophet (s.a.w.s.) with barley bread with some dissolved fat on it and he (the Prophet s.a.w.s.) had mortgaged his armour to a Jew in Madinah and took from him barley for his family.[4]

2. Ḥaḍrat 'Āishah narrated that the Prophet (s.a.w.s.) bought some foodstuff on credit from a Jew for a limited period and mortgaged him armour for it.[5]

Legal Status of the Pledged/Mortgaged Property

According to the viewpoint of the majority of Muslim jurists the pledged/mortgaged property assumes the status of trust in the hands of pledgee/mortgagee. Thus, if it is destroyed or lost without negligence, fault or wrongful action on his part he will not be held liable. He will remain entitled to his debt due on the pledger/mortgagor. The Ḥanafī jurists hold the view that the pledgee/mortgagee after taking the possession of the property becomes responsible in case of its being destroyed in his hands. The responsibility of the pledgee/mortgagee extends to the amount of the debt owing to the pledgee. Thus, if a pledged property equivalent to the amount of debt is destroyed in the pledgee's hand, his claim is rendered void and he is deemed to have obtained a complete payment. If, on the contrary the value of the pledge exceeds the amount of the debt, the excess is in that case considered as a trust for which the pledgee will not be held responsible in case of its destruction. But if the value be less

---

[4] Bukhārī, *Ḥaḥīḥ*, vol. 3, p.54.

[5] Ibid.

than the debt, the pledgee forfeits that part of his debt and the pledger will pay the remaining to the pledgee. [6]

In opposition to the above-mentioned opinion, the Shāfi'ī jurists maintain that the pledge is a trust in the hands of the pledgee. Thus, if it is destroyed in his possession, still he does not forfeit his due because it is recorded in the tradition that no pledge shall be distrained for debt and the pledger shall be liable for all risks.[7]

Conditions of pledged/mortgaged property

(i) It should be a thing having some monetary worth and legal value.

(ii) It should be a thing in which transactions are permissible in the *sharī'ah*. Thus, it should not be prohibited by Islamic law such as pork and wine.

(iii) It should be existent at the time of contract. Thus to pledge fruits on trees when their quality is yet to be established is not valid, because the object of pledge in this case is non-existent.

(iv) It should be deliverable. Thus, to pledge a stray animal is invalid, because its possession cannot be given to the pledgee.

(v) It should be precisely determined with regard to its essence, quantity and value. An indefinite part of any thing cannot be the subject-matter of pledge because the pledge is taken with a view to obtain payment of a debt. This objective cannot be realized if the pledge is an undefined part of property.

(vi) An article naturally conjoined cannot be pledged separately. Thus, it is not valid to pledge fruits without trees which bear it, crops without the land, trees

---

[6] Kāsānī, *Badā'i' al-Sanā'i'*, vol. 6, p.163.

[7] Shirbīnī, *Mughnī al-Muhtāj*, vol.2, p.137.

without ground, because the pledge in all these cases has connection with an article which is still unpledged, and the possession of which cannot be taken while the possession is a requirement of pledge.

(vii) It is not permissible to pledge the usufruct of a thing, such as to allow the creditor to stay in the house of debtor for some specified period in consideration of debt, these usufructs cannot be delivered at the time of the contract. Their continuation and permanence cannot be ensured from the time of the contract till the time of repayment of debt.

viii) Physical possession of the property by the pledgee/mortgagee is not necessary. Possession could also be constructive and legal through deposit of title of deed with the creditor such as registered/equitable mortgage in the banks.

ix) It should be of sufficient value to cover the amount of debt.

Mortgage of Financial Papers and *Ṣukūk*

AAOIFI has provided detailed rules on mortgage/ pledge of financial papers with the creditor institution. Some important rules are as follows:

1. It is permissible to mortgage the financial papers and *Ṣukūk* which are based on *Sharī'ah* principles such as Islamic *Ṣukūk* and shares of Islamic financial Institutions. The shares of the companies, whose original activities are permissible, also belong to this category.
2. It is permissible to mortgage usufruct-based *Ṣukūk* which represent common shares in the usufructs of specific assets, or assets in the form of a specific indebtedness.

3. It is not permissible to mortgage the financial papers that are not based on *Sharī'ah* principles such as interest-based bonds, preference shares and redeemable shares. Such financial papers include conventional investment certificates, certificates of conventional investment deposits and shares of the companies that pursue impermissible activities like manufacturing of alcohols, swine trade and dealing in *riba*. Among these financial papers also are shares of conventional financial Institutions, shares of conventional financial companies, shares of insurance companies.
4. The Institution can accept mortgage in the form of investment units in Islamic investment funds. In this case the Institution as a mortgagee can suspend the right of the client to get back or draw from the account, absolutely or in proportion to the amount of the debt, whichever is more suitable.
5. The income and growth earned by the units or the account are considered to be mortgaged along with the principal. This should hold true whether the contractual relationship between the client and the Institution or the fund is *muḍārabah* or investment agency, unless the two parties agree on other arrangement.
6. The mortgagee has the right at the time of signing the contract to request from the mortgagor to arrange Islamic insurance for the mortgaged asset whenever it is possible. When the mortgagor accepts to do so the compensation to be received on the damage of the mortgaged asset shall replace it. If the compensation is received in the form of a cash amount such amount shall be mortgaged along with its returns by depositing it in a frozen investment account owned by the mortgagor.

Conditions of claim or debt for which pledge/mortgage is given

- It should be an established and enforceable debt. Thus a pledge may be given for loan, price in credit sale, commodity of *salam*, claim after usurpation, damages in the torts against property, amount of dower, blood money and all the other binding and irrevocable claims.

- Pledge is not permitted for the things for which, there is no liability of compensation such as deposits, commodate loans, capital of *muḍārabah* and *mushārakah* partnerships, leased property in the hands of lessee .

- It is not permissible to give pledge for an amount, which the pledger will borrow, from the pledgee.

- It is not permissible to give pledge for a claim or debt, which is not recognized in the *Sharī'ah*. Thus, it is not permissible to give pledge for the remuneration of a dancer or singer, because hiring a woman to dance or sing is an invalid and impermissible act, hence pledge for an obligation arising from an invalid act is also invalid.

- The claim or debt should be known and defined. Thus, it is not permissible to give something as security for one of the two loans without specifying one of them.

Maintenance of pledged/mortgaged property

The Muslim jurists are unanimous on the point that the maintenance of pledged property is primarily the responsibility of the owner, i.e., pledger in this case. He will incur the cost of maintenance because the Holy Prophet (s.a.w.s.) has said: "To the pledger returns its profit, and he is held responsible for its loss."[8]

The Ḥanafī jurists, however, divide the expenses incurred on maintenance of pledge into two categories;

(i) Expenses required for its subsistence, improvement, and continuation of existence; and
(ii) Expenses incurred on its conservation and safekeeping.

In the opinion of Ḥanafī jurists the expenses of first category will be borne by the pledger. As such he is responsible for feeding the animal, the wages to be paid to the shepherd, expenses of the watering of the garden, its weeding, grafting and the cleaning of the water channels because these expenses relate to the improvement and continuation of the existence of the property.

The expenses of the second category are to be borne by the pledgee. Thus, the rent of the house wherein the pledge is kept as well as the wages of the keeper will be payable by the pledgee. However, if the pledge be a living animal and require a keeper and maintenance, the expenses of these will be incurred by the pledger.[9]

The other jurists do not accept this division. In their opinion all the expenses will be borne by the pledger.[10]

Benefiting from Pledged/Mortgaged Property

A. By pledger/mortgagor

The majority of Muslim jurists is of the view that pledger cannot benefit from the pledged property. The Ḥanafī jurists

---

[8] Ṣan'ānī, *Subul al-Salām,* vol.3, p.52.
[9] Kāsānī, *Badā'i' al-Sanā'i'*, vol. 6, p.151.
[10] Bahutī, *Kashshāf al-Qanā'* vol. 3, p. 326, Ibn Qudāmā, *al-Mughnī,* vol.4, p.392.

allow the benefiting from pledged property with the permission of pledgee. Mālikī jurists regard such benefiting invalid even with the permission of pledgee. In their opinion such permission amounts to termination of contract.[11] The Shāfi'ī jurists permit all kinds of benefits provided it does not cause devaluation of property.[12]

B. By pledgee/mortgagee

According to majority view the pledgee cannot use the pledge. The permission given by *ḥadīth* to milk or ride the animal will be availed only in a situation where the pledger, the owner of animal refuses to bear the expenses of its feeding. Ḥanbalī jurists allowed the benefiting from pledged property if it is animal. They allow the pledgee to ride it or milk it in consideration for fodder given to it. They support their view point by a *hadīth* that, "the pledged animal can be used for riding as long as it is fed and the milk of the animal can be drunk according to what one spends on it. The one who rides the animal or drinks milk should provide expenditures."[13]

The contract of *rahn* is basically meant for the security of debt, and not for investment and profitable use. Any profitable use of pledged property is regarded usury in Islamic law, because of the *hadīth* that "any loan which brings some benefit (for creditor) is a kind of *ribā.*"[14] Thus, if he earns any profit out of it, he is bound to return it to its owner. Mawlānā Mawdūdī in this connection writes;

> "If the pledge is productive, the creditor should keep a regular account of the produce and deduct it from the debt; otherwise any profit drawn from the pledged property

---

[11] Kāsānī, *Badā'i' al-Sanā'i'*, vol.6, p.146.

[12] Shirbīnī, *al-Mughnī al-Muhtāj*, vol.2, p.131.

[13] Ibn Qudāmā, *al-Mughnī*, vol.4, p.190.

[14] San'ānī, *Subul al-Salām*, vol.3, p.53.

would be interest. The only object in view of holding a pledge is the security of the repayment of the debt and it does not entitle the creditor in any way to make profit out of it. For instance, if a creditor lives in the houses which he holds as pledge for his debt or if he lets it to someone else, he is in fact guilty of taking interest, if he does not credit the rent of the house to the debtor, for there is no difference between taking direct interest on a debt or earning money from it or making use for the property delivered as a pledge."[15]

C. Benefit from pledged/mortgaged property under *bay' al-wafā'*

Bay' al-wafā' is a transaction in which a person in need of money sells a commodity to the lender on the condition that when he wishes the lender would return it to him upon the return of price.

According to Sir 'Abd al-Rahīm this contract partakes the attributes of a valid sale in as much as the buyer is entitled to the income of the property and of a vitiated sale as both the parties are entitled to annul it and of a pledge in as much as the buyer cannot sell or otherwise dispose of the property.[16]

But the fact is that it has the effect of pledge because the seller aims to raise commercial loan through this contract. He delivers commodities as pledge to the purchaser. He allows him to benefit from it during the period of indebtedness. In Islamic law the basis to be considered in contract is the meaning and spirit, not the name and form. *Bay' al wafā'* is not a real sale, instead it is a contract of pledge whereby the buyer (creditor) utilizes the commodity for the period during which it stays in his

[15] Abul A'lā Mawdūdī, *Tafhīm al-Qur'ān*, Lahore: Maktabā Ta'mīr Insāniyyat, 1983, vol.1, note # 331.

[16] 'Abd al-Rahīm, *Mohammadan Jurisprudence*, p.233.

possession. The Muslim jurists disapprove this transaction because it is a legal fiction for charging interest.

Legal consequences of pledge/mortgage

Some of the legal consequences of pledge are as follows:

1. The pledge has a right to keep possession until redemption of the pledge, and if the pledger has died, he has better right than the other creditors and can make full payment of the debt from the pledge.
2. The pledgee can sell the pledged property with the permission of pledger, when the debt becomes due in order to satisfy it out of the proceeds. He can also ask the court to have the pledge sold.
3. The pledger cannot sell pledge without consent of pledgee. But if he sells the pledged property without seeking his permission the sale will remain suspended and will come into force only after the debt is paid to the pledgee. Likewise, if the pledgee consents to the sale, it will become effective and debt will remain due to the pledger.
4. It is permissible for the pledger to appoint the pledgee his attorney to sell the property when the time of payment approaches. In such case the pledger cannot dismiss him from attornyship nor will he be dismissed by the death of either the pledger or pledgee.
5. The pledgee is not allowed to let out or give the pledge in loan because he is himself prohibited benefiting from it and consequently not authorized to confer the power of enjoyment upon others.
6. If after the discharge of the debt the pledge perishes in the hands of pledgee, he will be liable to return the money, he has received to the pledger, and the contract of mortgage is not dissolved until the property is restored to the pledger.
7. On the death of the pledger, his heirs of age will stand in his place and it will be their responsibility to free the thing

pledged by paying the debt from the property of deceased person.

Rahn in Pakistani Law

Meaning

A mortgage is security for the payment of debt. It is transfer of an interest or right in immovable property to the creditor.

Components of mortgage

1. Mortgagor: The transferor of interest in specific immovable property is called mortgagor.
2. Mortgagee: The transferee is called mortgagee.
3. Mortgage Money: The principal money, the payment of which is secured through mortgage is called mortgaged money.
4. Mortgage deed: The instrument, through which transfer is affected, is called a mortgage deed.

Simple mortgage

A transaction in which, the mortgagor, without delivering possession of mortgaged property, binds himself to pay mortgage money. Mortgagor agrees that in the case of default, he will cause the mortgaged property to be sold for the payment of mortgage money.

Essentials

Simple mortgage has following essentials:

1. Property is mortgaged.
2. Possession is not delivered.
3. A personal obligation to pay the debt.
4. Obligation may be expressed or implied.
5. No power of sale without out court but a decree for sale of mortgage property must be obtained.

Usufructuary mortgage

Where the mortgagor delivers possession to mortgagee and authorizes him to retain possession until payment of mortgage money; and to receive the rent or profits accruing from the property and to appropriate the same in payment of mortgage money.

Following are the salient features of usufructuary mortgage:

1. No personal liability on the mortgagor.
2. Possession is delivered.
3. No time period is fixed to pay mortgage money.
4. Mortgagee cannot sell out property.
5. Mortgagee is entitled for rents and profits of the mortgage money.

Rahn in Islamic Banks

Hypothecation charge

It is where the debtor client creates charge on his moveable assets. However, possession remains with the debtor. By virtue of his charge, client is under obligation to maintain sufficient level of assets to meet security requirement of the bank. In case of default by the borrower, the lender will have to take possession of goods first and then to sell the same.

Equitable mortgage

In equitable mortgage, the mortgagor deposits original documents of his property with the bank. The mortgage is registered with the registrar. He redeems these documents when he pays his debt. Equitable mortgage is used in cases of *murābaḥah*, *salam*, diminishing *mushārakah* etc. The bank may ask the debtor of *murābaḥah*, to deposit documents of his property as security with the bank.

Lien on investment account

By virtue of lien on investment account, the client cannot withdraw any amount equal to the amount of his debt from his account. The client allows the bank to retain that amount as security till he pays the debt.

Pledge of stocks

It is where a third party on behalf of Islamic bank, keeps pledged goods under his custody. The pledger, debtor is not allowed to take any benefit from it. It is commonly known as pledge with *muqaddam* arrangement. This is a pledge with possession.

Other forms of security

- **Right to repossess sold goods**

If the client of *murahabah* defaults and subsequently becomes bankrupt, while the sold goods are still available with him in the original condition, the bank has the right to repossess these goods. *Hadīth*: "If one party has sold an asset (on credit) and the other party (purchaser) becomes bankrupt, and the former party has managed to retain the asset, then he is more qualified to take possession of the asset in preference to other creditors."

- **Promissory notes & cheques**

In order to secure its debt, the Islamic bank may require the customer to provide postdated cheques or promissory notes. The bank is not entitled to use these cheques except on their due dates.

- **Future installments**

In order to secure its debt, the bank may stipulate that if the client delays in the payment without any genuine reason, the future installments will become immediately due, after serving a notice of reminder on the client.

- **Retention of sold property**

In order to secure its debt, the bank may retain the sold goods till the debt is paid by the client.

Conclusion

- *Rahn* (pledge) is to make a property security in respect of a right or claim.
- According to majority's standpoint the pledged property assumes the status of trust in the hands of the pledgee.
- Maintenance of pledged property is primarily the responsibility of pledger.
- The pledgee is not allowed to benefit from pledged property.

Part III

Issues in Islamic Finance

Chapter 21

Concept of *Ḥiyal* and its Applications in Modern Islamic Finance

Ḥīlah literally means an artifice, device and stratagem. Technically, it may be described as the use of legal means for extra-legal ends that could not, whether by themselves legal or illegal, be achieved directly within the means provided by the *Sharī'ah*. It enables person(s), who would otherwise have had no choice but to act against the provisions of sacred law, to arrive at the desired result, while actually conforming to the letter of the law. Thus, *ḥiyal* (legal artifices) constitute legal means, by which one can arrive at judicial results otherwise prohibited by the law.[1]

Ḥīlah in Islamic jurisprudence is used in two meanings. Firstly, as tricky solution(s) to difficult problem(s), without, *prima facie*, frustrating the purpose of law. They are clever uses of law to achieve legitimate ends. They are employed to overcome inconvenience in law. Such *ḥiyal* are considered to be lawful. The Ḥanafī and Ḥanblī jurists prefer to call them *makhārij* i.e. way out, rather than *ḥiyal*.[2] Secondly, as a device and subterfuge, used in order to circumvent certain *Sharī'ah* prohibition(s), or to evade certain obligation(s). Such *ḥiyal* are declared unlawful by the *fuqahā'*.

An example of a clever use of law is indirect exchange of superior dates with inferior dates, suggested in the *ḥadīth* of

---

[1] See Encyclopaedia of Islam, vol. 3, p. 510.

[2] Sarakhsī, *al-Mabsūṭ*, vol. 30, p. 209; *i'lām al-Muwaqqi'īn*, op.cit, vol.3, p. 148; Zafar Aḥmad Usmani, *I'lā' al-Sunan*, vol. 18, p. 423.

Haḍrat Bilāl (r.a.t.a).[3] The requirement of Islamic Law in the exchange of dates, with dates, is that dates on both sides should be equal. Now, if a person wants to exchange his inferior quality dates, with superior quality, he has to ignore quality difference and has to exchange it on the basis of equality in weight, on both sides. Any difference in the quantity will make the transaction, a transaction of *ribā al-faḍl.* The solution to this problem is to sell inferior quality dates in the market, and from the proceeds of this sale, buy the required superior quality. In this way, the parties can overcome a difficulty without jeopardizing the letter of Islamic Law.

Unlawful *ḥīlah* is used either to circumvent a prohibition, or to evade an obligation. An example of *ḥīlah* intended to circumvent *Sharī'ah* prohibition on *ribā* is *bay' al-'īnah. Bay' al-'īnah* is to sell a property on credit for a certain price, and then to buy it back at a price less than the sale price on prompt payment basis, both transactions take place simultaneously, in the same session of the contract.[4]

The majority of Muslim jurists consider this transaction invalid, because the intended objective of the transaction opposes the objective laid down by the Lawgiver.[5] This form of transaction, in their view, is nothing more than a legal device, aimed at circumventing the obstacle posed by the prohibition of *ribā*. It is a fictitious deal in usurious loan transaction, as it ensures a predetermined profit, without actually dealing in goods, or in sharing any risk.

The example of *ḥīlah* intended to evade some *Sharī'ah* obligation is gift of zakatable amount, before completion of one year in

---

[3] See, *Al-Bukhārī*, op.cit. Ḥadīth no. 2303; Muslim Bin Al-Ḥajjāj, *Ṣaḥīḥ*, p. 695, Ḥadīth no. 4081.

[4] 'Umar ibn 'Abd al-Azīz, *al-Ribā wa al-Mu'āmlāt al-Maṣrafiyyah fī nazar al-Sharī'ah al-Islāmiyyah*, p. 207.

[5] Badawī, *Naẓariyyah al-Ribā al-Muḥarram*, p. 203.

order to avoid *zakāh*. Similar to this is a situation, where, a person combines scattered animals to reduce the amount to be paid on account of *zakāh*. For example, a person owns forty sheep and his two sons also have forty sheep each. They combine them together as single property, to give one sheep instead of three sheep on account of *zakāh*. Conversely, a person has forty sheep. He sells two sheep to another person before the passage of one year so that he is exempted from obligation.

The last category of unlawful *ḥiyal* is reflected in a famous *sharī'ah* Maxim: *"Every legal artifice whereby nullification of a right, or affirmation of a wrong, is devised is unlawful"*.[6] It suggests that a legal artifice, which serves as means to violate some established principle of Islamic Law and defeats the intention of the law, is unlawful. Conversely, any legal artifice that does not contravene an established legal principle is valid and permissible in Islamic law.

A *ḥīlah* affected on a debt transaction is generally treated as unlawful *ḥīlah*, because it intends to give some extra benefit to the creditor. *Bay*' al-'īnah (buy-back agreement) and *bay*' *bi al-wafā* (sale with right of redemption) belong to this category. A famous maxim states: "*ḥīlah* affected on debt is a *ḥīlah* for *ribā*".[7] Some examples of *ḥiyal* on debt transaction can be to mortgage a house with the creditor and allow him to stay in it, or to sell an object to the prospective debtor for an exaggerated price and then immediately lending him some money, or to buy from him certain commodity at a lower price, or to lease to him some asset, at a rental higher than its prevailing market rate.

Ibn Qudāmah (d.620 H) alludes to the above stated categories in his celebrated work *al-Mughnī*. He writes:

---

[6] Walīd Ibn Rāshid al-Sa'īdān, *Talqīḥ al-Afhām al-'Illiyyah bi Sharḥ al-Qawā'id al-Fiqhiyyah*, p. 116.

[7] See, *Mawsū'at al-Qawā'id al-Fiqhiyyah*, op.cit. vol. 1, p. 201.

> "Unlawful *ḥīlah* means to do an act which is apparently permissible, with the intention to achieve some unlawful purpose, such as to do a prohibited thing, or to avoid some obligation or to nullify a right. The permissible *ḥīlah,* on the other hand, is sought to overcome difficulty and inconvenience (in law), with the purpose to abstain from an unlawful act or thing."[8]

Despite the fact that the word *ḥīlah* is a value-neutral word and it does not necessarily mean subterfuge, playing around law, wile trick, deception, circumvention of prohibitions etc., nonetheless, this meaning and nuance is prominent, both in the classical and modern Islamic legal usages of the term. Ibn Taymiyyah explains that when the word *ḥīlah* is used unqualified, then it conveys the meaning of subversive *ḥiyal* i.e the legal devices whereby *Sharī'ah* prohibitions are circumvented, like the legal devices used by Jews.[9] Ibn al-Qayyim says that in the common usage of *fuqahā',* *ḥīlah* means unlawful and reprehensible tricks.[10]

Treatment of *Ḥiyal* in Islamic Law Schools

Schools vigorously differ on the legitimacy of *ḥiyal*. Their views falling across spectrum. The Ḥanafī and Shāfi'ī take the most lenient position. They declare them valid. Even the apparently subversive artifices are valid in these schools although immoral. *Bay' al-'īnah* (buy-back agreement) for instance, is lawful in Shāfi'ī School. Their argument is that it is the external form of contract, and not the underlying intention, that determines the validity of a contract, or otherwise.[11] The Ḥanafī jurists allow

---

[8] Ibn-Qudāmah, *al-Mughnī,* vol. 6, p. 116.

[9] See, Ibn Taymiyah, *al-Fatāwā al-Kubrā,* vol. 3, p. 191.

[10] Ibn al-Qayyim *i'lām al-Muwaqqi'īn,* op.cit. vol. 3, p. 148, *Ighāthah al-Lahfān,* vol. 1, p. 385.

[11] *Al-Umm,* op.cit. vol. 7, p. 279-279; al-Nawawī, *Rawḍah al-Ṭālibīn,* vol. 3, p. 261.

nikāḥ taḥlīl i.e intervening marriage to facilitate remarriage between divorced couple after thrice repudiation (irrevocable divorce of major degree). They also allow *bay' bi al-wafā* i.e. sale with right of redemption, under need.

Ḥanblī jurists have taken a balanced position on the issue. They allow only those legal devices that provide a way out from a difficult situation, and consequently overcome inconvenience in law.[12]

Mālikī jurists condemn *ḥiyal* and declare them invalid. They even block ways that may lead to an evil. They call it *Sadd al-dharā'i'*. In the following lines, we will discuss the approaches of schools for the treatment of *ḥiyal* in some detail.

Ḥanafī approach in *ḥiyal*

As noted earlier, the Ḥanafī jurists have taken a liberal and flexible position on *ḥiyal*. Sarakhsī claims that majority of the *fuqahā'* regard *ḥiyal* lawful. Only a small group of rigid scholars disapproves it out of ignorance and lack of true understanding of the Qur'ān and Sunnah.[13] As such, Ḥanafīs are inclined towards permissibility of *ḥiyal*. In the classical Ḥanafī books, many instances of legal devices are observable where the boundaries between lawful *ḥiyal* and unlawful *ḥiyal* appear to have blurred. *Fatāwā Hindiyyah* (compendium of Ḥanafī legal opinions) offers many legal devices, whereby, a lender can charge certain increase on his amount from the borrower. In one case, Ibn 'Ābidīn author of *Radd al-Muḥtār*, suggests that if creditor wants to give extension in time to his debtor, against

---

[12] *I'lām al-Muwaqqi'n*, op.cit. vol. 3, p. 148. Ḥanblī Jurists are inclined towards impermissibility of *ḥiyal*. See, Ibn Tamiyyah, *al-Fatāwā al-Kubrā*, op.cit. vol. 3, p. 97-405; Faihān al-Matayri, ed. *Bayān al-Dalīl 'alā Ibtāl al-Tahlīl*, al-Madīinah al-Munawwarah: Maktabah Aḍwā al-Manār.

[13] *al-Mabsūṭ*, op.cit. vol. 30, p. 209.

some increase in amount, he may buy some commodity against the amount of debt from the debtor and then sell the same commodity to him on credit at a higher price. For example, he wants to increase the amount of loan from 10 dirham to 13 dirham for extension in time of repayment. Ibn 'Ābidīn suggests that he should do it by buying commodity for 10 dirham, (which is the amount of loan), from debtor, and sell it on credit for 13 dirhams. Ibn 'Ābidīn claims, that in this way, he has been saved from indulging in *ribā*.[14] We notice here that the solution suggested by Ibn 'Ābidīn, clearly violates the purpose of law. It is a subterfuge to circumvent prohibition of *ribā*.

In another case, *Fatāwā Hindiyyah* offers a tricky device, whereby, a lessor can shift the cost of renovation and major maintenance to the lessee. He suggests that if the building needs some repairs and renovation, and the landlord does not want to bear expenses, then the *ḥīlah* is that he should make estimate of the expenditures to be incurred on renovation, repair and maintenance and add them to the rent as supplementary rent. For example, if the rent is 10 dirhams, and another 10 dirhims are needed for repair and renovation, he may fix rent as 20 dirhams. Then, he may ask the lessee to use 10 dirhams and undertake renovation and repair work as his agent. Thus, the *ijārah* would be valid, because it is affected on a known and specified rent.

Ḥanafī jurists have also allowed *bay' bi al-wafā*, (sale with right of redemption), which carries the attribute of *ribā*. This is a transaction in which a person in need of money sells a commodity to a lender on the condition that whenever the seller wishes, the lender (the buyer) would return the purchased commodity to him upon surrender of the price.[15] The reason for its designation as *wafā*, is the promise to abide by the

---

[14] See Muḥammad Amīn, *Tanqīḥ Fatāwā al-Ḥāmidiyyah*, vol. 2, p. 245.

[15] *Radd al-Muḥtār*, op.cit. vol. 4, p. 341.

condition of returning the subject matter to the seller, if he too surrenders the price to the buyer. Like *bay' al-'īnah*, this too is a legal device for *ribā*. The purchaser in this case is a creditor, who benefits from the object held in his custody, as pledge, till the debtor pays him back his amount and retrieves his object. Islamic injunctions on pledge clearly provide that the creditor is not entitled to make any profit out of the pledged property. Any profit drawn from it is interest. The Muslim jurists generally treat *bay' bi al-wafā* as mortgage.

In another form of *ḥīlah*, the borrower who owns certain property, sells that property to the lender, lease it back, pays rent on it (equalling interest), and then invokes a right to repurchase the property for the original sale price.[16]

Mālikī approach in treatment of *hiyal*

Mālikī jurists take the strictest position on *ḥiyal*. They condemn *ḥiyal* and declare them invalid. Al-Shaṭibī writes:

> "The prominent meaning of *ḥīlah* is to do an act, which is apparently permissible, with the purpose to nullify and violate some *Sharī'ah* rule. Thus the ultimate purpose of the act is to offend established principles of *Sharī'ah*. For instance, when a person makes gift of *zakāh* just before completion of a year, he in fact does this, to evade the obligation. It goes without saying that to make a gift in itself is a permissible act, and abstention from *zakāh* is a prohibited act. Now, when he combines a permissible thing with a prohibited thing, he in fact intends to escape *zakāh*. Otherwise, making gift in itself is permissible but if it aims at avoiding *zakāh*, then it is unlawful.[17]

[16] *Al-Fatāwā al-Hindiyyah*, vol. 3, p. 209.
[17] *Al-Muwāfaqāt*, op.cit. vol. 4, p. 201.

To establish unlawfulness of *ḥiyal*, al-Shaṭibī argues that *Sharī'ah* was revealed for the purpose of regulating benefits, which are universally applicable. He further argues that the *aḥkām* of *Sharī'ah* are not the ends *per se*. They are meant to realize certain objectives. These objectives are, in fact, the interests which the *Sharī'ah* seeks to achieve by these *aḥkām*. Now when a person performs certain act that defeats that interest, he in fact violates the will of the Lawgiver.[18]

Mīlikī jurists are so strict on unlawfulness of *ḥiyal* that they do not acknowledge even the lawful means, which most probably lead to an evil, which is equal to benefit in its strength. Mālikī jurists call it *sadd al-dharā'i'*, which is permanent principle of legal reasoning in Mālikī School. Imām Shaṭibī has described *sadd al-dharā'i'* as use of a thing which has a benefit (*maṣlaḥah*), as a means to realize some unlawful end, or to get to an evil (*mafsadah*).[19] Another Mālikī jurist, al-Qarāfī defines it in the following words:

"*Sadd al- dharā'i'* is to annihilate the matter of means of corruption in order to eliminate it. If an act which is itself free from corruption (*mafsadah*) is used as means to corruption, Imām Mālik prohibited that act in many cases."[20]

Thus, *Sadd al- dharā'i'* refers to an act, which has a benefit but most probably leads to an evil which is equal to the benefit. The concept of *Sadd al- dharā'i'*, observes Kamālī, is based on the idea of preventing an evil, before it actually materializes. It is therefore, not necessary that the result should actually occur, or happen. It is rather the objective expectation that a mean is likely to lead to an evil result, which renders the means in

[18] Ibid. vol. 2, p. 385.
[19] Ibid. vol. 4, p. 199.
[20] *al-Furūq*, op.cit. vol. 2, p. 32.

question unlawful, even without realization of the expected results.[21]

The relationship between means (*dharā'iʿ*) and *ḥīlah* is that both lead to an evil. But the means, i.e. *dharā'* are not always associated with illegal motives. *Sadd al- dharā'iʿ*, basically contemplates preventing, or pre-empting, an evil before its possible occurrence. The question of intention to procure a particular result cannot be a reliable basis for assessing the means that leads to that result. The question of intention of perpetrator is not relevant to the objective determination of the value of means. A *ḥīlah,* on the other hand is always exercised with the intention and with the purpose to circumvent some *Sharīʿah* prohibition. In *bayʿ bi al-wafā,* as we have observed earlier, the goods sold are in the nature of mortgaged property. The transaction of sale authorizes the purchaser to benefit from the purchased goods, which would otherwise not be possible, or permissible, in the case of direct mortgage. Thus, sale with the right of redemption (*bayʿ bi al- wafā'*) was adopted as a tricky device, to circumvent the prohibition of benefiting from mortgaged property, held as security with the creditor. Now, since the *ḥīlah* violates the spirit of Islamic law, it should be condemned and discouraged. Similarly, a *dharīʿah* should also be discouraged, as long as it leads to an unlawful end.

Ḥanbalī approach

Ḥanbalī jurists make distinction between the *ḥīlah* to overcome inconvenience in law, and the one that circumvents *Sharīʿah* prohibitions. They call the former *makhārij,* and consider them valid.[22] Ibn al-Qayyim, a renowned Ḥanbalī jurist, has devoted full chapter to discussion on *ḥiyal* in his celebrated work *iʿlām al-muwaqqiʿīn*. Ibn al-Qayyim, like his contemporary Mālikī

---

[21] Hashim Kamali, *Principles of Islamic Jurisprudence*, p. 394.

[22] *iʿlām al-Muwaqqiʿīn*, op.cit. vol. 3, p. 148; *al-Mughnī*, op.cit. vol. 6, p.116.

jurist al-Shṭibī, emphasises the role of intentions in juridical acts. He writes:

> "Intention is the essence of every juridical act. The act follows the intention. If the intention is valid, the act will be valid, and if the intention is unlawful, the act would also be unlawful. Thus, if a person enters a sale transaction, which he intends to be a means for *ribā* transaction, the sale transaction would be treated as *ribā*. The outward form of contract does not make it a sale transaction."[23]

Ibn al-Qayyim regards *ḥiyal* inconsistent with the spirit of *sharī'ah*. He compares *ḥīlah* with *sadd al-dharā'i'*, (plugging means towards unlawful ends), and concludes that the doctrine of *ḥiyal* is in sharp contrast to the principle of *sadd al- dharā'i'*, in that the Lawgiver through *sadd al- dharā'i'* intends to block the means towards unlawful ends permissible, whereas, *ḥīlah*, opens means towards unlawful ends.[24] Ibn al-Qayyim does not allow a Muftī to use *ḥiyal* in legal reasoning.[25]

To prove the undesirability of *ḥiyal*, Ibn al-Qayyim cites the *hadīth* in which Holy Prophet (s.a.w.s.) cursed the Jews for circumventing the prohibition of fat of animals. The *hadīth* reads: "May Allāh (s.w.t) curse the Jews, when Allah (s.w.t) declared the fat of such animals unlawful, they melted it and enjoyed the price they received." The fat of animal was prohibited for Jews. So they melted it and changed its form. They thought that prohibition did not apply to this new form. Thus, they continued benefiting from fat. Another form of benefit they devised was to sell it and enjoy the price. Ibn al-Qayyim after quoting this *hadīth* writes:

---

[23] *i'lām al-Muwaqqi'īn*, op.cit. vol. 4, p. 217.

[24] Ibid. vol. 3, p. 190, See for the principle of *Sadd al-dharā'i'* Abū Zahrah, Muḥammad, *Uṣūl al-Fiqh*, p. 228.

[25] See, *i'lām al-Muwaqqi'īn*, op.cit. vol. 4, p. 230.

"Khaṭṭābī said: This *ḥadīth* provides a proof that a *ḥīlah* is invalid, when it leads to commission of prohibited act. The mere change of word, form and title does not change the *ḥukm*, and effect, if there is no change in substance."[26]

Thus, in the opinion of Ibn al-Qayyim, intention and purpose of law is the touchstone to determine the validity or invalidity of a juridical act.

Imām Ibn al-Qayyim in his book has given a number of solutions to difficult problems, which serve as precautionary measures, which a prudent person should take before entering a transaction. Ibn al-Qayyim's solutions are more close to *makhārij* than to stratagems and subterfuges. Following statement of Ibn al-Qayyim will explain the point.

> "If a person asked another person: Buy this commodity from this person, at this price, and I will buy it from you and will give you certain profit on it. The person thought that if he bought, the orderer might change his mind and refuses to buy it. In that situation, he would not be able to return it to seller. The *ḥīlah* in such situation is that he should buy it with *khayār al-sharṭ* (stipulated right of cancellation) for three days or more, and then present the goods to the orderer for sale. If he buys it at a stated price, the transaction will be enforced, but if he refuses, he can return goods to the original supplier by envoking his stipulated right of revocation i.e. *khayār al-sharṭ*."[27]

The case under discussion is that of "*Murābaḥah* to the purchase orderer". Imām Ibn Qayyim instructs that in case the buyer apprehends that the orderer will decline to buy promised goods, he should, as a precautionary measure, stipulate in the purchase contract his right to return. As such, this solution is more in

---

[26] Ibid. vol. 3, p. 138.
[27] Ibid. vol. 4, p. 24.

nature of a precautionary device, rather than as a stratagem or unlawful *ḥīlah*. It can also be described as a risk-management device. Thus, the *ḥiyal* in Ḥanbalī School are generally used in the sense of *makhārij*.

Use of *ḥiyal* in Islamic Banks

In Islamic finance, *ḥiyal* have been in practice since its inception. Many of them represented stratagems and subversive *ḥiyal*. But gradually, the size of such *ḥiyal* has decreased significantly. Now, most of the *ḥiyal* in practice are in the nature of *makhārij*. They are wise answers to difficult problems, rather than unlawful *ḥiyal*. They are clever uses of law, to achieve legitimate ends. There are, however, some devices which certainly fall under the category of unlawful devices, as they defeat the higher purposes of Islamic economics and finance. These legal devices have badly affected the originality and authenticity of Islamic banking. Here, we will deal with such *ḥiyal* in Islamic finance. It is pertinent to note that the opponents of Islamic banking, generally regard all the legal devices practiced in Islamic banks as unlawful *ḥiyal*, while the proponents identify them as *makhārij*, rather than as subversive *ḥiyal*.

Unlawful *ḥiyal* in Islamic Finance

The legal devices discussed under this title are the *ḥiyal* that frustrate the purpose of law and circumvent *Sharī'ah* prohibition on *ribā*. The list of such legal devices includes *bay' al-'īnah*, *tawarruq* and commodity *murābaḥah* transactions. Sale and lease back *ṣukūk* also partially fall in this category, as they have the properties of *bay' bi al-wafā'*, which has been declared invalid by the International *Fiqh* Academy.

1. *Bay al-'īnah*

Bay' al-'īnah i.e. 'Buy-Back Agreement (BBA)' is one of the transactions that defeat the purpose of Islamic law. In Pakistan, buy-back was one of the twelve modes of financing prescribed by the State Bank of Pakistan[28]. In 1992[29], the Federal Shariat Court and Sharī'ah Appellate Bench of Supreme Court in 1999[30] held buy-back void. Since then, it is no longer practiced by Islamic banks in Pakistan. However, the conventional banks in Pakistan, continue to practice buy-back agreements (*bay' al-'īnah*) in what they consider it as "Non-Interest Banking" (NIB). However, there is full consensus that this NIB banking is now considered interest based banking conventional banking *per se.*

Despite the claims of NIB banking which was introduced in 1986[31], in reality, Islamic banking's first genuine introduction in Pakistan started in 2003.[32]

It is pertinent to note that State Bank of Pakistan's Islamic Banking Department Circular No 2, dated 25th March, 2008, covers the minimum *Sharī'ah* regulatory standards, approved by the Sharī'ah Board of the State Bank of Pakistan. This circular's Annexure 1, Appendix A, page 7, on *murābaḥah*, Clause xiii) clearly states;

> "Buy-back arrangement is prohibited. Therefore, commodities already owned by the client cannot become the subject of a *murābaḥah* transaction between him and any financier. All *murābaḥah* transactions must be based on the purchase of goods from third party(ies) by the bank for sale to the client."

---

[28] State Bank of Pakistan's BCD Circular No. 13 of 1984

[29] Federal Shariat Court's decision on *Ribā* of 21st November, 1992

[30] Sharī'ah Appellate Bench of the Supreme Court of Pakistan vide its historic judgement on Ribā dated 23rd December, 1999.

[31] NIB, or "Non-Interest Banking" was introduced in Pakistan through State Bank of Pakistan's Circular No. 13 of 1984.

[32] Through SBP Circular No. 1 dated 1.1.2003 on Policy for promulgation of Islamic Banking in Pakistan

AAOIFI is also clear that *bay'al-'īnah* i.e. buy-back arrangement should not take place. AAOIFI's Sharī'ah Standard No. 8, '*Murābaḥah* to the Purchase Orderer' Clause 2/2/3 states;

> "The institution must ensure that the party from whom the item is purchased / bought is a third party, and not the customer or his agent. For example, it is not permitted for a customer to sell an ordered item to the institution and then repurchase it through a *murābaḥah* transaction. Nor may the party that is selling the item be wholly owned by the customer. If a sale transaction takes place and later on it is discovered that it was carried out through such practices, this would render the transaction void."

In order to avoid buy-back arrangement, Islamic banks in Pakistan are applying criteria strictly. Even SBP definition on 'Group'[33] is being strictly followed to ensure that no buy-back agreement takes place even with any co-owner/stakeholder(s) inadvertently.

"Group means any persons, whether natural or juridical, if one of them or his dependent family members of its subsidiary, have control or hold substantial ownership interest over the other. For the purpose of this;

- Subsidiary will have the same meaning as defined in sub-section 3(2) of the Companies Ordinance, 1984, i.e. a company or a body corporate shall be deemed to be a subsidiary of another company if that other company or body corporate directly or indirectly controls, beneficially own or holds more than 50% of its voting

---

[33] State Bank of Pakistan's Prudential Regulations for Corporate/ Commercial Banking (A) 14 defines Group, iner alia, as covering Subsidiary (same as in Subsection 3(2) of the Companies, Control and Substantial Ownership

securities or otherwise has power to elect and appoint more than 50% of its directors.

- Control refers to an ownership directly or indirectly through subsidiaries, of one or more than half of voting power of an enterprise.
- Substantial ownership/affiliation means beneficial shareholding of more than 25% by a person and/or by his dependent family members, which will include his/her spouse, dependent lineal ascendants and descendants and dependent brothers and sisters. However, shareholding in or by the Government owned entities and financial institutions will not constitute ownership/affiliation, for the purpose of these regulations."

Furthermore, in order to avoid, or pre-empt, or minimize any chances of "hidden" *bay' al-'īnah*, a prudent approach is also required by AAOIFI, as Sharī'ah Standard No. 8, *Murābaḥah* to the Purchase Order, Clause 2/2/4 states;

> "It is permitted for the institution to purchase the item from a party who has a blood relationship or marital relationship with the customer who is the purchase orderer, and then to sell the item to the customer on deferred payment terms by means of *murābaḥah* to the purchase orderer, provided that this does not amount to a legal device for covering the sale of '*īnah*. It is preferable that the institution's application procedures for *murābaḥah* to the purchase orderer be designed to avoid such a practice."

Sharī'ah Standard No 8, '*Murābaḥah* to the Purchase Orderer Agency', clause 3/1/3 only allows agency in case of 'dire need';

> "The original principle is that the institution itself purchases the item directly from the supplier. However, it

> is permissible for the institution to carry out the purchase by authorizing an agent, other than the purchase order to make the purchase; and the customer (the purchase orderer) should not be appointed to act as an agent except in the situation of dire need. Furthermore, the agent must not sell the item to himself. Rather, the institution must first acquire title of the item and then sell it to the agent."

Even though the SBP has started making AAOIFI's standards mandatory on all banks in Pakistan. Five standards, including *Sharī'ah* Standard No 8, *Murābaḥah* to the Purchase Orderer have been made mandatory so far. Rest are expected to be followed. Despite this, the treatment of customer as agent, only allowed by AAOIFI in case of 'dire need', remains the norm for most Islamic banks operating in Pakistan, as, inter alia, the Islamic banks do not have the requisite 'expertise' thereby justifying client's role as agent.

SBP's relevant clause seems to have been carefully drafted. The subtle nuances of change in roles is apparent;

> "v) In a *murābaḥah* transaction, the appointment of an agent, if any, the purchase of goods by or for and on behalf of the bank and the ultimate sale of such goods to the customer shall all be transactions independent of each other and shall be so separately documented.
>
> An agreement to sell, however, may embody all the aforesaid events and transactions and can be entered into at the time of inception of relationship.
>
> The agent would first purchase the commodity on behalf of his principal i.e. financier and take its possession as such. Thereafter, the client would purchase the commodity from the financier, through an offer and acceptance.

> According to *sharī'ah* it is sufficient in respect of the condition of 'possession' that the supplier from whom the bank has purchased the item, gives possession to the bank or its agent in such a manner that subject matter of the sale comes under the risk of the bank. In other words, the commodity will remain in the risk of the financer during the period of purchase of the commodity by the agent and its ultimate sale to the customer and its possession by him."[34]

2. *Tawarruq*

Tawarruq is a transaction whereby a person who is in need of money, buys a commodity on credit from certain person, and then sells it in the market on cash at a price less than the one at which he purchased it from the owner. It is called *tawarruq* because the purpose of this transaction is to obtain *wariq* (silver) i.e. money or finance by a needy person. For example, A is in need of Rs. 20,000. He approaches B with the request to sell him certain commodity on credit. B sells him a computer worth Rs. 20,000 for Rs. 30,000 on credit to meet his immediate need of money. A sells it in the market on cash for Rs. 20,000/- and gets money. He is indebted to B for Rs. 30,000/-.

The classical Muslim jurists have divergent views about its legal status. A considerable number of Muslim jurists hold it invalid. In their opinion, the motivating cause of the transaction is to get loan against certain increase. It is a subterfuge and a legal device to obtain money against a certain increase. Besides, it is an exchange of money for money with surplus from one side.

---

[34] State Bank of Pakistan's Islamic Banking Department Circular No.2, dated 25th March, 2008, Minimum Sharī'ah Regulatory Standards, Annexure 1, Appendix A, page 7, on Murabaha, Clause v)

Mālikī school holds *tawarruq* invalid. The authoritative Mālikī text *Mukhtaṣar Khalīl* explains *mālikī* position on *tawarruq*". The author writes:

> "If a person asks the other: Lend me eighty and I will return to you one hundred". The other person says: It is not lawful but I will sell you a commodity worth eighty for one hundred." This is disapproved in Mālikī school.[35]

Ḥanafī school has two divergent positions on *tawarruq*. Al-Zayla'ī (d.743) identifies *tawarruq* as *bay' al-'īnah* and disallows it. He says:

> "The form in which *bay' al-'īnah* is practiced is that a needy person approaches a merchant and requests him to lend him some money. The merchant wants to earn from the transaction, but at the same time, he does not want to be indulged in *ribā*. So, he sells him a cloth worth ten for fifteen on credit, so that person could sell it for ten (which is the real value of cloth), on cash and meet his need. This is unlawful and reprehensible."[36]

Ibn Humām (d.861), another Ḥanafī jurist, allowed it though considered it less preferable.[37]

Shāfi'ī jurists emphasise that external form of contract should be according to the requirement of Islamic law. They are not concerned with the underlying intention.[38] From this, it can be concluded that they acknowledge the validity of *tawarruq*.

---

[35] Al-Kharashī, Moḥammad 'Abdullāh *Sharḥ al-Kharashī*, vol. 5, p. 106; al-Dardīr, *al-Sharḥ al-ṣaghīr*, vol. 3, p. 89.

[36] *Tabyīn al-Ḥaqā'iq*, op.cit. vol. 4, p. 163.

[37] Ibn Humām, *Sharḥ Fatḥ al-Qadīr*, vol. 7, p. 212 & 148. See also, *Radd al-Muḥtār*, op.cit. vol. 5, p. 325-326.

[38] See, *Rawḍah al-Ṭālibīn*, vol. 3, p. 416.

Ḥanbalī scholars hold *tawarruq* valid. Al-Mardāwī, a renowned Ḥanbalī jurist writes:

> "If a person needs cash, and for that purpose he buys a commodity whose value is hundred for hundred and fifty, it is lawful. This is the ruling of Imām Aḥmad."[39]

Ḥanbalī jurists generally regard *tawarruq* permissible. Imām Ibn Taymiyyah and Imām Ibn al-Qayyim, two prominent Ḥanbalī scholars, however, do not agree with the acknowledged viewpoint of their school. They equate *tawarruq* with *bay' al-'īnah* (buy-back agreement).[40] Those who approve of *tawarruq*, rely on the texts that permit sale such as the verse: "Allāh has permitted sale and forbidden usury."

They, however, lay down certain conditions for its validity. These are:

There is a real need for transaction. The person undertaking *tawarruq* needs money and he is unable to get loan from any source. However, if he can get loan, then he is not allowed to enter *tawarruq*.

The contract in its form should not be similar to a *ribā* contract. This occurs where the seller expressly mentions that he is selling one thousand (which is the real price), for twelve hundred, because this amounts to exchange of money for money with excess. It is, however, lawful if he apprises the prospective debtor of its real price and his profit margin.

The debtor (buyer of commodity) should not sell it before taking its possession.

---

[39] Al-Mardāwī, *Kitāb al-Inṣāf*, vol. 4, p. 337.

[40] *I'lam al-Muwaqqi'īn*, op.cit, vol. 5, p. 86; *al-Fatāwā al-Kubrā*, op.cit. vol. 19, p. 302.

The commodity should not be sold to the same creditor (seller in this case) at a less price.

The '*Fiqh* Academy of Muslim World League' in its 15th session had also allowed *tawarruq* with certain conditions. It, however, reviewed its *fatwā* in its 17th session and declared current *tawarruq* practices by the Islamic banks invalid.

The procedure of *tawarruq* transaction in the Islamic banks is as follows:

The bank arranges a commodity for its customer from the international market and then sells it to him on credit. The bank also agrees with the customer that it will sell it in the market for him. This can be illustrated by the following examples:

A, a customer, approaches B, a bank, with a request to lend him Rs. 10,000/-. B purchases an item for Rs. 10,000/- from C, a dealer on cash, and sells it to A, for Rs. 12,000 on credit for one year. B, then in its capacity as the agent of A, sells it to C for Rs. 10,000/- on cash, and hands over Rs. 10,000/- to A, the customer.

It is worth-mentioning that Hong Kong Shanghai Banking Corporation (HSBC) and many other banks use *tawarruq* as a mode of personal financing. The working of *tawarruq* in HSBC is that it buys metals from international brokers, and then sells them on to customers at a pre-agreed price which is payable over an agreed term. The customer appoints the bank, as its agent, to sell the metals to a third party in the market. The proceeds are credited to the customer's account.

It is evident from the above mentioned practices of *tawarruq* in the banks that it is only a legal device (*ḥīlah),* to circumvent the obstacle posed by the prohibition of *ribā* by making it a sale transaction, while in fact it is an interest-bearing loan transaction. It is a credit vehicle and technique to provide cash liquidity to the customer, against an increase over and above the amount of finance. In the present *tawarruq*, even the possession of commodity is not taken by the prospective debtor. The commodity also does not move into his risk and liability. Main objections raised on *tawarruq* practice are as follows:

- This is a trick to get cash now, for more cash paid later.
- There are effectively only two parties i.e. no real, unconnected third party.
- There is a concealed buy-back.
- The metal, subject matter of *tawarruq*, does not move at all in relation to *tawarruq* sales; this renders the metal virtually, wholly irrelevant, since it serves simply as a prop, to enable these deals to be transacted.
- *Tawarruq* does not involve any kind of risks associated with normal and genuine commodity trading activities.[41]

The State Bank of Pakistan defines *tawarruq* as follows;

> "*Tawarruq* literally means to liquidate. In the *Fiqhi* term, it is to sell a commodity at spot, after its purchase on deferred basis. In practice, *tawarruq* is an arrangement in which one party sells a commodity to the other party on deferred payment at cost plus profit. The other party, namely, the buyer, then sells the commodity to a third party on cash with a purpose of having access to liquidity."[42]

---

[41] See, Salman H. Khan, *Organized Tawarruq in Practice: A Sharī'ah Non-Compliant and Unjustified Transaction*. See also Sāmī Ibn Ibrāhīm Swaylim, *Qaḍāyā fī al-Iqtiṣād wa al-Tamwīl al-Islamī*, p.313-435.

[42] State Bank of Pakistan's Islamic Banking Department Circular No.2, dated 25th March, 2008, Minimum Sharī'ah Regulatory Standards, Annexure 1, Appendix A, E, page 16, b

3. Commodity *murābaḥaḥ*

Similar to *tawarruq* is *commodity murābaḥaḥ* which is practiced by some Islamic banks in Pakistan. It is a treasury product, used mainly as a tool of liquidity management. The *commodity murābaḥaḥ* is practiced in the following manner:

Upon the requirement of funds, Bank 'ABC' approaches the Islamic Bank (IB) for the requirement of funds. After the required approvals, the IB and Bank 'ABC' enter into a Master *Murābaḥaḥ* Facility Agreement (MMFA) to execute *commodity murābaḥaḥ* transactions from time to time.

After signing the MMFA, Bank ABC submits an 'Order Form' to IB, for the total amount required. Upon receiving the order form, IB purchases the commodity from the commodity broker/seller, through telephonic recorded lines, on a spot basis, at the prevailing market rate. The commodity(ies) could be a mix of different items, such as pulses, fertilizer, rice etc.

At the time of such sale, IB appoints an IB representative, (*mucaddum*, or IB staff), for proper physical identification of the commodity, and taking its possession at the commodity broker's/sellers warehouse.

Upon taking possession by IB representative, the commodity broker/seller acting in its capacity as a seller, (or undisclosed agent), furnishes 'Delivery Order' and a Sale Invoice/Sale Warrant, entitling IB to hold the title of the commodities.
After taking possession, IB has the right to ask for physical delivery, if necessary, the broker may charge additional transportation charges, if he agreed to make the transportation of delivery, which will not be part of the selling price, as the sale takes place on an 'as is where is' basis.

IB credits the purchase price, against this purchase in a checking account of the broker, being maintained with the IB.

Before selling the commodity to bank 'ABC' on *murābaḥah* basis, the IB treasury office takes telephonic confirmation (on recorded lines), from IB representative, on whether he has taken possession of the commodity(ies) by signing the possession letter.

Upon affirmative confirmation, IB treasury office sells the same commodity, through recorded telephonic lines, to bank 'ABC', at cost plus profit on a deferred payment basis for 'x' number of days.

A separate authorized representative of bank 'ABC', (*mucaddum* or staff member), also takes the physical possession of the goods from IB representative at the commodity broker's/seller's warehouse.

After receipt of the title, and possession of the commodities, bank 'ABC' is free to hold, or sell, the commodity(ies) to any other third party in the ready market.

Bank 'ABC' pays IB for the commodity purchased, on the maturity date, i.e. after completion of 'x' number of days.

As mentioned above, commodity *murābaḥah* is a treasury product. Through commodity *murābaḥah*, the liquidity needs of a financial institution, generally a conventional bank, are met. Thus, the excess funds of Islamic banks are used by conventional banks. According to a survey, more than 70 billion rupees of Islamic banks are placed with conventional banks, through commodity *murābaḥah*. Since it has been devised to meet liquidity needs of a financial institution, it is an obvious thing that no party is interested in the commodity *per se*. The commodity does not come into the possession, or risk and liability, of bank that buys it. It is only a *ḥīlah*, to get a certain fixed increase on the amount lent to the financial institution.

At least some of those practicing the above arrangements, try to justify above by portraying it as sale part of the transaction to the bank 'ABC' as the "commodity *murabaha*", as "*Sharī'ah* compliant", without realizing that the second leg of the transaction, which *de facto* results in *tawarruq* simply cannot be ignored. Organized (i.e. banking) *tawarruq*, as discussed above in detail, is not an acceptable mode, based on latest *fatwas* also.

Furthermore, even if the transaction had been *Sharī'ah* compliant, the fact that the above is used for meeting the liquidity needs of the interest based conventional banks, brings it in direct conflict with the objectives of *Sharī'ah* i.e. *maqāṣid al- sharī'ah*, thereby attracting prohibition.

4. *Salam* in currency

A group of Muslim scholars in sub-continent hold the opinion that modern paper currency is not money. Thus, the *Sharī'ah* rules for the exchange of gold and silver (*dinar* and *dirham*) do not strictly apply to it. Some of these scholars even allow *salam* in currency. Some Islamic banks in Pakistan, on the basis of this *fatwa* use *salam* in currency as an alternative to discounting of trade bill. They buy the dollars evidenced by the bill at a lower price, pay the money in Pak rupees in advance, as a capital of *salam*, to the presenter of bill and then receive delivery of dollars at a prescribed future date. Please note that dollars in this case are the *muslam fih'* or the *salam* commodity. For example, the Islamic bank enters into *salam* with holder of bill, for the purchase of 1000 dollars at the rate of 140 rupees per dollar to be delivered after one month. The Islamic bank pays Rs. 140,000 as price of commodity i.e. 1000 dollars in advance at the time of contract. It receives the delivery of dollars on specified date and sells it in the market say for Rs. 150,000 and thus earns a profit of Rs. 10,000. Here we observe that paper currency has been equated with *fulūs* and not with gold and silver and thus the exchange has been exempted from the requirement of prompt possession of counter-values. It is worthy to note that AAOIFI in its standard on *salam* has clearly prohibited *salam* transaction in modern paper currency. Can modern paper currency be equated with *fulūs* of past time? Here we attempt to answer this question.

If we examine the position of *fulūs* in the early Islamic legal literature, we will be led to the conclusion that there is no point of similarity between *fulus* (copper coins) of the past and paper money of today. The status of *fulūs* as a currency has always been matter of dispute among the early jurists. A majority of them did not recognize them as a legal tender comparable to gold and silver currency. According to Abu Hanifah and Abu Yusuf sale of one *fils* for two is permissible. They also dispute their eligibility as capital of partnership. Imām Muḥammad al-Shaybānī attaches the status of currency to the circulating *fulūs* only. Imām Shāfi'ī does not treat them as currency even if they are in circulation. He, argues that the circulation of *fulūs* is merely a convention among people, a convention that changes from time to time.

Abraham Udovitch has discussed in detail the reasons which made *fulūs* a disputed currency among the *fuqahā'*. He writes: "unlike gold and silver coins, the minting of copper coins was decentralized and was entrusted to local authorities. There was no single standard governing the size, shape, or weight of the coins. Their value and acceptance varied widely from place to place. It was for this reason that the jurists casted doubt on the validity of their use in the conduct of commercial operations."

Paper money, on the other hand, carries a fixed/nominal value which does not vary from place to place. It is a legal tender which is acceptable by all, in commercial transactions. It commands the authority of the state. Is meets all the requirements of money. Hence, there is no point of similarity between *fulūs* and the paper money. Paper currency is a legal tender. It has a binding force. A seller cannot refuse to accept it when presented by the buyer as price or consideration in sale transaction. Nor, can a lessor refuse to accept money as rental in lease arrangement. As regards *fulūs*, a seller could insist to receive price in dirham and dinar only, because *fulūs* did not have any binding status. The acceptance of *fulūs* as medium of exchange merely depended on the agreement of the parties. *fulūs* of past time were used for small transactions only. For example, a person wanted to buy 100 grams of sugar, he would pay price in *fulus*. It never meant for high value transactions. *Fulus* were used as fraction of dirham, like *paisas* in relation to rupees. Besides, *fulūs* was supporting money not the original money. Thus, there is no point of similarity between *fulūs* of past time and dollars and riyals of modern age. All the prominent *fiqh* academies and AAOIFI consider the modern paper currency as gold and silver. The modern paper currency like dirham and dinar of old times, possesses full characteristics of money. It cannot be relegated to the position of *fulūs*. Dr. Yusuf al-Qardawi writes:

> We pay prices of goods, wages to workers, dower to wives, *diyat* in *qatl al-khaṭa'* in this paper money. If someone steals it, he is subjected to the punishment of theft in all codes of criminal law. Then why should we deny it the status of legal money?

Keeping all these facts in view the Fiqh Academy of Makkah in its meeting held in October, 1986 maintained that paper money has all the characteristics of gold and silver. It is *thaman* from the point of view of the *Sharī'ah* and consequently it is subject to all the rules of the *Sharī'ah* pertaining to *ribā* , *zakah*, *salam*, etc., which are applicable to gold and silver.

5. Sale and lease back - *Ṣukūk*

Ṣukūk have been defined by the Accounting and Auditing Organization for Islamic Financial Institutions (AAOIFI) in its Sharī'ah Standard No. 17 as:

> "Certificates of equal value, representing undivided shares in ownership of tangible assets, usufruct and services or (in the ownership of) the assets of a particular project or special investment activity, however, this is true after; receipt of value of *ṣukūk*, the closing of subscription and the employment of funds received for the purpose for which the *ṣukūk* were issued."[43]

The standard gives examples of fourteen different types of investment *ṣukūk*, such as *ijārah ṣukūk*, *salam ṣukūk*, *murābḥah ṣukūk*, *mushārakah sukūk* etc. Out of these *ṣukūk*, *ijārah ṣukūk* are the most popular Islamic investment certificates, which are rapidly gaining ground in the capital market.[44]

There are three parties to the structure of *ijārah ṣukūk*: The originator (beneficiary) of *ijārah ṣukūk*; the Special purpose vehicle (SPV)[45] and the investors (ṣukūk holders, primary subscribers, or can also later include secondary subscribers, if the *ṣukūk* is tradeable). The beneficiary creates SPV, as an independent legal entity, that acts as trustee for investors. The originator/ beneficiary sells specific asset(s) to the primary

---

[43] Sharī'ah Standard No. 17, Investment *ṣukūk*, Article 2, p. 307.

[44] Tradability is the main reason behind this popularity. *Salam* ṣukūk, being used as a 'Treasury Instrument' by the Bahrain Monetary Authority is non-tradeable, as all *Salam ṣukūk* are.

[45] Even though SPV is perceived as the issuer, however, in reality this may not be the case, since, depending on the documentation, the SPV is 'issuer' of the *ṣukūk* acting (as an agent) on behalf of the originator (beneficiary), i.e. hence, in the real sense issuer of *ṣukūk* is always the originator (i.e. beneficiary) *per se.*

subscribers, through the help of the SPV, acting as its agent. *ṣukūk* are issued against that asset. The proceeds of sale are paid by the primary subscribers, to the originator, through the SPV. The primary subscribers then lease back the asset to the originator and the latter pays rentals to investors (primary subscribers), through the SPV. The originator also gives undertaking to buy it back on expiry of lease. Pursuant to this unilateral undertaking, it buys the asset, at its face value, or residual value, depending on the price at which the undertaking to purchase was given in the first place.

In Pakistan, WAPDA and Motorway *ṣukūk* are two important sovereigns *ṣukūk* which were based on sale and lease back structure. WAPDA needed finance to enhance power generation capacity at Mangla. So, it issued *ṣukūk* worth 7,000 million rupees against ten turbines installed at Mangla. For this purpose, WAPDA First *ṣukūk* company was created to act as an SPV. The asset, i.e. ten turbines, were leased back to WAPDA for a period of seven years. WAPDA gave an undertaking that it would buy them back at the end of lease period at face value.

The above structuring of sovereign *ijārah ṣukūk* has been contested by many *Sharī'ah* scholars. In the analysis of these scholars, the most controversial and objectionable feature of this type of *ṣukūk* is the buy-back arrangement in it, in explicit, or implicit form.[46] As mentioned above, the SPV in case of sovereign *ijārah ṣukūk* is created by the government, which is the initiator of, and beneficiary from, the deal . The government gives undertaking to buy it, at its face value. This is in nature of a put option for the SPV. The SPV, being a subsidiary of government[47], is under obligation to exercise this option in

[46] Salman Syed Ali, *Islamic Capital Market Products, Developments and Challenges*, Occasional paper No. 9, p. 52-53.

[47] It is pertinent to note that SPV has many different roles. It is acting as a Facilitator for the transaction, without SPV, it may be difficult

favour of the government; i.e. the beneficiary.[48] So it is almost certain that assets are reverted back to the government on maturity. This is also similar to *bay' bi al- wafā,* i.e. sale with right of redemption, another controversial transaction of classical Islamic jurisprudence. In *bay' bi al-wafā*, a person, who is in need of money, sells an object on the condition that after a certain period, he will buy it back from the buyer at face value, i.e. at the price of first sale. The International Islamic *Fiqh* Academy has declared this transaction invalid. The reason of its invalidity is that it puts restriction on proprietary right of owner, as he is not allowed to dispose it off, through sale or gift; rather it binds him to sell it back to the first seller, at face value. This transaction is more close to lending, rather than selling. The seller in the first transaction is borrower, and buyer is lender. The property remains with the lender, as mortgagee from which he benefits. It is an established fact that any benefit drawn from mortgaged property is *ribā*. After the expiry of loan period, the first debtor, pays price and gets his asset back. The second sale in above structure, is in fact return of loan amount to the lender.

---

to manage the transaction. The SPV acts as an agent, on behalf of the Originator/Beneficiary/(Real) Issuer of the ṣukūk, when dealing with the primary subscribers (Investors i.e. ṣukūk holders). On the other hand, the SPV also acts as a Trustee and Agent on behalf of the primary subscribers (Investors i.e. ṣukūk holders), when dealing with the Originator/Beneficiary/(Real) Issuer of the ṣukūk. In this capacity, it may be holding property documents, lien, charges on behalf of the *ṣukūk* holders etc., as in the presence of large number of investors, who should create charges and hold the property documents, as a Trustee, if the SPV was not there in the first place? In some instances, SPV acts independently also, when it earns agency fee etc. and incurs expense in carrying out its duties, and paying its staff etc.

[48] Ibid.

Besides the above, buy-back and *bay' bi al-wafā* feature in above *ijārah ṣukūk*, there are also some other controversial features in the arrangement. Some of such features are as follows:

In most of the cases, the ownership of the sold asset remains with the originator. It is not clear in what way the certificate holders own the asset. Even though beneficial ownership/ beneficial interest has been suggested in this case.

Major maintenance of the leased asset is undertaken by the lessee (originator/beneficiary), which implies that the risk related to ownership has not been transferred to the owners.

On dissolution event, (even in case of destruction), the lessee is bound to purchase leased property. This means that the risk is borne by the lessee.

Almost all *ṣukūk* guarantee the return of principal, to the *ṣukūk* holders, at maturity in exactly the same way as in the case of conventional bonds. This is accomplished by binding promise(s) from, either the issuer, or the manager, to repurchase the asset represented by the *ṣukūk*, at the stated price at which these were originally purchased by the investors.

Moulānī Taqī Usmanī, a renowned and leading *Sharī'ah* scholar of Islamic finance, has expressed his dissatisfaction over a number of *ṣukūk*. His main concern has been that these *ṣukūk* violate the *maqāṣid al- Sharī'ah* i.e. higher objectives of Islamic Law and Islamic Finance. In a working paper, presented before the Sharī'ah Board of AAOIFI, Moulānā Taqī Usmanī describes current *ṣukūk*, inimical to objectives of *Sharī'ah*. He observes:

"If we consider the matter from the perspectives of the higher objectives of Islamic law, or the objectives of Islamic economics, then *ṣukūk*, in which are to be found nearly all of the characteristics of conventional bonds, are inimical in every way to these purposes and objectives. The whole objective for which *ribā* was prohibited is the equitable distribution among partners of revenues from commercial and industrial enterprise. The mechanism used in *ṣukūk* today, however, strikes at the foundations of these objectives, and renders the *ṣukūk* exactly the same as conventional bonds in terms of their economic results."[49]

In order to make *ṣukūk* transactions *Sharī'ah* compliant, it is necessary that these issues be addressed; otherwise, it may become a replication of conventional bonds.

Ḥiyal as *Makhārij* in Islamic Finance

As opposed to subversive *ḥiyal,* stated above, there are certain legal devices which do not frustrate the purpose and spirit of Islamic law. They are clever uses of law to achieve legitimate ends. Legal devices in Islamic banks predominantly belong to this category. Following examples can be cited to prove this proposition.

Case no. 1

In conventional banking, the financial institution discounts a trade bill and pays to the client; the holder of bill, an amount that is less than the face value of bill on account of payment before time of maturity. The bank for instance pays to the client, who holds a bill payable after three months, Rs. 45,000/- instead of Rs. 50,000/- when he wants money before the time of maturity of his bill. This is obviously *ribā*, prohibited by *Sharī'ah*.

Some *Sharī'ah* scholars in Pakistan, have proposed *qarḍ ḥasan* combined with *wakālah* as an alternative to conventional bill discounting. Thus, Islamic bank, instead of discounting bill, may give *qarḍ ḥasan* up to the value of bill to the client, and then, as agent of the client, collect the bill from the drawer, i.e.

---

[49] Taqī Usmanī,*ṣukūk and Their Contemporary Applications*, p. 13.

debtor of the client and charge agency fee for this task. In the above example, the bank will give him *qarḍ ḥasan* of amount Rs. 50,000/- and it will charge Rs. 5,000/- as collection fee. Here, we observe that Islamic bank through this mode has addressed the need of customer while abstaining from ribā. The Council of Islamic Ideology has approved this device as an alternative to discounting.[50]

Case no. 2

In conventional banks, hedging against fluctuation in value of currency is affected through forward and future currency contracts, in which both the counter-values are deferred to a future date, while the requirement of Islamic law is that both the counter values should be exchanged in the same session of contract.

In Islamic banks, hedging against future devaluation of currencies is affected through unilateral promise to buy/sell, given by the client i.e. importer or exporter. This is done in the following manner:

(i) A customer, (exporter/importer formally requests the bank for a forward promise to buy/sell foreign currency, to hedge against foreign currency rate fluctuation in future.

(ii) The bank issues to the customer, "promise to sell/purchase", as the case may be, as per approved format. This promise to sell/purchase records the promise between bank and customer, to sell/buy foreign currency, at a future date.

The customer signs and returns the "promise to sell/purchase" to the bank.

---

[50] See for the legitimacy of this transaction, Taqī 'Usmanī, *Takmilah Fatḥ al-Mulhim*, vol. 1, p. 363.

The actual transaction takes place on maturity date and both counter values are exchanged.

The hedging can also be done through the execution of back to back interest free loans, using different currencies, without receiving or giving any extra benefit, provided, these two loans are not contractually connected to each other.

In the above cases, the solutions provided by Islamic banks, are in fact clever answers to difficult problems whereby, difficulty in the law is overcome, without frustrating the purpose of the law.

Conclusion

Ḥīlah in Islamic jurisprudence is used in two meanings. Firstly, as tricky solution(s) to difficult problem(s), without, *prima facie*, frustrating the purpose of law. They are clever uses of law to achieve legitimate ends. They are employed to overcome inconvenience in law. Such *ḥiyal* are considered to be lawful. The Ḥanafī and Ḥanblī jurists prefer to call them *makhārij* i.e. way out, rather than *ḥiyal.* Secondly, as a device and subterfuge, used in order to circumvent certain *Sharī'ah* prohibition(s), or to evade certain obligation(s). Such *ḥiyal* are declared unlawful by the *fuqahā'*.

Schools vigorously differ on the legitimacy of *ḥiyal*. Their views falling across spectrum. The Ḥanafīs and Shāfi'īs take the most lenient position. They declare them valid. Even the apparently subversive artifices are valid in these schools although immoral. *Bay' al-'īnah* (buy-back agreement) for instance, is lawful in Shāfi'ī School. Their argument is that it is the external form of contract, and not the underlying intention, that determines the validity of a contract, or otherwise. The Ḥanafī jurists allow *nikāḥ taḥlīl* i.e intervening marriage to facilitate remarriage between divorced couple after thrice repudiation (irrevocable divorce of major degree). They also allow *bay' bi al-wafā* i.e. Sale with right of redemption, under need.

Ḥanblī jurists have taken a balanced position on the issue. They allow only those legal devices that provide a way out from a difficult situation, and consequently overcome inconvenience in law.

Mālikī jurists condemn *ḥiyal* and declare them invalid. They even block ways that may lead to an evil. They call it *sadd al-dharā'i'*.

In Islamic finance, *ḥiyal* have been in practice since its inception. Many of them represented stratagems and subversive *ḥiyal*. Some of the *ḥiyal* in practice are in the nature of *makhārij*. They are wise answers to difficult problems, rather than unlawful *ḥiyal*. They are clever uses of law, to achieve legitimate ends. There are, however, some devices which certainly fall under the category of unlawful devices, as they defeat the higher purposes of Islamic economics and finance. These legal devices have badly affected the originality and authenticity of Islamic banking. It is pertinent to note that the opponents of Islamic banking, generally regard all the legal devices practiced in Islamic banks as unlawful *ḥiyal*, while the proponents identify them as *makhārij*, rather than as subversive *ḥiyal*. The list of such devices includes *bay' al-'īnah*, *tawarruq* and commodity *murābaḥah* transactions. Sale and lease back *ṣukūk* also partially fall in this category, as they have the properties of *bay' bi al-wafā'*, which has been declared invalid by the International *Fiqh* Academy.

Chapter 22

Investment in Equities: *Sharīʿah* Appraisal of Screening Norms

Introduction

Investment in equities is an important area of investment for individuals and financial institutions under present financial system. It provides an opportunity to financial institutions to get financial resources without involving in interest on one side, and to the individuals looking for interest free investment opportunity, on the other. Generally, it is considered permissible to invest in stocks of a business company on the reason that it is an act of becoming partner in the business to share the actual returns of the business. Despite the general permissibility, there are certain *Sharīʿah* issues involved in stocks trading which warrant serious consideration by the *Sharīʿah* scholars:

a) Is it allowed to purchase shares of a company which is involved in any impermissible business activity? Will it not be like becoming partner in an impermissible business?

b) Under present financial system, each company arranges finance through debt as well as equity. In most cases debts are interest based. Is it allowed to become partner in a business in which interest based financing is involved?

c) Each company has liquid as well as illiquid assets. What is the *Sharīʿah* position of purchasing shares of a company against cash when shares represent liquid assets beside physical assets?

d) Normally each company has account of receivables in total assets representing company's outstanding debt against other organizations or individuals. Is it allowed to sell/purchase the share of such a company in the secondary market at a price different from its face value?

e) Each company invests its surplus funds in different investment avenues in order to earn some return on these funds. Shareholders receive income in the form of dividend, which contains some portion of impermissible income as well. Is it allowed to receive income containing some impermissible portion?

Strictly speaking, it is difficult to find a company free from all these issues. Hence, a committed Muslim investor finds it difficult to select equities which are fully *Sharī'ah* compliant. Keeping in view the need of investors and specially the Islāmic financial institutions, contemporary *Sharī'ah* scholars have addressed this issue and devised *Sharī'ah* screening criteria against which Islamicity or otherwise, a stock could be judged. For a stock to be *Sharī'ah* compliant, they require that it must meet certain conditions like that the core business of company should be *halal* or that the ratio of liquid assets to total assets should not exceed certain limit.

Presently investment in Islamic capital market is governed by a number of screening norms and methods such as Dow Jones Islamic Market Index criteria, FTSE criteria, Meezan's criteria for investment in stocks, AAOIFI's screening criteria and SEC Malaysia's screening criteria.

The common attribute in all these screens is the condition that the business activities of investee Company should be *halal*. Other filters such as debt ratio, liquid assets ratio, impermissible investment ratio and impermissible income ratio are disputed among *Sharī'ah* scholars, as well as the Islāmic financial institutions operating in the capital markets. As a result, a particular stock is treated as *Sharī'ah*-compliant and *ḥalāl* under one screen, whereas the same is considered unlawful and *ḥarām* under the other.

A considerable number of *Sharī'ah* scholars support these criteria, as they find their legitimacy in the Qur'ān, Sunnah and other sources of *fiqh*. While another group of scholars find some doubts about their Islāmicity and view them as compromises on *Sharī'ah* prohibitions to allow the Islāmic Capital market to exist to cater the requirements of Islāmic financial institutions. They may not be convinced with the justifications provided by the supporters of these screens.

The objective of this study is to examine the *Sharī'ah* legitimacy of these screening criteria, to critically evaluate the arguments of both the proponents and opponents of these filters and to suggest the way forward for healthy growth of Islāmic capital market.

1. Screening Norms for *Sharī'ah* Compliance

As pointed out earlier, the *Sharī'ah* scholars have laid down screening criteria for investment in shares and stocks. This criterion takes into account the following issues:

- Business activities of the investee company
- Debt to total assets ratio
- Liquid assets as a percentage of total assets.
- Investment in non-*Sharī'ah* compliant activities
- Income from non-*Sharī'ah* compliant activities
- Net liquid assets versus share price

These screening norms can be divided into two broad categories:

i) Screens for business and activity of the company and;

ii) Screens pertaining to financial ratios such as debt to total asset ratio and liquid to illiquid assets ratio, etc.

In the following, we will focus on these screens.

Screens for acceptable business of the investee company

An important criterion to judge whether a stock is *Sharī'ah* compliant or not, is the nature of business of enterprise. If the core business of investee company is lawful (*ḥalāl*), then it is included in the investable universe of *Sharī'ah* compliant equities. This implies that stocks of the companies which are engaged in unlawful (*ḥarām*) businesses are not eligible for investment in the capital market. Thus, investment in shares of conventional banks, insurance companies, leasing companies, pork-related products industry, alcohol industry, companies engaged in activities such as gambling, pornography, etc is not permissible.

The opinion of *Sharī'ah* scholars is, however, divided on the status of shares of a company whose core business is *ḥalāl*, but is involved in certain *ḥarām* activities as well; like interest based borrowing from conventional banks or holding some interest bearing securities or placing surplus funds in interest bearing bank accounts. It also includes companies involved partly in *ḥarām* activities such as hotels or airlines which may sell or serve alcoholic drinks as part of their operations though their main activity is to provide accommodation and transportation to its customers. The scholars have divergent positions on this issue. A group of scholars does not allow investment in such stock while the other allows it. These opinions and their arguments are discussed here:

2. Viewpoint of Opponents

The scholars belonging to this group maintain that investment in the shares of companies which are partly involved in un-

Islāmic activities is not permissible. *Fiqh* Council of World Muslim League, Makkah[1], International *Fiqh* Academy, Jaddah[2], Council of *Fatwā* and Research, Kingdom of Saudi Arabia[3], Sharī'ah Board of Kuwait Finance House[4], Sharī'ah Board of Dubai Islāmic Bank[5], Sharī'ah Supervisory Board of Islāmic Bank of Sudan[6], and a large number of renowned religious scholars like Sheikh Abdul 'Azīz bin Bāz, Shaik Ṣālih Fouzān, AllamahYusuf al-Qaraḍāwī, Dr. 'Ali Salūs, Shaikh 'Abdullah Ibn Bai,[7] etc. hold this view.

These scholars assert that just as an individual, it is not allowed to invest his capital or property in an impermissible business - in the same way, one is not allowed to subscribe shares of a company which undertakes some forbidden activity. This is a sort of assistance and cooperation in the act of sin, prohibited by the *Sharī'ah.* A Muslim is required to abstain from *ḥarām* and also which is doubtful as regards its permissibility and impermissibility. The Holy Prophet (s.a.w.s) has said: "*Ḥalāl* is clear and *ḥarām* is also clear and between them are certain doubtful things which may people do not recognize. He, who guards himself against doubtful things, keeps religion and honor blameless, but whosever, indulges in them falls into what is

[1] See, Resolution of *Fiqh* Academy, World Muslim League, Makkah, 1995, Resolution No.4, Session No. 14.

[2] See, Resolutions and Recommendations of International *Fiqh* Academy, Resolution, 401, Session No. 7, pp.135-140.

[3] *Fatwā* Council of KSA, *Fatwá* No. 7468, vol 13 p. 408.

[4] Sharī'ah Ruling on Economic Matters, Kuwait Finance House, *Fatwā* no. 532.

[5] Sharī'ah Rulings, Sharī'ah Supervisory Board of Dubai Islāmic Bank, *Fatwā* no. 49.

[6] Sharī'ah Rulings of Sharī'ah Supervisory Board of Islāmic Bank, Sudan, *Fatwá* no. 16.

[7] These scholars have presented their papers in the seventh session of International *Fiqh*, Academy Jeddah. See, *Majallah Majma' Fiqhī*, vol. 7 pp-1-415.

unlawful."[8] In one of its *Sharī'ah* verdicts, *Fiqh* Academy of Rabitah al-Alam al-Islāmi maintained that "It is not lawful for a Muslim to buy shares of companies or banks which partly deal in *ribā*, when the buyer is fully aware of the fact. The reason for its prohibition is that the Qur'ān and Sunnah prohibit dealing in *ribā*, no matter the amount of *ribā* is small or big. To purchase shares of company which deals in *ribā* knowingly, is to take part in *ribā* based activity, because the management of company while lending or borrowing money with interest, in fact acts as an agent of shareholders.[99]

In response to a question posed to the Permanent Committee for Research and *Iftā'* of KSA, about shares of companies which provide public services such as electricity, gas, transport etc., but deposit their surplus money in conventional banks, the Permanent Committee for Academic Research and *Fatwā* ruled:

"It is not permissible to subscribe shares of companies which deposit their surplus amount in interest bearing account, when the purchaser knows about it. It is a kind of cooperation in act of sin and disobedience."[10] It further provides, "Placement of funds of these companies in conventional banks is impermissible likewise, to be shareholder in companies that deal in *ribā*, is unlawful, even if such company was not originally founded for *ribā* activity."[11]

---

[8] Al-Bayhaqī, *al-Sunan al-Kubrā,* Shu'ab al 'īmān, vol.5, p.50 *ḥadīth* no.5740.

[9] See, Resolution no. 4, *Fiqh* Academy, *Rābiṭah al-'Ālam al-Islāmi*, 14th Session held on 1415H/1995 AD.

[10] See, *Fatāwā al-Lajnah al-Dā'imah li al-Buḥūth al-'Ilmiyyah wa al-Iftā'*, KSA, *Fatwā* no.7468 vol. 13, p 408.

[11] Ibid, *Fatwá* no. 8715, p.409

3. Viewpoint of Proponents

There is yet another group of scholars who allows investment in companies which carry out mixed activities including interest based borrowing and lending. They, however, prescribe certain conditions or rules for such investments. This position is taken by Shaikh Taqi Usmani, Shaikh Muḥammad Ibn Othaimīn, Shaikh 'Abdullah Ibn al-Mavī, Dr. Nazīh Ḥammād, and the organizations such as Sharī'ah Boards of Islāmic Bank of Jordan and Meezan Investment Management Ltd. In the following, rules prescribed by this group for investment in mixed business are discussed.

4. Rules for Investment in Mixed Business

The conditions and rules prescribed by them pertain to interest-based borrowing, placement of funds with conventional banks, quality of unlawful income, etc.

Rule no. 1

Borrowing with interest should not exceed prescribed limits. There is a difference of opinion regarding the permissible limit. Position of different Islāmic capital market indices providers on the issue is as follows:

a) Dow Jones position on the issue is that interest bearing debt should not exceed 33% of total market capitalization of company.

b) AAOIFI's position on the indebtedness of company is that it should not exceed 30% of total market capitalization.[12]

---

[12] AAOIFI, Standard No.21, Clause 3/4.

c) Meezan Index allows interest bearing debt up to 37% of total assets.[13]

Rule no. 2

Investment in non-*Sharī'ah* compliant activities, such as interest based lending and placement of funds with conventional banks, should not exceed certain limit.

The permissible ratio or tolerance benchmark ranges from 15% to 33% of total assets of the company. 15% benchmark was previously prescribed by the Sharī'ah Board of Rajhi Company but subsequently it was totally cancelled.

Dow Jones index does not acknowledge any unlawful investment up to 30% of total assets of company whereas Meezan Index sets acceptability limit for the ratio of interest bearing investment at 33% of market capitalization.[14]

Sharī'ah Advisory Council (SAC) of the Securities Commission Malaysia (SC) - Position on mixed activity

For companies with activities comprising both permissible and non- permissible elements, the SAC considers two additional criteria:

a) The public perception or image of the company must be good; and

b) The core activities of the company are important and considered *maṣlaḥah* to the Muslim *ummah* and the country, and the non- permissible element is very small

[13] See;www.almeezangroup.com/KnowledgeCentre/SharīahScreeningCriteria/tabid/124/Default.aspx visited on 22nd March, 2015.

[14] http://www.sc.com.my/wpcontent/uploads/eng/html/icm/Resolutions_SAC_2ndedition.pdf

and involves matters such *'umūm balwā*[15] (common plight and difficult to avoid), *'urf*[16] (custom) and the rights of the non-Muslim community' which are accepted by Islām.

Benchmarks of tolerance

The Sharī'ah scholars at Sharī'ah Advisory Council Malaysia have suggested following benchmarks of tolerance of mixed business:

a) Five percent benchmark

This is applied to assess the level of mixed contributions from the activities that are clearly prohibited such as *ribā* (interest-based companies like conventional banks), gambling, liquor and pork.

b) Ten percent benchmark

This is applied to assess the level of mixed contributions from the activities that involve the element of *'umūm balwa* which is a prohibited element affecting most people and difficult to avoid. For example, interest income from fixed deposits in conventional banks.

---

15 *'Umūm balwā* is a situation or action that affects most people and is difficult to avoid. Things are said to be the nature of *'Umūm balwā* when they affect the members of the society in general. They are matters of which people generally have definite needs that afflict people in general and recur relatively frequently in people's life. [al-Mausū'ah al- fiqhiyah al-Kuwaitiyah, 1st Ed (Dār al Ṣafwā: 1994), vol.31, p.6.

16 *'Urf* (العرف) is an Arabic Islāmic term referring to the custom of a given society. To be recognized in an Islāmic society if compatible with the Sharī'ah law.

c) Twenty-five percent benchmark

This benchmark is used to assess the level of mixed contributions from the activities that are generally permissible according to *Sharīʿah* and have an element of *maṣlaḥah* (public interest), but there are other elements that may affect the *Sharīʿah* status of these activities. For example, hotel and resort operations, shares trading etc., as these activities may also involve other activities that are deemed non-permissible according to the *Sharīʿah*.

Rule no. 3

Earning from impermissible investments/activities should not exceed 5% of total revenue. As mentioned earlier, this criterion applies to the companies whose core business is *Sharīʿah* compliant such as hotels which may also serve alcoholic drinks as a part of their main activity. In addition to that, they maintain account with conventional banks which fetches the company some interest. The company may also at times deploy excess short term liquidity in bank deposits and securities as a measure of treasury management. Such investments are allowed by the *Sharīʿah* scholars and Islāmic capital market indices providers, as long as the income from impermissible business activities and investments is less than or up to 5% of total revenue of company. But the shareholder is required to cleanse the actual percentage of impermissible income from his dividend income.

These bench marks of tolerance may be summarized in the form of table as follows:

Table 1: General Bench Mark of Tolerance

Islāmic Indices Providers	Debt to Total Assets Ratio	Liquid to Total Assets Ratio	Account Receivables to Total Assets Ratio	Impermissible Income
Dow Jones	Less than 33%	Less than 33%	Less than 45%	Less than or Equal to 5% of Total Revenue
FTSE	Less than 33%	Less than 33%	Less than 50%	Less than or Equal to 5% of Total Revenue
Meezan Islāmic Fund Index	Less than 33%	Less than 25%	Less than 75%	Less than 5% of Total Revenue
SEC Malaysia	Less than 33%	Less than 33%	N/A	5% - 25% of Total Revenue (depending on nature of activities)

5. Arguments of the Proponents of Mixed Activity

The scholars allowing mixed activity and mixed investments, rely on general - evidences of *Sharīʿah*, such as the principle of *ḥājjah* (need), *rafaʿ al-ḥaraj* (removal of hardship) and similar evidences. No specific evidence is adduced to prove validity of stocks of mixed companies. These scholars, for instance, argue that *Sharīʿah* acknowledges relaxation of rules in case of necessity and need. In *Sharīʿah*, sometimes a public need is treated like necessity that calls for relaxation of rules. On this basis, *bayʿ al-wafāʾ* [17](sale with right of redemption) has been allowed by later Ḥanafī jurists.

[17] *Bayʿ al-wafāʾ* is defined as an archaic sale with redemption.

The argument of these scholars is that a company has become a need of day. A company provides opportunity to investors to investment their surplus money. But it is also a fact that modern companies frequently resort to interest bearing borrowings to meet their liquidity needs. The companies also place their excess funds with conventional banks. This is true that it is not Islāmically desirable to deal with such companies. But to ignore them totally may cause a greater harm for the individuals and society. According to a known *Sharī'ah* principle a lesser harm is endured to avert a greater harm. Another *Sharī'ah* principle suggests that when two interests clash, one weak and other strong, latter prevails.[18] They also argue that borrowing with interest is not lawful but the borrower becomes lawful owner of the amount that he has borrowed. He can lawfully trade with it. The profit generated from it is also *ḥalāl.*[19]

In the opinion of these scholars, *ribā* occurring in the stocks of these companies, forms only a subsidiary part of stock which is composed of tangible assets, cash and interest bearing debt.

6. Screens for Acceptable Financial Ratios

As a general rule of *Sharī'ah*, a s hare can be traded at par only if it represents only cash. However, if it has been converted to some illiquid assets, then it can be traded at value different from its face value. The opinions of *Sharī'ah* scholars and Islāmic capital market indices providers are divided on acceptable limit of liquid assets, and the liquidity thresholds suggested by the *Sharī'ah* Boards range from 33% to 75% of total assets of company. Liquid assets include account receivables as well.

---

[18] Walīd ibn Rāshid, "*Talqīḥ al-afhām al-'illiyah bi sharḥ al-qawā'id al-fiqhiyyah*", vol.4, P.10.

[19] 'Usmāni, M. Taqi, "*Islām aur Jadīd Ma'īshat wa Tijarat*", p.87.

Following are some important screening criteria regarding acceptable liquidity ratios.

1) According to Meezan, for a company to be *Sharīʿah* compliant, the total illiquid assets of the investee company, should be at least 25% of the total assets.

2) According to Dow Jones, liquid assets should be less than 33% of market capitalization.

3) AAOIFI sets acceptable limit of liquid assets at 30% of total assets.

Sharīʿah basis of acceptable financial ratios

The main reliance of *Sharīʿah* scholars is on the juristic principle that provides: "A matter that cannot be ignored in independent contracts can be ignored in subsidiary contracts" (*yajūzo taba'n mā lā yajūzo istiqlālan*)[20], and the principle: "A thing which is not permissible in itself, may be permissible as accessory."[21] From these juristic principles and maxims they conclude that rules of *ribā al- faḍl* and *ṣarf* will be relaxed in cases where *ribā* does not occur in principal part of transaction. Thus, when the assets of company are composed of tangible assets, cash and debt, the rules of *ṣarf* will not be applied because the primary object of transaction is trading in tangible assets of the Company, not an exchange between two *rabwī* (*ribā* bearing) commodities. So, the size of cash and debt will be ignored, because cash and debts have subsidiary status in the contract. The AAOIFI also upholds this position, although its own view point about acceptable ratio of liquid asset is 30% of total assets. This implies that the scholars at AAOIFI require that illiquid

[20] Ibn Rajab, *al- Qawāʿid al-Fiqhiyah*, Commentary: Dr. M. Ali Al-Bannā, (Beirut, 1st Edition), P.363.

[21] Art., *Majallah al-Aḥkām al-ʿAdliyyah*, Karkhanah Tijārat e Kitāb, Karachi.

assets should constitute a significant part of combination. Section 3/19 of *Sharī'ah* standard No.21 lays emphasis on primary object of transaction. It states:

"If the purpose and activity pertains to trading in tangible assets, benefits and rights, trading in its shares is permitted, without taking into account the rules of *ṣarf* transaction in debts; irrespective of their size, as in such case these are secondary. If, however, the objective of corporation and its usual activity is dealing in gold, silver or currencies, it is obligatory to undertake trading in its shares in the light of the rules of *ṣarf.*

The evidential basis of above ruling of AAOIFI is a famous *ḥadīth* of Ibn 'Umar', and a number of *Sharī'ah* Maxims mentioned in the beginning of discussion. Here we will discuss a *ḥadīth* narrated by Ibn 'Umar and the opinion of Muslim jurists' on the issue.

It is narrated: by Ibn Umar (ra), that Prophet (pbuh) said: when a person buys a slave who has wealth, then the wealth is for the seller, unless the buyer stipulates this too.[22] [23]

In this *ḥadīth*, the word "Wealth": refers to cash, debt and gold. The *ḥadīth* indicates that cash or debts, less or more, will not be taken into account in the *ḥukm*, because in this case, cash possessed by slave is secondary and subordinate to the primary contract, which is a sale of slave. Thus, sale is affected, primarily on slave not cash or debt; which he possesses. Thus, cash will not be exchanged with similar amount. Ibn Ḥajar explains the *ḥadīth* in the following words;

> "The generality of the words indicates permissibility of sale of slave; in absolute manner. Thus, sale is lawful, even if the wealth held by the slave is a *rabwī* commodity (such as

[22] *Ṣaḥīḥ Bukhārī*, with commentary of *Fatḥ al-Bāri*, (Cairo: Salafi Publishers, 1380 AH), vol 2, p.81

> gold and silver): because, the sale transaction is affected on the slave and not on wealth i.e. gold and silver. Wealth in the transaction is subsidiary, which is irrelevant in the contract."[23]

Imām Mālik has also taken the same position in *al-Muwaṭṭā*. He comments on the *ḥadīth,* "It is our considered opinion, that if a buyer stipulated for wealth of slave in the contract, it would be the property of buyer; regardless of whether it is in cash form, or it is receivable, and regardless of whether the wealth of slave exceeds the price of slave, or is equal to it."[24]

The statement of Imām Mālik (Allah's Blessing be upon hi m) is explicitthat *ṣarf* rules will be ignored in this case because the gold possessed by the slave, is not the principal object of contract. Such sale is permissible, even if the price paid by the buyer, is also in the form of gold. There is yet another ruling in Mālikī law, which suggests that the value of gold content should not be more than one third of the value of the asset, slave in this case. In a statement in al-Muwaṭṭā, Imām Mālik rules that:

> "if a person bought a sword or ring with gold or silver content against dinars or dirhams as consideration, such sale would be permissible if the value of gold or silver content is one third and the value of remaining part is two third, provided the sale takes place hand to hand, without any delay, in the delivery of counter values. This is what the people of Madinah have been practicing till our time."[25]

---

[23] *Fatḥ al-Bārī*, Al-matba'h al-Salafiyah, (Cairo: 1380 AH) vol.5, p.51.

[24] 25 Malik bin Anas, *Al-Muwaṭṭā*: M. Fuad Abdul Bāqā, (Beirut: Dār Iḥyā al-turāth al 'Arabī, 1985), vol.2, P.775

[25] *Ibid*, Ibn Qasim, a senior pupil of Imām Mālik says: "it is lawful to buy slave along with money he holds, against dirhams or credit" [Ibn 'Abdul Barr, vol.19, p.32]

Renowned *Sharī'ah* scholar Maulana Taqi Usmani also subscribes to this view. He says that the illiquid part of the combination should not be in ignorable quantity. He, however, stipulates that the price of the combination should be more than the value of the liquid amount contained therein. For example, if a share of 100 dollars represents 75 dollars plus some fixed assets, the price of the share must be more than 75 dollars. In this case, if the price of the share is fixed 105, it will mean that 75 dollars are in exchange of 75 dollars owned by the share and the balance of 30 dollars is in exchange of the fixed assets. Conversely, if the price of that share is fixed as 70 dollars, it will not be allowed because the 75 dollars are represented by the share in this case, against an amount which is less than 75. This kind of exchange falls within the definition of *ribā*, and is not allowed.[26]

Other classical opinions

The Ḥanafī and Ḥanbalī jurists allow sale of a dirham and one *mudd* (a measurement) of *'ajwah* dates with two *dirhams*. In this case, one *dirham* will be against *dirham* and other *dirham* will be counted as price of *mudd 'ajwah. But* they do not allow sale of one *mudd 'ajwah* dates and one *dirham*, in exchange of one *dirham* or less than one *dirham*, because in case of its sale at par; or with discount, gives rise to *ribā al-faḍl* takes place which is prohibited.[27]

Shāfi'ī jurists do not allow exchange between two homogenous *ribā* bearing goods, such as sale of one *mudd* (a measurement of capacity) and *dirham* with two *dirhams*, or sale of sword studded

---

[26] Usmani, "*Islām aur Jadid Maeeshat wa Tijarat*", Idara-e- Ma'arif ul Qur'ān, (Karachi: 1996), p.86

[27] *Fatḥ al-Qadīr*, (Beirut: 'Ālam al-kutub), vol.6, p.266; *Al-Mughni*, (Riyadh: Maktabah Al-Riyadh al Ḥadīthah), vol.4, p.39, Ibn 'Ābidīn, *Radd al-Muhtār 'alā al-durr al-mukhtār* (Hashiat ibn 'Ābidīn), (Beirut: Dār al- fikr, 2nd edition, 1992) vol4, p.236

with gold against *dinars*[28]. They rely for their view on the *ḥadīth* of Fadālah Ibn 'Ubaid (r.a.t.a). It is narrated by Fadālah (r.a.t.a) that when Prophet (s.w.a.s) was in Khyber a gold necklace studded with the precious stones was brought to him. This necklace, a part of the war booty, was for sale. The Prophet (s.a.w.s) ordered that gold content of the necklace be separated from the rest. Thereafter, the Prophet (s.a.w.s) directed that the gold of the necklace be sold for gold on the basis of equality in weight.[29] From this, the Shāfi'ī jurists have concluded that sale of an object composed of illiquid and liquid asset is not allowed, unless the liquid content in it is separated from the rest, and the same is sold on the basis of equality in weight.

7. Analysis of Screens

We have explained above that two sets of Screens that govern modern capital market, first pertains to business of the investee company and second deals with financial ratios.

Screens for mixed activity

As noted earlier, mixed activity refers to that investee company whose primary business is lawful, but it is involved in some impermissible activity. Impermissible activity, besides other things, also include placing deposit and surplus money of the company in interest bearing accounts as well as carrying interest bearing debts. The scholars allowing mixed activity business, argue that *Sharī'ah* principles of *rafa'al-ḥaraj* (removal of hardship), '*umūm balwa* provide *Sharī'ah* jurisdiction for the above activity. These principles call for relaxation in the general rule of prohibition. Malaysian screening criterion tolerates forbidden portion of business even upto 25% invoking the principle of '*umūm balwa*, which in our view, is an out of

---

[28] Nawawī, *Rawdah al-Ṭālibīn*, (Damascus: Al-Maktabah Al-Islāmiah, vol.3, p.384-386, Al-Mughni, vol.4, p.39.

[29] Ṣaḥīḥ Muslim, (1955), Kitāb Al- Musaqāt, Vol.3 p. 1213-1214.

context use of principle. The principle speaks about a matter of common occurrence, which is though unlawful, but cannot be easily avoided, so relaxation in general rule is sought. It does not refer to a situation where a person deliberately involves himself in an unlawful business and justifies it on the plea that *ḥarām* is so prevalent that it is hard for him to avoid.

To justify interest bearing loans, some scholars also argue that though it is improper and abhorrent act to acquire interest bearing loan, yet the borrower becomes the lawful owner of borrowed amount. The borrowed money in consequence of loan contract moves into risk and liability of the borrower and; because of the risk and liability, he is entitled to profit resulting from it. It is, however, advisable according to these scholars that he should donate in charity that portion of profit which he earned from the investment as interest based loan. In *fiqhi* Symposium of Al-Barkah, Fatwá No.12, it was held that "If value of share of a company which sometime carried interest bearing borrowing, has risen, due to interest based loan and performance of company, any value addition in the company owing to injection of interest bearing loan/capital should be proportionately donated in charity." Commenting on the *fatwá*, Dr. Abdus Sattar Abu Ghuddah, a renowned scholar of Islāmic finance, held the view that such charity is only a recommended act not obligatory on the investee company. The company, because of the risk and liability in relation to borrowed amount is rightful owner of income arising from its investment. To declare it legitimate income Abu Ghuddah invokes famous *Sharī'ah* maxim: "*Al-Ghurmu bi al-Ghunm*" i.e. Gain is with risk and liability.[30] However, the verdict of Dr. Abu Ghudah, may not need any comment. One may easily

[30] Abu Ghuddah, Dr. Abdul Sattar, "*Al-Ajwibah al-Sharī'ah fī al-Taṭbīqāt al- Maṣrafiyyah*", Sharikah al-Tawfīq, (Majm'ah Dallah al-Barkah, 2002), p.140

conclude from it that he is unintentionally advocating the permissibility of interest bearing borrowing.

Similar to it is the opinion that suggests that the shareholder should raise his voice in Annual General Meeting against policy of the management of the investee company for interest based borrowing. After expressing his dissatisfaction, he is absolved of his responsibility towards Allah, and cannot be held responsible for this forbidden act. The scholars holding this opinion do not suggest an investor that he should disinvest his stock, immediately on knowing the fact that company is engaged in interest based borrowing. In our opinion, if he does not disinvest it, he is deemed to be a p art of impermissible business of company. Besides, the suggestions to record protest may not be practicable for minority shareholders who hold very small number of shares.

Conclusion

From the above discussion we may conclude that the *Sharī'ah* scholars may now need to review the basis of deciding the tolerance levels for the screens, particularly the relaxation about interest bearing borrowings, or placing surplus money in interest bearing accounts up to certain limits (one third) which is not justified in the light of Islāmic principles. Hence, such relaxation should be excluded from the list of approved Sharī'ah screens keeping in view the severity of prohibition of *ribā*. Needless to say those such screens were devised about two / three decades back when Islāmic financial institutions were very limited in number and did not have capacity to cater the needs of investee companies, which compelled them to resort to conventional banks for interest based borrowing for the development of their business. Today, the Islāmic banks have the potential and capacity to meet the working capital need of companies through *ijārah*, *salam* and *istiṣnā'*, and thus, need for interest based borrowing does no arise. The same can be said about placement of surplus funds in conventional banks. The opportunity is now available to place funds with Islāmic banks and earn income in *Sharī'ah* compliant manner. It would not be out of place to mention here that Dr. Husain Hamid Hassan, a renowned scholar of *Sharī'ah* from Azhar University, also subscribes to this viewpoint. In his paper presented in the 20th symposium of Al-Barakah on Islāmic Economics in Malaysia, he writes, "It is not allowed to take part in the business of a company whose objectives is lawful and permissible, but it raises interest based loans, against interest, or its contracts are irregular or void. The trading of such shares, and profit arising from it, is illegitimate. The reason is that it is a sort of cooperation in an act of sin and disobedience of Allah."[31]

As regards the proportion of cash and receivables in the assets of a company, the fact of the matter is that it cannot be treated with that strictness and rigidity which is required to be observed in cases of interest based borrowing and lending. We should bear in mind that cash and receivables are basically lawful components of company's business. Certain restrictions are, however, required to be observed in trading of companies' shares. But the strict rules of *ṣarf* and *ribā al- faḍl* cannot be applied on shares trading, when they are traded as a subsidiary part of the transaction. *Ḥadīth* of Ibn 'Umer and its explanation by Mālikī jurists and Ibn Ḥajar 'Asqalānī, clearly provides that quantum of cash is ignored when the purpose of business is not trading in cash. In *ḥadīth* of Fudalah bin 'Ubaid al-Anṣārī, on the other hand, the sale of golden necklace for equivalent *dinars* was a *Sharī'ah* requirement because gold was the principle object of sale and it was the principle part of transaction. In other

---

[31] Ḥassan, Hussain Ḥāmid, "*Components of Share and Effect Thereof on Trading*" paper presented in symposium on 3-5 Rabī'al-Awwal, 1422 AH, held in Kuala Lumpur.

words, sale was affected on gold i.e. necklace. On this analogy, if the primary objective of investee company is to trade in currency (Forex exchange business) or gold or silver, or debt instruments, then rules of *ṣarf* and *ribā al-faḍl* will be strictly applied on it. Similarly, if the company has not started its business and its whole capital is in form of cash, or in form of receivables at the time of liquidation, then rules of *bay'al-ṣarf* and *ribā al-faḍl* will be applied on it. Other than these situations, quantum of liquid vis-a-vis illiquid or accounts receivable in total assets of a company doing business and having some real assets will be ignored and rules of *ribā al- faḍl* will not be taken into consideration strictly in trading of its shares. However, *Sharī'ah* board of any bank or fund management company may like to determine any threshold for guidance of their treasuries.

Chapter 23

Islamic Microfinance: Fundamental Concepts and Principles

Introduction

Poverty has been a cause of concern in every society throughout the human history Islamic views poverty as a social ailment which has potential to create number of social and moral evils in the society. The Holy Prophet (s.a.w.s) always sought refuge in Allah from poverty. He warned against evil consequences of poverty.

Muslim society from its inception, has been concerned with eradication of poverty. The institutions such as *zakāh* and *waqf* played vital role in establishing economic and social justice in the society and helping the poor and the destitute to attain a respectable standard of living. Islamic microfinance, has emerged in recent past, as an effective tool for socio economic development in Muslim countries and has effectively contributed in the alleviation of poverty and economic uplift of the society. Through its multifarious charitable and business activities, it has shared the burden of governments and their responsibilities towards the poor and destitute segment of the society.

Concept of Islamic Microfinance

Microfinance refers to small loans available to poor people (especially those traditionally excluded from financial services) through programs designed specially to meet their particular needs and circumstances. Core objective of Microfinance is to eradicate poverty, to raise income levels and to broaden financial markets by providing financial services to the financially excluded people. Since conventional microfinance is interest based, a committed Muslim refrains from availing financial services offered by conventional microfinance institutions. For such religiously motivated people, Islamic microfinance is the only choice. It provides microfinance services to lower income groups in a *Sharī'ah* compliant manner through the religiously tailored products such as *qarḍ ḥasan*, *murābaḥah*, *muḍārabah*, *salam* etc.

Fundamental Beliefs and Values

A number of beliefs and social and moral values underlay the concept of Islamic microfinance. These values are the basic pillars of the institution of Islamic microfinance. Some important values are explained as under:

Man is custodian of wealth, not its real owner

According to Islamic law, the status of man in the universe is that of trustee of Allah. Thus, whatever is in the hand of man, is only a trust reposed by Allah in him.

The Qur'ān says: "Spend in charity out of the property of which He made you custodians" (or trustees)[1]. In another verse the Qur'ān attributes ownership of wealth to Allah. It says, "And give in charity out of God's wealth which He gave unto you."[2] The verse points to the fact that man has been given temporary right of ownership. He has the right of property over the things but his right is not absolute. He is bound to spend it according to instructions of its real owner. In another verse the Qur'ān has provided instructions about the obligation of a Muslim in his wealth. The Qur'ān says: "Seek the other world by means of what Allah has bestowed upon you, and do not be negligent about your share in this world, And do good to others) as Allah

---

[1] Qur'ān, 57:07

[2] Qur'ān, 24:33

has done good to you and do not seek to spread disorder on the earth."[3] The instructions mentioned in the verse are:

1- Allocation of a portion of wealth to others

2- Prohibition of use of wealth in a way that is likely to produce collective ills.

Social responsibility

Social responsibility, also known as *"kafālah 'āmmah"* suggests that society as a whole has responsibility and obligation towards less fortunate and deprived segment of the society. It is generally claimed that eradication of poverty and uplift of living standard of people, is the responsibility of state which ought to perform this duty through distribution of *zakāh*. The Holy Qur'ān and Sunnah refute this misconception. Holy Prophet (s.a.w.s) was asked whether the poor have any right to the wealth of the rich beside *zakāh*. He replied, yes, they have certainly right beside *zakāh*. Then he recited the following verse: "Righteousness is not that you turn your faces towards the east or the west, but [true] righteousness in [in] one who believes in Allah, the Last Day, the angels, the Book, and the Prophets and gives wealth, in spite of love for it, to relatives, orphans, the needy. The traveler those who ask for help. and for freeing slaves: [and who establishes prayer and gives *zakā*"[4] .

Hadrat Ali (r.a.t.a) narrated that Allah said:

> "Allah has made obligatory on the rich to provide the poor with what is adequate for them and if the poor are hungry or naked, this is only due to the fact that the rich have deprived them of their right."[5]

[3] Qur'ān, 28:77

[4] Qur'ān, 02:177

[5] *Majma' al-Zawā'id*, Kitāb al- Zakāh, Bab Farḍ al-Zakāh, vol. 3, p. 62

It is pertinent to note that according to the Qur'ān, the share of poor in the wealth of rich is his right, not a favour or benevolence from the rich. The concept has been emphasized in a number of Quranic verses. In *Sūrah Isrā*, the Qur'ān says: "In their wealth, there is a due share of the needy who asks and who is prevented from asking."[6] Here Qur'ān alludes to the obligation of *zakāh*. In *Sūrah al-ddhāriyāt* the Qur'ān says: "And in their wealth, there is a right for needy who asks, and who is prevented from asking."[7] Here Qur'ān clearly mentions that whatever a poor person receives from the rich he receives it as a matter of right.

Explaining the meaning of the above mentioned verse, renowned religious scholar Moulānā Muḥammad Shāfi'ī writes:

> Under materialistic economic systems, there is only one way of acquiring the right to wealth and that is by direct participation in the process of production. In other words, only those factors that have taken a direct part in producing wealth, are entitled to a share in wealth and none else. On the contrary, the basic norm of Islam in this respect is that wealth is in principle the property of Allah, and He alone can prescribe the rules as to how it is to be appropriated. Thus, according to the Islamic point of view. not only those who have directly participated in the production of wealth are entitled to its spoils, but also those to whom Allah has apportioned a share by His Command. Allah has made it obligatory upon others to help the needy, who are the legitimate sharers in the wealth of others. Hence, the poor, the helpless, the needy and the destitute, all have a right to wealth. Allah has made obligatory on all those producers of wealth, among whom wealth is in the first place distributed that they should pass

[6] Qur'ān, 70:24

[7] Qur'ān, 51:19

on to the less fortunate ones a part of their wealth. The Qur'ān makes it quite explicit that in doing so, they would not be obliging the poor and the needy in anyway. but only discharging their obligation, for the poor and the needy are entitled to share in wealth as a matter of right.[8]

Social and economic justice

Since all resources, according to the Qur'ān, are gift of God to all human being there is no reason why they should remain concentrated in few hands. Islam emphasizes distributive justice and gives a program for redistribution of income, so that every individual is guaranteed a standard of living that is humane and respectable. Holy Prophet (s.a.w.s) has said: "He is not a true Muslim who eats his fill when his next door neighbor is hungry." Islam prohibits concentration of wealth in few hands It demand that wealth should be circulated in the society as widely as possible, so as the distinction between the rich and poor is narrowed down. The Qur'ān says: "So that this wealth should not become confined to the rich amongst you."[9]

Hadrat 'Umar (r.a.t.a) the second Caliph in one public address emphasized that everyone had equal right in the wealth of the community, and that if he were to live longer, he would see to it that even a shepherd on mount of *San'ā* received his share from his wealth. This means that circulation of wealth among large number of people, and the attainment of well-being of the society, is the objective of Islam, which it seeks to realize through its institutions, such as *zakāh*. The above beliefs and values lie at the very root of Islamic microfinance. These very values make Islamic microfinance a really *Sharī'ah* -based finance.

---

[8] Muftī Muḥammad Shafī', Distribution of Wealth in Islam, Begum Aishah Bawani Waqf, Karachi, 1979, p.4

[9] Qur'ān, 59:7

Islamic Social Values in Islamic Microfinance

Islamic microfinance is based on number of islamic values:

- *Akhuwwah*/**Brotherhood**

According to teaching of Islam, Muslim are brotheren. This bond imposes a number of duties on the members of this community, prominent of these duties is that they should share the pain of each other. Holy Prophet (s.a.w.s) said:

> "The similitude of believers in regard to mutual love, affection, fellow feeling is that of one body, when any limb of it aches, the whole body aches, because of sleeplessness and fever."[10]

The Holy Prophet (s.a.w.s) after migration to Madinah, created *Muwakhāt* Institution, whereby *muhajirūn* were declared brotheren for *anṣār* and by virtue of this relationship, they were entitled to certain rights and privileges. *Muwākhat* is still a driving force for Akhuwat Islamic Microfinance Institution.

- *Ta'āwun fi Al-Khair*/**Cooperation in acts of goodness**

Islam encourages cooperation in acts of goodness and human welfare among members of human community. Allah says: "And cooperate in acts of goodness." The Holy Prophet (s.a.w.s) entered into treaties of cooperation with non-Muslims for the wellbeing of both communities. Islam treats human community as a family of God. The Holy Prophet (s.a.w.s):

"The creatures are the "Family of Allah" the most beloved to Allah among them is the one who is most beneficial to Allah's Family."[11]

---

[10] Ṣaḥīḥ Bukhārī, Ḥadith no. 6011

[11] Baihaqī, Shu'ab al-Īmān

- **Generosity**

Islam Promotes and encourages generosity in Muslim society. In number of Quranic verses, Muslims have been exhorted to be generous in spending in the way of Allah. "Spend your wealth for the cause of Allah "Similarly the Holy Prophet (s.a.w.s) said, "the generous man is near Allah, near Paradise, near men and far from Hell, but the miserly man is far from Allah, far from Paradise, far from men and near Hell. Indeed, an ignorant man who is generous is dearer to Allah than a worshipper who is miserly." In another *ḥadīth* He said, "Two traits are not combined in a believer: stinginess and bad manners."

In response to those commandments, Muslims have always been generous as a community. Even in present times, where Muslims are as a whole fare far from the practice of Islam, this continues to hold true.

- ***Al-'Adl* (Justice in distribution of wealth)**

Islam seeks equitable distribution of wealth in the society, and discourages concentration of wealth in few hands. *Zakāh, waqf* and Islamic microfinance institutions provide a mechanism for equitable distribution of wealth in the society. In the distribution of the property of *fai*, Qur'ān explains its rationale that its objective is to prevent concentration of wealth among the rich segment of the society.

- ***Iḥsān* and *īthār***

Iḥasān is the higher hierarchical stage of *'adl*. The Prophet said: "No one of you becomes a true believer until he likes for his brother what he likes for himself." The Prophet said "A Muslim is a brother of another Muslim. So he should neither oppress him nor hand him over to an oppressor. And whoever fulfilled the needs of his brother, Allah will fulfill his needs."

- ***Sadaqah Jāriyah***

Islam encourages charitable investment, or spending for social welfare which brings him reward in the world hereafter without expecting any worldly reward on it. It may take many forms such as: donations, *waqf*, *qarḍ ḥasan*, etc. *Qarḍ ḥasan* is spending in the path of Allah without expectation of return in this world. The Muslim jurists treat *Qarḍ ḥasan* as a gratuitous transaction not as an exchange or commutative transaction.

Islam ensures that the *ṣadaqah jāriyah* is a profitable investment and no risk of loss is involved in it. Allah says:

> "Devil threatens you with the prospect of poverty. Whereas Allah promises you his forgiveness and bounty and Allah is infinite, all knowing."[12] The fear of poverty will not materialize if we know that we will also be helped by our brothers in time of need.

Model of *qaḍ ḥasan* practices by Akhuwat and other Islamic microfinance institutions (IMFI's) is a manifestation of this value of *ṣadqah jāriyah*.

- **Prohibition of *Isrāf* and *Tabdhīr***

Islam prohibited wasteful consumption, in this way less money will be needed and more will be available to spend on the needy people. Allah says:

> "And give the relative his right, and (also the poor and the traveller, and do not spend wastefully. Indeed, the wasteful are brothers of the devils, and ever has Satan been to his Lord ungrateful."[13]

[12] Qur'ān, 2:268
[13] Qur'ān, 15:26-27

General Principles of Islamic Microfinance

Islamic microfinance is built on a number of *Sharī'ah* principles. The principles that predominantly pertain to *Sharī'ah* Contract Law, serve as criterion against which validity of a transaction or product may be judged. Some important principles that govern Islamic microfinance are as follows:

I. Lawfulness of business

It is necessary that the business for which loan or financing facility is given, should be halal and permissible. A microfinance institution is not allowed to finance wine or tobacco or musical instruments related business because such business or activity is not allowed in *Sharī'ah*. Any income or profit generated from such activity is regarded illegitimate and *ḥarām*. A Muslim can trade only in *ṭayyibāt* i.e. *ḥalāl* and pure substance. The Qur'ān says, "O believers, eat of the pure things which we have provided you for sustenance and give thanks to Allah, if it is Him that you serve[14]. *Ṭayyibāt* or pure substance are the things whose consumption and trading is allowed in *Sharī'ah*. This requires that financing facility should not be extended for unlawful commodity or business. In the same way, while providing loan, the institution should ascertain that the purpose for which loan is used, is lawful.

II. Prohibition of *ribā*

This is a fundamental principle of Islamic microfinance. Ribā literally means increase addition, expansion or growth. It technically refers to the premium that must be paid by the borrower to the lender along with the principle amount as a condition for the loan or for an extension in its maturity. Ribā may also be defined as a prefixed and stipulated increase of capital in a loan or debt transaction. Thus, for instance, if a

[14] Qur'ān, 2: 172.

person lends one thousand rupees and charges increase of five hundred rupees on it, he is in fact involved in *ribā* prohibited in Islamic law. In the same way, when a person sells a commodity on credit for certain period, and on maturity, due to failure of debtor to pay off his obligation, he (the creditor), increases the amount of debt, he in fact commits *ribā*.

Ribā has been prohibited in *Sharī'ah* because it entails a number of moral, social and economic evils. Islam wants to promote noble feelings of mutual care, cooperation sympathy in the society whereas *ribā* corrodes all those values and develops and promotes selfishness, greed, exploitation and injustice in the society. A main economic evil of *ribā* is that it causes concentration of wealth in few hands while Islam wants that wealth should be circulated as widely as possible in the society. It is important to note that under usurious system wealth assume superior position over human being. Under this system, man is relegated to secondary position and the satisfaction of his needs is given even lesser importance. Money and capital assume the first and foremost priority in life. This attitude reduces man's labour into a worthless and trivial thing, while capital becomes a value in itself.[15]

As explained earlier, *ribā* is in sharp contrast to the values of love, affection, help, assistance, cooperation and collaboration which Islam wants to promote in a Muslim society. It creates greed and excessive love for wealth.

While explaining verse 2:275, the exegetes have said that the eaters of usry become so much blinded by love of wealth and capital that this becomes their sole motive in life. This sick obsession with money erodes all moral virtues one after the other. Greed and niggardliness have been vehemently

[15] Justice (R) Khalil ur Rahman, Supreme Court's judgement on Ribā, p. 22)

condemned not only by the Qur'ān and the Sunnah but by all books of religion and morality. Their chief motive of life become hoarding of wealth through maximum exploitation and deprivation of others.[16]

The teachings of the prohibition of *ribā* require from Islamic microfinance practitioners that, while lending small loans to the poor they should not charge any increase on it or take any extra benefit from the borrowers. Taking gifts from the borrowers should also be avoided because it is also a form of *ribā* The teachings also imply that while selling any commodity to the client on credit the institution should not increase the amount of debt, in case the debtor fails to pay the amount in due time.

III. Prohibition of *gharar*

Gharar refers to uncertainty and lack of knowledge about necessary terms of contract. As a technical term it is applied to uncertainty about the ultimate outcome of a contract, which may lead to dispute and litigation. *Gharar* occurs in instances when there is a contract, which is not transparent between the two parties, involved and carries the risk of one party profiting more than the other. The prohibition of *gharar* ensures that all the profits from an investment and any losses accumulated, are eventually apportioned in order to avoid uncertainty on the returns or the profits of investment between the investors.

Gharar also constitutes the ambiguity ar unnecessary risk of a transaction and can further occur when contracted goods or services are inadequately specified; the price of a good may be unknown: or payment terms are uncertain in deferred sales. *Gharar* also refers to the uncertainty of a contract due to lack of disclosure and deliberate avoidance of transparency, which

---

[16] Supreme Court's judgement on Ribā, p.245

could have been avoided by simply adding more information to a contract.

Selling goods without proper description of promising a sale of products, which you are unable to deliver, also constitute *gharar* and it is strictly forbidden to mislead a party according to the ethical principles of Islamic finance. This is why most derivative contracts, which are short selling, are forbidden and considered invalid according to the principles of the *Sharī'ah* because of the uncertainty involved in the future delivery of the underlying asset.

IV. Principle of risk sharing

The principal is based on a famous *ḥadīth* of Holy Prophet (s.a.w.s.) which provides that "Entitlement to profit depends upon liability for loss." A person can get profit of project or enterprise only when he shares the risk and liability for loss.

Thus, when an institution invests money in a project on *mushārakah* or *muḍārabah* basis and gets increase on its investment, such increase is regarded *ḥalāl* in Islamic law, because he has earned that increase in a legitimate manner by sharing the risk and liability for loss.

It is not allowed in *mushārakah* or *muḍārabah* partnerships that the institution should get a prefixed increase on its capital and define its share as lump sum of its capital amount because in such case, he is in fact sharing the profit only, not the loss of business. In Islamic law sharing risk and liability for loss, is cause of entitlement to profit. The principle operates not only in *mushārakah* and *muḍārabah*, but the sale, *ijārah* and other business contracts as well. In *murābaḥah*, for instance, the financial institution, takes all risks related to commodity before it is sold to the beneficiary. This risk taking entitles it to earn increase on its cost price. In loan transaction, on the other hand, increase over and above principal sum is regarded unlawful because it is earned without bearing any risk by the creditor.

Modes of Islamic Microfinance

Islamic microfinance institutions, currently practice a number of methods for providing financial services to small entrepreneurs. The methods used by these institutions include *qarḍ ḥasan*, *murābaḥah*, *muḍārabah*, *mushārakah*, *ijārah* and *salam*. In Pakistan, *qarḍ ḥasan*, *murābaḥah* and *muḍārabah* are the most popular and frequently used methods.

Akhuwat, largely prefer *qarḍ ḍasan* over other methods, whereas Helping Hand for Relief and Development (HHRD), Islamic Relief and other Islamic microfinance institutions do not rely much on qard hasan. Due to issue of sustainability of organization, *murābaḥah* is preferred in these institutions. A brief description of these modes and methods is given below:

1. Qarḍ ḥasan

Qarḍ is synonymous to the term loan", *Qarḍ* may be defined as transfer of ownership in tangible property to a person who agrees to return a property similar to it in future. AAOIFI, in its standard on *Qarḍ* has defined *Qarḍ* as: "the transfer of ownership in fungible property to a person who is bound to return similar to it." It primarily takes places in form of money. However, other fungible consumable goods, can also be subject matter of loan. In Qur'ān, *qarḍ* has not been used in technical and legal sense. It has been used in the meaning of charity and spending in the way of Almighty Allah[17].

Qarḍ is an act of goodness and benevolence in a ḥadīth of Prophet Muḥammad (s.a.w.s.), *qarḍ* has been ranked higher than charity and donation because *qard* is given to the one who

[17] Qur'ān 2:245; 57:11; 18; 64:17

really needs it. Charity and donation on the other hand, may not be given to a person who really needs it.

It is not allowed to stipulate excess and increase on the principal amount of loan. A *Sharī'ah* maxim provides that every loan that entails benefit is *ribā*. The *Sharī'ah* does not allow the creditor, to derive any gain and benefit from the loan, which he has advanced to the debtor. Such benefit is a prohibited *ribā* in the eye of *Sharī'ah*. This should be however, borne in mind that the benefit which is prohibited by the *Sharī'ah* is the one that is prefixed, and stipulated in the contract, and is payable by the debtor as the part of contractual obligation.

The Islamic law allows paying some increase over and above the principal sum of loan to the creditor, voluntarily, provided it is not a part of the contract. This point has also been emphasized in *Sharī'ah* Standard No 19 on *Qarḍ* (loan). It states:

> "The stipulation of an excess for the lender in loan is prohibited, and it amounts to *ribā*, whether the excess is in terms of quality or quantity whether the excess is a tangible thing or a benefit, and whether the excess is stipulated at the time of the contract or while determining the period of delay for satisfaction or during the period of delay and further. whether the stipulation is in writing or is part of customary practice." (Article 4/1).

Islamic law also does not allow combining selling and lending concurrently. For example, if a person lends 10,000 rupees and at the same time sells to borrower a commodity for a price that is much higher than the prevailing market price, he has in fact charged increase on the amount lent. This is a *ḥīlah* or a back door for *ribā* because the increase which he wanted to charge on loan, he has now built it in the sale price. For this reason, Holy Prophet (s.a.w.s) has prohibited for combining loan and sell contract because such combination can easily be misused or abused for charging *ribā*. Islamic law also does not allow a creditor to charge increase on loan in case the debtor or borrower is unable to pay off his obligation in time due to his financial circumstances. In such case the Qur'ān instructs that insurgent debtor should be given time till the time of case. The Qur'ān says: "If the debtor is in difficulty then given him time till the time of case but if you remit it then it is better for you if you really know it." It is allowed in *Sharī'ah* to take some security or pledge from the borrower to secure the debtor.

Islamic microfinance institution, however, do not take any tangible security from their borrowers. Social collateral is considered sufficient to secure the debt.

2. *Murābaḥah* to purchase orderer

Murābaḥah to purchase orderer is the most popular form of Islamic financing techniques used by the Islamic microfinance institutions. They prefer it over *qarḍ ḥasan*. *Qarḍ ḥasan* is workable as a mode or instrument for microfinance services only when the institutions donations at large scale. But in situation where IMF does not have permanent source of income, it cannot practice *qarḍ ḥasan* for an indefinite period. *Murābaḥah*, a sale based mode, is a suitable alternative to the microfinance institutions, which provides the IFI some income sufficient to meet its administrative costs.

Under *murābaḥah* transaction, Islamic banks and Islamic microfinance institutions buy goods from the market at the request of client/beneficiary and then sell these goods by adding certain profit to the cost price. Under *murābaḥah*, Islamic microfinance institution at the request of client or micro entrepreneur buys goods, and then sells these goods at cost plus profit basis both disclosed to him separately. Since the institution does not own required goods at the stage of request. It cannot enter into *murābaḥah* contract because according to Islamic law, one cannot sell a thing which he does not own. Besides, it is a sale on a non-existent thing which is prohibited in *Sharī'ah*. The institution, therefore, does not conclude *murābaḥah* with client.

Instead, it takes a promise from him to buy goods from the institution when the later acquires the goods and owns them. Such promise is treated binding in the *fatwā* of International Fiqh Academy and Sharī'ah Board of Auditing and Accounting Organization of Islamic Financial Institutions (AAOIFI). It is important to note that the risk of purchased goods, before their sale to the client, is borne by IMFI not by the client. So, if the goods are destroyed while in the ownership and possession of IMFI, the loss is exclusively borne by the institution. An additional risk may be refusal by the client to buy promised goods.

After acquiring goods from the supplier, IMFI, enters into *murābaḥah* with micro entrepreneur in which cost price and profit are clearly stated. Period of payment of sale price and the mode of payment are also fixed. Usually, the client makes payment to the institution in installments.

To secure its debt, the institution has the right to take some security, but the IMFIs do not take any security of monetary value from the client. They only take social collateral. It is also worthy to note that after conclusion of sale transaction, selling price cannot be changed. *Murābaḥah* contract cannot be rolled over because the goods, once sold by the IMI, become the property of the client, and hence, cannot be resold to the same or another financial institution, for the purpose of obtaining further credit. The institution can however, extend the repayment date, provided that such extension is not conditional upon an increase in the selling price of goods, originally agreed.

Conclusion

Poverty has been a cause of concern in every society throughout the human history. Islam views poverty as a social ailment which has potential to create number of social and moral evils in the Muslim society. Islam, from its inception, has been concerned with eradication of poverty. The institutions such as *zakāh* and *waqf* played vital role in establishing economic and social justice in the society and helping the poor and the destitutes to attain a respectable standard of living. Islamic microfinance, has emerged in recent past, as an effective tool for socio economic development in Muslim countries and has effectively contributed in the alleviation of poverty and economic uplift of the society.

In Islam, the rich have responsibility towards the poor. This social responsibility sometime goes beyond the payment of obligatory *zakāh*. Social responsibility, also known as "*kafālah ʿāmmah*" suggests that society as a whole has responsibility and obligation towards less fortunate and deprived segment of the society. It is generally claimed that eradication of poverty and uplift of living standard of people, is the responsibility of state which ought to perform this duty through distribution of *zakāh*. The Holy Qur'ān and Sunnah refute this misconception.

Microfinance refers to small loans available to poor people (especially those traditionally excluded from financial services) through programs designed specially to meet their particular needs and circumstances. Core objective of microfinance is to eradicate poverty, to raise income levels and to broaden financial markets by providing financial services to the financially excluded people. As conventional microfinance is interest based, a committed Muslim refrains from availing financial services offered by conventional microfinance institutions. For such religiously motivated people, Islamic microfinance is the only choice. It provides microfinance services to lower income groups in a *Sharīʿah* compliant manner through the religiously tailored products such as *qarḍ ḥasan*, *murābaḥah*, *muḍārabah*, *salam* etc.

The role of Islamic microfinance in the alleviation of poverty can hardly be overemphasized. In the last few years it has played very significant role in the economic uplift of the people. Millions of people have benefited from microfinance services provided to them by Akhuwat, Helping Hands and other Islamic microfinance institutions operating in the country.

Chapter 24

Promise and Bilateral Promise in Islamic Finance

The predominant view point in classical Islamic law is that simple promises are not legally enforceable and binding, though morally and religiously, a promisor is bound to fulfill his promise. The Qur'ān enjoins upon every believer to fulfill his commitments. It says:

"And fulfill every engagement, for every engagement will be enquired into (on the day of reckoning)"[1]

It also says:"(But righteous) are those who fulfill the contract which they make."[2]

Thus, the breaking of promise is an act of sin and disobedience. It may also result in social disapproval, or ethical demerit. Its enforcement at law, however, cannot be demanded.

The Holy Prophet (s.a.w.s) said: "he who does not keep his word does not have faith."

Viewpoint of Classical Jurists

The Muslim jurists hold divergent views regarding the enforceability of a promise.

- *Shāfi'ī* and Ḥanblī jurists are of the view that promises are not mandatory. They just represent a moral obligation on a promisor to fulfil his promise.

---

[1] Qur'ān 17:34

[2] Qur'ān 2:177

- Mālikī jurists regard promises binding. This view is attributed to Ibn al 'Arabī and Ibn Shubrumah[3].

- The Ḥanafī jurists acknowledge the validity of *bay'al-wafā* which establishes the fact that Ḥanafī jurists also favour the concept of the binding nature of promises.[4] In *bay' al-wafā,* the purchaser of an immoveable property, undertakes that he will return it to the seller, if he, (the seller), returns the price to him. Such a promise is binding on the purchaser.[5]

The Muslim jurists are, however, unanimous on the enforceability of a promise that is made in a form of a guarantee such as, when a person asks a seller to sell a commodity on credit, to a particular person, and promises to pay its price. If the buyer makes payment at the stipulated time, the seller relying on this commitment sells commodity to the buyer. Here, the promisor has guaranteed the payment of price, on behalf of the buyer, and the promisee has taken certain action, and has incurred a risk, by relying on the promisee, so, he is entitled to demand its enforcement by law. Similar is the case of guarantee in *ju'ālah* (reward), promise. It is, where a person, offers a certain amount of money, or property, as reward to any person who brings about desired results. For example, "I will pay ten dinars to anyone who returns my lost camel."

In the contemporary context, an important area in the domain of *ju'ālah,* is the need for inventions, and innovations. An individual or company, already involved in research, may be motivated to work out a certain specific innovation, or invention against the payment of reward on realization of a

---

[3] Ibn Juzī, *al-Qawānīn al-fiqhiyyah*, p.258; *al-Mughnī,* op.cit. vol. 4, p.195.

[4] See, *Radd al Muḥtār*, op.cit. vol. 4, p.135.

[5] See, *al-Ashbāh wa al-Naẓā'ir*, op.cit. vol. 2, p.11; Atāsi, *Sharḥ al-Majallah*, op.cit. vol. 2, p.415.

task. Such promises, according to Muslim jurists, are binding and enforceable at law.

It may also be used for exploration of minerals, and extraction of water, in situations where entitlement to wages is contingent upon finding of water, or minerals, without reference to the amount of time, or the extent of period.

In the field of finance, it can be used for following purposes.

- Collection of debt(s), in cases where entitlement to compensation is contingent upon collection of debt(s).

- Securing permissible financing facilities, provided the subject matter of *ju'ālah* is valid, such as creation of debt through *murābaḥah*, on deferred payment, or *ijārah* with deferred rentals, raising of loans without interest, and issuance of letter of guarantee.

- For brokerage activities, in cases where the entitlement to compensation is contingent upon the conclusion of the contract, for which intermediation is undertaken.

Viewpoint of Modern Muslim Scholars

The modern Muslim scholars have applied the principle contained in this maxim to every such promise in which the promisee incurs some risk, and liability, and performs the act demanded in the promise. In modern Islamic law, the promises in commercial transactions are generally held enforceable at law. International Islamic Fiqh Academy is also inclined to this position. It has, however, laid down certain conditions for the enforceability of promises in commercial dealings. These conditions are:

- It should be a one-sided promise.

- The promisor must have caused the promisee to incur some liabilities.

- If the promisor is to purchase, or sell, something from, or to, the promisee, the actual sale must take place, at the appointed time, by the exchange of offer and acceptance. Mere promise should not be taken as a concluded sale.

- If the promisor backs out of his promise, the court may enforce specific performance from him, either to purchase or sell the commodity, as the case may be, or to pay actual damages.[6]

It is worth mentioning that in *murābaḥah* transaction, a customer asks the bank to purchase certain goods on the customer's specification from the supplier, and promises to purchase them from the bank, when the latter acquires goods.

Though the ruling of International Fiqh Academy, mentioned above, specifically deals with the particular case of *murābaḥah*, yet, it can be extended to all such cases, where the promisee takes some action, and incurs some risk and liability, as a result of the promise. The first al-Barakah seminar has also supported the notion of binding nature of promise. The declaration of the seminar provides that:

"The promise, and its binding nature, safeguard the transaction, and bring stability, and serve the interest of both, so it is lawful for the bank to insist on such promise."

In a *fatwā* of the Sharī'ah Board of Faisal Islamic Bank of Bahrain, the bank has been allowed to receive some security deposit from the *murābaḥah* to the purchase orderer (client), in order to compensate the loss of the bank, if the customer refuses to purchase the required goods after acquisition. If there is any remainder, after the bank has been compensated, it will have to be returned to the client. If the security deposit is insufficient as

---

[6] Resolution no.2, 3, Islamic Fiqh Academy, Academy's Journal no. 5, vol. 2, p.1509.

recompense, the rest should be paid by the purchase orderer, the client.[7]

Frank Vogel and Samuel have disagreed with the notion of unilateral promise, as prominently figured in the ruling of Islamic Fiqh Academy. The concept, in their opinion, has serious legal as well as financial implications for the contracting parties. To them, if promise in case of *murābaḥah* is binding for the customer, (promisor), and non-binding for the bank (promisee), it may prove to be an unjustifiable favour for the bank.

Thus, in the opinion of these authors, one-sided promise may prove harmful for the customer. In our view, the reason for Academy's emphasis on unilateral promise and its non-recognition of the concept of bilateral promises is that bilateral promises amount to a contract, and a contract cannot be made on a non-existent subject matter. Besides, in such an agreement both obligations are deferred.

Promise in Banking Transactions

The modern Islamic banks, and financial institutions, rely heavily on promises in their dealings, and have incorporated them in a number of transactions, such as *murābaḥah* and *ijārah muntahiyah bil tamlīk,* i.e. contract of lease which includes a promise, by the lessor to transfer the ownership in the leased property, at the end of lease period.

As mentioned earlier, in *murābaḥah* transaction, the customer gives undertaking to the institution, that it will purchase goods from the bank on the basis of *murābaḥah,* after the latter acquires the required goods from the supplier.

---

[7] Yūsuf Ṭalāl, A Compendium, of Legal Opinions on the Operations of Islamic Banks, p.22.

In *ijārah muntahiyah bil tamlīk,* the bank includes a number of promises in the contract, such as:

- A promise by the lessor, that he will transfer the ownership in the leased property to the lessee at the end of the term of the *ijārah* period, either for token price or to give it as a gift.

- The promise by the customer to take the asset on lease, whenever the institution acquires it for him. It is permissible for the institution, to require the lease promisor (customer), to pay an earnest money to the institution, to guarantee his commitment to accept lease on the asset.

Promise in Currency Exchanges

The contemporary Muslim scholars allow mutual promises, to sell or buy currency in future, provided the promises are non-binding. This opinion is based on the viewpoint of Zahirī jurists, who allow mutual promise for the exchange of gold and silver in future. Other jurists do not consider such promises permissible. Following are some important contemporary verdicts on the issue:

1. Question: Advance agreement on the rate

What is the *Sharī'ah* ruling, with regard to an agreement on the sale and purchase of foreign currency, at a rate that is agreed upon in advance, in which the transaction takes place at a later date, and in which the delivery and receipt of cash take place at the same time?.

Fatwā

Such a transaction will be considered the same as a promise to sell. Then, if both parties go through with the deal in the manner it is described in the question, there will be no legal impediment to its implementation. This is, because it is lawful to carry out the promise, as described. On the other hand, if the promise is linked to anything that suggests a contract of sale, like a down payment, the deal will then become like the sale of debt for debt, (a deferred payment for a deferred payment), which is absolutely forbidden. This is especially true in an exchange contract, because its validity depends upon the taking possession of both counter values at the time of transaction. In such a case, the stipulation of a deferment is considered by all the jurists to render the contract void.[8]

2. Question: Mutual promises to buy or sell currencies

What is your opinion with regard to a mutual promise for the sale of various currencies, at the rate of exchange applicable on the day of the agreement, (the day of the mutual promise), on the condition that delivery of both counter values will be delayed, so that the exchange may take place, on a spot (hand to hand exchange) basis, in the future? Will it make any difference, if the mutual promise is treated as binding, or, if it is treated as non-binding?

Fatwā

Such a mutual promise, if it is binding on both parties, is subject to the general prohibition against the sale of debt for debt, and is therefore, unlawful. If, however, the mutual promise is not binding on both parties, it is lawful.[9]

3. Question: A promise to purchase different currencies

What is the *Sharī'ah* opinion with regard to a mutual promise, to purchase different currencies at the rates current on the day of the promise? It should further be understood that the delivery of the two counter values will be delayed to allow for the exchange, hand to hand, in the future. What is the ruling,

---

[8] Kuwait Finance House, Fatāwā' *Sharī'ah*. Q. 211, p. 203.

[9] Dubai Islamic Bank, Proceedings of the Seminar on Islamic Economics, Madinah, 1983, pp. 53-54.

when such a promise is considered to be a binding? And what is the ruling, when such a promise is not considered binding?

Fatwā

Such a promise, if considered binding on both parties, will fall under the general prohibition, against the sale of debt for debt, and will therefore be unlawful. If, however, the promise is considered not to be binding on both parties, then it will be lawful.[10]

4. Question: Mutual promises in exchange

What is the ruling about mutual promises in the exchange of currencies?

Fatwā

It is necessary to emphasize the decisions taken by the Second Conference on Islamic Banking, held in Kuwait in March 1983, to the effect that a mutual promise, in the sale of currencies, involving a delay in payment of the price is lawful, as long as the mutual promise is not considered binding. This was the majority opinion.

If the mutual promise is considered binding, this transaction will not be lawful from a *Sharī'ah* perspective.[11]

5. Question: Agreeing to sell currency for a predetermined rate

As a facility for the pilgrims to Makkah, the Ministry of Awqaf, seeks an agreement with the Islamic Bank (of Jordan), under which, the bank would sell Saudi Riyals at a predetermined rate, todays for example. This (rate) would remain in effect, for a

[10] Ibid.

[11] The Sixth Albaraka Forum, Fatwā no. 23; al-Fatawā al-Shari'iyah li Majmu'ah al-Baraka, p. 70. Cf. A compendium of legal opinions, op.cit. pp. 79-80.

certain period of time (sixty days from the agreement, for example), and during this period, the Ministry would deliver to the bank, the price of Saudi Riyals in Jordanian Dinars. In return, the bank would deliver, on the same day, cheques for Saudi Riyals, drawn on the basis of the previously determined rate for this purpose, (which may be higher, or lower, than the exchange rate for the riyal, on any particular day).

Will it be lawful (for the Islamic bank) to carry out this transaction?

Fatwā

The agreement, to exchange currencies of different countries for a rate that is fixed, at the time of the agreement, with the understanding that exchange will take place between the bank and the ministry in future, on the basis of previously agreed upon rate, regardless of the current rate at the time of exchange, has been discussed by Imam Showkanī in *Nayl al Awṭār* (vol. 5, pp. 254-255). Showkani says, that in the opinion of the Ḥanafī and the Shāfi'ī schools, exchange at the current rate, or at a higher, or a lower rate is lawful. This view, though it contradicts the literal meaning of the *ḥadīth* by Ibn 'Umar, which allows the current rate only, appears to be based on the opinions of above two Imāms. I, therefore, agree to the Bank's going through with the transaction, in the manner explained, based on the opinions of Imām Abū Ḥanīfah and Imām al- *Shāfi'ī*. And Allāh most glorified and most high knows best.[12]

6. Question: A promise to purchase currency

What is the legal view of a promise to purchase a designated currency, in a designated amount, for a designated price, during a designated period of time, when the seller agrees to hand over

---

[12] Kuwait Finance House, Fatāwā *Sharī'ah*, Question 168, p. 165; A compendium of legal opinions, op. cit. pp. 80, 81.

the currency, on demand, at any time during the designated period, on the understanding that the purchaser will pay a certain amount in advance known as the "right to buy", which he/she will lose if the deal (to purchase the currency) is not concluded?

Fatwā

Such a transaction is not lawful, because it is no more than a promise to purchase currency. The only sale of currency allowed by the *Sharī'ah* is a straightforward sale, that is accompanied by direct receipt in money barter, or the exchange of price for price.

AAOIFI's position on unilateral and bilateral promises

AAOIFI in its *Sharī'ah* Standerd no 49 on unilateral and bilateral promise has explained the status of promise in financial transactions. In the opinion of *Sharī'ah* scholars at AAOIFI, a promise in a loan transaction that brings benefit to the lender or a promise in sale contract made by the buyer or seller that results in a repurchase of the commodity, (*'īnah*) is prohibited. A promise to perform an action or a financial transaction is binding on promisor only when promisor causes the promise to incur some liability as a result of the promise. Similarly, a benevolent promise such as a promise to make gift or lend an item is binding on promisor if the promise has incurred some financial liability as a result of that promise. For example, if the promisor says to the promise, "If you buy this item from me, I will give you a gift of another specified item." This promise is legally as well as morally binding.

A bilateral promise is generally not binding except in situations where an actual commercial transaction is not possible without a binding bilateral promise owing either to legal requirements or to general commercial custom and the objective is not merely providing financing, such as bilateral promises in international trade conducted by means of documentary credits or bilateral promise supply agreements. It is, however, not permissible to enter into back to back bilateral promises for the purpose of circumventing the prohibition by *Sharī'ah* of certain transactions such as back to back derivatives.[13]

Conclusion

The Muslim jurists hold divergent views regarding the enforceability of a promise. Shāfi'ī and Ḥanblī jurists are of the view that promises are not mandatory. They just represent a moral obligation on a promisor to fulfil his promise. Mālikī jurists regard promises binding. This view is attributed to Ibn al 'Arabī and Ibn Shubrumah. The Ḥanafī jurists acknowledge the validity of *bay'al-wafā* which establishes the fact that Ḥanafī jurists also favour the concept of the binding nature of promises. In *bay' al-wafā,* the purchaser of an immoveable property, undertakes that he will return it to the seller, if he, (the seller), returns the price to him. Such a promise is binding on the purchaser.

The modern Islamic banks, and financial institutions, rely heavily on promises in their dealings, and have incorporated them in a number of transactions, such as *murābaḥah* and *ijārah muntahiyah bil tamlīk,* i.e. contract of lease which includes a promise, by the lessor to transfer the ownership in the leased property, at the end of lease period.

The contemporary Muslim scholars allow mutual promises, to sell or buy currency in future, provided the promises are non-binding. This opinion is based on the viewpoint of Zahirī jurists, who allow mutual promise for the exchange of gold and

[13] See Articles 3/1 ,3/7 of *Sharī'ah* Standerd no 20 and *Sharī'ah* Standard no. 49, Articles 3/1, 3/2,3/6,4/1,4/2, and Article 6.

silver in future. Other jurists do not consider such promises permissible.

The *Sharī'ah* scholars at AAOIFI, hold the view that a promise in a loan transaction that brings benefit to the lender or a promise in sale contract made by the buyer or seller that results in a repurchase of the commodity, (*'īnah*) is prohibited. A promise to perform an action or a financial transaction is binding on promisor only when promisor causes the promise to incur some liability as a result of the promise. Similarly, a benevolent promise such as a promise to make gift or lend an item is binding on promisor if the promise has incurred some financial liability as a result of that promise.

Chapter 25

Takāful: Concept and Application

The word '*takāful*' means joint guarantee. The objective of *takāful* is cooperation, and mutual help, among the members of a defined group. In a practical sense, *takāful* can be visualized, as a method of joint guarantee, among a group of members, or participants, against loss, or damage, that may inflict upon any of them. The members of the group agree to guarantee jointly that should any of them suffer a catastrophe or disaster, he would receive certain sum of money to meet the loss or damage. All members of the group pool together to support the needy.

Malaysian Takāful Act defines it as: a scheme based on brotherhood, solidarity and mutual assistance which provides for mutual financial aid and assistance to the participants in case of need whereby the participants mutually agree to contribute for that purpose."[1]

Under *takāful* scheme, the participants annually deposit an agreed sum of money with the company. This contribution is divided into two parts. A larger portion goes into investment fund and remains the property of the contributor. The other part, which is nearly 2 to 5 percent of the contribution, goes into a *waqf* fund, and is considered as *tabarru'* (donation). The company invests the available funds in *muḍarabah* ventures, or some other approved modes. The profits, if any, are added to the investment and *waqf* funds, according to the previous ratios. The purpose of *takāful* may be life insurance, and it may also be insurance of property. If the insured person dies before the end of the covered time in case of life insurance, or, if an insured risk on the property materializes, then the company will pay back

---

[1] Section 2 of Act 312, Takāful Act 1984, Laws of Malaysia

the amount deposited in investment account by the policy-holder along with profits earned during that period.

As company uses islamically approved modes of investment, and distributes profit among the policy holders, element of is eliminated. The other objectionable element, *gharar* is still there, but as the company manages a separate *waqf* fund from the donations of the policy holders, for providing support to the needy member(s) of the group, this *gharar* will not invalidate the insurance contract. According to Malikī jurists, *gharar* in *'uqūd al tabarru'āt* (donation contracts) is acceptable, and does not invalidate the contract. Imam Mālik, while elaborating on the principle of *gharar,* and the effect it has on transactions, has given the rationale and wisdom at work behind the distinction between commutative contracts and gratuitous contracts.

Imam Mālik says:

> "The human transactions and dispositions are meant, either for reciprocal benefits that take place for some counter-value, or for promotion of goodness, and benevolence. The *gharar* should be avoided in the first type, as far as possible, except when there is compelling need for committing *gharar*. The dispositions of second category are not meant to be a source of augmentation of wealth. They only aim to promote goodness and benevolence towards others. Therefore, the divine law promotes and encourages such act, even though there is an element of uncertainty and lack of knowledge about the outcome of transaction. The reason for its permissibility is that they would be beneficiary has not spent any money to obtain the promised donation. If due to some reason he does not get the donation, he is still not a loser because he has not paid anything to acquire it. For example, if a person makes a gift of a runaway animal, such gift is lawful. It would be enforceable only when he finds it. But even if he does not

find it, he is still free from any obligation towards the donor. In contrast, the parties pay for counter-values in commutative contracts, therefore, *gharar* cannot be admitted in them."

Different Models of Takāful

Takāful (Islamic insurance) is practiced in the Muslim world, in a number of ways. The common feature in these methods, and models is the concept of *tabarru'* (donation), joint guarantees and assistance.

There are three important models, of *takāful* working in the Muslim world, namely:

- *Waqf model*
- *Wakālah model*
- *Murābaḥah model*

Waqf model

This model was proposed by the renowned religious scholar, Maulana Mufti Muḥammad Shāfi'ī and was later on endorsed by the Council of Islamic Ideology in 1992. The present legal framework of *takāful* in Pakistan is structured on the *waqf* principles.

Following are the prominent features of waqf model:

- The relationship of the participants and the operator is directly with the *waqf* fund. The operator acts as a *wakīl* of the fund on behalf of the participants.
- An initial donation is made by the company in order to create a *waqf* fund.
- The participants, or policyholders pay their contributions to the company by way of *tabarru'*,

which are credited to the same *waqf* fund (i.e. Participants' *Takāful* Fund, PTF).

- The combined amount is used for investment in different schemes in accordance with Shaī'ah rules and the profit earned from it is pooled back to the same fund which eliminates the issue of *gharar*.
- The company receives *takāful* operator's fee for providing *takāful* services and its share as *muḍārib*, out of investment income, from the *waqf* fund.
- Claims to the participants are paid by the company from the same fund.
- *Re- takāful* cost, business acquisition cost, and reserves are also maintained from the same fund, to cover and protect future losses.
- The balance or surplus in *takāful* fund is available for distribution among participants or policyholders proportionately, at the end of an accounting period. The matter is to be decided by the Sharī'ah board.
- The *takāful* company may reserve a portion of surplus to mitigate the future losses, and a portion of surplus may be utilized for charitable purposes every year.
- Any negative balance in participant's *takāful* fund, is made up by the company, out of its own capital in the way of *qarḍ-e-hasan*, which is redressed from the future surplus of the *takāful* fund.

Muḍārabah model

The *takāful* companies in Malaysia, generally follow this model. The companies use *muḍarabah* contract for operating *takāful* business. Prominent features of this model are, as follows:

- Under the *muḍārabah* model, participants will provide capital, (by paying contributions), to be invested by *takāful* operators (which play their role as entrepreneurs). Thus, *takāful* operator acts as *muḍārib* (entrepreneur), and participants as *rub-ul-māl* (capital provider).

- All management expenses, are met from the share holders fund, and therefore not borne by the policy holders.

- Claims, *re-takāful* cost and other claims related expenses are met from the *takāful* fund.

- When there is profit in the *takāful* fund, it will be shared between both parties, according to pre-agreed ratio.

- Under this type of contract, losses are borne by the participants as the capital provider. However, to protect the interests of the participants, the *takāful* operators are required to observe prudential rules, including provision of interest free loan by the operators, when there is deficit in the *takāful* funds.

Wakālah model

Wakālah model is generally practiced in Middle East. The fundamental concept which is at work behind this model is that the *takāful* operator acts as *wakīl* for the participants and charges a certain fixed fee. Such fee is credited to share holders's account. Surplus is distributed among the participants. Some important features of the model are follows:

- The *wakālah* concept is essentially an agent-principal relationship, where the *takāful* operator acts as a *wakīl* on behalf of the participants. He charges a certain fee for services rendered.

- The *wakālah* fee may be charged upfront, (generally in the range of 30 to 35% of the contributions), which is transferred to the shareholders' fund.
- The remaining portion of the contributions may be transferred to the *takāful* fund, which is used to pay claims, *Re-takāful* costs etc.
- The surplus, which remains, may be allocated 100%, for the benefit of the participants.
- Generally, a portion of the surplus may be retained as a contingency reserve, and the balance may be distributed to the participants in proportion to their contributions (to those who have not had a claim).
- In case of deficit in the *takāful* fund, the shareholders are required to provide interest free loan, which will be returned from future surplus.
- The shareholders would be responsible for all expenses of management and marketing etc.

Takāful Practice in Islamic Financial Markets

Takāful or mutual guarantee is generally considered as an Islamic alternative to the modern insurance business. *Takāful* refers to an agreement among group of people called participants to guarantee jointly that, should any of them suffer a catastrophe or disaster, he would receive certain sum of money to meet the loss or damage. Thus, it is a method of mutual help. Since the contributions in *takāful* business are invested on the basis of *muḍārabah,* it is also known as solidarity *muḍārabah.*[2] In *takāful,* the concept of donation is combined with that of

[2] See Chaudry Muhammad Sādiq, *Islamic Insurance (takāful) Concept and Practice, Encyclopaedia of Islamic Banking and Insurance*, p.198, London: Institute of Islamic Finance and Banking, 1995.

muḍārabah. A participant, while entering *takāful* business, concludes two contracts, i.e., (i) Contract of donation or *tabarru'* whereby he undertakes to donate a portion of his contribution in *tabarru'* fund, established to provide *takāful* benefits to any participant who suffers some material loss or damage; and (ii) Contract of *muḍārabah* whereby he undertakes to pay a portion of his contribution to the company for the purpose of business on the basis of *muḍārabah. Takāful* benefits, i.e., insurance benefits are paid from *tabarru'* (donation) fund. But if the fund proves insufficient, then the deficit is covered from the profits of *muḍārabah* business, if any, or from the capital of *muḍārabah.* The participants in *takāful* may also be required to make additional contributions for this purpose. Thus, the participants in *takāful* or solidarity *muḍārabah* have the right to share the profits generated by such *muḍārabah* business, but at the same time they are liable for contributing to amounts in addition to the premiums they have already disbursed, if their initial premiums paid during a particular year are not sufficient to meet all the losses and risks incurred during that year.[3] In other words the sharing of the profit or surplus that may emerge from the operations of *takāful* is made only after the obligations of assisting the fellow participants have been fulfilled.

Under *muḍārabah* agreement the participants pay their contribution to the entrepreneur or *muḍārib,* i.e., *takāful* company to invest that money in some profitable business in accordance with Islamic modes of investment. The profits are shared by the participants and the *takāful* company (in its capacity as *muḍārib*) according to a ratio agreed upon between contracting parties.

There are two types of *takāful* (insurance) business usually managed by *takāful* companies, i.e., life *takāful* (insurance) and

[3] Nabīl Sālih, *Unlawful gain and legitimate profit in Islamic Law*, p.126.

general *takāful.* Under life *takāful*, the company provides cover of mutual financial aid in the form of *takāful* benefits in case of untimely death of participant.

The general *takāful* provides various policies and schemes to a participant with a view to protect him against material loss or damage arising from catastrophies, or disaster inflicted upon his properties. General *takāful* are generally short-term contracts. Amount of *takāful* contribution varies according to the value of the property to be covered. Installments in general *takāful* are called *tabarru'* (donation). Company invests the *tabarru'* fund and the profits accrued are allocated between the fund and the management on the basis of *muḍārabah.* Indemnity is paid out of *tabarru'* fund. If the *tabarru'* fund generates net surplus, then unlike insurance, surplus is shared between participants and the company[4].

Here we will dilate upon the working of *takāful* business in Malaysia.

Working of the *takāful* business

Muḍārabah and *tabarru'*, involvement of these two Islamic forms of business eliminates the elements of *ribā* and *gharar* from the insurance contract. The operational details of different *takāful* businesses are as follows:

Family *takāful* (Life insurance)

Any individual between the ages of 18 to 55 years can participate in the family *takāful* business. Participants are required to pay *sharikah takāful* Malaysia regularly the *takāful* installments that are then credited into a defined fund known as the family *takāful* fund. Each *takāful* installment is divided and credited

[4] Muḥammad Anwar, *A Comparative Study of Insurance, and Takāful*, Islamabad: Pakistan Institute of Development Economics, 1994, p.14.

into two separate accounts namely, the Participant's Account (PA) and the Participant's Special Account (PSA). A substantial proportion of the installments is credited into the PA solely for the purpose of savings and investment. The balance of the installments is credited into the PSA as *tabarru'* for *sharikah takāful* Malaysia to pay the *takāful* benefits to the heirs of any participant who may die before his maturity of the family *takāful* plan. The amount accumulated in the PA is invested in various types of businesses carried out according to Islamic financing techniques, and the resultant profits are divided between the *sharikah* and the participants according to a ratio, e.g., 30-70 agreed upon between the parties. The participants' share is calculated according to their individual share in the PA, and credited into their respective accounts i.e. the PA and the PSA. For example, if a participant is paying RM 1000 to the *sharikah* as his installment the use of the amount could be shown with the help of the following chart:[5]

Family *Takāful* Fund RM1000	
Participant's Special Account RM2000	Participant's Account RM978.00
All Family *Takāful* Fund RM1000	
Investment profit (Example: RM70)	
70% (Example) Participant (RM49.00)	30%(Example) Company (RM21.00)
Participant's Special Account RM22.00 RM1.08 RM23.08	Participant's Account RM 978.00 RM47.92 RM 1025.92

In case of occurrence of an unhappy event, death or disability, the *sharikah* makes payment to the policy holder or his heirs.

[5] Chaudry Muhammad Sādiq, *Islamic Insurance (takāful) concept and practice, Encyclopaedia of Islamic Banking and Insurance*, pp.197-208.

The amount deposited in the PA along with the profits plus some amount from the PSA according to a formula is paid by the company. This scheme is explained as under by considering some cases.

Upon the occurrence of certain events the company will arrange *takāful* benefits to the rightful claimant in the following manner:

Case no. 1

In the event of untimely death of the participant or permanent and total disability suffered by the participant.

Should the participant die or suffer permanent and total disability in the fifth year of participation, *takāful* benefit will be paid in the following manner: -

(i)	From Participant's Account RM 978 x 5 (i.e. installments paid by the Participant into his participants account from the date of entry up to the date of death or suffering of permanent and total disability (PTD) together with profit if any, which have been earned from investment for during the same period, say	RM 4,890.00 RM 400.00
(ii)	From participant's special accounts (i.e. outstanding amount of *takāful* installments that would have been paid should the participant survive).	RM 5000.00
Total *takāful* Benefit Payable.		RM 10,290.00

For the PTD cover *takāful* benefit shall be paid in ten equal installments annually.

Case no. 2

If participant is still alive till the maturity.

Should the participant survive until the maturity of his family *takāful* FTP, payment of *takāful* benefit will be made to him as follows: -

i) From his Participant's Account = RM 9,780.00

RM 978 x 10 (i.e. total amount installments credited into his Participant's Account from date of entry to the maturity) together with the profit from investment if any, accumulated during the same period. RM 1,800.00

(ii) From Participant's Special Account's, surplus, if any as determined.

(b) By *Sharikah Takāful.* RM XXX

Total *Takāful* Benefit = RM 11,580.00 + surplus as determined by *Sharikah Takāful.*

Case no. 3

In the event of untimely death of participant due to accident:

Based on the above example, should the participant suffered death due to accident, then the total *takāful* benefits payable will be as follows:

(a) If the Participant died in the fifth year of participation, the payment of the benefit will be in the following order:

(i) From Participant's Account RM 4.890.00

RM 978 x 5, and profit from investment if any, accumulated in the Account during the same period, say RM 400.00

(ii) From Participant's Special Accounts RM 5,000.00 = RM 1000 x 5 (i.e. outstanding or balance of *takāful* installments to be paid by the participant should he had survived until maturity).

(iii) From Group Family *Takāful* Account.

RM 15,000.00 Total *takāful* Benefit. RM 25,290.00

(b) If Participant suffered bodily injury arising from accident, such as loss of arm or leg (rates of benefit fixed according to scale of disability or injury), then the amount of *takāful* benefits payable will be made from Group Family *Takāful* Account only, as follow: 50% x 15,000.00
RM 7,500.00

Case no. 4

In an event that the participant is hospitalized:

Based on the same example, should the participant be warded into any hospital for a period of 5 days the *takāful* benefit will be made from Group Family *Takāful* Account as follows: -

30 x 5 days. RM 150.00

General *Takāful* Business

General *takāful* schemes are basically contracts of joint guarantee, on a short-term basis, based on the principle of *muḍārabah* , between a group of participants to provide mutual compensation in the event of a defined loss. The schemes are designed to provide protection to both individuals and corporate bodies against any material loss or damage consequent upon a catastrophe or disaster inflicted upon properties, assets or other belongings of its participants.

In consideration for participating in the various schemes, participants agree or undertake to pay *takāful* contributions as *tabarru'* for the purpose of creating a defined asset as illustrated in the 'General *Takāful* Fund'. It is from this Fund that mutual compensation would be paid to any participant who suffers a defined loss or damage arising from a catastrophe or disaster affecting his property or belonging.

As the *Muḍārib, Sharikat Takāful* Malaysia invests the Fund. All returns on the investment are pooled back to the fund. In line with the virtues of mutual help, shared responsibility and joint guarantee as embodied in the concept of *takāful,* compensation or indemnity is paid to any participant who suffers a defined loss. Other operational costs for managing the general *takāful* business such as the cost of arranging re-*takāful* program and setting up of reserve is also deducted from the fund.

A participant who wishes to participate in a general *takāful* scheme such as Motor *takāful* to cover his motor vehicle, Fire *takāful* to cover his house from loss or damage against fire or Public liability *takāful* to cover against his third party liability, pays a certain sum of money called *takāful* contributions. The amount of *takāful* contribution varies according to the value of property or asset to be covered under the scheme. If no claims are made or incurred and after deducting all the operational costs, the fund registers a surplus, it is shared between the participants and *sharikat takāful* Malaysia according to an agreed ratio such as 6:4; 5:5. Profits attributable to the participants are paid on expiry of their respective general *takāful* schemes provided they have not received or incurred claims during the period of participation.

The general *takāful* business is different from family *takāful* as all the payments are credited to only *tabarru'* account, and not divided into two separate accounts. After deducting all administrative costs and claims, if this account shows some surplus (or profit) it is distributed among the policyholders as well. The problem here is that if the contributions of participants are *tabarru'*, then he should not get any profit on it, and if it is considered as a loan then the surplus amount earned by him, will amount to *ribā*. Therefore, the company should divide the available funds into two separate accounts. If due to short period of policy it is not possible to make investment and earn some profit *tabarru'* and subsequently no return should be given to them. If the surpluses accumulate, then the regulatory body can decide to reduce the amount of premium for next periods. It will indirectly help the policyholders.

Sharī'ah appraisal of takāful business

The *takāful* business of Malaysia is satisfactory from Sharī'ah point of view. It is constructed on the Islamic concepts of *muḍārabah* and *tabarru'*. It is also free from the element of *ribā*, because the participant or the policyholder does not get a fixed return on P.A. (Participant's Account), instead he gets a varied income. His capital is subjected to the principle of profit and loss sharing as enunciated in the tradition of the Holy Prophet (peace be upon him) "profit goes side by side with the risk". The amount accumulated in P.A. is invested in various forms of business strictly in accordance with Islamic techniques of financing and investment.

As regards participants in special account, this is the same fund which has been designated as *waqf* by the *'Ulamā* of Indo-Pakistan. Being a contract of donation, any uncertainty about the *takāful* benefits to be earned by any participant, does not affect the validity of contract. A contract of donation with *gharar* and *jahl* is permissible in the *Sharī'ah*. Thus a participant who dies or suffers from total disability in the fifth year of participation, is entitled to get his capital and profits along with five yearly installments from participants special account i.e. from donation fund. This benefit is lawful and does not form *ribā* because it has been paid as donation to him. The Muslim jurists are unanimous on the point that *gharar* (uncertainty), invalidates the exchange contracts only and not the contracts of donation. They say that the donation of stray or unidentified animal, or fruit before its benefits are evident, or usurped thing is permissible but their sale is unlawful. From this, we may conclude that *takāful* provides an Islamic alternative to the present insurance business.

Conclusion

'*Takāful*' is a method of joint guarantee, among a group of members, or participants, against loss, or damage, that may inflict upon any of them. The members of the group agree to guarantee jointly that should any of them suffer a catastrophe or disaster, he would receive certain sum of money to meet the loss or damage. All members of the group pool together to support the needy. It is a scheme based on brotherhood, solidarity and mutual assistance which provides for mutual financial aid and assistance to the participants in case of need whereby the participants mutually agree to contribute for that purpose.

Takāful (Islamic insurance) is practiced in the Muslim world, in a number of ways. The common feature in these methods, and models is the concept of *tabarru'* (donation), joint guarantees and assistance. There are three important models, of *takāful* working in the Muslim world, namely: *waqf model, wakālah model and murābaḥah model.*

A takaful company uses islamically approved modes of investment, and distributes profit among the policy holder. Thus it avoids riba in its operations element of riba. Being a contract of donation, any uncertainty about the *takāful* benefits to be earned by any participant, does not affect the validity of contract. A contract of donation with *gharar* and *jahl* is permissible in the *Sharī'ah*.

The Muslim jurists are unanimous on the point that *gharar* (uncertainty), invalidates the exchange contracts only and not the contracts of donation. They say that the donation of stray or unidentified animal, or fruit before its benefits are evident, or usurped thing is permissible but their sale is unlawful. From this, we may conclude that *takāful* provides an Islamic alternative to the present insurance business.

Chapter 26

Concept of *Maqāṣid al- Sharī'ah* Applications in Islamic Finance

Concept of *Maqāṣid*

The injunctions of *Sharī'ah* are based upon the interest of man here and in the hereafter. The laws of *Sharī'ah* are designed to protect and promote benefits of individuals and society. Thus, the *maṣlaḥah* or wellbeing of the mankind is the basic and fundamental objective for which the divine law was revealed.

Maṣlaḥah or well-being of people according to Imām Ghāzalī (505A.H) "lies in safeguarding their faith (*dīn*), their life (*nafs*). their intellect (*'aql*), their posterity (*nasl*) and their wealth (*māl*). Whatever ensures the safeguard of these five, serve as *maṣlaḥah* and is desirable."[1]

The theory of *maqāṣid*, thus, revolves around the concepts of *maṣlaḥah* and *manfa'ah* (benefits and utility). It is concerned with the acquisition of benefit and the repulsion of *haram*. This purpose is achieved through the preservation and protection of human's faith, life, intellect, progeny and material wealth as described by Imām Ghazālī. Imām Ibn Taymiyyah (728H/1262) has replaced "nasl" i.e progeny and posterity with human dignity and honor (*'irḍ*). He regards human dignity as one of the basic and essential benefits of mankind which *Sharī'ah* through its laws aims to promote and protect.

---

[1] Ibn 'Āshur, *Maqāṣid* al- *Sharī'ah*, p. 171

Definition of *Maqāṣid*

Drawn on Ghazali's 'Theory of *Maqāṣid*', the *Sharī'ah* scholars have formulated different definitions of *maqāṣid al- Sharī'ah*. 'Allama Ṭāhir Ibn 'Āshūr, a prominent Tunisian Muslim thinker and founder of revivalist movement for *maqāṣid* in 20th century, defines *maqāṣid* as: "the purpose and wisdom behind the enactment of all or most of the *Sharī'ah* rulings". Dr. Aḥmad al-Raysūnī, another modern *Sharī'ah* scholar has defined *maqāṣid al- Sharī'ah* as "the ends sought behind the enactment of each of the ruling of *Sharī'ah* and the wisdom and rationale underlying these rulings."

According to Dr. Yuūsuf Ḥāmid al-'Ālam, *maqāṣid* are: "the essential benefits of human beings pertaining to this world and the world hereafter. These benefits revolve around realization of *maṣlaḥah* (human interest) and repulsion of *mafsadah* harm, corruption etc.

In the analysis of Dr. Nūruddīn Mukhtār al-Khādimī, an expert of the science of objectives of *Sharī'ah*, *maqāṣid* are the purposes and objectives of *Sharī'ah* rulings regardless of whether these are general objectives of *Sharī'ah* (Macro objectives) or of a particular rulings (micro objectives).

Analysis of Definitions

From the definitions, we may conclude that the *Sharī'ah* scholars have used the phrase "*maqāṣid al- Sharī'ah*" to convey the following two meanings:

1. Macro and general objectives (*Maqāṣid 'āmmah*)

Maqāṣid in this meaning are the grand and essential benefits of human beings on which their wellbeing in this world and success and salvation in the world hereafter depends. These include: Preservation and protection of religion, preservation and protection of life, preservation and protection of human intellect, establishment of justice, equitable distribution of wealth etc.

2. Micro objectives (*Maqāṣid juz'iyyah*)

Micro objective means rationale and wisdom behind particular and individual *Sharī'ah* rulings. Micro objective provides answer to the question why was a particular law provided? For instance,

i) Why five prayers have been prescribed?
ii) What is wisdom behind obligation of fasting?
iii) What is the rationale behind prohibition of *ribā*?
iv) Why is *gharar* prohibited in transactions?
v) What is wisdom behind giving right of *ṭalāq* to men?
vi) Why is '*iddat* (waiting period) mandatory for divorced woman?

The Qur'ān, in a number of places has expressed the rationale, purpose and the benefit to be drawn from its laws. For example, with regard to prayer, Qur'ān declares: "Truly *ṣalāt* obstructs promiscuity of evil"[2]. With reference to fasting the purpose is "to guard against evil"[3]. The wisdom at work behind prohibition of gambling is that it stirs up enmity and hatred among the people and bars them from remembrance of Allah. The objective of *zakāh* is purification of soul and purification of wealth. The Qur'ān says: "take alms (*zakāh*) of their wealth so that you might purify them[4] .

With regard to law of *Qiṣāṣ* (justifiable retaliation) the Qur'ān says: "In *qiṣāṣ*, there is life for you, O, people of understanding"[5].

---

[2] Qur'ān 29:45
[3] Qur'ān 2:183
[4] Qur'ān 9:13
[5] Qur'ān 2:179

Thus, we observe that in number of cases the Qur'ān and Sunnah have explicitly mentioned the goal, justification, cause and the benefit of legislation.

Besides these two categories of *maqāṣid*, *Sharīʻah* scholars have also introduced field-specific *maqāṣid* such as objectives of criminal law of Islam. Objectives of political system and *siyasah shariyyah*, *maqāṣid* of family law, *maqāṣid* of economic system of Islam, philosophy of *'ibādāt*, etc. They call it *maqāṣid khaṣṣah* or specific *maqāṣid*. Dr. Bin Zaghībah, a prominent Muslim scholar on *maqāṣid*, has written his Ph.D dissertation on "*Maqāṣid al- Sharīʻah* relevant to financial matters". Dr. Yūsuf al-Qarḍawī has written extensively on the *maqāṣid* relating to *māl* and *milkiyyah*. Objectives of family law in Islam, has also been a subject matter of many intellectual debates.

Maqāṣid khaṣṣah have now emerged as a new category of *maqāṣid* which has attracted many intellectual discussions.

Sharīʻah Evidence of *Maqāṣid*

On what basis, a particular value or benefit may be chosen or identified as objective of *Sharīʻah*? The *Sharīʻah* scholars, have attempted to answer this question. A benefit (*maṣlaḥah*) that is supported by the explicit texts of the Qur'ān and Sunnah, or it is in conformity with the general dispositions of the Lawgiver, qualifies to be objective of *Sharīʻah*. All the five basic objectives of *Sharīʻah*, meet this criterion. *Ḥifẓ al-nafs*, for instance, is established by a large number of texts. *Ḥifẓ al-māl* as an objective has been proved by all such texts that prohibit usurping each other's properties unfairly and prohibit the acts like *ribā*, gambling, *gharar* etc. the objective of *Hifẓ al-nasl* is established by all such texts that prohibit extra martial relationship and emphasis procreation and continuation of human race through marriage contract.

Textual Evidence for *Maqāṣid*

Some of the verses of Qur'ān and *aḥādith* to endorse and support five basic *maqāṣid* are as follows:

(i) *Ḥifẓ al-dīn*

- 'And fight them on until there is no more tumult or oppression and there prevail justice and faith in God altogether and everywhere; but if they cease verily God doth see all that they do."[6]
- 'And slay them wherever ye catch them and turn them out from where they have turned you out; for tumult and oppression are worse than slaughter; but fight them not at the sacred mosque unless they (first) fight you there; but if they fight you slay them. Such is the reward of those who suppress faith."[7]

(ii) *Ḥifẓ al-nafs*: (Preservation and protection of human life)

- 'On that account: We ordained for the children of Israel that if anyone slew a person unless it be for murder or for spreading mischief in the land it would be as if he slew the whole people: and if anyone saved a life it would be as if he saved the life of the whole people. Then although there came to them our apostles with clear signs yet even after that many of them continued to commit excesses in the land."[8]
- 'Nor take life—which God has made sacred—except for a just cause. And if anyone is slain wrongfully, we have given his heir authority (to demand *qiṣāṣ* or to forgive) - but let

[6] Qur'ān 8:39
[7] Qur'ān 2:191
[8] Qur'ān 5:32

him not exceed bounds in the matter of taking life, for he is helped (by the law)."[9]

- Holy Prophet (s.a.w.s) said, "Allah has made the life, and property and honor of each of you unto the other sacred and inviolable like this day of this month in this territory."[10]

(iii) *Ḥifẓ al-nasl*: (Preservation and protection of progeny)

- "And among His signs is this, that He created for you mates from among yourselves, that ye may dwell in tranquility with them, and he has put love and mercy between your (hearts), verily in that are signs for those who reflect."[11]
- "The woman and the man guilty of adultery or fornication, flog each of them with a hundred stripes. Let not compassion move you in their case, in a matter prescribed by God, if ye believe in God and the Last Day. And let a party of the believers witness their punishment."[12]

(iv) *Ḥifẓ al-'aql* (Preservation and protection of human intellect)

- "Ye who believe! Intoxicants and gambling (dedication of) stones and (divination by) arrows are an abomination of satan's handiwork: eschew such (abomination) that ye may prosper."[13]
- Holy Prophet (s.a.w.s) said: "Every intoxicant is khamr, and every khamr is forbidden."

---

[9] Qur'ān 17:33
[10] Bukhārī, *Ṣaḥīḥ*, Ḥadīth no. 7447
[11] Qur'ān 30:21
[12] Qur'ān 24:2
[13] Qur'ān 5:90

(v) *Ḥifẓ al-māl* (Preservation and protection of wealth)

- "Ye who believe! eat not up your property among yourselves in vanities, but let there be amongst you traffic and trade by mutual good-will: nor kill (or destroy) yourselves, for verily God hath been to you Most Merciful".[14]

- "As to the thief male or female cut off his or her hands. A punishment by way of example from God for their crime and God is exalted in power."[15]

- "Children of Adam! Wear your beautiful apparel at every time and place of prayer: eat and drink: but waste not by excess for God loveth not the wasters."[16]

According to Dr. Wahbah Zuḥailī, the basic *maqāṣid* have been collectively mentioned in th *Sūrah al-Mumtaḥanah:*

> "O Prophet! When believing women come to thee to take the oath of fealty to thee, that they will not associate in worship any other thing whatever with God, that they will not steal, that they will not commit adultery (or fornication), that they will not kill their children, that they will not utter slander, intentionally forging falsehood, and that they will not disobey thee in any just matter- Then do thou receive their fealty and pray to God for the forgiveness (of their sins), for God is oft-forgiving, Most Merciful."[17]

Here we observe that prohibition of *shirk* is for *hifẓ al-dīn*, prohibition of theft is meant for *hifẓ al-māl*, prohibition of

---

[14] Qur'ān 4:29

[15] Qur'ān 5:38

[16] Qur'ān 7:31

[17] Qur'ān 60:12

murder stands for *hifẓ al-nafs*, while the prohibition of adultery establishes the objective of *hifẓ al-nasl*.

Classification of *Maqāṣid / Maṣālih* in Order of Priority

The *Sharī'ah* scholars have classified *maqāṣid* and *maṣālih* in order of priority into three categories:

(i) *Ḍarūriyyāt* i.e. Essential benefits

(ii) *Ḥajiyyāt* i.e. Complementary benefits

(iii) *Taḥsīniyyāt* i.e. Embellishments

1. Darūriyyāt

Darūriyyāt or esseantail interests are: faith (religiousity), life (sanctity of human life), progeny and lineage (protection and preservation of family unit), intellect and property.

Technically, *darūriyyāt* are those essential interests whose neglect may cause anarchy, and chaos in the society. "The *ḍarūriyyāt*, defines Kamali, are essential to normal order in society as well as to the survival and spiritual wellbeing of individuals, so much so their destruction and collapse will precipitate chaos and collapse of normal order in the society."[18]

By this definition, human life, human honor, sanctity of wealth, existence of family unit, etc. are the matters considered essential for the survival of human society, and maintenance of order in it. The *Sharī'ah aḥkām* essential for realization of *daruriyyat* such as obligatory prayers, obligatory fasting, *zakah*, prohibition of *ribā*, *qimār*, also fall under this category.

---

[18] Kamālī, Ḥāshim, *Maqāṣid* al- *Sharī'ah*, The objectives of Islamic law, p. 7.

2. *Ḥājiyyāt* (Complementary benefits)

These are need related interests, which if fulfilled, would bring relief to the hardship and create ease in the lives of the people. *Ḥājiyyāt* are required to support *ḍarūriyyāt* so as to enable the later's accomplishment to the highest standards.[19]

Sunnat rak'āt in prayers, *salam*, *istiṣna'* transactions and relaxation in *ṣalah* belong to this category.

Ḥājiyyāt also promote and protect the essential interests/objectives i.e. life, faith, progeny, intellect and wealth but at secondary level. Obligatory prayer is like necessity for promotion and protection of faith while *sunnat* prayer is a need for promotion of faith.

If *salam* or *istiṣnā'* are not allowed by *Sharī'ah* or relaxation in *salaht* for traveller is not granted, it will not create chaos or disorder but will only cause hardship and inconvenience for the individuals and society.

3. *Taḥsīniyyāt* (Embellishments)

Taḥsīniyyāt are in the nature of desire abilities as they seek to attain refinement and perfection in the conduct of people at all level of achievements.[20]

Taḥīiniyyāt include commendable acts and habits and observing high moral standards.

Sharī'ah aḥkam relating to the above categories

Sharī'ah has provided number of *aḥkām* for the promotion and protection of *maqāṣid*. These *aḥkām* serve the *maqāṣid* at different levels. Some *aḥkām* are primary and essential for

[19] See, Khaliq uzzaman, Ph,D Thesis, An Emperical Analysis of *Sharī'ah* Legitimacy of Islamic Banking Practices in Pakistan, p.19.

[20] Kamali, *Maqāṣid*, p.9

maqāṣid and some are of secondary nature, a complementary to the first category. From this aspect, *aḥkām* may be categorized into *darūrī aḥkām*, *hajiyyāt*-based *aḥkām* and *taḥsīnī aḥkām*.

The *aḥkām* which are very close and directly related to the objective and essential for its realization are *darūrī aḥkām* such as obligatory prayer, obligatory fasting, obligatory *ḥajj*, *zakah*, prohibition of *ribā* etc. As a rule, all obligations and prohibitions in conclusive terms, fall under *darūriyyāt*. *Ḥajiyyāt* are complemental and supplemental to *darūriyyāt*. *Sunnat rak'āt* of *fajr*, *zuhr*, *asr*, *magrib* and *Isha*, for instance, strengthens obligatory prayer in that their regular observance, complements the observance of obligatory prayers which leads to protection of faith and promotion of religiousness of people.

Observance of *tahajjud*, *ishrāq* prayers complements both the *sunnat* and *fard* prayers. Fasting on *'āshūrah*, *ayyam-e-bīḍ*, *'arafa* day etc. belong to the category of *tahsiniyyat* because these acts bring excellence in the accomplishment of one's religiosity, and contribute towards the realization of ḥifẓ al-dīn.

In the field of *mu'āmalāt* and transactions, the *aḥkām* with regard to their order of priority and closeness to the fundamental objective, may be categorized as follows:

Ḍarūriyāt based *aḥkām*

Prohibition of *ribā*, *gharar* (grave uncertainty), gambling, games of chance, sale of non-existent thing, sale of impermissible goods, prohibition of hoarding, combination of sale and loan, obligatory payment of *zakah*, inheritance laws and sale transaction also falls under *darūriyyūt* because they are necessary for every individual and society.

Ḥājiyyāt based *aḥkām*

Permissibility of *ijārah*, *ṣarf*, *salam*, *istiṣnā'*, *kafālah ḥawālah* (assignment of debt), *wakalah*, *wadī'yah*, *qarḍ* and contractual options such as option of defect, option of stipulation, option of inspection, etc. fall under this category. These *aḥkām* create ease in dealings and remove hardship from them. They promote and protect the objective of *hifẓ al māl* but in terms of importance, they are of lesser importance than *ḍarūrī aḥkām.* As a matter of principle all concessionary laws (rules established as exception to general rule) belong to the category of *ḥajyiyāt* such as *salam* and *istiṣnā'* which are considered an exception to the prohibition of sale of non-existent thing in *fiqh. Khiyārāt* or options are not a necessity for human beings, and the objective of *hifẓ al māl* is not affected or harmed if *khiyyarāt* or options are disallowed. But the absence of law of options certainly creates hardship and inconvenience for the people.

Taḥsīniyyāt based *ahkām*

In *mu'āmalāt*, *tahsiniyyat* include: *iqālah* in sale, giving time to poor debtor, remission in case he is unable to pay, to give commodate loan (*'āriyah*) to needy person, to repay debt in good quality, gentleness in dealing, encouragement of gratuitous transactions such as gift, *waqf*, *hibah*, tolerating *gharar* (uncertainty) in gratuitous contracts etc. From this we may conclude that *taḥsīnniyāt* are the recommendable habits in *mu'āmalāt*. This is a level of *iḥsān* (benevolence) and *taqwā* (peity) in *mu'āmalāt*. It would not be out of place here to mention that a matter of *ḥājah* (need or complementary benefit) sometimes assumes the status of *ḍarūrah* (necessity or essential benefit) when it becomes a general need. *Ijārah* may be a need for individuals but for society it is necessity. As such, in present day, *ijārah* is *ḍarūrah*, rather than mere *ḥājah* (need).

Other divisions of *aḥkām*

The *aḥkām* serve objectives from the following two aspects:

1. Protective and defensive aspect
2. Creative and promotive aspect

Obligatory prayers, obligatory fasting, obligatory *ḥajj* serve the objective of *ḥifẓ al-dīn* from promotive perspective, whereas *jihād* and penal laws serve this purpose from defensive and protective perspective. *Aḥkam* relating to the establishment of marriage institution serve the objective of *ḥifẓ al-nasl* form promotive and creative aspect while the prohibition of adultery serves the same objective from defensive and protective dimension.

The objective of *ḥifẓ al-'aql* may be realized through the promotion of education and awareness as well as through prohibiting and penalizing intoxicants. The objective of *ḥifẓ al-mal* is attained through promotive and creative *aḥkām* such as *Sharī'ah aḥkām* for commercial transactions as well as through protective *aḥkām* such as prohibiting and penalizing theft, embezzlement, bribery, hoarding, charging exorbitant profits etc.

Are *Maqāṣid* restricted to five objectives?

There has been debate in Islamic jurisprudence that whether *maqāṣid al- Sharī'ah* are restricted to five objectives expounded by classical jurists or some new *maqāṣid* can also be added to the list. It is evident from the above statement of Imam ibn Taymiyyah, that he does not insist on restricting them to the traditional list of five objectives. He, instead, favors to extend it to all matters of benefit to individuals and society. Imām Abū Isḥāq Ibrāhīm Shāṭibī (d-790H/1388AD), a renowned scholar of the science of *maqāṣid* has retained the list of Ghazālī, but he also does not regard it as an exhaustive and conclusive list. His only emphasis has been that a *mujtahid* while interpreting a text should not ignore the intention of law and the grand objectives and purposes of *Sharī'ah*. The "correct approach" suggests

Shatibi, "then, should be, to read the text, whether it is of a command or prohibition in conjunction with its rationale and objective, for this is most likely to bear the greatest harmony with the intention of the law-giver."

Revival of the Theory of *Maqāṣid*

In the last four decades of 20th century, the science of *maqāṣid*, received renewed attention by the Muslim thinkers and jurists. "This interest, observes Kamali, is partly due to somewhat restrictive and theoretical orientation of *uṣūl fiqh* and its methodology for *ijtihād* which has not responded well to the demands of Islamic revivalism and reform. This is because as a discipline of *Sharī'ah*, the *maqāṣid* are primarily concerned with the ends of *Sharī'ah* rather than conformity to technical details which seem to the dominant concern of various doctrines of *usul fiqh.*" Allamah Muhammad al-Tahir Ibn Ashur, renowned Tunisian *Sharī'ah* scholar, a founder of revivalist movement for *maqāṣid*, wrote treatise on *maqāṣid al- Sharī'ah* in which he contested many concepts of classical theory of *maqāṣid.* He proposed *maqāṣid* as a methodology for the renewal of the theory of Islamic law. He presented *maqāṣid* as a new paradigm for *ijtihād* and *fatwā* in contemporary issues of Islamic law. He gave new dimensions to the study of *maqāṣid al- Sharī'ah.* Ibn Ashur endorses the viewpoint of Ibn Taymiyyah that the old theory of *maqāṣid* is more focused on repulsion of harm (*daf' al-mafsadah*) than on acquisition of *maṣlaḥah.* It is pertinent to note that Juwainī and Ghazālī have identified those matters as *maqāṣid* for the violation of which, *Sharī'ah* has prescribed punishments. Preservation and protection of human life has been considered as objective of *Sharī'ah* because murder is strictly prohibited and *qiṣās* has been prescribed for it.

In the opinion of Ibn Taymiyyah, anything that brings about benefit to the people, may be classed under *maqāṣid al- Sharī'ah* regardless of whether *Sharī'ah* has fixed some punishment for its protection or not. Such benefit qualifies as objective of *Sharī'ah* provided the benefit is recognized by the *Sharī'ah*.

In line with this understanding of *maqāṣid*, Ibn 'Āshur has introduced many new *maqāṣid*. He has also re-designated many old *maqāṣid*. He has for instance, replaced "protection of life" with "freedom of faith", "protection of life" with "preservation of human dignity", "protection of intellect" with "propagation of scientific thinking", "avoidance of brain drain", "protection of wealth" with "well-being of society, minimizing income and wealth disparity".

Some other prominent scholars like Aḥmad al-Raysūnī, Ḥāmid al-'Ālam, 'Allāl al-Fāsī, Dr.Yūsuf al-Qaraḍāwī have also contributed to the revival of *maqāṣid* theory. They have not only emphasized the centrality of *maqāṣid* in *ijtihād*, but have also enriched the list of *maqāṣid*. Dr. Yousuf al-Qaradawi, in his list of *maqāṣid* has emphasized social welfare and solidarity, freedom, human dignity and human fraternity as objectives of *Sharī'ah*.

Some new objectives of *Sharī'ah* introduced by modern *Sharī'ah* scholars include:

1. Human honor and dignity
2. Fundamental rights and civil liberties
3. Establishment of justice
4. Elimination of poverty
5. Social welfare and security
6. Equitable distribution of wealth
7. Peace and security
8. Human fraternity and cooperation among members of human community

These scholars argue that the above values and ideals derive their legitimacy from the Qurān and Sunnah. These are legitimate essential benefits of an individual and society, thus, they qualify to be acknowledged as objectives of *Sharī'ah*. The modern scholars of *maqāṣid* also observe that adherence to apparent text in *fatwa* without pondering over its ultimate aims and objectives, may cause error in the ruling and judgment. Thus, a text should be interpreted in the light of ultimate ends and objectives. In case of *ṣadaqah al-fiṭr* (*fiṭrānh*), the requirement of Sunnah is that it should be in form of kind such as dates, wheat etc. Many *fuqahā'* insist that *ṣadaqah* or *zakah al-fiṭr* must be paid in kind and not in monetary equivalents, because *aḥādith* clearly specify this requirement. The Ḥanafī jurists maintain that *zakāh al-fiṭr* may be disbursed in monetary equivalents. The purpose of *zakāh al-fiṭr* is to satisfy need of the poor and this may be achieved through payment in kind or money form. Insistence on kind may defeat the purpose of law.

Applications in Islamic Finance

The *Sharī'ah* legitimacy of current Islamic banking from the perspective of *maqāṣid al- Sharī'ah* has been subject matter of debate among *Sharī'ah* scholars and Islamic finance experts for the last many years. A group of scholars holds the view that modern banking has ignored *maqāṣid al- Sharī'ah* (Higher purposes of *Sharī'ah*) in its scheme and agenda. They claim that a *Sharī'ah* compliant banking does not means mere compliance with the requirement of valid *Sharī'ah* contract or external form of contract. It rather extends to higher purposes of *Sharī'ah* relevant to Islamic finance which are held to be *ḥifẓ al-Māl*, augmentation of wealth in halal manner, observance of the values of justice, equity and fairness in dealings, realization of common good and wellbeing of society, generation of real economic activity, equitable distribution of wealth and discouragement of its concentration in few hands, avoidance of artifice and subterfuges etc. In brief, the socio-economic objectives of Islam, according to these scholars, are the objective of *Sharī'ah* in the field of Islamic banking and finance. These scholars assert that Islamic banks have introduced many controversial Islamic products which frustrate the spirit of *Sharīʻah* and oppose the objectives of *Sharīʻah*. These products have caused concentration of wealth in the hands of rich segment of the society. In the analysis of this group, the Islamic banking is presently working in capitalistic paradigm whose only motive is to maximize profit of its shareholders.

As against this, another group claims that observance of *maqāṣid Al- Sharīʻah* is not a valid criterion for judging the *Sharīʻah* legitimacy of Islamic banking. If Islamic banks comply with requirement of valid contracts approved by their *Sharīʻah* advisors, and avoid *Sharīʻah* prohibitions such as *ribā*, *gharar*, *qimār*, *maysir* etc. in their operations, then such banks are Islamic and their *Sharīʻah* legitimacy cannot be challenged. In the following lines, an attempt has been made to explore *maqāṣid* for Islamic finance based on *Sharīʻah* evidences and to examine their observance in Islamic banks.

Ideal *Maqāṣid* in Islamic Finance

As mentioned earlier that *maqāṣid al Sharīʻah* is not confined to five objectives advocated and expounded by Imām Ghazālī. Any value which promotes the *maṣlaḥah* and wellbeing of the society and averts harm from them, is the objective of *Sharīʻah*, provided it is acknowledged by *Sharīʻah* as objective through conclusive evidences from the Qur'ān, Sunnah and other sources. For example, establishment of justice is a primary objective of *Sharīʻah* although it is not included in the traditional list. The reason is that verses of Qur'ān and *aḥādith* of Holy Prophet (S.A.W.S) emphasize establishment of justice and promote values of equity and fairness in the society. In the similar way, elimination of poverty and equitable distribution of wealth and its circulation in the society are the objectives of economic system of Islam. This may be proved by the verses and *aḥādīth* which prohibit the concentration of wealth and emphasize the right of the poor in the wealth of the rich. We should also bear in mind that *ḥifẓ al māl* of Imām Ghazālī does not merely mean to protect the wealth through judicial, legal and penal system but also means to enhance and augment it through investment, trading and financial and commercial activities. The issue of *maqāṣid* in Islamic finance has been under discussion among the scholars for the last many years. Some scholars are of the view that socio economic objectives of Islam are the ideal objectives of Islamic finance. This has been generally the approach of prominent Muslim economists like Dr. Umer Chapra, Dr. Munzar Qaḥf. Dr. Nejatullah Siddiqui and many others. Dr. Chapra has identified the following objectives for an Islamic economic and financial system:

1. Economic development
2. Abolition of interest
3. Adherence to public interest
4. Promotion of economic wellbeing
5. Establishment of economic justice
6. Equitable distribution of income

According to the analysis of these scholars, the performance of Islamic banking industry and its *Sharī'ah* compliance should be measured and judged against this criterion. Some scholars are of the view that *hifẓ al māl* i.e preservation and protection of man is the prime objective of Islamic finance. It has many corollaries and sub-objectives, which are the integral part of the above mentioned fundamental objective. These sub-objectives and corollaries equally qualify to be the ideal *maqāṣid* for Islamic finance. The emphasis of Dr. Yūsuf Qaraḍāwī has generally been on *maqāṣid* relating to *māl* and wealth. He has mentioned a number of *maqāṣid* of *māl* in *Sharī'ah*. The economic and financial *maqāṣid* of *Māl* include fair distribution of returns of business, non-concentration of wealth, discouragement of injustice and exploitation and wellbeing of the society etc. While identifying *maqāṣid* of Islamic finance, some scholars have relied on Abū Zahra's theory, which has identified three values as *maqāṣid al Sharī'ah* that may be used for Islamic economics and financial system. These are educating the individual, establishing justice and public interest. Sheikh Abū Zahrā's theory has been generally adopted by Islamic finance experts for developing *maqāṣid* based index for Islamic finance industry.

Based on the current literature on *maqāṣid* and *Sharī'ah* evidences in support of *maqāṣid*, we may suggest the following values and objectives as the ideal *maqāṣid* for Islamic finance:

1. *Hifẓ al māl* i.e. to protect wealth and to augment it in halal manner
2. Justice and fairness in distribution of returns of business (to depositors, bank)
3. Circulation of wealth (financial inclusion)
4. Fair and transparent financial dealings
5. To fulfill social needs of the society and to achieve comprehensive communal prosperity to enhance the social wellbeing.
6. Linking of financial activity with real sector, value addition activity
7. To fulfill the form and substance of *Sharī'ah* in transactions to avoid stratagems (*ḥiyal*), and to maintain the real spirit and objective of Islamic law in a transaction.

Here we explain some of these objectives with supportive evidence from *Sharī'ah* sources and their applications in current Islamic finance.

Objective 1: *Hifẓ al-māl* i.e. Protection of wealth and its augmentation in *ḥalāl* manner

Islam emphasizes that every individual in the society should be engaged in some economic activity to earn the wealth and augment it. The Qur'ān says, "It is He who made the earth tame for you, so walk among its slopes and eat of His provisions and to Him is the resurrection"[21] He also said, "and when the prayer has been concluded, disperse within the land and seek from the bounty of Allah, and remember Allah often that you may succeed"[22]. Islam wants that wealth should not remain idle and unutilized. It should be augmented through trading and investment. Holy Prophet directed the guardians of orphans to invest the wealth of orphans, in profitable avenues before it is eaten up or consumed by *zakāh*. In one of the *aḥādīth*, Holy Prophet (s.a.w.s) has urged the land owner to cultivate it and if he does not cultivate it, then he should give it to someone else to cultivate.

This shows that augmentation of wealth is primary concern of Islam and consequently qualifies to be an objective of Islam. Holy prophet (s.a.w.s) and his companions practiced *muḍārabah* and *mushārakah* in order to earn profit and increase the wealth of the society. The realization of this objective is the main concern of Islamic banks as their primary function is to invest the money provided to them by the depositors i.e. *arbāb al amwāl*, in profitable avenues. This augmentation, however should take place in a *ḥalāl* manner which is a basic requirement of Islam for business and trading

The implication of the above objective is that an Islamic bank, while receiving funds from depositor, should not explicitly or implicitly guarantee fix return on this money to depositor because it is not a borrowing and lending arrangement. The saving deposits in Islamic banks are not the liability of the bank. If some profit emerges they share the profit in an agreed ratio. If the funds are destroyed without the negligence on the part of bank, it cannot guarantee the return of capital to him. On asset side, again the bank is not lender and the user of the fund is

---

[21] Qur'ān 67:15

[22] Qur'ūn 62 :9

borrower. The Islamic bank uses different Islamic modes for investment and trading. All these modes are asset-based and the bank has to bear the risk related to the asset. The Holy Prophet (s.a.w.s) said, "entitlement of profit depends upon liability for loss."

Islamic banks in Pakistan generally observe this objective in their operations. They use *Sharī'ah* compliant products such as *murābaḥah*, *ijārah*, diminishing *mushārakah*, *salam*, *istiṣnā'* etc. these products are free from prohibiting elements such as *ribā*, *gharar*, *qimār*, *maysir* and similar other elements that invalidate transactions. In line with the *ḥadīth* of Holy Prophet (s.a.w.s), which provides that a person is entitled to profit only when he bears risk and liability for loss, the Islamic banks bear all asset related and trade related risk.

This goes without saying that Islamic bank bears ability of loss and risk as stated in the above *ḥadīth* in a number of transactions in *murābaḥah* for example, all the risk associated with the asset, before its sale to the client is borne by the bank. If the asset does not remain in usable condition, the bank does not charge rental till it is brought back to usable condition. If the asset is destroyed, the loss is borne exclusively by the bank. In *salam*, after delivery of *salam* commodity by the seller to the bank and during the period of agency, if the asset is destroyed without the negligence on the part of agent, the loss is borne exclusively by the bank. As such this practice is in line with the instruction and spirit of the above *ḥadīth* of Holy Prophet (s.a.w.s).

The Islamic banks also avoid *qimār* (gambling) and *maysir* (games of chance) in their operations. They do not deal in derivatives, futures sale or debt which is frequently practiced by the conventional banks.

The nature of business to be financed by the Islamic banks is also very much important for them. They finance only those industries which are ethical and *Sharī'ah* compliant. Thus, they do not finance alcohol related industries, pork related industries, entertainment industries, tobacco business and other unethical and prohibited business. Islamic banks do not invest in conventional bonds, debentures and treasury bill etc. because they are *ribā* based transactions.

From this we may conclude that Islamic banks by and large comply with the objective of augmentation of wealth. The contracts used by the Islamic banks are largely free from the prohibited elements such as *ribā*, *gharar*, *qimār*, *maysir* etc.

Objective 2: Justice and fairness in distribution of returns of business and other dealings

Islam lays great emphasis in its commands and teaching on the value of justice. The Qur'ān says: "Behold! God enjoins justice and the doing of good."[23]

It also says, "We sent our apostles with clear signs and sent down with them the Book and the Balance (of right and wrong), that men may stand forth in justice."[24]

Allamah Ibn al-Qayyim says, "Verily, the *Sharī'ah* is founded upon wisdom and welfare for the servants in this life and the afterlife. In its entirety it is justice, mercy, benefit and wisdom. Every matter which abandons justice for tyranny, mercy for cruelty, benefit for corruption and wisdom for foolishness is not a part of *Sharī'ah* even if it was introduced therein by some remote interpretation."[25] In the opinion of Ibn al-Qayyim, a *Sharī'ah* verdict should be judged against the values of justice, equity, mercy, common good and wisdom. If any *fatwa* or *Sharī'ah* verdict contradicts these values, it does not qualify as

---

[23] Qur'ān 16:90

[24] Qur'ān 57: 25

[25] *I'lām al-Muwaqqiī'n* p.311

Sharī'ah ruling, though it is claimed to be so by remote interpretations.

The observance of the objective of justice and fairness in dealing has been frequently emphasized in the *Sharī'ah* Standards of AAOIFI. The *Sharī'ah* Standard on Iāarah no.8 states:

> "If the leased asset is destroyed or if the continuity of the lease contract becomes impossible up to the expiry period without the cause being attributable to the lessee in either case, then the rental is adjusted based on the prevailing market value. That is, the difference between the prevailing rate of rental and the rental specified in the contract must be refunded to the lessee if the latter rental is higher than the former. This is to avoid loss to the lessee, who agreed to a higher rental payment compared to the prevailing rate of rental in consideration of the lessor's promise to pass the title to him upon the expiry of the lease term. (Art. 8/8)

The observance of justice in Islamic bank can be judged and measured in its different operations such as the distribution of returns between the bank and the depositors. Some Indicators to measure justice in distribution of business returns are: profit sharing ratio, return on equity ratio and return on asset ratio. Some questions to judge compliance of Islamic bank with this objective could be: Does Islamic bank treat ordinary client and corporate client equally? Does it charge same rate on its financing from both the clients? How much return on corporate deposit is paid?

How far this objective is realized in Islamic financial institutions? The *Sharī'ah* scholars and Islamic finance experts have responded to this question in different ways but the common perception is that the values of justice, equity and fairness could not receive due attention in current Islamic finance industry. Many prominent Muslim economists entertain doubt about the compliance of Islamic banks with the ideals of justice and equity in dealings. We should bear in mind that banking industry is being financed substantially by small account holders, however, this hard earned resource is not being shared with them. In terms of financing, this class hardly gets financing from Islamic banks. They also get low returns on their funds. The products offered by the Islamic banks are not very much affordable for ordinary clients. The main beneficiary of Islamic banking services is corporate client. In Pakistan, the share of corporate client in total financing portfolio exceeds 75% while the share of SEME, agriculture and micro finance is hardly 5% of the total financing. It is important to note that a corporate client gets financing generally at the rate of 5% while the ordinary clients are charged at the rate of 12 to 13% on the financing.

SBP Governor in his speech on 29th January 2015, expressed his concern on the present state of unfair distribution of returns between Islamic bank and its depositors. He pointed out in his speech that Islamic banks earned Rs. 12 Billion (before tax) in the third quarter of last year which was about double the last year's amount, but the customers were not being rewarded accordingly. He advised that higher spreads should be reasonably rationalized. He said:

> "State Bank governor has urged the country's Islamic banks to develop ways to reward their customers in line with the surge in the sector's profitability or face regulatory action.... A growing client base and improving asset quality helped Islamic banks post profits before tax of 12 billion rupees in the third quarter of last year, almost double the year earlier amount. Central bank date shows.... But regulator wants to tackle customer perceptions that Islamic banks falter when it comes to social responsibility and ethical banking practices. The average financing to deposit spread - the difference between what banks charge for financing and what they pay their depositors - for all

> lenders, Islamic and conventional, remains high and should be reasonably rationalized."[26]

The objective of fairness in mutual dealings also implies that all material facts about the transaction should be brought into the knowledge of customer. He should have excess to all relevant information that may have bearing on his decision to enter the transaction or otherwise. The values of fairness and transparency are violated in many cases. 'Banca takāful' is one such product which contains active concealment of facts. In banca *takāful*, the client is not informed by the staff distributing or selling the product about the use of this money in commissions and benefits given to the staff and management. The product has been designed by the *takāful* companies and Islamic banks act as distribution channels against heavy commission which is deducted from the contribution of the participant (policy holder). If a participant has paid one lac rupees in first year, only 15% of this amount goes to investment pool. Remaining 85 thousand rupees are distributed among the staff and management involved in selling policy to an ignorant customer. In the second year, only 25% of the installment is invested for his benefit, remaining amount is distributed as commission. Banca *takāful* has become such a lucrative business that it has become a primary concern of every branch manager. (Meezan Bank has abstained itself from this practice. This is highly commendable stance.)

Banca *takāful* has become a common practice in the banks. It has reached a situation that a person comes for a deposit account, or to invest his small amounts for any earning scheme for his / her rainy days, the staff persuades him to get *takāful* policy, only to get a share in the commission. However, the issue is that due to high rate of commission (almost 80 % in first year), the policy holder might reach the break-even only after

---

[26] See, Dawn 30th January, 2015

4-7 years, as roughly 15 years' and 5 years' fees are taken in the first and the second years of 20 years *takāful* policies.[27] This may prove to be highly unjust and unfair in case some customers withdraw their policies in early years due to any reason where people might not have any option but to withdraw their funds from the banks / financial institutions. It is pertinent to note that while distributing banka *takāful*, the bank gets signature of client on disclaimer form, which is generally not explained to him and he himself does not have ability to understand it.

Objective 3: Circulation of wealth and discouragement of its concentration

One of the objectives of economic system in Islam is that wealth should be equitably distributed among all segments of the society. The Qur'ān says: "So that it (wealth) is not circulated among the rich among you."[28]

Islam prohibits *ribā* because it causes concentration of wealth. It prescribes *zakah* as an obligatory act because through *zakah* wealth moves from the rich to the poor. In the field of Islamic finance, the objective implies financial inclusion i.e. access to finance for large part of society or delivery of financial services to even low-income groups. This also implies that small business such as SME, micro finance be financed so that a large segment of the society benefits from it

The achievement of the objective of equitable distribution of wealth can be measured through the indicators, such as ratio of financing for corporate sector vis a vis SME, agriculture and micro finance. This can be measured through the questions such as how much Islamic banking products are affordable for a common individual in the society? What rate a bank charges on

[27] Journal of Islamic Business and Management, vol 6, no. 1, 2016
[28] Qur'ān 59:7

its financing to the corporate client? How much is gap between the highest paid and lowest paid employees?

Objective 4: Fulfilling both the form and spirit of *sharī'ah* principles and avoidance stratagems (*ḥiyal*) in transactions

Islamic law requires that a transaction should be *Sharī'ah* - compliant both in form and substance. In case of conflict, the substance should be given prime consideration. This *Sharī'ah* rule has been expressed in a famous maxim, "In contracts and transactions, prime consideration has to be given to meaning and objective not to external form, and phrases." This maxim closes the door for *ḥiyal* and subterfuges which are generally designed to frustrate the spirit and purpose of law.

In *Sharī'ah*, intention and purpose of law is the touchstone, to determine the validity, or invalidity of a juridical act.

It has primary role in determining its *Sharī'ah* status as to whether it is valid in the eyes of Law-giver, or invalid. If a transaction is done with illegal intention, it will be considered as an invalid act. For this reason, sale of grapes to winery has been prohibited by the *fuqahā'* because he will use these grapes to extract wine. A contract of marriage to facilitate re-marriage between divorced couple after triple repudiation is invalid because the parties do not intend lifelong companionship from this marriage.

The objective of fulfilling form and substance of *Sharī'ah* principles in transactions implies that products of Islamic banks should not be such that comply with the legal form but frustrate the substance and spirit of *Sharī'ah* like '*īnah* or organized *Tawarruq* based products. Some *Sharī'ah* scholars have termed such products as pseudo- *Sharī'ah* products. While assessing practices of Islamic banks from the perspective of *maqāṣid*, we should examine whether the products and practices of Islamic banks do fulfill both the form and substance of *Sharī'ah* principles or they merely conform to the letter of Islamic law and not to its spirit.

AAOIFI has also emphasized this position in its *Sharī'ah* Standards. It has identified many forms of *ḥiyal* and subterfuges and has urged Islamic financial institutions to abstain from them in designing their products as well as in their operations. Avoidance of *ḥiyal* (stratagems and subterfuges) occupies pivotal position in AAOIFI's methodology of legal reasoning (*ijtihād*) and *fatwā*. It is prominent policy principle for *fatwā* which dominates the whole *fatwā* activity of AAOIFI. AAOIFI frequently alludes to the forms of *ḥiyal*, and warns against *ḥīlah* based fictitious transactions in Islamic finance industry.

Some examples of the principle of prohibition of *ḥiyal* in *Sharī'ah* Standards are as follows:

1. *Sharī'ah* Standard no 8: "*Murābaḥah* to purchase orderer" identifies many situations of occurrence of *'īnah* in *murābaḥah*. This goes without saying that *'īnah* is *ḥīlah* to circumvent the prohibition of *ribā*. Articles 2.2.1 to 2.2.5 exclusively deal with *ḥiyal* in *murābaḥah*.

2. *Sharī'ah* Standard no 9 on *ijārah* also identifies cases of *'īnah* in *ijārah*. Articles 3.3 and 3.4 deal with prohibited *'īnah* in *ijārah*. In sale and lease back, *Sharī'ah* Standard requires passage of reasonable period between the first sale and last sale with a view to avoid *'īnah*.

3. In *istiṣnā'*, AAOIFI's verdict is that *istiṣnā'* transaction should not be concluded in a way that they become a *ḥīlah* for *ribā*.

4. In the standard on 'Combination of Contracts', AAOIFI has prohibited many such combinations which may lead to *ribā* or *gharar*.

5. The standard on *tawarruq* clearly prohibits the return of commodity to the first seller either through agreements, collusion or *'urf* because it is a form of *'īnah*

6. The Standard on 'Shares and Bonds' clearly prohibits two binding promises in futures and forwards, because this is *heelah* to circumvent the prohibition of *bay' a-kāli' bil-kāl'* (Sale of debt for debt, or sale of one obligation for another obligation).

AAOIFI is so concerned about *ḥiyal* that it has adopted prohibition of *ḥiyal* as permanent principle for its legal opinions. It would not be out of place to mention here that AAOFIF does not oppose *makhārij shar'iyyah* or genuine alternatives "that do not frustrate the *maqāṣid al- Sharī'ah*, do not lead to *mafsadah* (evil consequences) or conflicts with clear *Sharī'ah* evidence".

As mentioned earlier, that Islamic banking products and operations are largely *Sharī'ah* compliant. There are, however, certain products and operations which do conform to the requirements of a valid contract of Islamic law, but frustrate its purpose and spirit. These products are in fact subterfuges to circumvent certain *Sharī'ah* prohibitions.

A prominent *ḥīlah* practiced in Islamic banks is 'Running *Mushārakah*'. It is a prominent financing mode in Pakistan. Running *mushārkah* (RM) is an Islamic banking product that was introduced as an alternate to interest based product of running finance. In RM, an Islamic bank joins the business of client as sleeping partner through contractual partnership (*shirkah al 'aqd*). Islamic bank specifies a credit limit that is considered Islamic bank's investment. Two stage profit rates are determined in RM. For the first stage, Islamic bank gives the client its target rate/profit ceiling that is usually equal to the KIBOR rate. It is mutually agreed that up to the profit ceiling, profit would be distributed according to investment shares of bank. For second stage, Islamic bank agrees to reduce its profit share as low as .0001% in over and above profit of target profit and to give 99.999% to the client. Usually this remaining profit is more than the total profit that is distributed between Islamic bank and corporate client at first stage.

Example: RM limit is Rs. 120M and maturity period is 6 months. It is decided that profit will be distributed according to their investment shares. But at the same time, Islamic bank gives its target profit rate, say KIBOR 7%, which implies that in future, Islamic bank will take an amount that would be equal to the 7% of Islamic bank's capital which is called target rate or profit ceiling. After getting target rate, remaining profit will be distributed according to .0001% and 99.999% between Islamic banks and client. RM starts and corporate client withdraws amount as and when needed. Three days prior to the maturity, it is calculated how much capital the corporate client has withdrawn from bank. This utilized amount is considered as Islamic bank's capital share, say it is Rs. 100M. At this stage, corporate client presents all his business details to determine his capital share in joint business and it is found that his capital share is Rs. 40M. Suppose business profit is 30 M. Now total investment is Rs. 140M. Islamic banks investment share is 71.43% and client's investment share is 28.57%. According to these shares, Islamic bank's share in profit is Rs. 21.43M (71.43% x 30M) and client's Share in profit is Rs. 8.57M (28.57% x 30M). But Islamic bank will not take Rs. 21.43M, because according to target rate Islamic bank has to take Rs. 7M (7% x 100M). Now remaining profit Rs. 23M (30M- 7M) will be distributed between Islamic bank and client according to second stage profit rate which is .0001% and 99.999%. Islamic bank will take Rs. 230 and client will get Rs. 22,999,770 out of Rs. 23M.

Here we observe that Islamic bank actually wants to give the remaining profit as *hibah* (gift) to corporate client but it cannot do it, *Sharī'ah* does not allow pre-agreed *hibah* in favour of any partner. To circumvent such prohibition, Islamic bank adopts a *ḥīlah* through which it is decided that remaining profit will be distributed according to .0001% and 99.999% between Islamic bank and client. Though, they use the words *shirkah* or *profit sharing* in RM but actually it is *hibah*.

Here we observe that RM, in its meaning, purpose, effect and end results is not substantially different from running finance of conventional bank, where the bank gets a fixed return i.e. interest on its investment, which is 7M rupees on the capital of Rs.100M provided by the bank, in the above example. The only difference is that Islamic bank, under running *mushārakah* receives additional amount of Rs. 230 which is insignificant for the bank.

This goes without saying that *mushārakah* in Islamic law is a partnership to share real returns of business to the partners. If this purpose is frustrated by some fictitious profit sharing ratio such as 99.999% and 0.0001% then in substance it is not real *musharakah* but a transaction close to running finance.

This should also be noted that in running *mushārakah*, the bank provided the funds of *rabb al-māl* to the corporate client. Thus, it acts as *muḍārib* partner in the transaction. Any profit earned on the funds of *rabb al-māl* is basically the right of *rabb al-māl* i.e. depositors. The bank, as *muḍārib* has no right to waive the right and entitlement of *rabb al-māl*, by giving this profit as gift to the corporate client. The *Sharī'ah* Standard number (13) on *muḍārabah*, clause 9/6 states:

> "It is not permissible for the *muḍārib* to make a loan or a gift or a charitable donation out of the *muḍārabah* funds. Likewise, the *muḍārib* is not entitled to waive a right associated with the *muḍārabah* operation unless the capital provider has consented to his doing so."

As mentioned earlier, the primary objective for which *mushārakah* is instituted in Islamic law is to give opportunity to the partners to share real returns of business in just and fair manner. The *fuqahā'* are so sensitive about this objective that some of them do not allow a profit ratio which is not strictly in proportion to the investment. According to Malikī and Shāfi'ī jurists, both the profit and loss should follow the investment of the parties. In the instant case, a large portion of profit goes to the corporate client without any counter value, defeating the purpose of *Sharī'ah* behind instituting *mushārkah*. This arrangement clearly frustrates the objective of fair distribution of returns. So, from the perspective of form, it is *mushārakah*, but by substance and meaning it is not the *musharakah* or more specifically *shirkah al-'inān*, as contemplated by early jurists.

The proponents of running *mushārkah* generally place their reliance on the clause of *Sharī'ah* Standard on *mushārakah* which allows Islamic bank to allocate its share of profit to the client, if the profit of bank is beyond the desired rate. The desired rate has been interpreted as KIBOR linked fixed return on capital. It means if the bank wants 7% of its capital, then whatever profit is above this rate, may be allocated to the other partner.

The above argument may not be accepted on the ground that here the bank has entered into partnership with corporate client as *muḍārib* for *rabb al-māl*. So, all the rules relevant to *muḍārib* are applicable to the transaction. One of such rules is that *muḍārib* cannot withdraw or surrender any financial right belonging to *rabb al māl*. How Islamic bank deprives depositors of their due right in profit, may be judged from a running *mushārakah* transaction of an Islamic bank which earned a profit of RS.10 billion above desired rate i.e. KIBOR related rate (9% of bank's capital). The bank received from this amount Rs.2000 only. Remaining all profit went to the client in line with the profit distribution ratio of 99.9999% for client and 0.0001% for bank. This means that Islamic bank received one paisa on every one million rupee of extra profit i.e above target profit. A negligible amount of Rs.2000 out of one billion is only a deception and *ḥīlah* intended to prove that there was a real profit sharing and that it was a *mushārakah*, but the fact of the matter is that it is just running finance arrangement. The client at the inception of contract knows clearly that he has to pay 9% of bank's financing. This is how the parties agree at the time of contract. If the client has paid 2 thousand rupees, it does not change the nature and reality of transaction.

Some other *ḥīlah* based products are: *bay' muajjal* of *ṣukūk*, commodity *murābaḥah* and PMEX *murābaḥah* transaction, etc. The issue of *ḥiyal* and its applications in Islamic finance has been discussed in detail in the chapter on "Ḥiyal and their Applications in Islamic Finance".

Objective 5: Enhancing social wellbeing

This goes without saying that society as a whole has responsibility and obligation towards less fortunate and deprived segment of the society. It is generally claimed that eradication of poverty and uplift of living standard of people, is the responsibility of state which ought to perform this duty through distribution of *zakah*. The Holy Qur'ān and Sunnah refute this misconception. Holy Prophet (s.a.w.s) was asked whether the poor have any right to the wealth of the rich beside *zakah*? And he replied that yes, they have certainly right beside *zakah*.

Haḍrat 'Alī (r.t.a) narrated that Allah said: "Allah has made obligatory on the rich to provide the poor with what is adequate for them and if the poor are hungry or naked, this is only due to the fact that the rich have deprived them of their right."

It is pertinent to note that according to the Qur'ān, the share of poor in the wealth of rich is his right, not a favour or benevolence from the rich. The concept has been emphasized in a number of Quranic verses. In *Sūrah al-Isrā,* the Qur'ān says: "In their wealth, there is a due share of the needy who asks and who is prevented from asking."[29] Here Qur'ān alludes to the obligation of *zakah.* In *Sūrah al-dhāriyāt,* the Qur'ān says: "And in their wealth, there is a right for needy who asks, and who is prevented from asking."[30]Here Qur'ān clearly mentions that whatever a poor person receives from the rich, he receives it as a matter of right.

Thus, by virtue of these texts, contribution towards fulfilling needs of the society becomes a religious obligation for the rich segment of the society. This injunction applies to the individuals as well as financial institutions operating in Muslim state. Now it is the responsibility of regulatory authorities to direct financial institutions to allocate some amount from their profits for fulfilling social needs of the society and to achieve communal prosperity. To meet the distributive justice, the Islamic banks should help the needy in their self-employment pursuits by financing micro and small enterprises and allocating some amount of *qarḍ ḥasan* from the profits.

It is pertinent to note that now even the conventional finance experts and scholars acknowledge that financial institutions created for earning profit for shareholders, have responsibility to contribute in the welfare and wellbeing of the society. They believe that banks and business corporations have obligation towards social development that add value to peoples' lives and the communities around them.

Conclusion

Maqāṣid al- Sharī'ah are the essential benefits of individual and society on which their wellbeing in this world and their success and salvation in the world hereafter depends. *Maqāṣid* are not

[29] Qur'ān 17:24

[30] Qur'ān 51:19

restricted to five objectives identified by Imam Ghazali. Any essential benefit of human-being endorsed by *Sharī'ah* evidences qualifies to be an objective of *Sharī'ah*. In the last three decades, science of *maqāṣid* has received renewed attention. The modern scholars like Ṭāhir Ibn 'Āshūr, Aḥmad al-Raysūnī, Yuūsuf al-Qaraḍāwī and many others, have developed and identified many new *maqāṣid* not contemplated by the early jurists. They have also introduced *maqāṣid* as a method of legal reasoning and *ijtihād*. The modern *Sharī'ah* scholars have not only introduced new list of higher purposes of *Sharī'ah* like establishment of justice, peace and security, human dignity, etc. but have also attempted to develop *maqāṣid* for different fields of Islamic law such as *maqāṣid al- Sharī'ah* of family law, *maqāṣid* of criminal law of Islam, *maqāṣid* of Islamic commercial law etc. In the recent past, *maqāṣid* in Islamic finance has been a subject matter of debate and discussion among the *Sharī'ah* scholars, economists and Islamic finance experts. Many indices have been developed based on these *maqāṣid*. There has been a difference of opinion as to what exactly are the Islamic finance related *maqāṣid al- Sharī'ah*. Based on the current literature on *maqāṣid* and *Sharī'ah* evidence in support of those *maqāṣid*, the following values and objectives may be held as ideal *maqāṣid* for Islamic finance.

1. *Hifẓ al māl* i.e. to protect wealth and to augment in halal manner
2. Justice and fairness in distribution of return of business and other dealings.
3. Circulation of wealth (financial inclusion)
4. Fair and transparent financial dealings
5. To enhance social wellbeing
6. Linking of financial activity with real sector value addition activity

The implication of these objectives for Islamic finance is that the products, contracts, and operations of an Islamic bank should be in conformity with the *maqāṣid al- Sharī'ah*. *Sharī'ah* legitimacy of an Islamic bank should not be judged by its mere compliance with the contact mechanics, but it should be judged by its observance of the *maqāṣid al- Sharī'ah*. A true Islamic finance is expected to be a value-oriented finance. It should avoid subterfuges in its products and operations. Islamic finance should help in development of national economy. It should be linked with real sectors of economy.

Bibliography

Al-Qur'ān al-Karīm

'Abd al-Latīf 'Āmir, al-Duyūn wa Tawthiquhā fī al-fiqh al-Islāmī, Cairo: [n.d]

'Abd al-Karīm Zaydān, al-Madkhal li-Dirāsah al-Islāmīyyah; Beirut: Mu'assasah al-Risālah, 1402 H. 1982.

Abd al-Rahim, Sir, The Principles of Muhammadan Jurisprudence, Lahore, All Pakistan Legal decision, 1977.

'Abd al- Razzāq al-Sanhūrī, Dr., Maṣādir al-Ḥaqq fī al-Fiqh al-Islāmī, Cairo: Dār al-Ma'arifah, 1967;

_______al-Wasīt, fī Sharḥ al-Qanūn al-Madnī, Cairo: Dār al-Nahḍa al-'Arabiyyah, 1964

'Abdullah 'Alawī Hājī Ḥassan. *Sale and Contracts in Early Islamic Commercial Law.* Islamabad: Islamic Research Institute, 1994.

'Abdullah al-Mūṣilī. *Al-Ikhtiyār li Ta'līl al-Mukhtār.* Karachi: Qadīmī kutub Khānah, n.d.

'Abdullah Yūsuf 'Alī. *The Holy Qur'ān: Text Translation and Commentary.* Islamabad: Da'wah academy, 1983.

Abu al-Ala Mawdudi, Tafhīm al-Qur'ān:Maktabā Tameer Insaniyyat, 1983.

Abū-Dāwūd. *al-Sunan.* Syria: Dār al-Ḥadīth, 1973.

Abu Ghuddah, A. S. (2002). *Al-Ajwibah al- Shariah fi al-Tatbiqat al-Masrafiyyah.* Sharikah al-Tawfuq, Majmu'ah Dallah al-Barkah.

Abū ʻĪsā bin Saurah. *Sunan al-Tirmidhī*. Beirut: Dār Iḥyā' al-Turāth al-Islāmī, n.d.

Abū Muhammad Bin Ghānim. *Majma' al-ḍamānāt*.

Abū Zahrah, Muhammad. *Uṣūl al-Fiqh*. Cairo: Dār al-Fikr al-'Arabī, 1958.

Accounting and Auditing Organization for Islamic Financial Institutions. (2015). *AAOIFI's Shari'ah Standards*. Bahrain.

'Adil Muṣṭafā Basyūnī, al-Tashrī' wa al-Nuẓum al-Qānūniyyah al-Waḍ'iyyah, Cairo.

Aḥmad bin Ḥanbal. *Musnad*. Egypt: Dār al-Ma'ārif, 1956.

Aḥmad bin Muḥammad al-Ḥamawī. *Ghamz 'uyūn al-Baṣā'ir: Sharḥ kitāb al-Ashbāh wa al-Naẓā'ir*. Beirut: Dār al-kutub al-'Ilmiyyah, 1985.

Aḥmad Ḥasan. *Principles of Islamic Jurisprudence*. Islamabad: Islamic Research Institute, 1993.

Aḥmad Ibrāhīm Bik, al-Iltizāmāt fī al-Shar' al-Islāmī, Cairo: Dār al Ansār, 1944.

Aḥmad Yūsuf, Dr., 'Uqūd al-Mu'āwaḍāt al-Māliyyah, Cairo: Dār al-Naṣr, Cairo University.

Al-Jaziri, Al-Fiqh 'alā al-Madāhib al-arba 'ah, Dār Iḥyā al-urāth al-'Arabī, Beirut, 1963.

'Alī Aḥmad al-Nadawī. *al-Qawā'id al-Fiqhiyyah*. Damascus: Dār al-Qalam, 1991.

__________. *Jamharah al-Qawā'id al-Fiqhiyyah fī al-Mu'āmalāt al-Māliyyah*. Al-Riyāḍ: sharikat al-Rājiḥī al-Maṣrafiyyah, 2000.

Ali Hayder. *Durar al-Ḥukkām Sharḥ Majallat al-Aḥkām*. Dār al-kutub al-'Ilmiyyah, n.d.

Anwar Iqbal Qureshi. *Islam and Theory of Interest*. Lahore: Sh. Muḥammad Ashraf Publishers, 1991.

Amīr Bādshāh, Taysīr al-Taḥrīr, Cairo: Muṣṭafā al-Bābī al-Ḥalabī, 1351 A-H.

'Āshūr. *Maqāṣid al-Sharī'ah al-Islāmiyyah*. Tunisia: al-Sharikah al-Tūnisiyyah li al-Tawzī', 1978.

Atāsī. *Sharḥ al-Majallah*. Quetta: Maktabah Islamiyyah, 1403 H.

Babilli, Maḥmūd Muḥammad, al-Māl fi al-Islām. Beirut: Dār al-Kitāb al-Lubnānī, 1975.

Bacha, O. (2001). Financial derivatives markets and application in Malaysia. *Serdang, Penerit University Putra Malaysia*.

Badawī. *Naẓariyyah al-Ribā al-Muḥarram*. Cairo al-Majlis al-A'lā li Ri'āyat al-Funūn, 1940.

Al-Bahūtī. Manṣūr bin Yūnus, *Kashshāf al-Qinā' 'alā Matn al-Iqnā'*. Maṭba'ah Anṣār al-Sunnah al-Muḥammadiyyah, 1366 H.

Al-Bājī, al-Imām. *Al-Muntaqā Sharḥ al-Muwaṭṭa'*. Egypt: Maṭba'ah al-Sa'ādah, 1331 H.

Al-Barwari, S. M. (2002). *Burasah al-Awraq al-Maliyyah min Manzoor Islami*. Damascus: Dar al-Fikr al-Mu'asir.

Al-Bayhaqī. *al-Sunan al-Kubrā*. al-Riyāḍ: Maktabah al-Rushd, 2004.

__________. *Shu'ab al-'īmān*. Beirut: Dār al-Kutub al-'ilmiyyah, 1990.

Baz, Salim Rustum. *Sharḥ al-Majallah*. Beirut: Dār Iḥyā al-Turāth al-'arabī, n.d.

Black, William, E.A. Law Dictionary, U.S.A.:West Publishing Company, 1979 A.D.

Bossaerts, P., & Odegaard, B. A. (2006). *Lectures on Corporate Finance.* Singapore: World Scientific Publishing Co. Pte. Ltd.

Brealey, R. A., Myers, S. C., & Allen, F. (2011). *Principles of Corporate Finance.* New York: McGraw-Hill/Irwin.

Al-Bukhārī, Muhammad Bin Ismā'īl. *Ṣaḥīḥ*. al-Riyāḍ: Maktabah al-Rushd, 2004.

Al-Burnū, Muhammad Sidqī. *Mawsū'at al-Qawā'id al-Fiqhiyyah.* Beirut: Mu'assasat al-Risālah, 2003.

__________.*al-Wajīz fī Īḍāḥ Qawā'id al-Fiqh al-Kulliyyah.* Beirut: Mu'assasat al-Risālah, n.d.

Al-Būṭi, M. T. (1998). *Al-Buyu Al-Shaai'ah wa Asaru Dhawabit Al-Mabie 'Alaa Shariyyatihaa.* Damascus, Syria: Dar al Fikr.

Chisholm, A. M. (2002). *An Introduction to Capital Markets, Products, Strategies, Participants.* Baffins Lane, Chichester: John Wiley & Sons, Ltd.

Council of Islamic Idiology. 14th Report on Contract Act, 1872 Islamabad: 1983.

Al-Dardīr. *al-Sharḥ al-Ṣaghīr*. Beirut: Dār Ṣādir, n.d.

Al-Dasūqī. *Ḥāshiat al-Dasūqī 'Alā al-Sharḥ al-Kabīr*. Cairo: Dār Iḥyā' al-Kutub al-'Arabiyyah, n.d.

Al-Dhareer, S. M.-A. (1997). *Al-Gharar: In contracts and Its Effects on Contemporary Transactions.* Jeddah: Islamic Development Bank.

Dubai Islamic Bank. Proceedings of the Seminar on Islamic Economics, Madinah, 1983.

Dusūqī, Muḥammad ibn Aḥmad, Hāshiyah 'alā al-Sharḥ al-Kabīr, Cairo: 'Isa al-Bābī al-Ḥalabī, 1350 H.

El-Gari, M. A. (1993). Towards an Islamic Stock Market. *Islamic Economic Studies, 1*(1), 1-20.

Encyclopaedia of Islam.

Fabozzi, F. J., & Drake, P. P. (2009). *Finance Capital Markets, Financial Management, and Ivestment Management.* Hoboken, New Jersey: John Wiley & Sons, Inc.

Faheem Khan. *Islamic Futures and their Markets.* Jeddah: Islamic Development Bank, 1995.

Faihān al-Matayri, ed. *Bayān al-Dalīl 'alā Ibtāl al-Tahlīl.* al-Madīinah al-Munawwarah: Maktabah Aḍwā al-Manār, n.d.

Al-Fārisī, 'Alā'uddīn *al-Iḥsān bi Tartīb Ṣaḥīḥ Ibn Ḥibbān*. Beirut: Dār al-kutub al-'Ilmiyyah, n.d.

Al-Fatāwā al-Hindiyyah. Cairo: al-Maṭba'ah al-Amīriyyah, n.d.

Federal Shariat Court, Suo-Moto Examination of Laws in the Contract Act, Islamabad: 1986.

Frank B. Vogel and Samuel L. Hayes. *Islamic Law and Finance: Religion, Risk and Return*. Kluwer Law International, The Hague, 1988.

Ghazi, Dr. Mahmood Ahmad, Muḍarabah Financing: An appraisal, Paper read at Conference on Islamic Corporate Finance: based solutions Nov.21,22,1998 at Karachi.

Ghulām Murtaza, Dr., Socio-Economic System of Islam, Lahore Malik Sons Publishers, 1990.

Al-Harīrī, Ibrāhīm Muḥammad. *al-Madkhal ilā al-Qawā'id al-Fiqhiyyah al-Kulliyyah: Tārīkhuhā, Nash'atuhā, ṭaṭawwuruhā wa Shar'iyyatuhā*. Jaddah: Dār 'Ammār, n.d.

Hasanuzzaman. *Economic Relevance of Sharī'ah Maxims.* Jeddah: Islamic Development Bank.

__________. *Sharī'ah Maxims.*

Hashim Kamali. *Al-Qiyās (Analogy), and its Modern Applications.* Islamic Development Bank, Islamic Research and Training Institute, 1999.

__________. *Islamic Commercial Law: An Analysis of Futures.* American Journal of Islamic Social Sciences, No. 1, 13, 1996.

__________. *Principles of Islamic Jurisprudence.* Cambridge: Islamic Texts Society, 2003.

__________. *Qawā'id al-Fiqh: The Legal Maxims of Islamic Law.* The Association of Muslim Lawyers.

Ḥaṣkafī, Alāuddīn. *al-Durr al-Mukhtār Sharḥ Tanwīr al-Abṣār,* Bombay: al-Maṭba'ah al-Ḥaydariyyah, 1309 H.

Haṭṭāb al-Mālikī. Taḥrīr al-Kalām fī Masā'il al-Iltizām.

Al-Haythamī. *Majma' al-Zawā'id.* Beirut: Dār al-Fikr, 1412 H.

Al-Hindī, 'Alā'uddīn. *Kanz al-'ummāl fi Sunan al-Aqwāl wa al-Af'āl.* Beirut: Mu'assasah al-Risālah, 1979.

Ḥussain Ḥāmid Ḥassān. *al-Ḥukm al-Sharī 'ind al-Uṣūliyyīn.*

__________. *An Introduction to the Study of Islamic Law.* Islamabad: Sharī'ah Academy, International Islamic University, 1977.

__________. *Uṣūl al-Fiqh.* Islamabad: Dār al-Ṣidq, 2003.

Ibn 'Ābidīn. *Radd al-Muḥtār.* Quetta: Al-Maktabah al-Mājidia, 1982.

Ibn Ḥajar al-'Asqalānī. *Fatḥ al-Bārī Sharḥ Saḥīḥ al-Bukhārī.* Beirut: Dār al-Kutub al-'ilmiyyah, 2004.

Ibn Ḥazm, *al-Iḥkām fī Usūl al-Aḥkām,* Beirut: Dār al-Āfāq al-Jadīdah, 1347 H.

_________. *Al-Muḥallā.* Beirut: Dār al-Āfāq al-jadīd, n.d.

Ibn Humām. *Sharḥ Fatḥ al-Qadīr.* Beirut: Dār Ṣādir, n.d.

Ibn Juzy. *al-Qawānīn al-Fiqhiyyah.* Beirut: Dār al-Fikr, n.d.

Ibn Mājah. *Sunan.* Beirut: Dār al-Fikr, n.d.

Ibn Manī', A. I. (n.d.). Hukm Tadawul ashum al-Sharikat al-Musahimah, bayan wa Shira'an wa tamallkan wa tamilikan. *Majalla al-Buhuth al-Fiqhiyyah al-Muasirah, 7.*

Ibn Nujaym. *al-Baḥr al-Rā'iq sharḥ Kanz al-Daqā'iq.* Egypt: al-Bābī al-Ḥalabī, n.d.

_________. *Al-Ashbāh wa al-Naẓā'ir.* Karachi: Idārat al-Qur'ān wa al-'Ulūm al-Islamiyyah, 1978.

Ibn Qudāmah. *al-Mughnī.* Beirut: Dār al-Fikr, 1985.

_________. *al-Sharḥ al-Kabīr.* Beirut: Dār al-Fikr, 1984.

Ibn al-Qayyim. *Al-Ṭuruq al-Ḥukmiyyah.* Lahore: Dār Nashr al-kutub al-Islamiyyah, n.d.

_________. *Ighathah al-Lahfān.* Beirut: Dār al-Ma'rifah, 1975.

_________. *'i'lām al-Muwaqqi'īn 'an Rabb al-'ālamīn.* Cairo: Maktabat al-Kulliyyah al-Azhariyyah, 1968.

_________. *Tahdhīb Sunan Abī Dāwūd* [Maktabah Shāmilah Version].

Ibn Rushd. *Bidāyat al-Mujtahid.* Lahore: al-Maktabah al-'Ilmiyyah, n.d.

_________. *Bidāyat al-Mujtahid,* tr. Imran Nyazee. UK: Garnet Publishing Ltd. 1996.

Ibn Taymiyyah. *al-Fatāwā al-Kubrā*. Beirut: Dār al-Kutub al-'Ilmiyyah, 1987.

_________. *Majmū' al-Fatāwā*. Dār al-Wafā, 2005.

_________. *Naẓariyyah al-'Aqd*. Cairo: Markaz al-Kitāb li al-Nashr, 1998.

Ismā'il al-Ḥasani. *Nazariyah al-Maqāṣid 'Ind al-Imām Muḥammad al-Ṭāhir bin 'Āshūr*. Washington: International Institute of Islamic Thought, 2007.

Jāmāluddīn 'Aṭiyyah. *Naḥwa Ṭaf'īl Maqāṣid al-Sharī'ah*. Damascus: International Institute of Islamic Thought, Dar al-Fikr, 2001.

al-Jibālī, 'Abd al-Sattār *Aḥkām 'aqd al-Bay'*. Cairo: Jāmi'ah al-Azhar, 1993.

Kamali, M. H. (1990). *Islamic Commercial Law: An Analysis of Futures and Options*. Cambridge: Islamic Texts Society.

Kamali, M. H. (1996). Islamic Commercial Law: An analysis of futures. *The American Journal of Islamic Social Sciences, 13*(2), 197-224.

Kamali, M. H. (2007). Commodity Futures: An Islamic Legal Analysis. *Thunderbird International Business Review, 49*(3), 309-339.

Al-Kāsānī. *Badā'i' al-Ṣanā'i' fi Tartīb al-Sharā'i'*, Cairo: Maṭba'ah al-Imām, 1972.

Khalil Muhammad. *Islamic Law Maxims*, Islamabad: *Islamic Studies*, vol. 44, No. 2, 2005.

al-Kharashī, Mohammad Abdullah. *Sharḥ al-Kharashī*. Beirut: Dār al-Fikr, n.d.

Khut S.S. Vikor. *Between God and the Sultan: A History of Islamic Law*. New Delhi: Cambridge House, 2005.

al-Kurdī, Aḥmad *al-Madkhal al-Fiqhī*. Damascus: Maṭba'ah al-Inshā, 1984.

Kuwaiti Finance House, *Fatāwā Sharī'ah*.

Majallah al-Aḥkām al-'Adliyyah. Karachi: Kārkhānah Tijārat-e-Kutub, 1968.

Majallat al-Buḥūth al-Islāmiyyah. Saudi Arabia: al-Ri'āsah al-'āmmah li al-Buḥūth al-'ilmiyyah wa al-Iftā'.

Mahmassani, S. (1983). Al-Mujibat wa al-uqud fi al-fiqh al-Islami. Beirut: Dar al-Ilm li al-Malayin.

Mālik bin Anas. *al-Mudawwanah al-Kubrā*. Beirut: Dār Ṣādir, n.d.

__________. *Al-Muwaṭṭa'*. Damascus: Dār al-Qalam, 1991.

Al-Maqqarī, Moḥammad b. Aḥmad. *al-Qawā'id*. Makkah: Umm al-Qurā University, n.d.

Al-Mardāwī. *Kitāb al-Inṣāf*. Beirut: Dār Iḥyā' al-Turāth al-'Arabī, n.d.

Al-Marghinānī. *al-Hidāyah*. Cairo: Dār al-Salām, 2000.

Al-Mawdūdī. Abul A'lā, *Tafhīm al-Qur'ān*. Lahore: Maktaba Ta'mīr-e-Insāniyyat, 1983.

Mohammad Amīn. *Tanqīḥ Fatāwā al-Ḥāmidiyyah*. Cairo: al-Maktabah al-Maymaniyyah, n.d.

Moḥammad Amīn 'Ubādah. *Tārīkh al-Fiqh al-Islāmī*, Cairo: Dār al-Ṭibā'ah 1395 H.

Moḥammad Anīs 'ubādah. *Tārīkh al-Fiqh al-Islāmī*. Cairo: Dār al-Tibā'ah, 1395 A.H.

M. Fahim Khan. *Islamic Futures and Their Markets*. Jeddah: Islamic Development Bank, 1995.

Mullah, D.F. *The Contract Act (IX) of 1872*. Commentary by Ahsan Suhail Anjum. Lahore: Mansoor Book House, 1987.

Muslim Bin Al-Ḥajjāj. *Ṣaḥīḥ Muslim*. Al-Riyāḍ: Dār al-Salām, 2000.

Muṣṭafā al-Zarqā'. *Al-Istiṣlāḥ wa al-Maṣāliḥ al-Mursalah wa uṣūl Fiqhihā*. Damascus: Dār al-Qalam, 1988.

Al-Nasā'ī. *al-Sunan al-Kubrā*. Al-Riyāḍ: Maktabah al-Rushd, 2006.

Nasā'ī, Al-Ḥāfiz Abu 'Abdur Reḥmān. *Sunan Nasā'ī*, Istanbul: Dār al-Da'wah, n.d.

Nawawī, Muḥayyuddīn Abū Zakariyyah. *Minhāj al-Ṭālibīn*, translated into English by: E.C. Howard. London: 1977.

__________. *Kitāb al-Majmū'*. Cairo: Maktabah al-'Āṣimah, 1966.

__________. *Rawḍah al-Ṭālibīn*. Cairo: al-Maktabah al-Tawfīqiyyah, n.d.

Nayla Comair Obeid. *The Law of Business Contracts in the Arab Middle East.* Kluwer Law International, 1996.

Nyazee, Imran Ahsan Khan. *Outlines of Islamic Jurisprudence*. Rawalpindi: Federal Law House, 2008.

Qanūn al-Muamalat al-Madaniyyah li Dawlah al-Imārāt al-'Arabiyyah al-Muttaḥidah.

Al-Qaradaghi, A. M. (1983). *Buhoos Fi Fiqh Al-Bunook Al-Islamiah.* Berut, Lebnon: Dar Ul Basha'air al-Islamiyyah.

Al-Qarāfī, Shihāb al-Dīn. *Kitāb al-Furūq*. Cairo: Maṭba'ah Dār Iḥyā al-Kutub al-'Arabiyyah, 1346 H.

Qarārāt al-Majma' al-Fiqhī li Rābiṭah al-'ālam al-Islāmī, 1410/1998.

Al-Qurṭubī. *al-Jāmi' li aḥkām al-Qur'ān*. Cairo: Dār al-Kutub al-'ilmiyyah, 1353 H / 1935 AD.

Rahmani, Khalid Saifullah. ed. *Nay Masā'il Awr 'Ulama-i-Hind key Faisaly*. Delhi: Ifa publications, 2004.

Al-Ramlī, Mohammad. *Nihāyat al-Muḥtāj*. [Maktabah Shāmilah Version].

Al-Raysūnī, Aḥmad *Nazariyah al-Maqāṣid 'ind al-Imām al-Shāṭibī*. Riyāḍ: al-Dār al-'Ilmiyyah li al-Kitāb al-Islāmī, 1992.

Salman H. Khan. *Organized Tawarruq in Practice: A Shariah Non-Compliant and Unjustified Transaction*. New Horizon: Oct-Dec. 2010.

Salman Syed Ali. *Islamic Capital Market Products, Developments and Challenges*. Occasional paper No. 9. Saudi Arabia: Islamic Research & Training Institute, IDB, 2005.

Sāmī Ibn Ibrāhīm Swaylim. *Qaḍāyā fi al-Iqtiṣād wa al-Tamwīl al-Islamī*, Riyāḍ: Dār Kunuz Ishbalia, n.d.

Ṣan'ānī. *Subul al-Salām*. al-Riyāḍ: Maktabah Nazzār Muṣṭafā al-Bāz, 1995.

Al-Sanhūrī, 'Abd al-Razzāq. *alwasīṭ fi Sharḥ al-Qānūn al-Madanī al-Miṣrī*. Cairo: Dār al-Nahḍah al-'Arabiyyah, 1964.

__________. *Maṣādir al-Ḥaqq fi al-Fiqh al-Islāmī*. Cairo: Dār al-Ma'rifah, 1967.

Sarakhsī, Abū Bakr. *al-Mabsūṭ*. Beirut: Dār al-Ma'rifah, 1978.

Al-Shāfi'ī, Muḥammad Bin Idrīs. *al-Umm*. Beirut: Dār al-Fikr, 1983.

Al-Shanqiti, M. A.-A. (1992). *Dirasah Shar'iyyah li Ahkam al-Uqood al-Maliyyah al-Mustahdathah.* al-Madinah tul Munawwarah: Maktabah al-Uloom Wal Hikam.

Al-Shāṭibī. *al-Muwāfaqāt*. Damascus: Dār al-Fikr, n.d.

_________. *Al-Muwāfaqāt.* Shaikh Abdullah Darāz (ed). Beyrūt: Dār al-Ma'rifah, 1994.

Shariah Standards. Accounting and Auditing Organization for Islamic Finance Institution, 1429 H / 2008 AD.

Al-Shawkānī. *Nayl al-Awṭār*. Cairo: Dār al-Ḥadīth, 2005.

Al-Shīrazī, Abu Isḥāq. *Al-Muhadhdhab.* Cairo: Dār al-Naṣr, n.d.

Al-Shirbīnī. *Mughnī al-Muḥtāj*. Cairo: Sharikah wa Maṭba'ah Muṣṭafā al-Bābī al-Ḥalabī, 1933.

Al-Ṣiddīq al-Ḍarīr. *al-Gharar fi al-'uqūd wa Āthāruhū fi al-Taṭbīqāt al-Mu'āṣirah*. Jaddah: Islamic Development Bank, 1993.

Al-Siyūṭī, Jalāl al-Dīn. *al-Ashbāh wa al-Naẓā'ir fi'l Furū'*. Dār al-Fikr, n.d.

Slayman, A. (1426H). *Akham al-Ta'amul fi al-Aswaq al-Maliyyah al-Mu'asirah.* Riyadh: Kunuz Ashbaliyyah li al-Nashr wa al-Touzi.

Al-Shubaili, Y. (2005). *Al-Khadmat al-Istithmariyyah fi al-Masarif wa Ahkamuha fi al-Fiqh al-Islami* (Vol. 2). Dar Ibn al-Jouzi.

Al-Suwailem, S. (2000, April). Towards an objective measure of Gharar in exchanges. *Islamic Economic Journal, Islamic Research and Training Institute, Islamic Development Bank*.

Al-Ṭabrānī. *Al-Mu'jam al-Kabīr*. [Maktabah Shāmilah Version].

'Umar ibn 'abd al-azīz. *al-Ribā wa al-Mu'āmlāt al-Masrafiyyah fī nazar al-Sharī'ah al-Islāmiyyah*. Al-Riyāḍ: Dār al-'Āṣimah, 1997.

Al-'Umranī, A. I. (n.d.). *Al-Istithmar wa al-Mutajarah fi Ashum al-Sharikat al-Mukhtalatah*. Riyad: Kunuz Ashbeliya.

'Usmānī, Muhammad Taqī. *An Introduction to Islamic Finance*. Karachi: Maktabah Ma'ārif al-Qur'ān, 2008.

__________. *Ṣukūk and Their Contemporary Applications*.

__________. *Takmilah Fatḥ al-Mulhim*. Karachi: Maktabah al-Ḥijāz, n.d.

Wael. B. Hallaq. *A History of Islamic legal Theories*. Cambridge University Press, 1997.

Walīd al-Sa'īdān. *Qawā'id al-Buyū' wa Farā'id al-Furū'*.

Walīd Ibn Rāshid al-Sa'īdān. *Talqīḥ al-Afhām al-'aliyyah bi Sharḥ al-Qawā'id al-Fiqhiyyah*.

Yūsuf Ḥāmid al-'Ālam. *al-Maqāṣid lil al-Sharī'ah al-Islāmiyyah*. Washington: International Institute of Islamic Thought, 1415 H/1994.

Yusuf Talal. *A compendium of legal opinions on the operations of Islamic Banks*. London: Institute of Islamic Banking and Insurance, 1998.

Zafar Ahmad Usmani. *I'lā'i al-Sunan*. Karachi: Idārat al-Qur'ān wa al-'Ulūm al-Islamiyyah, n.d.

Zainuddin Zafar. *Bay' al-Ma'dūm; An Analysis*. Paper presented in the International Islamic Capital Market Conference, Malaysia, 15-16 July, 1997.

Al-Zarqā, Muṣṭafā Aḥmad. *'Aqd al-Ta'mīn*. Damascus: Demascuss University Press, 1962.

__________. *al-Madkhal al-Fiqhī al-'āmm*. Damascus: Demascuss University Press, 1959.

Al-Zarqā, Aḥmad. *Sharḥ al-Qawā'id al-Fiqhiyyah*. Dār al-Gharb al-Islāmī, 1983.

Zaydān, 'Abd al-Karīm *al-Madkhal li Dirāsat al-Sharī'ah al-Islāmiyyah*. Beirut: Mu'assasah al-Risālah, 1402 H/1982.

Al-Zayla'ī, Jamāl al-Dīn. *Naṣb al-Rāyah*. Lahore: Dār Nashr al-Kutub al-Islāmiyyah, n.d.

Al-Zayla'ī, Fakhr al-Dīn. *Tabyīn al-Ḥaqā'iq sharḥ Kanz al-Daqā'iq*. Multan: Maktabah Imdādiyyah, n.d.

Al-Zuḥayli, Moḥammad. *Maqāṣid al-Sharī'ah*, Majallah Kulliyat al-Sharī'ah wa al-Dirāsat al-Islāmiyyah. Makkah: Umm ul-Qurā University, 1402 H.

Al-Zuḥaylī, Wahbah. *Naẓariyyah al-Ḍarūrah al-Shar'iyyah*.Beirut: Mu'assasah al-Risālah, n.d.

__________. *al-Fiqh al-Islāmī wa adillatuhū*. Damascus: Dār al-Fikr, 1984.

__________. *Naẓariyyah al-Ḍamān*. Damascus: Dār al-Fikr, 1982.

Index

A

AAOIFI, xxiii, 144, 346, 372–74, 383–85, 399, 405–6, 427, 430, 442, 444, 487–88
Abū Qatādah, 315
adultery, 39, 466–68, 472
agency, 65–68, 71–72, 77, 82, 91, 194, 196, 198, 200, 202, 268, 272, 282, 293, 295
  contract of, 34, 65, 67, 71, 82, 268
  mutual, 274, 277
  subject matter of, 67, 82
agreement, 14, 16–17, 22–25, 97–98, 162, 179–81, 190, 229, 236, 260–61, 269, 274–75, 327, 334, 437–41
  buy-back, 12, 158, 361–62, 372, 377, 391
  mutual, 21, 25, 71, 82, 191, 320
ahādith, 4, 6, 11, 132–34, 136–37, 157
al-faḍl, 135, 140–43, 145, 360
al-Fikr, 498, 502–4, 507–8, 510
al-Fiqhiyyah, 361, 498, 500, 509–10
aqd, 19, 21–25, 40, 172, 174, 181, 188, 202, 265, 267, 488, 504
Arabiyyah, 57, 86, 497, 500, 506–7
assets, 254–57, 263, 272, 277, 286, 291, 346, 354–55, 361, 385–88, 405–7, 412, 438, 456–57, 480
  fixed, 408
  leased, 251, 255, 388, 482
  mortgaged, 347
  tangible, 385, 404–6

B

Badā'i'al-sanā'i, 40, 42, 46, 48, 114, 116, 182,184,250, 252, 254, 268, 300–301, 303, 320, 329–30, 349–50
bay, 42, 99, 109–10, 145–47, 212–15, 217–18, 223–24, 228, 351, 360–65, 367, 370–71, 376–77, 387–88, 391–92
  properties of, 370, 392

Beirut, 4–6, 10, 126, 132–33, 139, 405, 407–8, 497–505, 507, 510
benefit, 8, 12–13, 102–3, 176, 207–8, 349–51, 355–56, 365–68, 428, 455–56, 458–61, 463–64, 472–74, 481, 484
  pecuniary, 120
  takāful, 451–56, 458–59
bay' al-wafā, 363–65, 367, 370, 387–88, 392
Bidāyat al-Mujtahid, 108, 110, 112, 114, 238, 240, 246, 285
bilateral promises, 433, 435, 437, 439, 441–43
Board of Dubai Islāmic Bank, 397
business law, xxii, xxiv, 49, 168
buy-back arrangement, 146, 371–72, 386

C

Cairo, 6–7, 13, 29, 45, 49, 55, 58–59, 66, 70, 113, 119, 147, 406–7, 497–501, 503–8
charity, 75, 125, 128–31, 142, 145, 410, 416, 427–28
coercion, 4–5, 58, 62–63, 92–93, 159, 167–70
Combination of Sale and Loan, 12
commercial transactions, 14, 59, 339, 383, 435, 472
  medium of, 329, 338
commodity, 39–40, 135–37, 146–47, 151, 157–58, 163, 215–19, 221–26, 229–30, 234, 239–44, 351, 364, 374–81, 424–26
  ascertained, 270
  measurable, 134
  price of, 153, 382
  salam sale, 224
commutative contracts, 44, 96, 115, 123, 175–76, 193, 195, 201–2, 446–47
company, 117, 119, 121–22, 262–63, 296, 346–47, 372, 393–400, 402, 404–5, 409–13, 445, 447–48, 451–54, 458
  construction, 235
  investee, 394–96, 405, 409–11, 413
  shares of, 396, 398
  takāful, 451
Condition of Ahliyyah-al-adā, 54
Condition Relating to Subject-Matter, 39
conditions, 11–12, 16–17, 31–32, 66–67, 85–86, 95–97, 100–101, 149–50,

171–80, 223–25, 270, 272, 286–88, 300, 306–8
ancillary, 92, 95, 171–72
basic, 73, 224, 267
contractual, 173
essential, 46, 92, 100, 105, 169, 186
extrinsic, xxiii, 96, 171, 173, 175, 177–78
invalid, 92, 95–96, 105
irregular, 95–96, 175–76
Conditions for
Validity of Sale, 210
Agency, 66
Effective Coercion, 168
Murābaḥah, 239
Conditions of pledged/mortgaged property, 345
Contract
Muḍārabah, 299–300, 307
Sarf, 218–19
gratuitous, 44, 96, 104, 116, 123, 175–76,193, 196, 202, 446, 471
mawqūf, 87–88
void, xxiii, 86–87, 92, 102, 104
fāsid, 47, 92
Contract Act, 23, 28, 33–34, 314, 500–501, 506
Contract of
Agency, 65
Ijārah, 231, 245–47, 249, 251, 253, 255, 257
Kafālah, 311, 313, 315, 317, 319, 321, 323, 325
Muḍārabah, 295, 297, 299, 301, 303, 305, 307, 309
Mushārakah, 259, 261, 263, 265
Rahn, 343, 345, 347, 349, 351, 353, 355
Sale, 39–40, 46, 70–71, 93–94, 96, 99, 115, 195, 200–201, 207–9, 211–13, 215, 237, 243–44, 246
authorisation, 194
guarantee, 194
salam, 104
suretyship, 197
credit partnership, 286, 288, 293–94
credit sale, 217, 297, 319, 333, 348

D

Damascus, 22, 122, 409, 498–500, 504–6, 508–10
Dār al-Ma'rifah, 503, 507–8
debt contract, 132, 143
debtor, 130–32, 146–47, 149, 312, 315–16, 322, 324, 327–33, 335–37, 340–41, 351, 354–55, 363–65, 424–25, 428–29
insolvent, 315–16

new, 23, 327, 329, 331, 334
original, 311, 327, 329–30, 332, 334–36, 340
principal, 23, 311, 313–16, 321–22, 330, 334, 340
prospective, 146, 361, 377, 379
debt transactions, 134, 143, 361, 423
declarations, 21–26, 28, 166, 264, 436
unilateral, 22, 24, 319
Defect of Consent, 159, 161, 163, 165, 167, 169
deferred payment, 109, 132, 134, 151, 153, 219, 221, 379, 435, 439
Delegated Authority, xxiii, 65, 67, 69, 71, 73, 75, 77, 79, 81–83
Diminishing Partnership in Islamic Banks, 291
Division of profit, 268, 283, 285, 303
divorce, 21, 24, 55, 62, 69, 71, 95, 181, 193–94, 200, 202, 392
donation, 40, 96, 98–99, 104, 116, 123, 193, 196, 422, 427–28, 445–47, 450–52, 458–59
contract of, 458–59
Dubai Islamic Bank, 439, 500

E

Effect of Gharar on Contracts, 115
Elements of Contract, 27, 29, 31, 33, 35, 37,86,101
Encyclopaedia of Islamic Banking and Insurance, 450, 453
exchange, 126–27, 139–41, 155, 198, 207, 213–15, 217–18, 220–21, 243, 245–46, 335–38, 340–41, 360, 408, 439–42
medium of, 136, 219–22, 384
transaction of, 81, 134, 140
unequal, 135–36

F

Fāsid and Bāṭil, 85, 87, 89, 91, 93, 95, 97, 99, 101, 103, 105
Federal Shariat Court, 28, 32–33, 501
finance lease, 254–55, 258
financial institutions, 256, 373, 381, 393–95, 411, 426, 430, 437, 443, 485, 493
Fiqh, , xxiv, 152 119, 180, 222, 228, 368, 395, 397,

471, 473 497–98, 502, 507
Fiqh al-Islāmī wa adillatuhū, 78, 90, 93, 95, 100, 179, 194

G

General Principles of Contracts, 5, 7, 9, 11, 13, 15, 17
ghabn fāḥish, 164–65, 170
gharar, 5–6, 43–45, 85–86, 92, 101, 107–8, 110–11, 114–16, 118–23, 201–2, 425–26, 446–48, 458–60, 463–64, 480–81
  effects of, 115–16
  element of, 44, 110, 119, 122, 177, 200, 244
  contract of, 108, 119, 123
Gharar fī al-'Uqūd, 47, 107, 110–11
gharar sale, 6
gharar transactions, 110
Gharar wa Atharuhū fi al-'Uqūd, 119–20
guardianship, 65, 78–80, 82–83

H

hadīth, 44–46, 57, 114, 174, 189, 216–18, 315–16, 320, 350
Ḥanafī jurisprudence, 94–95
Ḥanafī jurists, 70, 86–87, 92–93, 99, 101, 112–14, 161, 163–64, 175–76, 232, 234, 267–70, 286, 288, 349
Ḥanafīs, 27, 29–30, 54–55, 73–75, 77, 79, 82, 85–87, 100, 183–87, 275, 277, 299–300, 334, 336
Ḥanbalī jurists, 61, 70–71, 113–14, 116, 172, 190, 242, 303, 306, 316, 334, 350
Ḥanbalīs, 30, 67, 73, 79, 87–88, 174, 181, 183, 187, 240, 275, 300, 306–7
Ḥawālah , 327–34, 336, 338–39,340, 359–62, 364–65, 367–70, 378, 389, 391, 434–35, 470–71, 487–88, 490, 492, 500, 502, 510
  restricted, 341
ḥarām, 39, 173, 395–97, 410
Ḥassān, 47, 57–58, 61, 75–77, 85, 87, 90–91,389–90, 416, 422, 427, 429, 431, 493, 498
ḥawālah, 23, 96, 193, 197, 200, 321, 324, 327–41
ḥawālah al-ḥaq, 332
ḥawālah al-dayn, 332
ḥiyal, 359, 361–63, 365–71, 373, 375, 377, 379, 381,

383, 385, 387, 389, 391–92, 486–88, 492
hoarding, 135–36, 425, 470, 472
Holy Prophet, 5–6, 10–11, 142–43, 145, 148–49, 172–73, 214–16, 223–25, 247–48, 264, 297–98, 312, 320–21, 419–21, 479–80
ḥukm al-Sharʿī, 57–58, 502

I

ibādāt, 17, 53–55, 174
Ibn al-Qayyim, 43–44, 50, 108, 200, 202, 362, 367–69, 377, 503
Ibn Juzy, 104, 108, 110, 243, 269, 503
Ibn Qudāmah, 70, 73, 102, 110, 114, 243, 246, 250, 254, 259, 264, 296, 302, 316, 318
Ibn Taymiyyah, 4, 16–17, 45, 172, 174, 202, 362, 461, 473, 504
Ījāb, 28, 31, 35–36, 86, 100
ijārah, 116, 198, 231–33, 245–49, 251, 253–55, 257–58, 303, 411
Ijārah in Islamic Banks, 255
ijārat al-ashyā, 196, 248–49
ijmā, 172, 247–48, 264, 297, 311–12
illah, 43, 45, 137–40, 221
Imām Abū Hanifa, 32, 56, 59, 59, 99, 181, 184, 234–35, 315-16, 318, 325,329, 334
Imām Mālik, 113, 139, 250, 272, 407
Imām Shāfiʿi, 139, 147
Imam Ḥanbal, 66, 111, 139, 144, 318, 331, 367, 370, 377, 408, 498
IMFI, 422, 430
inān, 197, 267, 270–71, 273–76, 283, 288, 293
inah, 146–47, 158, 360–62, 365, 370–73, 376–77, 391–92, 442, 444, 486–88, 497
Indexation of Loans and Ribā, 150
Institute of Policy Studies, xxiv
insurance, xxiii, 116–23, 254, 450–53, 509
  amount of, 119, 121, 123
  contract of, 116–17, 121–22, 446, 452
Investment in Equities, 393, 395, 397, 399, 401, 403, 405, 407, 409, 411, 413
sharḥ, 503, 510
Irregular contract, 87, 92–93, 96–99, 105
Irregularity in Fāsid Contracts, 92

al-Islāmiyyah, 360, 498–99, 505, 507, 509–10
Islamic Banking, 371, 475–76
  authenticity of, 370, 392
  opponents of, 370, 392
Islamic banking products, 485, 488
Islamic banks, 255–57, 289–90, 292, 323, 355, 370, 374, 378, 380–82, 389–92, 440–41, 475–76, 479–83, 488–91, 493–95
Islamic Commercial Law, 494, 497, 502, 504
Islamic Development Bank, 156, 223, 500–502, 506, 508
Islamic Finance, xxiv, 230, 245, 249, 291, 370, 388–89, 392, 426, 475–78, 485, 492, 494–95, 509
Islamic Fiqh Academy, 243, 436–37
Islamic Insurance, 347, 447, 450, 453, 459
Islamic Jurisprudence, 76, 359, 367, 391, 472, 498, 502, 506
Islamic Law, 28–30, 33–34, 39–41, 98–100, 104–5, 118–19, 220, 244, 335–37, 360–61, 388–89, 426, 428–29, 486–88, 490–91
Islamic Law of Contract, xxii, xxiv, 4, 6, 8, 10, 12, 14, 16, 20, 22, 24, 26, 116–18, 160
Islamic Law of Options, 179, 181, 183, 185, 187, 189, 191
Islamic Microfinance, 415–17, 419–21, 423, 425, 427, 429, 431–32
Islamic microfinance institutions, 416, 421–22, 427, 429, 432
Islamic Research Institute, 215, 497–98
Islamic Texts Society, 502, 504
istisnā, 196, 231–32, 234–35
  contract of, 231–32

J

Jeddah, 47, 151, 156, 223, 500–501, 506
juridical act, 168–69, 172, 174–76, 178, 368–69, 486

K

kafālah, 91, 96, 194, 197, 200, 311–19, 321, 323–25
  contract of, 311, 314
kafālah bi al-māl, 312–13
Kamali, 468–69, 473, 504

Karachi, 8, 118, 247, 316, 405, 408, 419, 497, 501, 503, 505, 509
Kāsānī, 40, 42, 74–75, 114, 116, 181–82, 184, 250, 252, 270, 272, 300–301, 303, 329–30, 349–50
Khayārāt, 179, 181, 183, 185, 187, 189, 191
khiyār al-sharṭ, 37, 175, 179–82, 184–85
KIBOR, 489, 491
Kuwait Finance House, 243, 397, 439, 441

L

Lahore, 28, 41–42, 66, 118–19, 125, 136, 198, 351, 497, 499, 503, 505–6, 510
Law of Business contracts, 162, 506
lāzim contract, 91
lease, 249–50, 252, 254–56, 258, 291–92, 361, 365, 370, 385–86, 392, 437–38, 443, 487
  conventional, 256–57
  operating, 254–55, 258
    contract, 93, 200–201
liability, 14, 70–71, 261–63, 283–84, 286–87, 293–94, 314–18, 321–22, 327–30, 332, 336–40, 410, 426, 435–36, 479–80
  limited, 261, 263
  personal, 354
  principle of, 14–15, 216
liability insurance, 118
life insurance, 117–18, 445, 452
liquidity, 379, 381–82, 404
loan, 12, 125, 127, 130–32, 140–46, 150–51, 155–56, 172–73, 249, 323–24, 328–29, 348, 377, 423, 427–29
  amount of, 132, 140, 319, 364, 387
  bearing, 410
  commodate, 91, 193, 196, 198, 319, 348, 471
  free, 141, 391, 449–50
  interest-free, 142
  payment of, 144, 328, 335, 341
  transfer of, 328–29
loan contract, 49, 86, 131, 145, 193, 196, 303, 410
loan transaction, 96, 125–27, 130, 140–43, 157, 249, 426, 442, 444
  interest-bearing, 143, 378
  usurious, 360
loss, 14–15, 57–58, 117–18, 152–54, 164–66, 256–57, 268–69, 275, 279–81,

284–87, 425–26, 445, 448–51, 456–59, 480
defined, 456–57
excessive, 164–65
material, 451–52, 456
Loss of capital, 280
lunatic, 54–55, 57, 78, 194, 197

M

al-Madkhal, 47, 53, 56, 72, 75–77, 80, 90–91, 100, 169, 176, 180, 182, 194–95, 198, 201
Madkūr, 86, 160, 174, 185, 187, 195, 198, 201
Majallah, 23, 28, 97–98, 119, 165, 168, 265, 267, 283, 299–300, 304, 307–8, 332, 343, 405
Majallah Kulliyat al-Shar, 510
majlis, 25, 27, 30–33, 36, 47–48, 100, 239
makfūl lahū, 311, 314, 318
Makkah, 122, 215, 397, 440, 505, 510
Mālikī jurists, 30–31, 74–75, 77, 82, 104, 108, 112, 114, 116, 169, 174, 178, 285, 294, 302
marriage contract, 19–20, 25, 29, 50, 62, 69, 71, 95–96, 104, 161, 173, 464, 486
Maṣādir al-Ḥaqq, 87–88, 90, 92, 108
mawqūf, 73, 87–89, 169, 182
maysir, 8, 17, 476, 480–81
murābaḥah, xxiv, 8, 166,197, 203, 217,223, 236–41, 244,269, 276, 293, 259-309,348, 450–52,447, 456, 458, 459
investment, 302
partnership, 289, 301, 306
conditions of, xxiv, 239
mushārakah, 194, 259, 261, 263, 265, 281, 289–90, 293, 354, 426–27, 479–80, 488, 490–92
muḍārib, 297, 299–300, 302–6, 308–9, 451, 457
Muslim jurists
modern, 27, 193
opinion of, 112, 171, 177, 240
al-Muwaqqi, 359, 362, 367–68, 481, 503

N

nāfidh, 87–88, 91
nafs, 464–65, 468
Nayl al-Awṭār, 42, 172–73, 180, 187, 189, 213–15,

218–19, 225, 247, 298, 312, 316, 328, 508
Negotiable Instruments Act, 336–38
NIB banking, 371

O

objectives of shariah, 13, 382, 388, 462, 474–76
obligatory prayers, 468–70, 472
orphans, 80, 250, 317, 417, 479
ownership, 44–45, 70, 75, 96–98, 100, 249–50, 254, 256, 265, 271, 286–88, 290–92, 385, 388, 437–38
  ratio of, 287
  transfer of, 70, 208, 218, 427

P

Pakistan, 119, 152, 198, 370–71, 374, 386, 389, 427, 447, 458, 483, 488
paper currency, 220, 382–83
  modern, 382–84
partners, 15, 98, 242, 259–62, 264–66, 268–70, 273–90, 293–94, 300, 307–9, 389, 393, 488, 490–91
  inān, 275–76
Partnership Act, 260, 262, 278–79
Partnership and profit in Medieval Islam, 238,302, 304–5
partnership contracts, 15, 93–94, 197, 202–3, 280
person, 54–63, 65–69, 72–76, 78, 101–4, 164–68, 249–52, 259–63, 304, 312–15, 317–22, 327–28, 359–61, 375–77, 426–28
  accused, 313, 321–22
  deceased, 315, 353
  drunken, 61
  insolvent, 194, 318
  insured, 118–20, 122, 445
  intoxicated, 61–62
  needy, 6, 375, 471
pledge, 42, 46, 68, 94, 98, 102, 147–48, 194, 198, 203, 277, 343–46, 348–52,355–56, 365
poverty, 415, 422, 430–31, 474, 476
  eradication of, 415, 417, 431, 492
price, 96–97, 99–100, 108–12, 146–47, 166–67, 216–17, 225, 229–30, 234–40, 286–88, 368–69, 384, 386–88, 407–8, 440–43
  agreed, 98, 105
  fixed, 183, 231, 246
  higher, 146, 216, 230, 364

inflated, 166, 170
lower, 165–66, 361, 382
pre-agreed, 230, 378
real, 238–39, 377
Principles of Islamic Jurisprudence, 367, 498, 502
profit, 14–15, 236–42, 260–61, 267–70, 274–76, 279–81, 283–91, 293–96, 298–99, 301–5, 425–26, 451–55, 457–58, 479–80, 488–91
profit ceiling, 488–89
profit margin, 236, 241, 377
profit principle, 241, 458
progeny, 12, 102, 461, 466, 468–69
Prohibited Sale Contracts, 212
Prohibition of gharar, 5–6, 425
Prohibition of Ribā, 6
Promise and bilateral promise in Islamic Finance, 435, 437, 439, 441, 443
Promise in Banking Transactions, 437
Promise in Currency Exchanges, 438
promise to sell, 232
property insurance, 118, 445
public property, 40, 211
purchase contract, 369

Q

qarḍ, 55, 140–41, 143–45, 277, 389–90, 416, 422, 427–29, 431, 448, 470, 493, 507
Qawānīn, 104, 361, 404, 434, 498, 500-501, 503, 505, 509–10
quality, 6, 41–42, 47, 155, 160–62, 179, 211, 217, 224, 228–29, 234, 244, 251, 302, 304
substantial, 159–60, 170
quantity, 42, 47–48, 109, 113, 121, 123, 134–35, 138–39, 141, 155–56, 213–14, 224, 228, 234, 244
quantum, 6, 108–9, 120, 412–13
Qur'ān, xxii, 5,7,9-11,13-17, 19–21, 78, 80, 128–29, 131–32, 151–53, 157, 247, 252–53, 264, 297, 416–19, 421–23, 427, 433, 463–67, 478–79, 481, 492–93,311–12, 343 497, 505, 507

R

Rahn, 197, 324, 343, 345, 347, 349, 351, 353, 355–56
Rahn in Islamic Banks, 354

remuneration, 276, 319, 348
rent, 15, 95, 115, 245, 247, 249, 252–53, 255–57, 290–93, 305, 319, 349, 351, 354, 364–65
revocation, 33–34, 74, 97–98, 160–61, 165, 181–82, 228, 369
reward, 53, 55, 128–29, 284, 422, 434, 465, 483
ribā , 6,11–12, 86–87, 96–97, 101, 125, 130–36, 138–43, 145–47, 149–50, 156–58, 222–23,360–61, 364–65, 368, 370–71, 376–77, 389–90,398, 401, 404–5, 423–25, 428, 480–81, 487, 490–91
  prohibition of, 6–7, 140, 143,147, 149,360, 364, 378, 411,425, 463, 468, 470, 487
ribā al-faḍl, 132, 134–35, 137–38, 155, 157, 408, 413
Riyād, 498–500, 506–7, 509
Rules for Mixed Business, 399

S

sadd al-dharā'i', 366–68
salam, 42–44, 217, 222–24, 226–32, 234, 244, 348, 354, 382–85, 411, 416, 427, 431, 469–71, 480
  object of, 225–26
  parallel, 230–31
salam commodity, 229, 348, 382, 480
salam contract, 223, 226–27, 229, 232, 234
  parallel, 230–31
salam sale, 42, 112, 224–25
Sale of absolute price, 218
sale transaction, 86, 109, 134, 141–42, 146, 217, 367–68, 372, 378, 384, 407, 430, 470
Sanhūrī, 27, 87–88, 90, 92, 108, 159, 166
Sarakhsī, 107, 167, 174, 176–77, 271, 286–87, 299, 301, 305–6
ṣarf, 125, 139–41, 143–45, 193, 195, 217–18, 222, 244, 405–6, 412–13, 470
Screening Norms for sharī'ah, xxiv, 393–95, 397, 399, 401, 403, 405, 407, 409, 411, 413
services, 15, 39, 51, 102, 214, 220, 231, 233, 237, 240, 245, 248–49, 252, 276, 324
  financial, 415–16, 427, 431, 485
  microfinance, 416, 429, 431–32

Shāfi'ī jurists, 30–31, 58, 80, 144, 164–65, 207, 238, 306, 345, 408–9
Shāfi'īs, 29–30, 48, 70, 73, 87, 88,114, 116, 169, 174, 178, 181, 183, 186–87, 211,269, 271, 275, 277, 299, 303,306, 433, 443
Sharī'ah, 34, 36, 39, 101–2, 104–5, 174–76, 178–79, 219–22, 252, 255, 258, 345, 402–4, 406, 411–12 439, 441, 505
Sharī'ah Appraisal, 118, 393, 395, 397, 399, 401, 403, 405, 407, 409, 411, 413
Sharī'ah Board, 397, 399–400, 413
Sharī'ah scholars, 393–96, 401–2, 404–5, 411
Sharī'ah Supervisory Board, 397
sharikah, 91, 203, 259–60, 264–65, 267, 270, 275–79, 282, 295, 452–53
Sharikat al-a'māl, 197, 265, 267, 273–74, 276, 281, 283,293-94
sharikat al-amwāl, 267, 269–70, 273, 288, 293
  hah, 280
Sharikat al-milk, 265–66, 271
Sharikat al-wujūh, 197, 267, 286, 293–94
Ṣīghah, 27–29, 31, 33, 35, 37, 86, 100, 110
slave
  sale of, 406
  wealth of, 407
State Bank of Pakistan, 296, 371, 375,379
substituted debtor, 330–33, 335–36, 340–41
subterfuges, 146, 359, 362, 364, 369, 375, 391, 475, 486–88, 495
Subul al-Salām, 163–64, 166, 328, 349–50
Sunnah, xxii, 5, 7, 9, 13, 15–17, 43, 171–73, 177–78, 247–48, 297, 311–12, 343–44, 464, 474–76
suretyship, xxiii, 68, 91, 94, 194, 197–98, 200, 282, 311–13, 315, 317–25, 330
  contract of, 96,203,317–18, 330, 321–22

T

tabarru', 143, 445–47, 451–53, 457–59
takāful , 450–52, 456–57,458
tawarruq, 370, 375–80, 382, 392, 488
Theory of contracts in Islamic Law, 22

Traditional Forms of Fraud in Islamic Juristic Literature, 163
transactions, xxii, 10–13, 41–43, 54–55, 109–11, 140–43, 145–48, 270, 360, 368–72, 374–77, 386–87, 436–43, 486–87, 490–92
  barter, 96, 126–27, 134–35
  commutative, 143, 422
  financial, 442, 444
  gratuitous, 143, 422, 471
  usurious, 50, 134
  valid, 211
transfer, 39, 245, 262, 295, 302, 327–30, 337–41, 353, 437–38, 443

U

Unlawful Gain and Legitimate Profit in Islam, 127, 240, 307,331, 334,451,
Uqūd, 47, 110, 119–20, 196, 200
usufructs, 8, 160–61, 171, 193, 198, 200, 245–46, 248–50, 253, 257, 346, 385
usury, 7, 92, 125, 128, 130, 350

V

valid contract, 4, 44, 46, 53, 87–88, 93, 96, 98, 103–5, 169, 199, 225, 234, 239, 249
validity of contract, 49, 51, 93, 159, 169, 458–59
value, 47, 97–98, 153, 155–56, 218–19, 221–22, 344–46, 385–87, 404, 407–8, 416, 419, 424, 476, 481
  measure of, 153, 221
  particular, 464
verses, 4, 15, 19–20, 78, 80, 128–30, 143, 149, 157, 264, 343, 377, 416–18, 424, 476
Void conditions, 176, 178

W

wakālah, 69, 278,447,449,459
WAPDA, 386
waqf, 21, 24, 55, 59, 96, 123, 193, 196–98, 200, 202, 211, 250, 415, 421–22, 431
waqf fund, 445, 447–48
wealth, 58–59, 270, 273, 281, 406–7, 416–19, 421, 424–25, 461, 463, 467–69, 474, 476–79, 485, 492–94

augmentation of, 446, 475, 479, 481
concentration of, 419, 421, 424, 476, 485
equitable distribution of, 156, 421, 463, 475–76, 485
work partnership, 282, 284, 293–94

Z

zakah, 384, 468, 470, 485, 492–93
Zarqā, 506, 509–10

Made in the USA
Las Vegas, NV
25 January 2023

66223582R10319